Ancestral Books in the Management of Organizations

A 31-volume facsimile series
reproducing classic works in the field.

Edited by

Arthur P. Brief

Graduate School of Business Administration
New York University

A Garland Series

Higher Education for Business

Robert Aaron Gordon,
James Edwin Howell

Garland Publishing, Inc.
New York • London
1987

For a complete list of the titles in this series
see the final pages of this volume

This facsimile has been made from a copy
in The New York Public Library.

Library of Congress Cataloging-in-Publication Data

Gordon, Robert Aaron.
Higher education for business.

(Continuity in administrative science)
Reprint. Originally published: New York :
Columbia University Press, 1959.
Bibliography: p.
Includes index.
1. Business education—United States.
I. Howell, James Edwin. II. Title. III. Series.
HF1131.G6   1987   650'.07'1173   86-25813
ISBN 0-8240-8207-9   (alk. paper)

The volumes in this series are printed on
acid-free, 250-year-life paper.

Printed in the United States of America

HIGHER EDUCATION
FOR BUSINESS

HIGHER EDUCATION FOR BUSINESS

BY *Robert Aaron Gordon*

AND *James Edwin Howell*

COLUMBIA UNIVERSITY PRESS

NEW YORK CITY · 1959

119541

Published in Great Britain, Canada, India, and Pakistan by the Oxford University Press London, Toronto, Bombay, and Karachi

Manufactured in the United States of America

FOREWORD

HIGHER EDUCATION FOR BUSINESS in America is essentially a product of the twentieth century. It represents the response of a democratic society to the educational needs of its industrial system. In recent decades business education at the college and university level has grown at a phenomenal rate. At present in the United States one out of every seven degrees awarded by institutions of higher education is in business administration. The number of degrees awarded in this field is second only to the number in education.

Although schools of business administration have now been assimilated into the academic structure of the United States, contrary to the situation abroad, many problems remain to be solved. The vocational approach that has all too often characterized these schools in the past is now considered inadequate. A few institutions have been experimenting with new curricula designed to provide a more rigorous professional training within the context of a liberal education. The results achieved to date are highly promising. In such programs, increased emphasis is being placed on the application of the fundamental disciplines of the social and behavioral sciences to the problems of business administration. Previously only the relevance of economics had been fully appreciated. Another promising development is the growth in the application of modern mathematical and statistical methods to business problems.

These changes have generally been associated with a research orientation. Business educators in increasing numbers are recognizing that it is insufficient to transmit and apply present knowledge. It is the function of higher education to advance the state of knowledge as well. A professional school of business that aspires to full academic status must meet this test.

The Ford Foundation has been concerned with business education since 1954, when its Program in Economic Development and Administration was established. Although recognized at the outset, it became increasingly evident as the program evolved that an objective and comprehensive survey of business education in the United States was needed. Such a study would build upon the factual survey of member schools of the American Association of Collegiate Schools of Business that was conducted by Dean Richard L. Kozelka of the University of Minnesota.[1] R. A. Gordon, Professor of Economics at the University of California (Berkeley), was appointed to the Foundation staff in 1956 to direct the study while on leave from his University. With the cooperation of J. E. Howell, formerly a staff member at Yale and now Associate Professor of Economics at the Graduate School of Business at Stanford, and others, Mr. Gordon examined the objectives and educational methods of schools of business in relation to the requirements of business and society. This report is the culmination of their combined efforts.

A preliminary draft of the report was presented to a small panel of business executives and general and business educators for their constructively critical review. It was their consensus that the report's usefulness was such that it should receive widespread distribution. Certain suggestions for modification were made. The report was prepared in its final form by the authors in the light of these and other suggestions and of their further reflections. It does not in any sense represent a statement of Ford Foundation policy or of the opinions of its trustees, officers, or professional staff members.

Despite its youth in the American educational family, business education has become a numerical giant. The need for its improvement in the years ahead is evident. Its effective development can bring rich rewards to business and society both at home and abroad. This report is being published in the hope that through broad dissemination and discussion of the authors' findings and of a companion report on a study financed by the Carnegie Corporation,[2] a constructive contribution will be made.

On behalf of the Ford Foundation, I wish to express sincere appreciation to Messrs. Gordon and Howell for the time and thought they have invested in this important undertaking.

Thomas H. Carroll
Vice President
The Ford Foundation

New York, New York
July 15, 1959

---

[1] *Professional Education for Business,* Report on Pilot Field Survey (1954).
[2] Frank Pierson *et al., The Education of American Businessmen,* A Study of University-College Programs in Business Administration (to be published in the late fall of 1959).

PREFACE

THIS REPORT embodies the results of a three-year study of collegiate business education which was undertaken at the request of The Ford Foundation. Our concern is with education for business at the college or university level, primarily although not exclusively as it is offered by university schools of business administration. This report does not deal with commercial education in the secondary schools or with the proprietary "business colleges."

One token of the widespread interest in collegiate business education is offered by the fact that surveys of the subject were commissioned almost simultaneously by two major national foundations. The other survey was undertaken by Professor Frank C. Pierson of Swarthmore College at the request of The Carnegie Corporation. Both surveys were carried on during the same period, and the two reports are scheduled for publication at about the same time.

We are happy to express our appreciation to Professor Pierson for his unstinted cooperation at all stages of the two studies. While some duplication was unavoidable, there has been a division of labor between the two projects, and he and we have provided for an exchange of information. It need hardly be added that, except for consultation in the early planning stage and the exchange of information, the two studies have been conducted entirely independently.

It would take many pages to list the names of all the persons and organizations that have helped us in the course of this study. We take this opportunity to express our thanks to all of them. During the course of this investigation we have talked to more than a thousand businessmen and educators, and they have all generously supplied us with information and counsel where they could.

We are particularly grateful to the deans of the business schools that we visited. Without exception, they patiently tried to answer our innumerable questions and courteously arranged for us the interviews we sought with members of their faculties and with representatives of the university administration. We owe a similar debt of thanks to the officials of about 100 companies who gave generously of their time when we interviewed them. The names of the schools visited are given in Appendix E; those of the companies interviewed are listed in Appendix B. Appendix B also lists the names of a number of individuals and organizations that were very helpful to us in planning and carrying out the analysis in Part II.

Through the good offices of The Ford Foundation, we were fortunate enough to have the preliminary draft of this report reviewed by a distinguished group of businessmen and educators. Their comments and suggestions were extremely helpful in the final revision. The members of this group, who, it hardly needs to be added, assume no responsibility for any part of this report, were:

G. L. Bach, Dean, Graduate School of Industrial Administration, Carnegie Institute of Technology

Robert D. Calkins, President, The Brookings Institution

Charles W. Cole, President, Amherst College

Paul Davies, President, Food Machinery and Chemical Corporation

Richard Donham, Dean, School of Business, Northwestern University

Russell H. Hassler, Associate Dean, Graduate School of Business Administration, Harvard University

Charles E. Odegaard, President, University of Washington

Ewing W. Reilley, Director, McKinsey and Company, Inc.

Harold F. Smiddy, Vice President, General Electric Company

Arthur M. Weimer, Dean, School of Business, Indiana University

Logan Wilson, President, University of Texas

James C. Worthy, Vice President, Sears, Roebuck and Company

The Ford Foundation also arranged for us to meet on two separate occasions with a group of business educators, who were asked to comment on various aspects of our study. Our sincere thanks go to all of these two dozen or so individuals for their helpful advice and for the time they were willing to give us.

Helpful comments on substantial parts of the preliminary draft were also received from E. T. Weiler, Dean, School of Industrial Management, Purdue University; Lewis Ward, Director, Executive Study, Educational Testing Service; and members of the staff of Arthur D. Little, Inc.

We are also indebted to Donald S. Bridgman, formerly Director of College Relations, American Telephone and Telegraph Company, and Professor Thomas L. Whisler, School of Business, University of Chicago. Both provided very helpful comments and in addition conducted for us many of the intensive company interviews described in Appendix B.

Professors George Kuznets and Lyman Porter, both of the University of California, were of considerable assistance on some of the technical problems that arose in connection with the analysis in Part II.

We wish particularly to express our appreciation for the efficient research assistance contributed by Frederick C. Schadrack, James K. Nettles, Irving Krauss, Eugene Brady, and Robert Stephenson, and for the equally efficient secretarial help provided by Mrs. Paul Grunland, Mrs. Charlotte Christofferson, and Miss Gaye Sorensen.

Our thanks are due to the Ford Foundation on several counts. Not only did the Foundation provide the funds for this study, but it facilitated our work in every way possible. Special mention should be made of Thomas H. Carroll, Vice President with special responsibility for the Program in Economic Development and Administration, whose efforts to improve the quality of collegiate business education considerably antedate this report, and his colleagues Lloyd G. Reynolds and Neil W. Chamberlain, former and present Director, respectively, of the Program in Economic Development and Administration. We should also like to acknowledge the help of Oscar Harkavy and Kermit Gordon, members of the Foundation's staff during all or a part of the study.

We also wish to thank the publishers listed below for permission to reproduce material from the following books and articles.

Kenneth R. Andrews, "Executive Training by the Case Method," *Harvard Business Review*, xxix (September, 1951).

G. L. Bach, "Some Observations on the Business School of Tomorrow," *Management Science*, iv (July, 1958).

C. E. Barnard, "Education for Executives," *The Journal of Business*, xviii (October, 1945).

J. H. S. Bossard and J. F. Dewhurst, *University Education for Business*. University of Pennsylvania Press, 1931.

Robert D. Calkins, "Objectives of Business Education," *Harvard Business Review*, xxv (Autumn, 1946).

Commission on Standards of Education and Experience for Certified Public Accountants, *Standards of Education and Experience for Certified Public Accountants*. University of Michigan Bureau of Business Research, 1956.

Joel Dean, *Managerial Economics*. Prentice-Hall, Inc., 1951.

R. E. Doherty, *The Development of Professional Education*. Carnegie Press, 1950.

Education for Business Beyond High School. The American Business Education Yearbook, vol. xiv, 1957. Published by the Eastern Business Teachers Association and National Business Teachers Association.

Frank S. Endicott, *Trends in the Employment of College and University Graduates in Business and Industry, 1957.* Northwestern University, 1957.

Ernest Havemann and Patricia Salter West, *They Went to College.* Copyright 1952 by Time, Inc. Reprinted by permission of Harcourt, Brace, Inc.

J. G. March and H. A. Simon, *Organizations.* John Wiley and Sons, Inc., 1958.

L. C. Marshall, "The School of Commerce," in R. A. Kent, ed., *Higher Education in America.* 1930. By permission of Harvard University Press.

O. W. Phelps, "Academic Research in Business Administration," *The Journal of Higher Education,* xviii (February, 1947).

National Industrial Conference Board, *Executive Development Courses in Universities.* Studies in Personnel Policy No. 160, 1957.

H. A. Simon, *Administrative Behavior.* 2nd ed. The Macmillan Company, 1957. Copyright 1945, 1947, 1957 by Herbert A. Simon.

Elliot D. Smith, "The Education of Professional Students for Citizenship." In *Education for Professional Responsibility.* Carnegie Press, 1948.

Alfred North Whitehead, *The Aims of Education.* Mentor edition, published by The New American Library of World Literature, 1949. Copyright 1929 by The Macmillan Company.

William H. Whyte, Jr., *The Organization Man.* Simon and Schuster, Inc., 1956.

Because of administrative convenience, the authors served as members of the Foundation's staff during the larger part of the period devoted to the study. The research and writing were carried on in all respects, however, as if there had been a research grant administered by a university. The authors are completely responsible for the planning of the project, the conduct of the field work and library research, and the final analysis and recommendations. Indeed, officials of the Foundation went to considerable lengths to insure that we were completely free to plan the study as we wished and to draw any conclusions that seemed to us appropriate. Thus, we are glad both to thank the Foundation for its assistance and cooperation and at the same time to absolve it from any responsibility for what follows.

This report is in all respects a joint product, for which both authors take full responsibility. While the senior author was asked to undertake the direction of the study, both authors participated fully in the planning, research, analysis, and formulation of recommendations. One or the other author wrote the first draft of particular chapters, but what then emerged was jointly revised, rewritten, and again revised until neither author can say that any particular section is his own creation.

We have not thought it necessary to provide a separate summary of our conclusions and recommendations in the body of the report. To a considerable extent, this summarizing role is played by Chapter 7, which brings together the conclusions drawn from the analysis of Part II and translates them into a series of educational recommendations, which are then considered in detail in the remainder of the volume.

R. A. Gordon

J. E. Howell

Berkeley, California
Palo Alto, California
July 15, 1959

CONTENTS

LIST OF TABLES

PART I

The Present State of Business Education

chapter 1

THE REASONS
FOR THIS STUDY

> The extraordinary advances in the application of science to modern life which have made possible the remarkable economic progress and vast improvement in human well-being during the present century have created a multitude of economic and social problems for the solution of which our business leaders must assume primary responsibility. Hence the task to which the collegiate schools of business have addressed themselves, that of training young men for the heavy responsibilities of the business leadership of the future, constitutes an educational problem of paramount importance.[1]

THE QUOTATION with which we begin this report could have been written yesterday instead of nearly thirty years ago. The importance of the role of the businessman in American society needs no elaboration here. In a world that looks forward apprehensively as well as expectantly to the closing decades of the twentieth century, the American businessman will play a dominant role—not only as the leader in the insistent drive for greater economic output, but as a shaper of opinion and public policies that will affect the welfare of the American people in a thousand directions, from local action to cope with juvenile delinquency to national policy in the precarious field of international relations.

How well prepared will the businessman be for this role of leadership, and will he have the skill and vision needed to cope with the critical decades that lie ahead? It is fair to say that a significant part of the answer lies with the colleges and universities. A large fraction of tomorrow's businessmen will be college educated; this will be particularly true of the leaders among them. A very substantial proportion of these college educated businessmen will be the products of a peculiarly American kind of higher education—the curriculum in business administration, which is today offered on some 600 college campuses in every part of the country, in the ivied halls of many liberal arts colleges as well as in schools of business in the teeming state universities and the grimy downtown universities of the large cities.

[1] J. H. S. Bossard and J. F. Dewhurst, *University Education for Business* (1931), p. 565.

Business Education Adrift

Collegiate business education is largely a product of the twentieth century. Today it is a restless and uncertain giant in the halls of higher education. It enrolls considerably more male students than either engineering or the natural sciences and mathematics combined. Approximately one in seven of all bachelor's degrees are in business; the figure approaches one in five if we take men only. There is no question but that the school or department of business has established itself firmly on the college campus. Teachers in the humanities look glumly on while students flock to its doors.

But it is an uncertain giant, gnawed by doubt and harassed by the barbs of unfriendly critics. It seeks to serve several masters and is assured by its critics that it serves none well. The business world takes its students but deprecates the value of their training, extolling instead the virtues of science and the liberal arts. It finds itself at the foot of the academic table, uncomfortably nudging those other two stepchildren, Education and Agriculture. It is aware of its ungainly size and views apprehensively the prospect of still further growth, knowing that even now it lacks the resources to teach well the horde of students who come swarming in search of a practical education.

It is no wonder, then, that "Schools of Business Administration across the nation are trying, sometimes almost desperately, to find their souls."[2] They are "bedeviled by the problems of whom to teach and what to teach."[3] They seek to clarify their purpose and to find their proper place in the educational world. They search for academic respectability, while most of them continue to engage in unrespectable vocational training. They seek to be professional schools, while expressing doubt themselves that the occupations for which they prepare students can rightfully be called a profession.

This is the problem of business education in these latter decades of the twentieth century. The need for competent, imaginative, and responsible business leadership is greater than ever before; the need becomes more urgent as business grows ever more complex and as the environment with which it has to cope continues to change at an accelerating tempo. Business educators debate with each other and with their critics as to how

[2] Clark Kerr, "The Schools of Business Administration," address delivered at the University of Pittsburgh, May, 1957. Published in *New Dimensions of Learning in a Free Society* (1958). See p. 63.

[3] Richard Hofstadter and C. DeWitt Hardy, *The Development and Scope of Higher Education in the United States* (1952), p. 92.

this need can best be met, or at least be met better than is now being done. That is, the more thoughtful and alert ask the question and debate the issue. The others plod in a rut they dug long ago. For them it is enough to tell their students what business did yesterday and the day before.[4]

It is not only the business schools that are concerned about their purpose and their future. Business itself is showing an unparalleled interest in the educational process, and it too is asking the question: How should businessmen be educated? At commencement time company recruiters swarm over the college campuses, frequently seeking that non-existent paragon, "the broadly educated specialist," but settling for an engineering or business degree and a pleasant personality. Company officials are sent back to the colleges to participate in "executive development programs" and even to study the humanities. Employees in all ranks go to school within the company walls. Aspiring candidates for advancement throng the evening classes conducted by the urban universities and technical schools, frequently at their employers' expense.

Business itself is pulled in two directions. It feels increasingly the need for educated men who have the breadth, perspective, and flexibility of mind to cope with a business environment that grows in complexity and changes with bewildering rapidity. Yet it also feels the pressure for more and better trained specialists who can master the technical problems that have been spawned by the technological and organizational revolution of the twentieth century. Thus business looks to the colleges to give it generalists and specialists, if possible embodied in the same person.

But business does not speak all with the same voice, any more than do educators. Nor do businessmen, any more than ordinary citizens, always practice what they preach. While some business leaders praise the virtues of a liberal education, operating supervisors on the firing line look for the technical training that will enable the young college graduate to earn immediately his very first salary check. Thus the uncertainty within the business schools is compounded by the uncertainty which business itself feels. There is agreement only that business needs *more* and *better* educated young men and women. The dimensions of "more" are simple to understand; they have to do with bricks and mortar, dollars, students, and, above all, teachers. But what is a "better" education—in general as well as for a career in business?

The problem of business education is thus one of both quantity and, much more important, of quality. Many deans and presidents concern themselves chiefly with the quantitative issues, which are serious enough.

[4] In all fairness we should add that a similar situation prevails in other fields also.

Some worry a bit about the effect of such numbers on the quality of the education they provide. The more thoughtful deans concentrate their attention on the qualitative issues, on how to provide a better education. While the uncertainty we have noted exists as to what is the best kind of education for business, some things do seem to be clear. One of them is the low level and narrow vocational character of much collegiate business education. Nearly as well documented is the failure of most business schools to develop in their students the qualities of mind and character and the kinds of professional-type skills for which business and society have the greatest need.

For these and other reasons, there is, as we have noted, strong and widespread dissatisfaction with the quality of business education in American colleges and universities today. What passes as the going standard of acceptability among business schools is embarrassingly low, and many schools of business do not meet even these low standards. While the schools are still bedeviled by uncertainty, there is growing recognition that the present situation is intolerable. The gap between what society needs and what the business schools are offering has grown wide enough for all to see.

The Need for Reappraisal

While the feeling of dissatisfaction is widespread, it is important to stress the even stronger feeling of uncertainty. It is probably safe to say that in no other area of professional education (unless it be education for teaching) is there so much uncertainty as to what constitutes a proper educational background for professional practice, or are existing educational standards and practices viewed with greater skepticism. Despite their size and entrenched position, the business schools have not yet reached agreement as to what their objectives should properly be and how these objectives might best be attained. At one extreme are the best of the graduate schools. At the other extreme are the worst of the vocational schools that find residence on a college campus. Within this wide range there may be a moderate amount of consensus as to what is unacceptably bad, although the worst can apparently always find some local justification. There is also some agreement on a safe level of mediocrity which yields academic respectability. But there is yet little agreement as to what constitutes the best sort of education for a business career or whether there is any single "best." The most thoughtful and imaginative programs in business education have attracted more comment than imitators.

Hence there is clear need for a careful reappraisal of the state of business education in the United States. The purpose of this study is to provide the basis for such a reappraisal. This may suggest to the reader a "Flexner Report" on business education, but the parallel is a relatively weak one. The circumstances that led to Abraham Flexner's famous report on *Medical Education in the United States and Canada* some fifty years ago were rather different from those with which we are concerned here.[5]

First of all, there is no clear-cut model of what a good business school should be, as there was for medical schools in 1910. Flexner could take for granted the nature of medical practice and the kind of training such practice required. He also had the German universities and the Johns Hopkins Medical School to use as guides. In this respect our task is more difficult and must lead to less certain answers. The very heterogeneity of business makes this inevitable; so does the embryonic state of the social sciences, which bear somewhat the same relation to the practice of business that the natural sciences bear to the practice of medicine.

In the second place, as bad as much collegiate business education must be judged to be, it has a legitimate status such as many medical schools did not have at the turn of the century. We do not have to worry about proprietary schools misleading their students and the public, which was in good part Flexner's concern. The schools and departments of business which are the focus of our attention are affiliated with universities, have at least a core of full-time faculty, and offer courses of study which meet the standards of the host institution. Even admittedly poor business education does not involve so obviously the dangers inherent in the hopelessly inadequate medical preparation Flexner found in many institutions.

Let it be said also that one major purpose of Flexner's report has no parallel at all in our study of business education. Flexner wanted to do more than improve the average quality of the medical schools then extant. He set out to eliminate the worst of them, believing both that there was an oversupply of doctors and that the poorest of the medical schools were beyond redemption. This he succeeded in doing by naming names in a brilliant and acid appraisal. But our problem is different. There are not too many businessmen, but there are too few well educated ones. While we have no doubt that the students in the worst of the business schools are to a considerable extent wasting their money and their time, we have not tried to appraise every school and department. The American economy is perhaps wealthy enough to afford the waste of resources involved, although it badly needs the talent that a better education might

---

[5] Flexner's report was published in 1910 as Bulletin Number 4 of the Carnegie Foundation for the Advancement of Teaching. With the help of foundation funds to implement the changes it proposed, the Flexner Report can fairly be said to have precipitated a revolution in the teaching of medicine in the United States.

provide. A large fraction of American college students get a poor education in any event. The right of poorly prepared students to spend four years in a college program of indifferent quality or worse is what many Americans mean by democracy in higher education. We do not deny the right of the poorer business schools to cater to this demand, as Flexner did deny the right of the worst of the medical schools of his day to perpetrate poorly trained doctors on an unsuspecting public. But we do argue that, whatever other needs they may be serving, most schools and departments of business are not providing the kind of education tomorrow's businessmen will need.

This report is aimed at the entire range of business schools, from the very poor to those which are generally judged to be among the better schools. The very best schools have, perhaps, less to gain from this report than those which are less distinguished. Nonetheless, we think that there is something in this report for virtually every school and department of business.

Only a very few schools substantially meet the standards of excellence we propose in this report. Even the best schools have no reason for complacency. Education for business must be a dynamic thing, sensitive both to the changing character of business itself and to the advances in the fields of knowledge on which an understanding of business should be based. The need for experimentation and for keeping up with and applying new knowledge never ends.

It is also true that the "best" schools are almost never best in all respects. The school which has pioneered in teaching methods may do little significant research, or it may pay too little attention to the substantive content of its courses. The research oriented school may have a poorly designed curriculum, or its faculty may do a poor job of teaching. And so on.

The point we would stress most is the universal need for improvement. The best schools can do better than they are now doing. Even more important, the better-than-average school leaves much to be desired, and the need for improvement becomes progressively greater as we move down among the poorer schools. In varying degrees, today's business schools are not providing the kind of education tomorrow's businessmen will need, and the record with respect to research is even less satisfactory.

The Issues in Greater Detail

The debate over how best to educate future businessmen resolves itself into a formidable array of issues. In considerable part these have to do with objectives and the best means of implementing them. Uncertainty about objectives has plagued business educators almost from the begining.[6]

The debate has many facets. What, for example, should be the relative emphasis on general education and on specific training for a business career? Further, should business education be of a general, management-oriented sort, or should stress be placed on one or another of the special fields of business? What emphasis, if any, should be put on preparation for the first job? Should all students planning a business career be educated in the same way, regardless of mental ability or aptitude for business, or should business schools limit themselves to educating only the most able? What are the relative roles of experience and formal education in developing the knowledge, skills, and aptitudes required for successful business careers? How shall we combine the teaching of underlying principles and the development of the kinds of skills which the practitioner needs? Should business education be offered at the undergraduate or graduate level or at both?

There are other issues. As a part of a university, a business school can perform some combination of the following functions: educate future practitioners, engage in research, train future teachers and research workers, and perform a variety of service activities (such as educational programs for persons already in business and consulting for business firms and government agencies). Should all schools try to perform all four functions? What kinds of research need to be emphasized, and should all or most members of a business school faculty be expected to engage in research? What is the best kind of training for teachers and research workers, and who should provide this training? Given limited resources, how far should the schools go in their service activities, and when does faculty consulting cease to make a contribution to a teacher's own education and become merely a source of extra income?

The debate currently going on regarding curriculum, teaching methods, and the like is in many respects a healthy sign, and it has already led to some good results. While many business schools show little desire to break out of the rut in which they have long plodded, the field of business education *is* in ferment. An increasing number of schools are re-examining their curricula, their teaching methods, their objectives, the content of their courses, and other aspects of their programs. In the last few years

---

[6] Nearly thirty years ago, Bossard and Dewhurst complained of "the lack of clear-cut objectives" and urged that "schools of business need to define their objectives more definitely and more specifically." *University Education for Business*, p. 568. This was still being urged in 1955. See American Association of Collegiate Schools of Business, *Faculty Requirements and Standards in Collegiate Schools of Business* (1955), pp. 5–10.

important self-studies have been undertaken at a number of institutions, and from these some significant changes in curriculum and other aspects of educational policy have resulted.

Thus progress is being made, although it is discouragingly slow. The uncertainty we have described is only part of the problem. Educational institutions do not escape the heavy hand of inertia, and vested interests develop in established ways of doing things. Lack of communication is also a problem, particularly for the more isolated campuses. A variety of local pressures may make it difficult to initiate particular reforms.

Four conditions are necessary for the kind of widespread and radical change that is needed in the majority of institutions. There must be the will to improve; there must be knowledge of the better alternatives available; there needs to be confidence that these alternatives do represent improvement; and, finally, sufficient resources must exist to make improvement possible.

To help create these conditions for further improvement is largely the purpose of this study. Obviously it is easier for a report of this kind to affect the first three factors mentioned than the last; but, if the will to improve is strong enough, the resources needed can usually be found.

Probably none of the proposals we shall make is new, and virtually all of our recommendations for educational reform are now in effect on one or another campus. But by synthesizing the best of current opinion, by adding some new evidence of our own, and by being blunt where bluntness is called for, we may be able to make some contribution to the progress that has already begun.

The recommendations we make in later chapters, particularly with respect to needed curriculum changes, are quite specific. The reason we prescribe in detail, however, is not that we think there is only one route to a better business education. Our concrete proposals are to be interpreted merely as illustrative of the ways in which the basic educational values and objectives we believe important can be implemented. We have no desire to impose a standard pattern on the business schools. Variety and experimentation are needed, and each school must take account of its own particular environment, including the human and financial resources at its disposal. Not only must there be variety; there needs also to be continuous experimentation and change. Knowledge does not stand still, and neither does the world of affairs in which business students will practice their careers.

Thus we do not suggest that our proposals be followed in every detail by all schools. Equally important, our recommendations are to be interpreted dynamically and not statically. They are the base from which further improvement is to be made in the light of new knowledge and the recognition of new needs.

But while it is important to stress the need for variety and change, it is even more essential to emphasize the fact that the general direction in which the business schools need to move is becoming increasingly clear. In later chapters of this report we shall try to indicate what this direction is and what it implies in terms of educational objectives, curriculum, teaching, and research in the business schools.

Does Business Education Belong in the Colleges?

The American business system is already the most efficient the world has ever known. Its efficiency has been achieved despite the admitted weaknesses of collegiate business education. More to the point, the majority of American businessmen never went to a business school or took a formal program in business administration.

In light of this situation, is it clear that the American economy needs the kind of business training that can be offered in college? Let us ignore for the moment the demand from students and their parents for business courses and the fact that employers seek out the products of the business schools, for there is no doubt that the demand for collegiate business education exists. But is society wise to satisfy this demand as freely as it has been doing and at the cost of alternative forms of education that have been foregone? This question has been raised most pointedly about the value of business training in the undergraduate years.[7]

At this juncture, we shall confine ourselves to the question of whether training for business careers deserves a place in the scheme of American higher education. If the answer is in the affirmative, we can consider later whether such training belongs in the undergraduate college or should come at a more advanced stage.

We think a strong case can be made for providing some professional education at the university level for those planning on careers in business. The primary reason is that in a meaningful sense business is rapidly becoming "professionalized." In Peter Drucker's words, "The days of the

---

[7] Thus, in commenting on the recent expansion in undergraduate business education, William H. Whyte, Jr. has been led to observe: "Something has had to give and it has been fundamental education. The great increase in business education has not been channeled into graduate schools of business administration which, like those of Harvard and the University of Chicago, require a basic education as a prerequisite. The increase has been in the undergraduate 'schools of commerce,' and the students who are enrolling in them include many who ten years ago would very likely have majored in economics or politics or history." *The Organization Man* (1956), pp. 84–85.

'intuitive' managers are numbered."[8] Since the closing decades of the nineteenth century, the problems facing the businessman have become increasingly complex. At the same time, as more rational attitudes have been introduced into business, as record keeping has improved and the supply of information about business and economic affairs has increased, business has developed a body of knowledge which can be studied and from which significant generalizations can be made. To paraphrase a comment of Howard Bowen's, formal knowledge, however acquired, is becoming a practical necessity for the practice of business.[9] This is particularly true in the large corporation, but it is becoming increasingly true of small business as well. As the need for a more rational approach to the practice of business grows, the opportunities to develop and teach such an approach also increase.

Until a half century or so ago, this was not nearly so true. Business firms were much smaller; organizational problems were simpler; it was easier to adjust to technological developments and to the economic, social, and political environment; and under the growth conditions prevailing through the eighteenth and most of the nineteenth century in the United States, profits came easily to the businessman with a new idea or to one possessing more than an average amount of shrewdness and aggressiveness.

The situation has been changing rapidly during the last fifty years. A "managerial revolution" has occurred, although without all the political implications James Burnham predicted. As we think this report will show, the training required by today's and tomorrow's managers can be provided in part in the university. Even the imperfect business education offered today has been of some help, particularly in the lower levels of business, and it has been supplemented by a variety of forms of post-college training offered both by business and the universities. Business will need the help of higher education even more in the future.[10]

The new situation does not necessarily mean that all future businessmen should attend a business school. There is no disagreement that a variety of roads to a business career must be left open. But it does suggest that the educational requirements for the practice of business are

---

[8] *The Practice of Management* (1954), p. 9.

[9] Cf. *Social Responsibilities of the Businessman* (1953), p. 95.

[10] As Robert Calkins has put it: "Imagine any projection of recent trends you like, and you are forced to the conclusion that the men who are shortly to exercise authority in the direction of affairs must have a degree of knowledge, intellectual skill, and administrative competence exceeding anything we have regarded as adequate heretofore." "Objectives of Business Education," *Harvard Business Review,* xxv (Autumn, 1946), p. 48.

becoming more rigorous and that some combination of a general and a professional education can make businessmen better businessmen, although no form of education, business or otherwise, can ever guarantee business success.

THE CHANGING CHARACTER OF AMERICAN BUSINESS

We should like to say a bit more about the important trends that have been "professionalizing" the practice of business. While numerous observers have commented on them, further consideration of these developments may suggest some of the kinds of education college students contemplating careers in business are likely to need. Since these trends will not soon be reversed, they also tell us something about the kind of environment in which businessmen will have to operate in the years ahead.

1   As business firms have grown in size, increasing emphasis is being placed on organizational problems. There has been an enormous increase in the importance of the administrative function. The process of decision-making has been diffused, greatly increasing the need for coordination and planning within the enterprise.

2   With the separation of ownership and management in the large firm, business leadership has largely been taken over by salaried executives. Capital or family connection is no longer necessary for a top position in business. For success in large-scale business, a "college degree has become more important than great wealth, and easier to obtain."[11]

3   The accelerating tempo of scientific and technological change is having a profound effect upon the practice of management. Businessmen increasingly need some technical background so that they can communicate with scientists and engineers. Long-range planning becomes more difficult but at the same time more essential. Increasing flexibility, of organization and of mind, is needed to permit rapid adjustment to new situations. "Automation" in the factory, data processing equipment, and the like are revolutionizing production methods and office procedures, radically changing the composition of manpower demands, and increasing "the need for intellect and skill among all who plan, produce, operate, and maintain the process."[12] "If all these changes in industry are bewildering for the operative, they throw even more problems of adjustment on to the shoulders of the manager. Indeed, one of the most press-

[11] Mabel Newcomer, *The Big Business Executive* (1955), p. 146.
[12] Cf. National Education Association, *Manpower and Education* (1956), p. 22.

ing of contemporary needs is to produce a sufficient number of enterprising and competent leaders of industry and society, capable of facing up to the demands of the increasingly complex and science-based economy which we are now entering."[13]

4   Related to these developments in engineering and the physical sciences has been, since the days of Frederick Taylor, a growing scientific attitude toward management problems. At first confined to production management in a narrow sense, the scientific attitude has now spread to all aspects of management activities. At the same time, there has been a concomitant growth of usable knowledge in the social sciences and in statistics that is providing an increasingly substantial basis for rational decision-making. The new "management sciences" are still in their infancy, but in a broader sense management science is increasingly being practiced in the various functional areas of business.

5   While today's "other-directed" world may, as Riesman and Whyte suggest, be increasing the pressure for group conformity, it is also true that there has been a growing emphasis on the role of the individual in organizations. Instead of being taken as given, the individual and his contribution to the organization have become variables which are related to other variables that students in the field of human relations attempt to analyze and that "human-relations engineers" attempt to manipulate in the interest of organizational harmony and higher output. Skill in human relations has become an essential ingredient of effective management. This new emphasis on the psychological needs of the individual and on his capacity to influence his organizational environment is certain to become even stronger in the future than it is now.

6   There is growing need for highly trained staff specialists, as well as for administrators to coordinate the work of such specialists. The complexities and ramifying activities of modern large-scale business create a dilemma. Specialization, which is essential in today's large complex organizations, is coming to rest on an increasingly technical and rapidly changing body of knowledge that derives from the physical and social sciences and from mathematics and statistics. On the other hand, the need for the broader kind of administrative abilities, particularly in the upper levels of management, is also becoming more urgent. There is a growing recognition that the

---

[13] Alexander King, "Management as a Technology," *Impact of Science on Society*, VIII (June 1957), 70. See also H. J. Leavitt and T. L. Whisler, "Management in the 1980's," *Harvard Business Review*, XXXVI (November-December, 1958), 41–48.

solution to this dilemma is to be found in training which emphasizes both the fundamental disciplines and the development of
problem-solving ability and flexibility of mind. The need for training in the relevant basic disciplines and for a high level of analytical
and problem-solving ability will certainly continue to grow.[14] In
addition, business itself is taking increasing responsibility for meeting its specialized training needs, both by intra-company educational programs and by sending its employees back to school for
special courses.

7 The increasing complexity of the firm's external environment has
steadily added to the difficulties of the businessman's task. This is
by now a familiar story: the increase in the power of organized
labor and the steady upward pressure on wages; the expanding
role of government; the Cold War and the precarious state of international relations; changes in the distribution of political and economic power and in the climate of public opinion; and so on.

As a result of these changes, the social responsibilities of the businessman are greater and more complex than they once were. The business
manager, particularly in the larger firm, possesses great power for good
or harm, and public opinion demands that this power be exercised with
responsibility, even though the goals to be served are not always clearly
discerned or generally agreed upon. In this respect, the large corporation, directed by salaried managers but owned for the most part by
passive stockholders, presents grave problems with which we have only
begun to grapple. Our legal institutions still impose on the executive (at
least implicitly) the primary obligation of seeking maximum profits for
his firm and his stockholders. He is also under increasing pressure from
a variety of groups to further their particular sets of interests. Cutting
across these pressures is the growing demand that the business leader
adopt broad social criteria, aimed at benefiting the weaker groups in the
economy and society at large. To these goals we must add the personal
goals of the business leader himself and of his subordinates. In an economic world that lacks the automatic regulation which the classical economists' concept of perfect competition was supposed to provide, the business executive must try to reconcile these partially conflicting goals, a

---

[14] In a similar fashion, the engineering schools are now finding that fundamental training
in mathematics, physics, and the theoretical aspects of engineering carry an engineer further
in coping with new and difficult problems than does a detailed familiarity with the details of
current engineering practice. See, for example, R. B. Adler, "Science and Engineering Education," *Journal of Engineering Education*, XLVII (October, 1956), 121–28.

task which may well be impossible.[15] In any event, the task calls for men of broad knowledge and sensitive perception, with a well-developed philosophy and set of ethical values, and with the ungrudging willingness to accept the responsibilities inevitably associated with the possession of power.[16]

It can be taken for granted that the trends described in the preceding paragraphs will continue in the years ahead and that they will be reinforced by other kinds of change which can as yet be imperfectly foreseen. Today's student who will be tomorrow's businessman must be flexible of mind and adaptable to change. He needs not so much a specialized knowledge of present business practice as the qualities of mind and the kinds of basic knowledge that will permit him to understand and adapt himself to the kind of world in which he will live and work in the years ahead.

While it has been the large corporation that has been emphasized in this discussion, much of what has been said applies to the small firm also. The rational and scientific approach is needed in firms of small and moderate size as well as in the largest concerns. Indeed, the approach is even more necessary in the small concern if the competitive advantage in favor of the great corporation is not to increase still further. Even in enterprises of only a hundred employees, administrative and organizational problems can be troublesome; the factors previously mentioned call for a scientific approach to marketing, production, and financial problems; and the small businessman, equally with the large, needs a well developed sense of his broader responsibilities and a perceptive knowledge of the ways in which a continuously changing environment is likely to affect the present course and future prospects of his business.

It would seem, then, that American businessmen would benefit from a professional-type education. They should be able to do a better job, for their firms and for society at large, with the right sort of education—if we can determine what the "right sort" is. While the preceding discussion suggests that there is room for some sort of program at the university level which is geared to the needs of businessmen, it leaves open the question whether this should be at the graduate or undergraduate level, and it says nothing about whether the present offerings of American

[15] Cf. R. A. Gordon, *Business Leadership in the Large Corporation* (1945), pp. 340–42; A. A. Berle, Jr., *The 20th Century Capitalist Revolution* (1954), particularly p. 181; and F. X. Sutton *et al.*, *The American Business Creed* (1956), p. 358.

[16] Cf. J. A. Bowie, *Education for Business Management* (1930), particularly pp. 10–11. For a general discussion of some of the issues raised in this paragraph, see Bowen, *Social Responsibilities of the Businessman;* Berle, *The 20th Century Capitalist Revolution;* and Sutton *et al.*, *The American Business Creed.*

business schools come close to meeting these needs. So far, the success of American business has depended very little on either the teaching or research activities of the business schools. However, while most of today's businessmen did not graduate from a school of business, the number who did is increasing; and business school graduates now form a significant fraction of those in the lower and middle ranks of business. Given the acceptance and appeal which business schools have as a part of our system of higher education, this trend is certain to continue.

We have, in the preceding paragraphs, put our stress on education for *business* careers, and, as its title suggests, this report is primarily concerned with the education of businessmen. But the educational needs of businessmen are not radically different from those of the administrators of other types of organizations. Organizational skill, problem-solving ability, imagination and foresight, a rational approach to the use of resources under the control of the organization, breadth of perspective, and a sense of social responsibility are qualities that are needed in all types of organizations—for example, in labor unions, government agencies, hospitals, and the military services. Much of what we shall have to say in later chapters applies in varying degrees to preparation for management careers in nonbusiness as well as in business organizations. Indeed, the business schools are increasingly coming to realize that they can make a significant contribution to training young men and women for administrative and some types of staff careers in more than just business concerns. This is a trend which clearly deserves to be encouraged.

A Brief Preview

This chapter has been concerned with some of the broad issues that confront American colleges and universities in attempting to provide an education geared to the needs of the businessman. Against this background we are now ready for the more detailed analysis in the chapters that follow. Chapter 2 provides some factual background and a broad survey of the types of institutions now offering programs in business administration. Part II (Chapters 3–7) is concerned with the nature of business competence and how it can be developed by formal education. Part III (Chapters 8–12) presents a critical survey of existing curricula and indicates the directions in which we believe change is needed. Part IV (Chapters 13–17) deals with students, faculty, teaching, and research, while a final chapter comprising Part V summarizes some of our more important recommendations and suggests possible lines of action which might help to bring about the kinds of improvement that are needed.

Perhaps it should be added that Chapter 7, by providing both a summary of the findings in Part II and a preview of the detailed educational recommendations which follow, serves also as a partial summary of the volume as a whole.

Let us now turn and take a closer look at the dimensions of this restless and still growing giant in American higher education. As we shall see in the next chapter, collegiate business education is not a very homogeneous phenomenon. Diversity, as well as bigness, is one of its conspicuous characteristics.

chapter 2

HIGHER EDUCATION FOR

BUSINESS: ITS GROWTH AND

PRESENT MAGNITUDE

BUSINESS and the businessman play a more important role in American life than in that of any other country. Also unique is the American system of higher education, which at the undergraduate level combines in a peculiarly American mixture elements of three types of European institutions: the university, the *lycée* or *gymnasium*, and the non-university technical school.[1] Within this framework the United States continues beyond the secondary school its great experiment in education, providing some combination of general and practical education to a large proportion of its citizens. More than half of the students then move out into the world of business.[2]

Against this background, it is not surprising to find that academic business education has been more extensively and highly developed in the United States than anywhere else. The United States, it is fair to say, is the first country in the world to prepare young people, formally and on a large scale, for careers in business.[3] The American business school has become an object of study for a stream of visitors from all parts of the free world, and some of its features are now being fitted into the edu-

[1] Cf. James Bryant Conant, *The Citadel of Learning* (1956), particularly chap. 2, and Abraham Flexner, *Universities—American, English, German* (1930).

[2] Ernest Havemann and Patricia Salter West, *They Went to College* (1952), p. 32.

[3] It is not correct, however, to assume that the early development of business education in the United States had no counterparts in Europe or that various forms of a professional type of business education did not exist in some other countries before the Second World War. See the learned and interesting paper by Fritz Redlich, "Academic Education for Business," *The Business History Review*, XXXI (Spring, 1957), 35–91; cf. also Heinz Hartmann, *Education for Business Leadership: The Role of the German "Hochschulen"* (Organization for European Economic Cooperation, 1955), and James A. Bowie, *Education for Business Management* (1930), chaps. 4 and 5.

cational systems of many other countries, not only in the industrial countries of Western Europe but also in the less developed areas.[4]

The Growth of Collegiate Business Education

Yet collegiate business education in the United States is not so very old—younger by a considerable margin than engineering education and, of course, much younger than the traditional forms of professional education long favored by the universities. The detailed story of the development of collegiate instruction in what was first called "commerce" and is now called "business administration" has been told a number of times.[5] We need not repeat the details of that story here. Excluding a few abortive attempts, the story begins with the founding of the Wharton School in 1881. But the rapid spread of business education in American colleges and universities did not begin until the First World War. After that, expansion was continuous and rapid, marked by particularly sharp spurts immediately following each of the two World Wars. (See Table 1.)

The expansion in the number of business students has been accompanied by a corresponding increase in the number of institutions offering work in business administration. At the close of the nineteenth century, there were only three separately organized schools of business.[6] There were over a dozen by 1910, a hundred by 1929, and about 120 by 1939.[7] Today there are about 160. In addition, formal degree programs in business are now offered by more than 400 departments or divisions not

[4] Cf., for example, discussions appearing in various publications of the European Productivity Agency in recent years. For a short summary of developments in Western Europe, see Herbert B. Schmidt, "Developing Business Leadership in Europe," *Business Horizons* (Supplement to the *Indiana Business Review*, December, 1956); Harold J. Leavitt, "On the Export of American Management Education," *The Journal of Business*, xxx (July, 1957), 153–61.

[5] See J. H. S. Bossard and J. F. Dewhurst, *University Education for Business* (1931), Part III; Benjamin Haynes and Harry Jackson, *A History of Business Education in the United States* (1935), chap. 8; Dorothy E. Lee, "Historical Development from Colonial Times," in *Education for Business Beyond High School* (*The American Business Education Yearbook*, xiv [1957]), chap. 2; Leverett S. Lyon, *Education for Business* (3rd ed., 1931), chap. 12; and "The Road Thus Far in Business Education," in *The Challenge of Business Education* (papers published in celebration of the Fiftieth Anniversary of the founding of the School of Business of the University of Chicago; 1949), pp. 30–35; L. C. Marshall, *The Collegiate School of Business* (1928); Meeri Marjatta Saarsalmi, *Some Aspects of the Thought Underlying Higher Education for Business in the United States* (Indiana Readings in Business, No. 16, 1955), particularly Part I; and Alfred Bornemann, "The Development of Economics and Administration in the School of Business," *The Journal of Business*, xxx (April, 1957), 131–40.

[6] At Pennsylvania (1881), California (1898), and Chicago (1898).

[7] Cf. The Carnegie Corporation Survey of Business Education, *Summary of Preliminary Findings* (as revised to August 1, 1958), p. 12, and H. G. Wright, "The Professional Schools of Commerce and Business Administration of Today," *The Deltasig of Delta Sigma Pi*, xxxvi (May, 1947), 93.

TABLE I

EARNED DEGREES IN BUSINESS

1919–1920 THROUGH 1957–1958

Academic Year	Degrees in Business*				Master's Degrees in Business as % of All Business Degrees	Business Degrees as as % of Degrees in All Fields	
	Bachelor's	Master's	Doctor's	All Levels		Bachelor's	All Levels
1919–20	1,576	110	0	1,686	6.5	3.2	3.2
1921–22	3,595	192	0	3,787	5.1	5.8	5.5
1923–24	5,091	267	0	5,358	5.0	6.2	5.9
1925–26	5,467	390	0	5,857	6.7	5.6	5.4
1927–28	6,748	460	3	7,211	6.4	6.1	5.8
1929–30	6,376	578	4	6,958	8.3	5.2	5.0
1931–32	9,755	1,017	35	10,807	9.4	7.1	6.8
1933–34	9,657	897	35	10,589	8.5	7.1	6.7
1935–36	9,973	698	38	10,709	6.5	7.0	6.5
1937–38	14,289	951	34	15,274	6.2	8.7	8.1
1939–40	18,549	1,139	37	19,725	5.8	10.0	9.1
1947–48	37,328	3,357	41	40,726	8.2	13.7	12.8
1948–49	61,624	3,897	29	65,550	5.9	16.8	15.5
1949–50	72,137	4,335	58	76,530	5.7	16.6	15.3
1950–51	58,237	4,355	65	62,657	7.0	15.2	13.7
1951–52	46,683	3,826	92	50,601	7.6	14.1	12.6
1952–53	40,706	4,035	109	44,850	9.0	13.4	12.0
1953–54	39,827	4,231	118	44,176	9.6	13.6	12.3
1954–55	40,350	4,641	144	45,135	10.3	14.0	12.7
1955–56	41,035	4,266	121	45,422	9.4	13.3	12.1
1956–57	45,455	4,575	93	50,123	9.1	13.4	12.2
1957–58	50,090	5,205	109	55,404	9.4	13.7	12.6

* "Bachelor's degrees" is the same as the Office of Education's category "Bachelor's and First Professional degrees" except that adjustments have been made so as to include master's degrees in business ("First Professional" degrees) as "master's degrees."
Source: See Appendix D.

organized as separate schools or colleges, as well as by more than a score of technical (engineering) institutes.

We commented in Chapter 1 on the growth of collegiate business education. This growth can be followed in Table 1. Not only did total college enrollments expand more or less continuously up to the Second World War and then jump sharply after the war, but business students have tended to constitute a larger and larger fraction of the total. At least this was true until the tide of veterans began to subside around 1950. Since then bachelor's degrees awarded in business have represented about 13 per cent of all bachelor's degrees, compared to about 16 per cent in 1948–50.

It is no secret that, as the proportion of college-age students going to college has risen, the relative emphasis on the practical aspects of a college education has also increased. Thus the expansion in collegiate business enrollments reflects the great increase both in the total college population as well as in the fraction of college students who seek to use their college education as the opening wedge into a business career and thus as a first step up the socioeconomic scale.

Despite the increasing attention being paid to business training at the post-baccalaureate level, business education is still very much an undergraduate affair. Of the 55,000 business degrees awarded in 1957–58, only about 5,000 were master's degrees. The general impression that graduate work in business has been expanding rapidly is correct. But it started from a very small base, and it has grown not much faster than undergraduate business enrollments. Thus, while the number of advanced business degrees now awarded annually is several times as great as in the 1930s, this is true also of the number of bachelor's degrees. The ratio of master's to bachelor's degrees is now only slightly larger than it was in some of the depression years, but significantly higher than in the 1920s or late 1930s.

By the standards of other fields, the ratio of advanced to bachelor's degrees in business is low. Table 2 brings this out clearly. The contrast stands out even in comparison with a field like engineering, in which professional training is also primarily at the undergraduate level. Clearly, graduate work in business is still not a very popular route to a business career. Perhaps even more alarming for the future is the small number of doctor's degrees in business. A smaller fraction of those receiving master's degrees go on to the doctorate in business administration than in any of the other fields shown in Table 2. Again, the contrast with engineering and the other professional fields is striking.[8]

Business Education in the Future

The number of business degrees awarded at all levels in 1956–57 was about 50,000, and business enrollments were nearly 400,000.[9] That is, enrollments were about this figure if we count students enrolled in busi-

---

[8] The very small number of doctorates in business is less alarming than it seems because a significant fraction of the needed college teachers and research workers is composed of those holding doctor's degrees in the social sciences, particularly economics. This is a subject we shall examine further in Chapter 14.

[9] The enrollment figure was obtained by taking 13 per cent of total collegiate enrollments in Fall, 1956, as reported by the U. S. Office of Education (*Higher Education*, XIV [January, 1958], 76). A figure of 383,100 was obtained. The ratio of 0.13 comes from Professor John P. Lewis of Indiana University; we shall have more to say about this figure later in this section.

TABLE 2

DISTRIBUTION OF EARNED DEGREES BY FIELD OF STUDY, 1955-1956

Field of Study[a]	Total No. of Degrees	Distribution by Level of Degree			Doctorates as Proportion of Master's Degrees
		Bachelor's	Master's	Doctor's	
All fields	379,641	81.7%	16.0%	2.3%	14.7%
Education	102,337	69.0	29.4	1.6	5.3
Business and commerce	*45,422*	*90.3*	*9.4*	*0.3*	*2.8*
Social sciences— basic[b]	41,915	88.5	8.9	2.6	28.2
Social sciences— applied	4,788	80.5	17.2	2.3	13.7
Engineering	31,646	83.1	14.9	2.0	12.9
Physical sciences and mathematics	21,787	75.0	16.3	8.7	53.5
English and journalism	19,304	87.2	10.7	2.1	18.7
Fine and applied arts and architecture	15,453	81.9	16.6	1.5	9.3
Biological science	15,350	81.9	11.4	6.7	58.3
Agriculture and home economics	11,517	85.5	11.2	3.3	29.3
Psychology	7,272	77.9	13.4	8.7	65.2
Foreign language and literature	5,130	77.6	17.5	4.9	28.2
Philosophy	3,017	88.4	8.8	2.8	30.7
Forestry	1,209	80.7	16.5	2.8	17.1

[a] A few fields (e.g., law) are excluded because of non-comparability of degree designations. Degrees in "business and commerce" and in "all fields" have been adjusted to include as master's degrees those degrees reported by the United States Office of Education as "Bachelor's and First Professional degrees" which are, in fact, master's degrees in business. Such an adjustment does not appear necessary for the remaining fields.
[b] Includes geography.
Source: See Appendix D.

ness programs plus those not yet enrolled but who will eventually take degrees in business. Exclusion of the latter group yields an estimate for 1956–57 of about 200,000.[10]

[10] Figures on enrollments for business students are, in the last analysis, neither reliable nor very meaningful. Since enrollments by field of study must be estimated from total enrollment data, the common procedure of using the ratio of degrees awarded in business to all degrees awarded yields estimates of dubious value. The problem, of course, is that students who eventually receive degrees in business may be registered as business students for two, three, or all four of their college years.

Total college enrollments, of course, will be rising considerably in the next fifteen years. It is generally assumed that the relative increase in the number of business students will be fully as great, perhaps even larger.[11] There is, we suspect, more than a fair possibility that these forecasts may be somewhat on the high side. A glance at Table 1 suggests that the proportion of total bachelor's degrees going to business students has been stable at around 13 or 14 per cent for the last six or seven years. Moreover, the proportion has not shown any significant increase since the total number of degrees began to rise again after 1953–54.

Professor John P. Lewis of Indiana University has prepared estimates of enrollments through 1970 on the assumption that the proportion of degrees awarded in business in 1950–54 could be extrapolated.[12] Dean Herbert Hamilton, although using quite different figures, also seems to prefer the assumption that the business share of total enrollments will not change considerably.[13]

We shall not try to add our own projections of future business enrollments to those that have already been made. While the absolute number of business students is certain to rise further and thus increase the pressure on already strained facilities, the possibility must at least be considered that the ratio of business to all college students may decline. There are a number of reasons for believing that this may turn out to be the case. Students are becoming aware of the recent widespread criticism of undergraduate business education, some of which they will find reflected in faculty discussions in the business schools themselves. To this we can add the flood of recent statements in praise of a liberal education, including the many testimonials by businessmen. The pressure to match the quality

[11] In August, 1954, a questionnaire was sent to 76 deans of business schools belonging to the American Association of Collegiate Schools of Business (AACSB). Forty-five replied to a question about what they expected business enrollments on their campuses to be relative to total campus enrollments fifteen years hence. Twenty-one expected the share to stay about the same. And 24 expected it to rise; no one expected a decline. *Faculty Requirements and Faculty Supply in Collegiate Business Teaching, 1954–1970* (AACSB, 1955), Appendix B.

[12] *Faculty Requirements and Faculty Supply in Collegiate Business Teaching, 1954–1970*, p. 15; later digested as "The Need for Collegiate Business Faculty, 1955–1970," in *Faculty Requirements and Standards in Collegiate Schools of Business* (AACSB, 1955), pp. 41–59.

[13] "The Present Status of Higher Education for Business," in *Education for Business Beyond High School*, p. 37. Dean Hamilton estimated "conservatively" a 1970 enrollment in business and commerce of 325,000. Professor Lewis projected "quite conservatively" a 1970 estimate of 619,000. (Using slightly more recent data, the two methods now yield estimates of about 370,000 and 640,000 respectively.) The large difference between these two estimates arises out of the complication mentioned previously. The larger figure includes all students who will eventually receive business degrees, whatever program they are currently enrolled in, whereas the smaller includes only those currently registered in business programs. The latter figure thus excludes many freshmen and sophomores who have not yet formally begun to "major" in business.

of scientific and technical training in Russia points in the same direction. The occasional public warning that we must not overdo the emphasis on science comes from those who argue the cause of liberal arts, not business administration. It may be, also, that our own report will slow the rush of students to the undergraduate business schools and accelerate the development of business training at the post-baccalaureate level. An attendant result would be some shift at the undergraduate level from business to other fields. A general rise in standards such as we advocate, and which is already occurring in some institutions, would also operate to hold down the rise in business enrollments.

None of this should cause any apprehension in the schools of business. Resources are hardly adequate to cope with even present enrollments, and present faculties are clearly inadequate, in both quantity and quality, to deal with the much larger numbers of students predicted for the 1960s. Indeed, if the enthusiasm for undergraduate business education should subside somewhat, while college enrollments generally are rising, the transition to the kind and quality of educational program we recommend in this report might turn out to be less difficult than we should otherwise expect it to be.

The Diversity of Business Education

Business education is a term with many meanings—from secondary school work to doctoral programs, from the education of future corporation executives to the training of high school teachers, and from the teaching of typing and filing to instruction in business policy and organization theory. This variety in instruction is matched by the diversity in the types of institutions which offer educational programs in business: secondary schools, proprietary commercial colleges, junior or community colleges, colleges and universities, and private business firms and their associations. Even if we look only at collegiate business education, heterogeneity is still the keynote. Business degrees are conferred by four-year colleges ranging from converted normal schools to some of the better liberal arts colleges, by technical institutes, and by multipurpose universities. These institutions are public and private, urban and rural, large and small, old and new, good and bad. The programs may be administered by academic departments or divisions, or by semi-autonomous schools or colleges. Work may be offered at the graduate or the undergraduate level or at both. Students may be full-time or, as in the case of the urban schools, a significant number may be part-time.

Our concern is only with collegiate business education, particularly but not exclusively as it is offered by separately organized schools or colleges of business administration in the universities. We shall, however, pay brief attention to the business programs of the junior colleges in Chapter 10, where we shall also consider the business-type programs offered by the engineering schools.

Business programs leading to the bachelor's or master's degree are today available in about 600 four-year colleges and universities. About 160 of them have separately organized schools or colleges of business, and these award about three-fourths of all business degrees. In addition, there are more than 400 departments or divisions of business administration (frequently combined with the department of economics), accounting for a bit more than a quarter of all business degrees. (See Table 3.)

As a general rule, departments of business tend to be relatively small. The average number of degrees awarded by business departments in 1956 was about 30; for schools of business, the average was about 200. Few departments graduate as many as 50 students per year; not many schools graduate fewer than this number.

As we should expect, colleges (as distinct from universities) offer their work in business primarily through departments. The separately organized schools of business are usually units of universities which offer both graduate and undergraduate instruction and also include professional schools in other fields.[14]

The particular institutional setting within which a business program is offered helps us to understand the limitations and pressures with which the business faculty must cope in shaping its educational policies. Most schools of business, for example, are more or less independent in terms of administrative discretion; they also tend to reflect a professional orientation which is common on university campuses but relatively rare among four-year colleges. Departments, of course, are more likely to have an undergraduate, liberal arts orientation.

In line with this difference in resources and orientation, schools are more likely to offer graduate work than are departments. About 60 per cent of the schools have master's curricula, while fewer than 10 per cent of the departments do. The latter accounted for only 8 per cent of the master's degrees. The schools of business are increasingly becoming fully

[14] The exceptions are less important than they seem on the surface. Some of the "universities" having departments of business actually are more like colleges than universities; a similar statement is true of the "colleges" reported as having schools of business. The U. S. Office of Education classifies institutions of higher education by "type of program." It recognizes eleven types of programs which we have combined into three categories. For details, see Appendix D.

TABLE 3

NUMBER OF EARNED DEGREES IN BUSINESS AND NUMBER OF
CONFERRING INSTITUTIONS BY TYPE OF INSTITUTION AND
LEVEL OF DEGREE, 1955–1956

Type of Institution and Level of Program[a]		No. of Institutions Conferring Earned Degrees in Business			No. of Earned Degrees Conferred in Business		
		Through Schools of Business	Through Depts. of Business	Total No. of Programs	Through Schools of Business	Through Depts. of Business	Total No. of Degrees
Colleges	B	28	386	414	2,960	10,019	12,979
	M	9	20	29	118	137	255
	D	0	0	0	0	0	0
	Any level	28	386	414	3,078	10,156	13,234
Technical	B	6	17	23	694	835	1,529
institutes	M	2	3	5	37	59	96
	D	0	0	0	0	0	0
	Any level	6	18	24	731	894	1,625
Universities	B	119	31	150	23,658	2,204	25,862
	M	81	12	93	3,747	143	3,890
	D	20	1	21	120	1	121
	Any level	123	31	154	27,525	2,348	29,873
All institutions	B	153	434	587	27,312	13,058	40,370
	M	92	35	127	3,902	339	4,241
	D	20	1	21	120	1	121
	Any level	157	435	592	31,334	13,398	44,732

[a] The letters "B," "M," and "D" stand for bachelor's, master's, and doctoral programs, respectively.
Source: Appendix D. (The slight difference between the total of all degrees granted in 1955–1956 shown here and that shown in Table 1 is explained in Appendix D.)

integrated, offering degree work at three levels. Few schools in the future, we predict, will be content to offer only an undergraduate degree, although it must be confessed that many of them hardly have the resources to offer adequate work at the bachelor's level.

Collegiate business programs are affiliated with institutions which vary in a number of ways. Some are privately-controlled; others are publicly-supported. The bulk of the departments are in private institutions, while only a trifle more than half of the schools are. Most of the programs are coeducational even if they enroll many more men than women; yet there are forty women's colleges with business curricula—all but one (Simmons College) conferring business degrees through departments.[15]

There are slightly more business schools in private than in public institutions, but Table 4 reveals that the latter award a larger total of business

TABLE 4

DISTRIBUTION OF BUSINESS SCHOOLS BY REGION AND

NATURE OF CONTROL, 1955-1956[a]

		All Public Institutions				All Private Institutions		
		Degrees				Degrees		
		Business		All Fields		Business		All Fields
Region	No. of Institutions	Bachelor's	All Levels	All Levels	No. of Institutions	Bachelor's	All Levels	All Levels
New England	3	432	447	2,534	11	1,621	2,403	10,586
Middle Atlantic	6	1,892	1,967	11,195	24	5,192	6,649	33,811
Southeast	20	3,208	3,342	19,979	11	845	869	5,025
Central	18	4,617	5,148	40,789	21	2,677	3,152	17,450
Southwest	9	1,740	1,821	11,602	4	634	644	2,994
Northwest	13	1,387	1,434	10,969	3	604	643	2,707
Pacific Coast	5	1,611	1,740	14,446	9	852	1,075	6,343
Totals	74	14,887	15,899	111,514	83	12,425	15,435	78,916

[a] Includes only separately organized schools or colleges of business and excludes departments and divisions of business.
Source: See Appendix D.

degrees, particularly at the bachelor's level. The business school looms larger in the private than in the public university: in 1956 about 14 per cent of all degrees awarded in the public institutions having business schools went to business students, while the comparable figure in the private universities was 19 per cent.

About half of the schools of business conferring degrees in 1956 were members of the American Association of Collegiate Schools of Business

[15] Altogether, women's colleges account for about 1 per cent of all business degrees. Only one of the 40 conferred master's degrees in 1956, and only 10 confer more than a dozen or so undergraduate degrees annually. Over 90 per cent of all degrees awarded are to men, even though women receive over a third of all degrees in all fields. Only about 3 per cent of the degrees currently being earned by women are in the field of business.

(AACSB).[16] They accounted for something less than half of all bachelor's degrees, for the bulk of all master's, and for all but one of the doctor's degrees conferred in that year. The typical member school of the Association offers both graduate and undergraduate work, has a large undergraduate enrollment, and is of the multipurpose or comprehensive type described later in this chapter. About two-fifths are schools in state universities; a considerable part of the remainder are schools in the larger metropolitan areas.

Two types of universities tend to dominate collegiate business education in the United States. One is the state university, particularly in the Midwest, South, and Far West. The other is the large urban university, usually privately supported. Both types attract students covering a wide range of ability. In both, students' interests tend to run toward what is practical. The urban schools have particular problems of their own—for example, large numbers of part-time students, many students who come from working class families in which the parents had little education, the need to offer extensive evening programs, a large demand for vocational-type courses, considerable use of businessmen as part-time faculty members, and a tendency for the full-time faculty to become heavily involved in consulting. Some of the worst examples of overspecialization and course proliferation are found in these large urban schools.

Table 4 provides some indication of the regional distribution of business students in so far as they are enrolled in schools rather than departments of business. Students in the privately supported schools were concentrated in the East and Midwest. More than half the degrees awarded by the publicly supported schools went to students in the Midwest and Southeast, but there were a substantial number in every region except New England. The large business school is a particularly important phenomenon in the Middle Atlantic, Central, and Southeastern states. Although colleges and universities in these three areas combined confer only 49 per cent of all degrees, they account for about 65 per cent of all business degrees awarded by schools of business and for nearly 70 per cent of all business degrees conferred by members of the AACSB.

It is the separately organized schools that provide the bulk of the undergraduate and nearly all of the graduate instruction in business administration. It is they who are responsible for selecting and preparing the future teachers of business subjects and to whom we must look for

[16] There were 80 member schools in 1956. This figure had risen to 93 by 1958. (Letter to the authors from James A. M. Robinson, Executive Secretary of the Association, August 5, 1958.)

research.[17] This report, therefore, is primarily concerned with these schools of business. Business education under other administrative arrangements is not unimportant, but it is the collegiate school of business which must carry the bulk of the burden and which ultimately sets the pace and tone for all formal education for business. In the remainder of this chapter we shall examine the various forms which the school of business can take. Business education in departments of business, junior colleges, and engineering schools will be dealt with in Chapter 10, although much of what is said in other chapters will also be relevant to the teaching of business in these contexts.

Types of Business Schools

Even when we concentrate upon the separately organized schools of business administration, the factor of diversity stands out. Of course, many elements of similarity exist. Instruction is more or less autonomously organized in a separate school or college under its own dean. Schools of business tend to be fairly large, averaging, as we have noted, about 200 graduates annually. They tend to be multipurpose operations, although there are wide differences in the degree to which various types of activity are emphasized. Most offer degrees at two levels and all except a few teach undergraduates. Nearly all have or participate in service-type educational activities in addition to their regular degree programs. These additional educational activities include the offering of separate courses for part-time students in an evening college or extension division and various types of training programs, conferences, and institutes for businessmen. The training of future businessmen and some degree of service to the business community are objectives virtually all business schools have in common. But the schools differ widely in the degree to which the research function is emphasized. About half have formalized research units, which, however, are as often concerned with community service as with research in a real sense.

The variation among schools is so great that the concept of a typical school is not very useful. We can, however, distinguish a few broad types, each having significant elements of diversity.

The simplest basis of differentiation is by the level of instruction offered. We can distinguish exclusively graduate schools, the integrated or comprehensive schools that offer both graduate and undergraduate instruction, and those which are almost exclusively undergraduate schools, although some may have a very small and weak master's program attached

---

[17] Except in so far as the training of teachers and research go on outside of business schools entirely, as, for example, in social science departments.

as an appendage. In each of these three types, the following elements of diversity should be taken into account: the school's general orientation and its approach in teaching business subjects, the emphasis on research, the range of service activities offered and the nature of the faculty's contacts with the business community, and the quality of the students. We have already noted some other elements of diversity, for example, whether the school is in a publicly or privately supported institution and whether it operates in an urban setting. Certain other organizational characteristics which may be differentiating factors, such as the location of the economics department and the degree of departmentalization within the school, will not be dealt with in this chapter. Our purpose here is only to sketch in broad strokes the major elements of diversity among business schools.

THE EXCLUSIVELY GRADUATE SCHOOLS

A few business schools are organized to give work only to students who already have bachelor's degrees. At the moment there are nine such schools: at Carnegie Tech, Chicago, Columbia, Cornell, Harvard, New York University, Stanford, the University of Virginia, and Dartmouth.[18] The Amos Tuck School at Dartmouth is included in this list even though, because of its "three-two" program, most of its students do not receive their bachelor's degrees until the end of their first year at the school.

Although these graduate schools differ considerably, most of them have certain things in common besides the requirement that their students must already have a bachelor's degree. In so far as overall quality can be measured, they are among the best of American business schools; only a few of the schools offering undergraduate instruction can be said to rate as highly. With one exception, these schools offer fairly broad training and neither require nor encourage undergraduate work in business.[19] Virtually all have close ties to the business community, and most have

[18] It is not easy to compile a list of exclusively graduate schools. In the above list, Chicago, Harvard, and Stanford are clearly eligible; Dartmouth is, with the proviso mentioned. At Carnegie Tech, Columbia, and Cornell some undergraduate instruction in business is given somewhere on the campus, although in each case the school of business administers only graduate degrees. At New York University there are two schools of business, one undergraduate and one graduate, each with its own faculty and dean. The University of Virginia, which has long had an undergraduate school, now also has a completely separate graduate school with its own dean and faculty. The latter graduated its first students in 1957. Some universities, such as the University of California (both Berkeley and Los Angeles), and Northwestern, have graduate schools which share faculties with the undergraduate schools. We have not classified such schools as being exclusively graduate. The school at M.I.T. offers instruction leading to both graduate and undergraduate degrees, but has an emphasis that nearly qualifies it as an "exclusively" graduate school.

[19] The graduate school at New York University is unlike the other exclusively graduate schools in a number of respects.

well developed management development programs. Except for Dartmouth and Virginia, all award the doctorate as well as the master's degree.

While a narrow kind of specialism is frowned on by this group of schools, there is still some variation in their general orientation and approach to teaching. In this respect, two lines of differentiation may be drawn. Business teaching may have a managerial and clinical emphasis and concentrate on decision-making with respect to the internal problems of the firm. Or it may have an external emphasis, concentrating on analysis or description of a firm's activities in its broader setting. Secondly, the approach may be broad, with little intensive cultivation of particular business specialties, or it may be narrow, emphasizing work in one or another special area of business.[20]

Several graduate schools (for example, Harvard and Stanford) emphasize both breadth and managerial decision-making. The viewpoint is almost exclusively that of the general manager faced with the need to make decisions. Significantly, these schools have not been notable for pioneering research (although some exception must be made for Harvard), and all make extensive use of the case system of teaching.

Other graduate schools (for example, Chicago and Columbia) are more "academic" in their approach. While a managerial, decision-making approach is not completely neglected, there is more of an external and analytical emphasis than at the schools in the first group; more attention is put on explaining why and how firms function in and adjust to their environment. There is also more emphasis on subject matter than in the first category. This emphasis on subject matter leads the schools in the second group to require students to have a field of specialization. And in line with their more academic orientation, they place more emphasis on faculty research.

The graduate offerings at Carnegie Tech (and at M.I.T.) differ from other master's programs in their technical setting and the consequent fact that their students have backgrounds in engineering or science. In their orientation toward research and their emphasis on significant subject matter, they resemble the second group, but both also put a fair amount of emphasis on managerial decision-making. However, both stress analysis and the search for principles considerably more than the first group. Research is emphasized in both schools and particularly at

[20] It should be noted that a "business specialty" can be either internal (e.g., personnel management) or external (e.g., transportation), just as an internal approach can be either broad or narrow depending on whether it emphasizes or deemphasizes functional or departmental lines.

Carnegie Tech, which has been a pioneer in bringing the behavioral sciences and some of the newer mathematical and statistical techniques to bear on business problems.

THE INTEGRATED MULTIPURPOSE SCHOOLS

More than half (about a hundred) of all business schools offer both graduate and undergraduate instruction. It is among these schools that the bulk of the membership of the AACSB is to be found. In their manifold activities, problems, and limitations, they represent the quintessence of collegiate business education.

Schools of this type have a number of characteristics in common. They are generally large and engage in a wide range of activities. They offer degree programs at the bachelor's, master's, and frequently (about a fourth of the time) the doctoral level. They have (or participate in) extensive educational offerings outside their degree programs, including extension courses, a variety of conferences for business groups, and frequently a management development program. Some members of the faculty engage in consulting activities for private business firms. A large part of the business textbooks come from institutions of this type. A majority of these schools have a "bureau of research" in some guise or another, although the activities of the bureau usually fall more under the heading of community service than research. Nearly all of these schools offer at least lip service to the objective of furthering research. For some, it is only lip service; in others, the goal is followed assiduously but with results which are frequently more noticeable in terms of quantity than quality.

Internal diversity is a common characteristic of these schools: a wide range in the abilities of students and in the quality of the faculty; a variety of approaches and teaching methods in the courses given; differences in the interests of faculty members ranging from those who do nothing but teach to those with extensive outside activities and to those who spend most of their time on library research.

What we are describing, obviously, is not only the business school in the large state university, but also the business school which is part of a large urban university. It is this type which Clark Kerr has referred to as the "split personality" business school: "It must be several things to several people. Its soul must belong, in part, to both God and Mammon, and considering the pressures it is under, it may remain in this state forever."[21]

[21] "The Schools of Business Administration," in *New Dimensions of Learning in a Free Society* (1958), p. 72.

So much for the prototype of the "comprehensive" business school. It is only a prototype, and there is even wider variation among individual schools in this category than among the purely graduate schools.

Few of these comprehensive schools approach business administration as broadly as do most of the exclusively graduate schools. The emphasis on managerial decision-making is growing and is stronger at some schools than at others; but for most the primary emphasis is still on command of subject matter. Most of these schools tend to fragment business into special fields, although some take a rather broad approach.[22] In general, the range is from schools which emphasize a fairly broad, analytical (but not necessarily managerial) approach, to those which emphasize narrow, vocational-type skills and description of prevailing business practice. In something of an intermediate position are those schools which, while emphasizing a considerable degree of specialization, approach these special fields at a respectable level of analysis.

The majority of these schools are conventional in their emphasis on subject-matter specialization, their neglect of the newer developments in some of the underlying disciplines, their neglect of a managerial emphasis, and their failure to integrate their curricula.[23] But in all these respects signs of improvement and of a "new look" are beginning to appear in a number of them. Although some comprehensive schools are not much more than vocational schools, others attempt to maintain reasonably high standards at both the graduate and undergraduate levels.

At the master's level, with a few exceptions, the comprehensive schools offer a program which in varying degrees is also conventional. The equivalent of the undergraduate core is usually a prerequisite; typically there is little if any graduate core of required courses. The degree tends to be oriented toward subject-matter specialization; by implication, the emphasis is on training staff specialists rather than general managers. Some schools are moving, at varying rates of speed, toward the newer type of "professional" M.B.A. program, which is described in detail in Chapter 11.

There is also wide variation in the quantity and quality of the research output among the comprehensive schools. In most, such research as does go on tends to be largely descriptive. In many schools, there is little if anything that can properly be called research, even when a bureau of

[22] The approach may be either "broad and external to the firm" or "broad and internal." Failure to distinguish between these two aspects of a general approach to business education has sometimes resulted in confusion.

[23] A few attempt integration through a business policy course in the senior year (see Chapter 9). Indiana has recently inaugurated a comprehensive examination at the end of the junior year which seeks, among other things, to consolidate what the student has learned in his core courses.

business research occupies a prominent place in the building. In only a few schools is there a noticeable amount of significant research output.

Needless to say, these schools vary widely in the quality of their faculty and student bodies. Some expect their faculty to have doctorates, to publish, and to maintain contacts with the business community. In others, most of the faculty is less well trained, and instructors do less than they might to keep up with the scientific literature and current business practice.

There is similar variation in the quality of students. A few schools are fairly selective in admitting students, both graduate and undergraduate. Others admit virtually all applicants, particularly to the undergraduate program. Some schools attempt to maintain high academic standards even in the face of a non-selective admissions policy, with consequent high attrition rates; others make little pretense at maintaining high standards.

THE UNDERGRADUATE BUSINESS SCHOOLS

The schools with exclusively undergraduate programs cover a wide range. While a few are large, most are not. Only a few are members of the AACSB. They operate in a variety of settings and ways: some are in the smaller state universities; a number are publicly or privately supported metropolitan schools; there are a number of Catholic institutions, and some affiliated with Protestant denominations.

Needless to say, the general quality of schools in this group is not high. Almost no research emerges from them, and, with some exceptions, the quality of both students and faculty tends to be low, although in many cases no lower than in the poorer of the comprehensive schools. (And often no lower than in the liberal arts departments on the same campus.)

In their general orientation and approach to teaching, these schools show considerable variation. A few view their teaching broadly, but usually without much depth of analysis and with little emphasis on maagerial problem-solving. A larger number, particularly the urban schools, go in for a good deal of specialization, and some are quite narrowly vocational. In general, teaching tends to be on the descriptive side with a heavy reliance on textbooks.

Except in some of the urban schools, service activities tend to be limited. Full-fledged management development programs are the exception, although special programs may be run for particular business groups. Faculty contacts with the business community are generally not extensive. Most of these schools have modest pretensions and limited objectives. The highest aspiration of many is eventual membership in the AACSB. With very few exceptions, they are followers, not innovators, and significant improvement in their programs will inevitably wait on action by their big brothers, the multipurpose schools, particularly as such action is reflected in the standards of the Association.

Closing the Gap

Such is the population of business schools that seek to educate tomorrow's businessmen, to serve the business community and society at large, and to add to our store of knowledge about the functioning of business. In a sense, diversity has been the theme of this brief survey—diversity and the very wide gap between the poorest and the best.

We think that the beginning of a consensus as to what is good and bad in collegiate business education is beginning to emerge. So is the feeling of a need to narrow the gap between the poorest and the best—or, more realistically, between the average and the best. There is increasing agreement on the desirability of greater breadth in both the senses in which it has been used in this chapter, higher standards and more analytical rigor, more emphasis on managerial problem-solving and organizational and communication skills, a reduced emphasis on subject-matter, and a greatly lessened degree of specialization.

The need for widespread reform is clear, although the diversity we have emphasized makes reform difficult. The avenue to improvement does not require that all business schools be remade in a common image. But they all can, within the limitations of their environment, judge themselves (and be judged) by standards of excellence that have general approval and reflect the most informed opinion as to how particular objectives can best be achieved. The key to widespread improvement lies with the integrated, multipurpose business schools. They are the great middle class of collegiate business education. They account for most of the membership of the AACSB and thus are largely responsible for the minimum standards by which most business schools govern themselves. A major task is to find in this group the needed leaders and innovators. A few, we think, are beginning to emerge.

Reform in collegiate business education requires a more general agreement than now exists regarding the needs the business schools should try to serve. The next several chapters are concerned largely with an analysis of these needs.

PART II

The Needs to be Served:

The Development of Business Competence

chapter 3

THE AIMS OF BUSINESS

EDUCATION

How DO business educators themselves evaluate their role in the scheme of American higher education? What needs do they attempt to serve, and how do they assess the educational requirements of the heterogeneous collection of occupations we call "business?" Public and private statements of educational objectives throw some light on these questions. Current practice is even more informative.

For What Careers Are Business Students Being Prepared?

The official statements of American business schools indicate a greater agreement about career objectives than does their practice. If we examine the official catalogues and bulletins, prepared largely for the benefit of prospective students, we find considerable repetition of a common theme. The objective is to prepare students "for positions of responsibility in business," or "for executive responsibility," or, even more broadly, "for careers in business."

Actually, these broad statements of career objectives hide a certain amount of diversity, both among schools and even within the same school. Broadly speaking, there are three types of career objectives which business schools have in mind in planning their educational programs.

The first objective stresses preparation for a career in business without regard to the kind of business or job, except that it assumes that eventually the future businessman will attain a position involving a significant amount of administrative responsibility. The stress here is on the fact that the student will become a "manager" or "administrator," although what this means is often not very clear.

The second objective also implies preparation for a lifetime career but puts the emphasis on imparting knowledge of subject matter in some particular area of business, such as accounting, marketing, production, or insurance. This objective is narrower than the first; it emphasizes the need for specialized knowledge more, and the broader types of knowledge and abilities less, than does the first objective. On the other hand, the second objective recognizes the need of business for specialists and the fact that the earlier years of a business career are likely to be spent in more or less specialized jobs.

The third objective is not often admitted publicly and is never the sole career objective of a school or department of business. This is training for the first job after graduation. This objective plays a considerable role in probably the majority of undergraduate schools and a major role in many, although it is openly disavowed by the better graduate and undergraduate institutions.

PREPARATION FOR THE FIRST JOB

Inevitably, there is a high inverse correlation between the emphasis placed on the third objective and the quality of the school. This is true for two reasons. First, preoccupation with the need to prepare the student for his first job is greatest in institutions which attract students of inferior native ability or those with a poor educational or cultural background. Secondly, concern with a vocational objective leads to overemphasis on a narrow range of factual knowledge and the development of largely routine skills, with a consequent neglect of more fundamental knowledge and the broader, more basic skills, including general problem-solving ability and the capacity to learn from new experience.

Emphasis on the narrow and short-range vocational objective is tending to diminish, although its influence is still all too apparent in the course offerings and teaching in many business schools. Among the leaders of educational opinion, the view is unanimous that preparation for the first job is not a legitimate objective of business education at the collegiate level. At best, training for the first job should enter only as an incidental byproduct of training for the entire career. Otherwise, purely vocational rather than professional education is being offered.[1] On this point, the evidence is overwhelmingly in one direction, and we shall add some further evidence of our own in later chapters.

PREPARATION FOR GENERAL AND SPECIALIZED CAREERS

Let us return to the other two objectives: preparation for a general business career with emphasis on preparation for positions of administrative responsibility, and training for specialized careers emphasizing

[1] There would be no dissent among leading educators with the following forceful statement by Robert Calkins. "The issue is between training for a job and training for a career. On this issue I shall be emphatic. Any student with intelligence enough to benefit from college education should be prepared for a career." "Objectives of Business Education," *Harvard Business Review*, xxv (Autumn, 1946), 48.

technical competence. The recent trend, particularly among the "prestige" schools, is to concentrate on the first. The rank and file of schools put considerable weight on the second, although recognition of the first objective is noticeably growing. The following statement by one state university is typical. "Academic training for business is directed primarily toward preparation for future business, industrial, and civic leadership; secondarily, for professional competence in the fields of accountancy, finance, marketing, management, and others."

The exclusively graduate schools concentrate primarily on the first type of career objective, not only in their published statements but also in their practice. These schools tend to attract better students, who are assumed to be capable of moving eventually into positions of considerable responsibility. The emphasis is on a broad base of fundamental knowledge (more so in some schools than others) and the development of certain basic skills on which the student can build through experience obtained after college. Specialization is, in general, eschewed. Most of these schools put their emphasis on training for "management and administration," although the possibility of a high-level staff career is not ignored.

This is increasingly the emphasis at a few of the undergraduate schools. The same sort of emphasis on a broad training, but not necessarily the same concentration on management or administration, is found in some of the other better undergraduate programs.

A larger number of undergraduate schools emphasize preparation for specialized careers, although this is not always clear from the statements of educational philosophy appearing in their official bulletins. Occasionally, the preparation is at a reasonably high level; what is apparently envisaged are careers which, while specialized, involve technical competence of a fairly high order. All too often, however, the training is at a low level, involving detailed descriptions of current practice and the development of low-level skills. When this is so, the assumption is being made implicitly that the student will not rise very far in the business world. For the less capable students this assumption is undoubtedly justified. It is not justified, however, to assume that the student will not need new skills and knowledge as he grows older, either because of job changes he will make or because business practice itself will change. The narrower a student's training and the more it emphasizes current practice, the less well equipped he will be to cope with change and to learn from experience.

Some schools see themselves as training such technicians and low-level supervisors; their programs would not look much different if they were openly preparing their students for narrowly defined specific jobs, as some of them openly admit doing. Among the more specialized curricula that some schools make available are property insurance, marketing of building products, light construction, fashion merchandising, airline and airport management, restaurant management, and executive secretary-ship. More common are the more broadly defined but still specialized fields such as public accounting, advertising, banking, insurance, pur-chasing, real estate, and traffic management. Specialization is still less marked when the student majors simply in accounting, finance, market-ing, personnel, or production; it virtually disappears when the field of concentration is defined as "management" or "general business."

Some schools are quite open in avowing the objective of specialized training. Thus one business school in the South announces that it "has the staff, curricula, and facilities to offer any degree of specialization in the respective fields of business endeavor." The school in a neighboring state announces in a brochure a four-point program which lists, in this order, preparation for the first job, training for promotion on the job, "the opportunity to specialize," and guiding the student's interests "toward an active civic and cultural life."

It is typical for a business school to profess in its catalogue a set of broad objectives and in the same publication to list a wide variety of narrow courses and fields of specialization, in which a large part of the student's time will be spent. For example, one large urban school, a member of the AACSB,[2] claims "to give the student both a broad back-ground of understanding of his social and economic environment and a basic knowledge of the structure of business." It adds that the "class-room cannot substitute for business apprenticeship" and that "the work in the School is intended to help the student develop breadth and pene-tration in his thinking so that his early business experience will be more meaningful." The student "is encouraged to postpone specialization to the graduate year." Yet the nonbusiness (general education) require-ments of this school are clearly inadequate to implement these stated ob-jectives. And despite the reference to breadth, the student is offered his choice of fifteen fields of concentration within business, in one of which he is expected to take a large number of specialized courses. Among the courses required in some of these specialized curricula are such offerings as Salesmanship, Advertising Copy and Mechanics, Advertising Cam-

---

[2] The fact that this school is a respected member of the Association should be noted. We have the impression that the strongest supporters of specialization are some of the members of the AACSB. The weakness of nonmember schools lies in such matters as standards, faculty, and students, but not necessarily in more specialized curricula than those of member schools.

paigns, Air Cargo Economics and Operation, Credits and Collections, Industrial Safety and Hygiene, Retail Store Operation, Employee Training, Advanced Shorthand, Office Appliances, and the like. Some of these courses are standard fare in many undergraduate business schools

BROAD VS. SPECIALIZED TRAINING

The issue between breadth and specialization has not yet been resolved, but it is clear that the advocates of highly specialized training are increasingly on the defensive. As we pointed out at the end of Chapter 2, there is growing agreement on the need for greater breadth and higher standards in collegiate business education. As standards are raised and as the emphasis on analytical rigor and problem-solving ability grows, we can assume that there will be a concomitant decline in the kind of specialized training that concentrates on descriptive detail and low-order skills. The need to prepare some students for specialized careers that call for mastery of a body of technical subject matter will, however, continue to exist. As we shall point out later, such technical training will increasingly require the foundation of a broad undergraduate education, with an appropriate emphasis on various of the underlying disciplines, and is therefore best obtained at the graduate level.

Another reason for emphasizing breadth of training is suggested by the fact that the business schools are in a position to assist in the training of future administrators in nonbusiness organizations; a number of schools have adopted this as one of their subsidiary objectives. The more specialized and narrow the business curriculum, the less the business school has to offer future government officials, trade union leaders, or hospital administrators. But as we noted in Chapter 1, the educational needs of such administrators are not radically different from those of businessmen.

Development of the Qualifications
That Make for Business Competence

As we shall see later, business competence can be viewed as a bundle of skills, which in turn derive from some combination of knowledge, the ability to apply that knowledge, and personal traits. A good part of the difficulty which business schools have in formulating a satisfactory educational program stems from lack of knowledge regarding these ingredients of business competence and how any particular set of qualifications can best be developed.

The problem involved in relating educational programs to the qualifications needed for the practice of business can be resolved into several component elements. First of all, what do we know about the kinds of business careers in which college graduates engage, including the particular succession of jobs they hold as they move upward in the business world? Second, what are the qualifications common to all or most business occupations, and to what extent do the qualifications vary according to the career and the job? Third, what should be the role of formal education in developing the qualifications needed? What is the most effective division of labor between undergraduate and graduate education, on the one hand, and experience on the job and special training after college, on the other?

The lack of verified answers to these questions is depressing. Relatively few business schools know very much about the careers their graduates follow, and they lose contact with students very quickly after graduation. Frequently even information about the initial placement is unavailable in any detail.[3] Since most business schools have not made a careful analysis of the kinds of careers their students will follow, they have been handicapped in determining the kinds of qualifications they should seek to develop.

Detailed information on the career histories of college graduates who go into business is both difficult and expensive to obtain, and in this report we have not been able to add much to what is already known. Even without precise quantitative data, however, we think it is possible to do more than business educators have done so far to analyze the ingredients of business competence.

THE SKILLS AND KNOWLEDGE NEEDED

There is a modest amount of consensus among business educators as to the qualities they should seek to develop in their students, but in many institutions very little thought has been given to the matter. Some schools emphasize the need to develop the ability to analyze and solve problems. In a sense, the spread of the case method of teaching is a measure of the growing emphasis on this objective, although it is clear that analytical ability can also be developed in other ways.

Some schools refer to the need to develop "administrative skills." What is meant by this term is not always apparent. Increasing reference is made to the need "to get along with other people" or "to get things done through other people," but systematic work to develop this capacity is required in only a small minority of schools.

---

[3] What information does exist comes from the placement office and seldom is widely disseminated among the faculty. In several schools we visited, the dean's impressions regarding the nature of the first jobs taken by his school's graduates conflicted with what we were later told by the placement office itself.

In general, business schools are content to say that they seek to develop "the basic skills" needed for responsible careers in business. Neither their published statements, their educational programs, nor our conversations with deans and faculties in all parts of the country revealed a clear awareness of what these skills are or how they may best be developed.

Somewhat the same situation prevails as to the kind of knowledge the schools believe their students should acquire. Emphasis is put on a "knowledge of business fundamentals," "an understanding of business principles and practices," and the like. The core of business subjects specified by the AACSB, with all its incompleteness and vagueness, represents the present consensus as to the knowledge of "business fundamentals" required. Even here there is considerable variation in practice. To some schools, "fundamentals" mean generalizations that serve as a basis for analysis; to others, they mean description of existing institutions and practices. The analytical content of business courses varies widely among schools and even within the same school. In most business courses the analytical content is not high. The kinds of knowledge of the underlying disciplines that may be desirable or necessary for the understanding of business problems is still a debated issue, and a number of business schools scarcely seem to be aware that the issue exists (except for the traditional relationships between economics and business administration).

While the emphasis business schools put on the need for specialized knowledge of particular business fields varies widely, in most schools it is fairly heavy. However, few systematic studies have been made of the kinds of training which are most appropriate for various types of specialized careers.

Some schools place importance on a broad type of understanding of the interrelationships between business and its economic, social, and political environment. This is frequently related to the need to develop in the student a sense of social responsibility and a code of business ethics. Thus a major objective at one school is to develop in the student "a philosophic outlook and historical perspective on the place and responsibilities of business in society." A more conventionally stated objective of another school is "to foster an appreciation of sound ethical and professional conduct in business affairs." In most schools, emphasis on the development of ethical standards and a sense of social responsibility does not go much beyond the statement in the official bulletin. A few schools, however, have inaugurated courses that seek to develop an awareness in the student of the role business plays in the broader society of which it is a part.

THE ROLE OF GENERAL EDUCATION

Another issue on which business schools are still badly divided is the amount of liberal or general education which should be required of future businessmen and what, precisely, the function of such education is when combined with professional training. This is a problem particularly for the undergraduate schools. But it is also an issue in which the graduate schools should be more interested than they now seem to be.

The amount of general education required by undergraduate schools of business varies greatly. The content of the requirement also shows a wide variation. Even more important, substantial disagreement exists as to what should be the role of general education in an undergraduate business school. We find frequent references to such phrases as "training for citizenship," "provision of an adequate cultural background," "well rounded social and mental development," and offering a "foundation of fundamental knowledge, disciplined mind, and character" for future personal growth. Few schools have a well thought out philosophy of the role of general education in their programs. Most recognize it is important but do not go much beyond that. In a good many schools, general education, aside from a few essentials and such other requirements as may be imposed by the central university administration, represents a residual claim on the student's time. Quite a few deans and faculty members protest that the "liberal values" of their business courses are as great as those of most nonbusiness courses their students take. While undoubtedly true of some business courses in some schools, this claim is in part merely a rationalization of a situation in which between a third and a half of the members of the AACSB fail to meet the Association's requirement that 40 per cent of a student's work should be in nonbusiness subjects.

The attempt to provide professional training at the undergraduate level makes it particularly essential that the undergraduate business school take seriously its responsibility to insure that the student obtains a satisfactory amount of general education. To paraphrase John Stuart Mill, men are men before they are businessmen, and the first objective of undergraduate education should be to provide for the student an education which "looks first of all to his life as a responsible human being and citizen."[4] But the argument for stressing the importance of general

[4] The quotation is from *General Education in a Free Society* (Harvard University, 1945), p. 51. See also *Fifty-first Annual Report of the Carnegie Foundation for the Advancement of Teaching*, 1955-56; R. A. Goldwin, ed., *Toward the Liberally Educated Executive* (The Fund for Adult Education, 1957); Robert D. Calkins, "Professional Graduate Education and the Liberal Arts," *The Georgia Review*, VI (Summer, 1952), 3-19; and W. M. Kephart and J. E. McNulty, *Liberal Education and Business* (Institute of Higher Education, Teachers College, Columbia University, 1958, mimeographed).

education rests on professional as well as cultural grounds. A business-man cannot be well trained unless he is also reasonably well educated. A general education provides knowledge and develops qualities of mind and spirit that are directly useful to the businessman. In addition, parts of a general education cover the essential "preprofessional" disciplines on which the practice of business is built, in somewhat the same way that the natural sciences are necessary preprofessional subjects for the doctor or engineer.

The undergraduate school of business, therefore, cannot avoid accepting responsibility for general as well as for professional education. This is recognized by the better business schools, and this recognition lies behind the requirement of the AACSB that a minimum fraction of the total work required for the undergraduate degree in member schools must be in nonbusiness subjects.

Thus wide uncertainty exists both as to the qualifications the business schools should seek to develop and how students should be trained to acquire these attributes. There is also doubt as to how far the colleges can go in developing in the student the ability to use the knowledge he acquires. It has been said that knowledge without the ability to use it is sterile. In this respect, collegiate business education presents some striking contrasts. Some vocationally minded schools give their students intensive practice in using a narrow body of knowledge that will soon be out of date. At the other extreme, a number of well intentioned schools offer a broad education, but the students seldom have the opportunity to apply what they learn. We shall in subsequent chapters emphasize the happy medium in which the emphasis is put on breadth of knowledge, but in which the student is also made to apply what he has learned so that he can develop the analytical and organizational skills he will need.

The Educational Objective: A General Statement

Despite the uncertainty and the variation among schools, it seems to us that the basis for agreement on a general statement of educational objectives does exist and might be stated along these lines. *It should be the primary objective of collegiate business education to prepare students for personally fruitful and socially useful careers in business and related types of activity.*[5] ("Related types of activity" include any sort of career—for example, in public administration—in which organizational skill and the management of economic variables are important.)

[5] J. H. S. Bossard and J. F. Dewhurst use almost the same words: ". . . the primary aim of the university school of commerce is to prepare its students for successful and socially useful careers in business." *University Education for Business* (1931), p. 55.

The competence required for "personally fruitful and socially useful" careers calls for some combination of knowledge, skills, and attitudes, to the development of which collegiate business education can make a limited but important contribution. In the development of business competence, experience and training after entrance on a career play an even more important role than in the traditional professions. Hence, it is particularly important that schools of business concentrate on the educational foundations upon which a student can develop competence through continued self-education, since, as many have suggested, the most important thing a student can take away from college is the capacity to learn for himself. These educational foundations should emphasize the kinds of fundamental knowledge and those skills and attitudes which are most common to all types of business positions, are the more important the more responsible the position, and are the most difficult for a student to acquire after college.

Within the framework of some such statement of objectives, variation in detail can allow for differences in the abilities and aspirations of students and diversity in the educational resources which different business schools and departments have at their command. But a significant uniformity is also suggested, and in Part III we shall describe in detail the set of minimum standards we believe are implied by this statement of objectives.

First, however, we must meet some of the issues raised in the preceding section. In particular, what are the kinds of knowledge, skills, and attitudes that make for business competence? And what does the answer to this question imply as to the kind of education the future businessman should receive? One of the main purposes of this study, and particularly of the remainder of Part II, is to throw some additional light on the answers to these two questions.

The limitations of the analysis attempted in the next several chapters scarcely needs to be emphasized. The conceptual apparatus employed will not be universally accepted and undoubtedly contains defects. The factual information available is incomplete; and the first-hand collection of facts that we have been able to make, largely through intensive interviews with a modest sample of business enterprises, leaves much to be desired. Clearly, there is room for much additional research. Our purpose is not to offer definitive and final answers, but to suggest the directions in which workable answers may lie and to urge the need for a more active and concerted effort to find documented answers to the questions raised.

Other Objectives of the Business School

Up to this point we have dealt with the objectives of business education only in so far as they concern the education of future practitioners. Actually, there are three additional objectives to be considered: the training of future teachers and research workers in the field, furthering the accumulation of knowledge through research, and service activities for government, business, and the community at large. The first two functions usually go together. The training of future college and university teachers involves education at an advanced graduate level and speedily carries both faculty and students to the frontiers of what is known. There teaching merges into research, and each strengthens the other.

The urgency of the need to train future teachers of business administration is being recognized more and more.[6] As in the training for practice, there is much uncertainty as to how the job can best be done. The issues will be examined in Chapter 17.

The performance of the business schools on the side of research is even less satisfactory than with respect to teaching. Ideally, professional schools should blaze the way for the practitioner, continuously creating knowledge which in time becomes the basis for improvements in professional practice. Such, for example, is the relation between the medical schools and the practice of medicine, or between the engineering schools and engineering practice. Unfortunately, this has not been true of the business schools and the practice of business. Little fundamental research has so far come out of the business schools, and the research that is done is more likely to be descriptive of what business is now doing than the sort of pioneering research that provides the basis for what business will be doing ten years from now. This situation, however, is slowly improving.

One final objective remains to be mentioned—service to business, to other groups, and to the community at large. A business school, as part of a university, can make many valuable contributions to the life of the community, including a host of special educational programs for people already in business. The provision of technical consulting services to particular firms and government agencies is another type of service activity in which some schools are heavily engaged.

Here, again, schools vary widely in their practices. Virtually all busi-

---

[6] See, in particular, American Association of Collegiate Schools of Business, *Faculty Requirements and Standards in Collegiate Schools of Business* (1955).

ness schools engage in some service activity. But some pursue the service objective so intensively that it probably affects their ability to fulfill satisfactorily their other objectives, particularly those concerned with regular teaching and research. A related issue in many business schools is the excessive amount of private consulting performed by some faculty members. In their zeal to elicit support from the local business community, some schools go too far in the amount and variety of services they are willing to provide.

The simultaneous pursuit of a variety of objectives helps to create in a business school the sort of "split personality" described by Clark Kerr.[7] Many business schools attempt at one and the same time to educate future businessmen (offering instruction at both the graduate and undergraduate levels), push fundamental research, train future teachers and research workers, and spread themselves in a variety of service activities. Actually, there is ample room for business schools to combine these important objectives in different ways. But it is neither essential nor wise for all business schools to pursue all these objectives with the same intensity.

[7] "The Schools of Business Administration," in *New Dimensions of Learning in a Free Society* (1958), p. 72.

chapter 4

BUSINESS AS AN

OCCUPATION

IF BUSINESS SCHOOLS exist to educate students for personally fruitful and socially useful careers in business and related types of activity, we cannot avoid asking: what is a business career and what is a businessman?

The Market for Business School Graduates

To ask this question is to suggest the wide and multifarious range of activities that constitute the business world: managing a small business; selling, from the itinerant peddler and the clerk behind the counter to the top sales engineers and sales managers of the largest companies; the "line" activities of foremen and factory superintendents; the direction and coordination by "top executives" in companies with from hundreds to tens of thousands of employees; the work of a host of staff experts; all the kinds of work that go on in advertising agencies, in real estate firms, in banks and insurance companies, in railroads, airlines, and shipping companies, in all kinds of retail establishments, not to mention the varieties of manufacturing and mining, gas and electric and telephone companies, and all the other industries listed in the census classifications.

What are the common elements in this vast congeries of activities? One answer might run as follows. Business firms are organizations which engage in some sort of socially useful activity primarily for private gain. A person can be said to be engaged in the practice of business when his position requires that he be concerned with *how* some aspect (or all) of a business firm's activities contributes to the firm's organizational objectives, particularly to the objective of profit-making. Or, in more familiar terms, we are concerned with those who manage or administer the affairs of business concerns—and of nonprofit organizations that govern themselves to an important degree by economic criteria. By "manage" we mean three things: 1) making the decisions that determine the course of a firm's activities, including determining and evaluating the alternatives from which choices are to be made, 2) supervising the organizational arrangements that lead to action in response to decisions, and 3) evaluating the results of decisions in terms of the firm's objectives.[1]

This definition would lead us to include as businessmen those who are owners, managers and supervisors, and most staff specialists—but exclude those, like workmen and routine clerks, who are not charged with some responsibility, direct or indirect, for determining how the firm's physical activities relate to its objectives. Even so, this still leaves us with a tremendously wide range of activities—those of line supervisors at various levels, general managers and executives, independent entrepreneurs, and a host of staff specialists—which are carried on in all the different kinds and sizes of businesses that serve the economy. Literally interpreted, our definition would probably exclude most salesmen but would, of course, include sales managers. It would exclude many but not all engineers. It would include most supervisors, including foremen, and also all persons concerned with the various functional areas of business, even though they may have no responsibility for the decisions which their "staff" work helps to influence. It would include all owner-managers of small firms in their capacity as managers of their enterprises, but not in their activities as workmen or salesmen.

This definition of businessmen may be somewhat too broad from the point of view of the business schools. Not all persons who would qualify as businessmen by our definition would necessarily benefit from a technical business education. This is particularly true of the owners of very small businesses who are more craftsmen or salesmen than managers. It is also true of probably a good many in the lowest salaried ranks of large firms.

What has been said so far suggests that the business schools should be concerned with educating students for any sort of career in business that involves either direction of some aspect of a firm's activities or securing and analyzing the information on which such direction must depend. This corresponds substantially to what the larger business firms themselves mean by the "management group" (including first-line supervisors) plus the owners of small businesses in which the managerial function is of some importance.

Actually, as we have already suggested, the market for business school graduates is larger than "business" as we have defined it. It includes also a variety of positions in nonbusiness organizations, particularly positions

---

[1] There is considerable vagueness in the notion of decisions that "determine the course of a firm's activities." We mean approximately those decisions which serve as directives to some group within the firm. The second element, supervision, also involves decision-making, but it involves something more, particularly the coordination that comes from possession of authority. Other definitions of businessmen or business managers are available, most of which aim to characterize approximately the same group we are seeking to describe.

that are concerned with some aspect of "economic management." Thus business schools should and do train accountants and financial and personnel experts for government agencies (including the military services), educational institutions, hospitals, and the like. In addition, some business training is frequently considered a desirable background for the practice of law, much of which is concerned with the legal problems of business firms. The potential nonbusiness market for business school graduates is a large one, which the business schools should cultivate in the future more than they have in the past.

The Size of the Market

ESTIMATES FROM THE AVAILABLE DATA

Unfortunately, we do not have much of a basis for judging how many "businessmen" there are in the United States. Table 5 summarizes what can be learned from the official census statistics. Briefly, we selected from the Census of Occupations all the occupations under the headings of "professional, technical, and kindred" and "managers, officials, and proprietors" that seemed relevant; to these we added salesmen other than salesclerks in retail trade. The result is the formidable total of approximately 6,600,000. If we exclude the engineers and all salesmen, the total is still well over four and one-half million. In addition, about 750,000 foremen (excluding those in professional service industries and government) are listed in the Census.

Even this latter figure is clearly too large for our purpose. How much we reduce the figure depends, of course, on how we interpret our definition. Under a restrictive interpretation, we might include only salaried managers and owners of firms over some minimum size. If we arbitrarily exclude two million of the self-employed listed in the table and all the engineers and include only a fourth of the salesmen, we get a total of around three million. This should probably be raised to 3.7–3.8 million to allow for expansion since 1950. While somewhat arbitrary, this is probably a not unreasonable estimate of the population of businessmen which the colleges have in mind in planning their programs in business education. The figure becomes larger as we add more of the self-employed and include more salesmen.[2]

It also becomes larger as we include persons in nonbusiness organiza-

---

[2] It might be noted that there are many more self-employed than those reported in Table 5. In 1951, there were three million firms with three or fewer employees; there were about four million firms of all sizes. (*Survey of Current Business*, May, 1954, p. 18.) The difference is due to the fact that many self-employed persons report themselves not as proprietors, but as optometrists, jewelers, plumbers, etc.

TABLE 5

NUMBER OF PERSONS IN SELECTED BUSINESS OCCUPATIONS,
EXCLUDING PROFESSIONAL SERVICES AND GOVERNMENT, 1950

(In thousands)

Occupation	Total	Male	Female
Managers, officials, and proprietors:			
Categories identified by the Census which are relevant[a]	270	219	51
N.e.c. group—salaried[b]	1,689	1,498	191
N.e.c. group—self-employed[b]	2,425	2,101	325
Professional, technical, and kindred workers:			
Relevant categories including engineers[e]	886	814	72
Relevant categories excluding engineers[d]	331	271	60
Salesworkers:			
Advertising, real estate, insurance, and stock and bond	483	429	54
Other, excluding retail trade	830	766	64
Totals:			
Excluding engineers and all salesworkers[d]	4,715	4,189	627
Excluding engineers only[d]	6,028	5,284	745
Including engineers and salesworkers	6,583	5,827	757

[a] Includes buyers and department heads, store; buyers and shippers, farm products; credit men; floormen and floor managers, store; purchasing agents and buyers, not elsewhere classified.

[b] "N.e.c." stands for not elsewhere classified.

[e] Includes accountants and auditors; engineers, technical; natural scientists; personnel and labor relations workers; social scientists; professional, technical, and kindred workers, not elsewhere classified.

[d] Natural scientists as well as engineers are excluded.

Source: U.S., Bureau of the Census, *Census of Population: 1950, Occupation by Industry.* Data are for all industry categories except "professional and related services" and "public administration."

tions. For example, the 1950 Census reported more than 45,000 "accountants and auditors" in public agencies and more than 150,000 public officials not elsewhere classified, a considerable number of whom were undoubtedly engaged in some aspect of economic management.

Business schools increasingly think of themselves as being concerned with training "managers"—both those with "line" responsibilities and the staff specialists who work with them. In the interviews we conducted with officials of nearly 100 business firms, we asked our respondents to indicate what they meant by management and to report the number of

TABLE 6

NUMBER OF PERSONS IN THE "MANAGEMENT GROUP"

BY SIZE OF FIRM, 1951

(*In thousands*)

Size of Firm (Number of Employees)	Estimated Number in "Management"[a]
0 to 3	3,040
4 to 19	830
20 to 49	260
50 to 99	120
100 to 499	700
500 to 999	190
1,000 and more	1,120
Total	6,260
Owners of retail trade and service establishments with less than four employees	2,040
Total, excluding very small retail and service concerns	4,220

[a] For firms with less than twenty employees, one manager per firm was assumed; two per firm were assumed for the twenty to forty-nine employees group; and three per firm were assumed for the fifty to ninety-nine employees category. For firms with 100 to 999 employees, we took the average ratio of managerial to total employees as reported by the firms in these size groups in a sample of companies, and applied these ratios to the total number of employees in all firms in these size groups. In the case of companies with more than 1,000 employees, we used the same technique but were able to apply a different ratio to each major industry group before taking a total for all firms in this size category. Data on the number of firms by size are from Betty C. Churchill, "Size Characteristics of the Business Population" in *Survey of Current Business*, May, 1954, p. 23. Figures on the ratio of managerial to total employees were supplied by some but not all of the companies interviewed in the course of this study. For the nature of this sample of companies, see Appendix B. We should also remark that several alternative estimates were tried varying the assumptions somewhat, but the alternative calculations yielded results similar to those shown here.

employees in the "management group." Some firms included foremen in "management," and others did not. All included staff specialists above some level, generally with salaries equal to those received by persons who were included in the supervisory group.

We have experimented with some calculations, applying the ratios of management personnel to total employees derived from our sample to all firms with more than 100 employees. The results, which are summarized in Table 6, suggest that in firms of at least this size there were about 2,000,000 persons in the management group in 1951, of which an unknown number were first-line supervisors.[3] The figure had risen to perhaps 2,300,000 by 1958. Over half of these would be in firms with more than 1,000 employees. There are perhaps another 400,000 "managers" in firms with from 20 to 100 employees, and we undoubtedly should include the owners of some firms with less than twenty employees. If we include those with more than four employees and adjust upward the estimates in Table 6 to allow for some increase since 1951, we get a total for all firms of nearly 4,000,000 "managers." Allowing for the differences in implied definitions, this is roughly consistent with the estimates derived from the Census data which were summarized in Table 5.

Wolfle has offered a much smaller estimate of the number of "professional-level" workers in business for 1953. His estimate is 1,372,000, but he included only those occupations which met two criteria: 1) many but not all of those in the occupation "must have had extensive formal education of the kind which is normally secured in" college, and 2) the occupation must "require reasonably high intelligence." He thus confined himself to "professional accountants and the more generalized management group."[4] Of the group he included, slightly more than half were college graduates.

This is clearly too restrictive a concept for our purpose. The proportion of the total business population with some college education will continue to grow, and many of those in business occupations that Wolfle excluded can benefit from both a college education and formal business training. This is all the more true in light of the increasing complexity of business operations and the growing opportunities for a rational approach to business decision-making.[5]

OPENINGS IN BUSINESS IN RELATION TO BUSINESS DEGREES

What do all these figures mean in terms of the openings "in business" likely to be available in a given year? The colleges and universities are now graduating around 50,000 business students annually, of which 90 per cent are men, and it has been estimated that this figure may about double by 1970. Should we share the fear expressed by Professor Seymour

[3] This is about 10 per cent of the twenty-three million employees in firms of this size in 1951. There is other evidence supporting this 10 per cent figure. For example, a survey of 460 companies reported about 250,000 "management and supervisory personnel" and approximately 2.5 million non-management employees. *Current Practice in the Development of Management Personnel* (American Management Association Research Report No. 26, 1955), p. 3.

[4] *America's Resources of Specialized Talent*, Report of the Commission on Human Resources and Advanced Training, Dael Wolfle, Director (1954), pp. 10–11, 114–15.

[5] See Chapter 1. In all of the census categories included in Table 5, the median years of schooling for the men in 1950 were more than twelve except for the self-employed group, and the trend toward more formal education is clearly continuing.

Harris that the expansion in college enrollments will leave us with a glut of college graduates who cannot find positions that will make the most effective use of their education?[6] So far, the evidence is in the other direction, both because of the fact that the "managerial" group in business is increasing relatively more rapidly than the total labor force and because the demand for college-trained men is increasing more rapidly still. Indeed, these trends have accelerated since the Second World War.

Here, again, there is a paucity of data on which to base any quantitative judgments. Some guesses, however, may be made on the basis of calculations made by Jaffe and Carleton.[7] They estimated, for the decade of the 1950s, the manpower requirements for each major occupational group, taking account of deaths, retirements, and the net gain in the number employed. (The study covered males only.) For both of the broad groups, "managers, officials and proprietors" and "professional, technical and kindred," the total number of male entrants required during the decade was about 40 per cent of the number in 1950 or about 4 per cent each year.[8] If we use a figure of, say, 2,700,000 businessmen for 1950 (men only), this would suggest the need for about 110,000 new businessmen per year.[9] It would be, of course, significantly larger in the 1960s, perhaps about 150,000—less early in the decade and more in the neighborhood of 1970. Thus there is room for a much larger number of business graduates than are now coming from the colleges, while at the same time leaving opportunity for college graduates with other types of training. But if the number of male business graduates does rise to eighty or ninety thousand by 1970 and if there is also an increase in the number of other college graduates going into business, the percentage of all businessmen who are college graduates will be much larger than it is today, and many will have to spend all or part of their lives in occupations or types of firms in which college graduates are today in a small minority. This, clearly, is the trend.[10]

[6] S. E. Harris, *The Market for College Graduates* (1949).

[7] A. J. Jaffe and R. O. Carleton, *Occupational Mobility in the United States, 1930–1960* (1954), particularly pp. 24–25.

[8] We use those of their estimates which assumed that in 1960 the military establishment would be small rather than large, and that business conditions would be prosperous rather than depressed.

[9] We used the figure of three million on p. 53; of these, perhaps 90 per cent were men.

[10] However, there are several offsetting considerations to take into account. Some fraction of the business graduates will go into business occupations not covered by the estimates in the text. For example, the estimate in the text excludes three-quarters of the salesmen listed in Table 5 and most of the self-employed. Business graduates also go into nonbusiness pursuits, for example, government and education, and a fair number go into the law. From scattered alumni surveys we judge that perhaps as many as 15 per cent of all business graduates wind up in government, education, or some other profession.

The Variety of Business Occupations

Positions in business differ in at least four respects: the kind of function performed within a firm, the level of authority involved, the kind of business in which the enterprise is engaged, and the size of the business with which an individual is connected. In Chapter 5 we shall try to determine in what respects these elements of diversity are important for business education. At this juncture we are concerned only with a description of these elements of heterogeneity and with some indication of the number of persons involved in different kinds of business positions.

As to the kinds of business functions to be performed, we cannot add much to what is generally known. In the larger firms there is an increasing degree of specialization within the management group. In addition to functional specialization, a broad line can be drawn between persons with primarily administrative responsibilities and those whose chief task is to compile and analyze the information on the basis of which decisions are made. This corresponds very roughly, but only roughly, to the conventional distinction between "line" and "staff."

We know of no data that would permit us to estimate, even as rough orders of magnitude, the number of persons holding positions in the various functional areas of business. The scraps of evidence we collected in our company interviews suggest that, at least in manufacturing and mining, the largest single category is production management in its various aspects. This is true even if the first level of supervision is excluded. Marketing management and supporting staff positions constitute the second largest group.

We are better informed about the distribution of businessmen by type of industry. If we take all business firms, even the very smallest, the largest total is in retail trade, followed by manufacturing and the service industries. If we consider only firms with 100 or more employees, manufacturing is far and away the most important group, followed by the public utilities and retail trade. If we can rely on the evidence presented in Chapter 5, the kind of business education required is much the same in different industries.

Table 6 provides some information regarding the distribution of businessmen by size of business. If we use our broadest definition, a large proportion of businessmen are simply the owners of very small retail and service establishments. But there are something like two million or more with firms having 100 or more employees, and more than half of these are with firms having 1,000 or more employees. As the proportion of the adult population who are college graduates continues to increase, so will the fraction of small businessmen who have gone to college. While the chief market for business school graduates is in firms with more than 100 employees, the business schools are paying increasing attention to the educational needs of those in the smaller concerns.

Management hierarchies, by definition, resemble pyramids. There are many more persons at the bottom than at the top. College graduates typically enter near the bottom of the pyramid and, depending upon the success they have, move upward. Their first position after college may be outside the management group as we have defined it. Beginning as a salesman, first-line supervisor, or low-level staff specialist, the graduate will gradually rise in the management hierarchy, perhaps shifting across functional lines and sometimes even changing his employer as he moves upward. For a fortunate few, the terminal position will be at the very top, but for the great majority the ultimate position held will be in the lower and middle levels of management. Some will move out of salaried positions in the larger firms into business for themselves.

We know almost nothing about the distribution of the ultimate positions business school graduates achieve before they retire. The graduate schools, particularly the better ones, think in terms of training for ultimate positions in top and middle management. The undergraduate schools recognize that many of their graduates will not do this well and that many who go into the business world will not get into the management group at all, spending their lives instead as salesmen, in routine clerical operations, or as the owners of very small enterprises.

We judge, from the scattered replies on this question that we received from the companies we visited, that perhaps a quarter to a third of the management group in large firms may be considered as belonging to middle and top management. The proportion seems to vary widely, as do the criteria used for determining who should be included in this upper group. If our estimate is right that there are over two million members of the "management group" in firms with more than 100 employees, then there would be perhaps a half to three-quarters of a million in the middle and top management groups. In firms with more than a thousand employees, there would be three or four hundred thousand with the responsibilities and income that we associate with middle and top management. Our companies' replies lead us to guess that, for firms with more than 100 employees, something like 5 per cent of the total management group are considered to be in top management—approximately 100,000 executives.[11]

[11] These guesses can be compared with Perrin Stryker's attempt to estimate the number of "executives" in the United States. Depending on the method used, he obtained a range of from 75,000 to more than 400,000. *Fortune*, December, 1955, p. 232.

These figures understate the opportunities open to college graduates. Many of those in the lower ranks at any particular time still have a good part of their careers ahead of them and will gradually move upward into positions of greater responsibility. Yet it is undoubtedly true that the majority of those who enter business never rise to positions of very great responsibility; professional training at the university level is hardly necessary for performing adequately in the positions that are likely to be open to many of them.

Undoubtedly, such technical training as the less able students are likely to require can frequently be obtained on the job, in technical institutes or junior colleges, or in other ways than in a graduate or undergraduate business program. Yet, without question, many of these students can derive substantial benefit from the kind of broad and rigorous undergraduate business program that is recommended in later chapters. They can do better the jobs they are asked to do, and many will be able to reach positions they could not have achieved without such education. Also, as we pointed out in Chapter 1, the directions in which business is moving increasingly require the kind of education which must be obtained in college, and this is becoming true even of the lower ranks of business. As business decision-making becomes more rational, with greater emphasis on the collection and analysis of information about an increasingly complex environment, even lower ranking jobs in management will need to be filled, to a greater degree, with college educated men and women.[12]

Robert Calkins, more than a decade ago, urged that the business schools train men for positions of leadership in economic affairs, both in business firms and in other types of organizations.[13] The plea for "economic statesmen" has been echoed by others. At the same time, the business schools cannot help but wonder to what levels of management they should gear the preparation they offer students and whether a broad education is the best sort of training for those who will not rise very far.

Our own answer on this point is twofold. The business schools should emphasize breadth and seek to develop future economic statesmen, but these "statesmen" can find a useful place for themselves in business and

[12] This argument in favor of a reasonably rigorous college education for many of those who will not ascend into the upper levels of management is not inconsistent with the picture of future management needs drawn by Leavitt and Whisler in a recent article. While what they call the new "information technology" may, as they predict, lead to the routinizing of many middle-management jobs, it will also increase the need, at lower as well as higher levels, for technically trained staff specialists and for those who, without having a highly specialized training, will have a moderate degree of sophistication in those disciplines which are becoming increasingly important to business. See H. J. Leavitt and T. L. Whisler, "Management in the 1980's," *Harvard Business Review*, XXXVI (November-December, 1958), 41–48.

[13] See his articles in the *Harvard Business Review*, Winter, 1945, and Autumn, 1946.

nonbusiness positions at *all* administrative levels. There is need for breadth of outlook and qualities of leadership, in addition to technical competence, in the lower as well as in the highest levels of business and nonbusiness organizations. We need "little economic statesmen" as well as those who will sit in the top councils of business and government. However, these "little economic statesmen" need humility as well as breadth of outlook. Too often business school graduates begin to act like vice presidents while they are still little more than glorified clerks.

The Basic Elements in the Practice of Business

In the chapters that follow we shall be concerned with what constitutes business competence and with how such competence can be developed through formal education. Business competence rests upon the possession of some combination of skills, i.e., of some array of knowledge combined with the ability to use it. The nature of the needed skills depends, obviously, on the kinds of problems with which businessmen must deal—on what it is that constitutes the practice of business.

In this connection, several aspects of the structure and functioning of the business firm need to be emphasized. First, the business firm is an *organization*. Second, the firm operates in an *environment* to which it is tied by both *market* (i.e., buying and selling) and *nonmarket* relationships. Third, within this environment and continuously adjusting to it, the firm is engaged in procuring and combining the services of men, money, and physical resources in order to create something for sale. If a primary objective of the organization is to make a profit from these activities, it is a business enterprise, even though it will have also other important objectives. If we eliminate the profit objective and the consequent need to generate sales revenues in excess of costs, the elements listed above will apply to all organizations, the more so as they engage in strictly economic activities.

With respect to each of these aspects of business, it is essential to emphasize the additional element of *change*. The model of the business world we are drawing is a dynamic one. The firm's organizational problems and needs are continually changing; change is the most important characteristic of the market and nonmarket environment in which it operates; the decisions involved in combining economic resources for the purpose of production and sale must continuously take account of changes which have already occurred or are anticipated. The businessman creates change and must adjust to change. He lives in an uncertain world that is in part of his own making.

We shall now consider these elements in greater detail. For convenience, we shall treat the market and nonmarket aspects of the firm's environment separately, so that, apart from the factor of change and uncertainty, we shall have four elements with which to deal. The factor of change will be considered in connection with each of these four elements.

ORGANIZATIONAL ASPECTS

First, the firm is an organization. It is a "system of consciously coordinated personal activities."[14] The successful functioning of any organization implies the planned and conscious coordination of the efforts of a group of persons toward a common set of goals. Hence, the practice of business, since it is carried on through organizations, implies the need for dealing with organizational and administrative relationships. To quote a comment that has been made perhaps too often, management or administration is "getting things done through people."

It is worth pausing for a moment to compare the role which organizational problems play in business with that which they play in the other fields for which the universities offer professional training. In the attention that must be paid to the organizational factor, business resembles military leadership, the church, and various other forms of institutional administration, private and public. It resembles much less medicine and even law and engineering. Although they all encounter administrative problems in varying degrees, doctors, lawyers, and engineers tend to concentrate their attention on the substantive aspects of their practice. It is different with the typical businessman. He must "manage" a set of economic variables, but within an organizational context that helps to determine the choices available to him and how he selects among the alternatives. The decisions he makes are affected by the fact that he operates within a system of consciously coordinated activities.[15]

Thus business education must concern itself with two kinds of professional preparation. It must provide the knowledge and skills to deal with substantive problems of finance, production, and the like. It must also seek to develop the organizational knowledge and skills that are needed. To put the same thing a bit differently, business students should learn

---

[14] C. I. Barnard, *The Functions of the Executive* (1938), p. 72. As one authority has put it, "the term *organization* refers to the complex pattern of communications and other relations in a group of human beings. This pattern provides to each member of the group much of the information, assumptions, goals, and attitudes that enter into his decisions, and provides him also with a set of stable and comprehensible expectations as to what the other members of the group are doing and how they will react to what he says and does." H. A. Simon, *Administrative Behavior* (2nd ed.; 1957), p. xvi. Cf. also J. G. March and H. A. Simon, *Organizations* (1958), chap. 1.

[15] In the need to deal with other human beings as individuals, business does have some resemblance to law and medicine but not to engineering.

how to make wise decisions regarding substantive questions within the kinds of organizational contexts they will encounter in practice.

Let us review briefly some of the kinds of organizational problems the businessman (or anyone concerned with administrative problems) must face. These problems affect the businessman at all levels, but he becomes more conscious of them as he rises in the organizational hierarchy.

The successful functioning of an organization implies the setting of organizational goals and the reconciliation of these goals with the changing demands of the environment and with the goals of subordinate groups and individuals within the enterprise.[16] It also implies the establishment of administrative relationships, including the assignment of authority and responsibility and the development of a system of communications so that the need for action can be recognized, alternatives evaluated, orders transmitted, and the implementation of decisions controlled. Since organizations imply cooperative effort and hierarchical relationships, there must be supervision and personal leadership, including the recruitment, training, and development of personnel. As most writers on the subject have pointed out, the achievement of objectives through organizations requires that there be planned coordination of the efforts of individuals. An adequate system of communication is as essential to the organization as the nervous system is to the human body. And since the cooperators in organizations are human beings, the element of "human relations"—of inducing loyalty to and identification with the organization and its goals—becomes an essential element in the efficient functioning of any organization.

Organizational behavior takes place in a world characterized by change and uncertainty. To be viable, organizations must be able to cope with uncertainty. They must be able to generate the information needed to identify changes in their environment and to predict future change. They must be flexible enough to adapt to both internal and external change. They should be able not only to adjust to perceived changes in their environment, but also to plan and initiate new types of activity—in short, to innovate.[17]

All this implies that the businessman needs some grounding in such knowledge as we have regarding how human beings function in organizations, the conditions necessary to secure continuously effective action within organizations, and the problems that arise when one at-

[16] See, for example, J. D. Thompson and W. J. McEwen, "Organizational Goals and Environment: Goal-Setting as an Interaction Process," *American Sociological Review*, XXIII (February, 1958), 23–31.

[17] For some discussion of the dynamic aspects of organizational behavior, see, for example, March and Simon, *Organizations*, chaps. 6–7.

tempts, in the face of change and uncertainty, to make and to implement rational decisions within organizations.[18] The organizational factor suggests also that the businessman needs not merely certain kinds of knowledge or understanding, but also such types of skills as administrative skill in planning the design of organizational relationships, skill in devising communication systems and in communicating, and skill in eliciting cooperation from colleagues and subordinates. One of the large unsettled questions has to do with how the necessary organizational skills can best be developed; this is a matter we shall look into later.

THE NONMARKET ENVIRONMENT

Let us turn now to the second element in our conceptual scheme. The business firm, like any organization, operates within a set of environmental influences. There is continuous interaction between the firm and the various parts of its environment, and, taking all enterprises together, economic history is the record of this interaction. Let us concern ourselves first with what earlier we called the nonmarket environment.

This aspect of the business environment includes all those external influences which do not involve the firm's buying and selling relationships. The elements of this environment are almost too numerous to list: for example, the legal and political framework within which business must operate, the aggregate of economic influences which determine the level of national income and employment and the way in which these change with the passage of time, the whole field of international developments, and the development of science and technology, which for many firms becomes the dominating force determining what they produce and the technical processes they utilize. A variety of pressures from private groups also are a part of the nonmarket environment, and these pressures exert themselves not merely through prices and the terms of contracts. Thus the influence of such groups as labor unions, farm groups, trade associations, and banks affects the way in which the firm carries on its business and the kinds of decisions which are made within the firm. Perhaps even

---

[18] Argument exists among the experts as to whether there is a systematic and clearly delineated body of knowledge which can be called "organization theory," or whether what we have are merely scraps of knowledge and hypotheses from the various "behavioral sciences," lacking the integration which would make of them a separate and self-contained body of knowledge. The argument regarding this issue has not been particularly fruitful. What is clear is that here is a range of problems of great importance to the businessman, that these problems must be dealt with in one way or another, and that from a variety of sources we are in the process of developing a greater understanding of the nature of these problems and how they affect the "substantive" decisions that business operations entail. For further discussion, see Chapter 9, where some references to the literature are also given.

more important is the intangible something we call the climate of opinion, both the widespread social attitudes that comprise present public opinion and the ideas of individuals and groups that will shape the public opinion of the future.

There are two points to stress about the relations between business firms and their environment. One is the fact of mutual interaction. The environment helps to determine the alternatives on the basis of which business decisions are made and also affects the value systems which supply the criteria for choosing among these alternatives. At the same time, business firms, individually and particularly collectively, react upon their environment. It is this fact that makes it so important for businessmen to bring a keen sense of social responsibility to their jobs. More than economic effects ensue from their decisions. Business activity affects government policy in a variety of ways. It helps to determine the conditions of community living; it has been largely responsible for the kind of urban civilization in which we live; it helps to shape the intellectual and moral tone of the times.[19]

Another important aspect of the interrelations between business and its environment is that these relations are continuously changing, evolving out of the past into a future that can be but vaguely foreseen. Change and uncertainty are the very essence of the businessman's life. It is a truism that the world which today's students will have to manage a generation hence will be much different from the world which they and their teachers know at present. Businessmen clearly have to be equipped to deal with unforeseen change, to have some idea of the sources of change in their environment, and, so far as this is possible, to anticipate change.

All this suggests something about the kinds of knowledge and abilities required of the businessman. To cope with a continuously changing nonmarket environment he needs breadth of knowledge, a sense of historical perspective, and flexibility of mind. He needs also to have a sensitive and sophisticated appreciation of the role which business does and can play in our kind of society. All this implies some familiarity with the more relevant branches of history and perhaps philosophy, and some knowledge of the social sciences, particularly economics, political science, and sociology. Implied also is some appreciation of the nature and significance of scientific and technological developments. The acquisition of knowledge in these different areas ought to bring a sense of historical perspective, contribute to flexibility of mind, and help to develop a sense of responsibility to the larger society of which the businessman is a part.

[19] See, in this connection, F. X. Sutton *et al.*, *The American Business Creed* (1956).

THE MARKET ENVIRONMENT

The business firm operates in a market as well as a nonmarket environment. This is the third element in our conceptual scheme. Human, financial, and physical resources are acquired in markets, and the terms on which these resources are made available are set in these markets. The economist's factors of production must be procured before they can be combined into something which the firm will attempt to sell. How much it can sell, and on what terms, will also be determined in a set of markets.

Thus the business enterprise is surrounded by an environment of market as well as nonmarket influences. Here also are mutual interaction and continuous change. The individual firm is affected by, and in turn has an effect on, the markets in which it operates, the more so the larger it is in relation to the market. Conditions in these markets are continually changing, thereby making highly uncertain the future consequences of present action and creating the need for prompt and frequent adjustment.

The critical importance of the market environment calls for both general and specialized knowledge. There are some types of knowledge about the market environment that probably all businessmen should have. They need some analytical tools which will give them a start in understanding in a general way how any kind of market functions.[20] They also need a broad familiarity with the kinds of institutional arrangements under which goods and services (including labor and money) are bought or hired. Furthermore, a great deal of specialized knowledge about particular markets is required, depending on the things a particular firm buys and sells and on the division of labor within any given enterprise. Thus there will be specialists in finance, in personnel and industrial relations, in purchasing, and in marketing. In so far as this specialized knowledge involves knowledge of immutable facts and command of particular analytical skills, it can profitably be acquired through formal education. But much of it involves a mastery of detail which is continually changing and must be acquired through actual experience.

ECONOMIC MANAGEMENT

Knowledge of markets is closely related to the fourth element in our conceptual scheme, which for brevity we can call economic management. The firm must manage the resources it procures, combine them,

---

[20] Such understanding rests in part, but only in part, on economics. The other social sciences, particularly those called "the behavioral sciences," are also very much involved. See, for example, the recent advanced text by Wroe Alderson, *Marketing Behavior and Executive Action* (1957).

and arrange for the sale of what it produces. Economic management in this sense has several aspects.

First, there is the need to procure and to conserve each of the types of resources used: labor, money, and physical resources. While the term "conserve" may seem awkward in this context, it accurately describes what is involved in much of financial management, in the management of raw materials and work in process, in the maintenance of physical equipment, and in personnel management.

There is, secondly, the job of "production," of planning the systematic combination of labor and materials with the help of plant to create the final utilities which the firm intends to sell. The "conservation" of labor, materials, and plant goes on very largely during the act of production; thus there is an extremely close relation, both in practice and in business education, between these functions.

The last aspect of economic management involves sale of the final product. This is the larger part of the so-called marketing function. Here the business firm is concerned with decisions as to what and how much can be sold and by what means. Since the viability of a business enterprise depends on its ability to secure a continuous stream of sales receipts which exceed its costs by a satisfactory margin, the marketing function will naturally be heavily stressed. Obviously, also, this aspect of (internal) economic management must depend heavily on knowledge of the (external) market environment.

Efficient economic management requires the identification, weighing, and choice of relevant alternatives. It also requires some guarantee that decisions, once made, will be properly implemented. Hence there must be an "information system" which will yield data as a basis both for decision-making and for evaluating the results of decisions already made. Statistics, accounting, and techniques of interpretation and analysis based on numerical data are essential tools in the kinds of economic management we are now discussing. All managers require some working familiarity with these subjects. In addition, there is the need for specialized technicians capable of generating the necessary information in its most useful form, and capable also of analyzing it to extract the kinds of information the decision makers need for planning and control. These informational and analytical tools, however, are of no help unless there is a logical system of analysis to use in the evaluation of alternatives. The logical system most relevant here is that of formal economics. Some ability to work with economic criteria and some knowledge of basic economic relationships, however acquired, are essential for the various kinds of "functional management" and for the overall management which integrates these functions from the point of view of the enterprise as a whole.

Economic management requires both general and particular skills and general and particular kinds of knowledge. There is need for general problem-solving ability and skill in the use of analytical tools, especially those derived from accounting, statistics, and economics. There is also need for more particularized kinds of knowledge dealing with the various functions of business and their interrelationships. Needed also are the kinds of technical knowledge which the natural sciences and engineering provide. Depending on its size and internal organizational relationships, the firm will need both generalists and specialists. The specialists may be concerned with any one of the aspects of economic management mentioned earlier, and, within any one of these aspects, may concentrate on the management of a particular kind of economic resource, such as labor, plant, or financial resources.

Economic management obviously requires also some familiarity with the other elements in our conceptual scheme. For instance, marketing or financial decisions are made in an organizational context; they must also take into account the pressures which impinge on the firm from its market and nonmarket environment. Economic management must, of course, be particularly sensitive to the market environment. This helps to explain why, in dealing with the various "functional" areas of economic management, business schools frequently deal with the "managerial" and the external market aspects together. For example, the same course may deal with "financial management" and the operation of the money and capital markets.

This discussion of economic management must of course be interpreted in a dynamic context. The management of economic resources takes place in a continually changing environment. It must try to anticipate a future that can be but imperfectly foreseen. It must not only react to past and current change but also try to anticipate future change. Imagination, the ability to make decisions on the basis of incomplete information, and a semi-intuitive skill in anticipating the future all have to be combined with the kinds of knowledge we have described.

Some recapitulation may be useful at this point. The practice of business at what might be called a professional level centers around the making of decisions about economic variables in an organizational context and within a market and nonmarket environment that is continuously changing. Such decision-making has both a "line" and a "staff" aspect. Decision-making implies not only the final act of choice and the exercise of authority to insure that the decision is carried out. It involves also the compiling, processing, and interpretation of information which permits the listing and evaluation of the alternatives from which a choice can be made. Thus "staff work" is an integral part of business administration and is the only kind of work in which a good many men in business will engage.

As we noted in Chapter 1, business decision-making is becoming increasingly rational and, in this sense, "scientific." But, in view of the complex and continuously changing environment within which business operates, complete rationality is impossible. Decisions must be made on the basis of incomplete information and in the face of goals which may to some degree conflict. Therefore, decision-making in business requires a generous helping of "judgment." By this we mean the ability to sense what is relevant and to grasp intuitively what cannot be formulated precisely—in brief, a feel for what is possible.

Business as a Profession

Our discussion of the attributes of business as an occupation raises a question which is sometimes embarrassing to the business schools. We speak of "professional" education for business, but in what sense is business a profession? The problem is illustrated by a recent study of professional education published by the United States Office of Education. The introductory chapter on the professions does not mention business or business administration. Yet a chapter on business schools holds a prominent place in the volume.[21] While the question is largely a semantic one, the issues involved do bear on the kind of training which the colleges might appropriately provide for future businessmen.

What is a profession? Definitions are numerous and varied, but most tend to stress the same points. Virtually all agree with Mary Parker Follett that "The word 'profession' connotes . . . a foundation of *science* and a motive of *service*."[22] This simple statement can be elaborated into the following four criteria.[23] First, the practice of a profession must rest on a systematic body of knowledge of substantial intellectual content and on the development of personal skill in the application of this knowledge to specific cases. Second, there must exist standards of professional con-

---

[21] U. S. Office of Education, *Education for the Professions*, L. E. Blauch, ed. (1955), chaps. 1 and 6.

[22] In H. C. Metcalf, ed., *Business Management as a Profession* (1927), p. 73.

[23] These criteria have been variously stated by different writers, and the weight given to each criterion also varies considerably. For a survey of the literature on how to define a profession, beginning with the criteria suggested by Abraham Flexner in 1915, see Morris L. Cogan, "The Problem of Defining a Profession," *The Annals of the American Academy of Political and Social Science*, January, 1955, pp. 105-11.

duct, which take precedence over the goal of personal gain, governing the professional man's relations with his clients and his fellow practitioners. These two primary criteria have led in practice to two further ones. A profession has its own association of members, among whose functions are the enforcement of standards, the advancement and dissemination of knowledge, and, in some degree, the control of entry into the profession. Finally, there is a prescribed way of entering the profession through the enforcement of minimum standards of training and competence. Generally, the road leading to professional practice passes through the professional school and is guarded by a qualifying examination.

Let us now apply these four criteria to the practice of business.[24] Clearly, business does not satisfy the fourth criterion. There is no single way of entering into a business career, and, in the view of most thoughtful observers, there never should be. Schools of business supply only a modest (but increasing) fraction of those who enter the business world. Even today a college education is not absolutely necessary, although it is becoming increasingly essential for those who aspire to the higher administrative levels of the larger firms. (And for many types of technical positions, of course, training at the university level is necessary.) Obviously, also, no sort of qualifying examination is required, although to this public accounting is an important exception.

Our second criterion involved the question of personal goals and professional standards. Here again business fails to qualify as a profession. There is no clearly agreed and generally accepted standard of professional conduct for business as a whole. Some minimum standards of honest dealing are embodied in the law; beyond this, businessmen, like all other members of our society, subscribe in varying degrees to the traditional moral standards of western civilization. Increasingly, also, business leaders speak of their obligations to their employees, their customers, and the public at large, as well as to their stockholders.[25] In entering on a business career, one does not undertake to live up to a

[24] The question as to whether business is or can become a profession has been treated by many writers. The bibliography is a long one, but see, for example, Louis Brandeis, *Business— A Profession* (1914); H. C. Metcalf, ed., *Business Management as a Profession;* Howard Bowen, "Business Management: A Profession?" *The Annals*, January, 1955, pp. 112–17; J. F. Bradley, "The Emergence of Business as a Profession," *Collegiate News and Views*, March, 1958, pp. 11–15; and Bernard Barber, "Is American Business Becoming Professionalized?" (mimeographed copy made available to us by the author).

[25] See, as one illustration, Frank W. Abrams, "Management's Responsibilities in a Complex World," in T. H. Carroll, ed., *Business Education for Competence and Responsibility* (1954). Here the professionalization of management is made to rest on its growing sense of responsibility to the various groups that have an interest in the business firm.

Hippocratic Oath or otherwise to meet clearly stated standards of professional conduct.[26]

One difficulty is that, unlike the traditional professions, the businessman's client is not clearly defined. First and foremost, a businessman's loyalty is to the enterprise with which he is associated, and the company can be taken to be his client. (In this sense, perhaps, we can speak of the motive of "service.") But a business enterprise can have a complex of objectives, only one of which is profits for the owners. Are the businessman's goals of service and his standards of conduct to be geared solely to the objectives of the firm, whatever they may be, or are there to be standards expressed in terms of the quality of the particular kind of service the individual contributes? And, if there is a conflict in goals, how is "quality of service" to be interpreted? A company doctor is first a physician and only second an employee of the company. The standards of his profession take precedence over the objectives of the company. This is not necessarily true of the business manager or staff specialist and least of all true of the owner-entrepreneur.

So far as the third criterion is concerned, business clearly has no governing body similar to those of the medical and bar associations. Various branches of business activity have their associations, but, with some exceptions, such groups do not serve the same functions as the truly professional societies. This is particularly true with respect to the enforcement of standards, the dissemination of knowledge, and the control of entry into the occupation.

From the standpoint of business education, it is not too important that business does not meet these three criteria of a profession. Schools of business cannot afford to forget that theirs is not the only road to a business career. The matter of professional standards is something with which the business schools need to concern themselves more than they have in the past. But for the business school seeking the most effective means of training future businessmen, the crucial criterion of a profession is the first one: the existence of a systematic body of knowledge of substantial intellectual content and the development of personal skill in the conscious

[26] See Talcott Parsons' argument that personal motivation in business and in the traditional professions is basically similar. "The Professions and Social Structure," in *Essays in Sociological Theory* (rev. ed., 1954). However, he recognizes that while personal goals may be similar in the two cases, there is a difference in the paths to the similar goals which reflect "the differences in the respective occupational situations" (p. 44). Parsons' position does not contradict that which we take here. The doctor's and the corporation executive's goals may be quite similar, both reflecting the same degrees of altruism and ambition. But their respective occupations impose on them somewhat different "rules of the game." Part of the problem arises out of the difference in the nature of the services provided by the two. In this connection, see the next paragraph in the text.

application of this knowledge to specific cases. In what sense does business meet this criterion?

The earlier discussion in this chapter and the description in Chapter 1 of the forces making for a more rational kind of decision-making help us to answer this question. The elements of the conceptual scheme elaborated in the preceding section require that businessmen deal with a range of problems toward the solution of which a wide array of systematic knowledge and analytical tools can make a contribution. This is increasingly the evidence from business practice itself. The growth of rational decision-making through the use of such systematic knowledge is what we meant by the "professionalization of management" in Chapter 1.

Businessmen and research workers are still seeking to determine what bodies of knowledge are of greatest relevance to business and how this knowledge can best be put to use. Clearly relevant are economic analysis and the analytical and informational tools of accounting, statistics, and mathematics. There is no question about the importance of the physical and engineering sciences. And increasingly the potential contributions of the social sciences other than economics—both to our understanding of organizational behavior and to our ability to solve "substantive" problems in the various business fields—are being recognized.

Uncertainty does exist as to how all of this knowledge is to be organized for the purpose of "professional" training for business. In particular, how can what is needed be reworked into a set of business "sciences" which apply to business problems the lessons of the underlying disciplines? Some agreed-upon answers have been reached, as in such standard business fields as marketing and finance, although these fields still need to be further enriched by what is most relevant in the underlying social sciences and in mathematics and statistics. At the moment the greatest areas of uncertainty center around two points. Is there a basis for a separate field of "organization and administration" from which generalizations can be drawn that can be applied in actual practice? A related point concerns the best way of developing skill in problem-solving or decision-making in business situations. One view, associated particularly with the Harvard Business School, holds that "business is an art rather than a science" and stresses the need for "judgment rather than the accumulation of knowledge." The opposing view stresses the importance of developing a command of relevant principles, although it does not deny that there is also an important nonrational element in much business decision-making. The difference between these two viewpoints is tending to diminish as the body of knowledge usable in business situations continues to grow.

One can conceive of a spectrum of "professional" occupations that ranges from the creative arts at the one extreme to the traditional professions such as medicine at the other. Each involves some particular bundle of skills. They vary widely, however, in the extent to which the skills required represent the conscious application of an underlying body of systematic knowledge. In this respect, business stands somewhere between the creative arts and the traditional professions. It still bears many of the attributes of a creative art, and this until recent years was the prevailing view of businessmen themselves. But it is slowly moving toward the other end of the spectrum where professional skill rests on the conscious application of a systematic body of knowledge. As one businessman has put it, management "is no longer merely an art." It is "fast acquiring the character of a profession," which "means that its principles can be increasingly discovered, stated, verified and taught systematically. They can be learned, and they can be applied."[27]

Business is not yet a profession, but in this respect it is beginning to resemble one. However, business competence is a complex mixture of a number of ingredients, of which skill in rational decision-making is only one, although an increasingly important one. In the next chapter we shall analyze this mixture in considerable detail.

[27] H. F. Smiddy, "General Electric's Philosophy and Approach for Manager Development," in American Management Association, *Fitting Management Development to Company Needs* (General Management Series No. 174, 1955), p. 16. See also our earlier discussion in Chapter 1.

chapter 5

THE QUALITIES NEEDED BY BUSINESS: THE EMPIRICAL EVIDENCE

In Chapter 4 we suggested an array of kinds of knowledge and skills which are needed, or at least desirable, for the practice of business in virtually all its forms. Our conclusions were reached deductively from premises, derived from observation and reflection, regarding the nature of business operations. Now we turn to more empirical evidence. What do businessmen themselves say on this subject, and what conclusions regarding the qualities needed for success in business have been reached by other qualified observers?

Verified knowledge in this area is discouragingly slim. More than a decade ago, Robert Calkins, then dean of the School of Business at Columbia, was moved to say: "What qualifications make for competence in the careers for which we train? Frankly, I do not know, and I can think of no one who does. But it is high time we found out."[1] The situation is not a great deal better today.

The evidence currently available is of several sorts. There are the personal views of individual businessmen, all highly subjective and to some extent contradictory. There is the experience of individual companies in using various procedures and criteria in evaluating, selecting, and promoting management personnel. And there are the studies made by psychologists, personnel experts, and others of the characteristics that are presumably correlated with successful executive or leadership performance.

There is a growing body of literature of this third type, out of which few generally accepted conclusions have as yet emerged.[2] The work so

---

[1] "Objectives of Business Education," *Harvard Business Review*, xxv (Autumn, 1946), 49–50.

[2] With a few exceptions, the schools of business administration have done relatively little in this field. Harvard has probably done more systematic work on the personal characteristics that make for success in business than any other business school, but some research in this area has also been going on at a few other schools.

far done has been of highly uneven quality. Among its results thus far have been a number of psychological tests which are presumably predictive of successful administrative performance. While some companies seem to have found such tests useful, there is also a good deal of negative evidence regarding their value; and some observers have expressed more than skepticism.[3]

The Present State of Opinion Regarding the Qualifications for Success in Business

Let us consider first the more systematic studies that have been made of the qualifications successful executives should presumably possess.[4] One type of study attempts to identify the personal traits which universally seem to identify successful executives and other types of leaders. Studies of this type suffer from a number of limitations: vagueness as to what constitutes an executive, failure to differentiate among businessmen according to the nature of the position held, lack of adequate criteria as to what constitutes successful performance, and so on. These studies emphasize personality traits. In utilizing various sorts of tests to uncover such traits, they run the risk of merely uncovering the stereotype-image of a successful executive which the persons tested happen to hold. In addition, they suffer from the fact that personality depends not merely on the possession of certain traits, but also on the way in which those traits are combined in an individual.[5]

In recent years, there has been some reaction against this kind of search for universal traits. More recent studies emphasize the importance of interaction between an individual's personal attributes and the nature of the situation in which he is expected to perform. According to this "situational" approach, leadership is not a passive phenomenon which automatically emerges out of a given bundle of personal traits but is the result of the interaction between the nature of the organizational position to be filled and the particular characteristics of the person asked to fill it. As one student has put it, "the performance of an individual depends on what the *man* is, what the *job* is, and what the *situation* is."[6]

[3] Notably William H. Whyte, Jr., in *The Organization Man* (1956). Cf. also M. L. Mace, *The Growth and Development of Executives* (1950), p. 84.

[4] The next several pages are based on a memorandum prepared for this study by Professor L. W. Porter and Mr. Irving Krauss of the University of California.

[5] For one useful critique of studies of this sort, see A. W. Gouldner, ed., *Studies in Leadership* (1950), pp. 21ff.

[6] Renato Tagiuri, "Research in Executive Selection," paper presented at Symposium on Management Selection Research, Sixty-sixth Annual Convention of American Psychological Association (1958, mimeographed).

Somewhat related to these "situational" studies are several which attempt to discover whether managers at different administrative levels reveal significant differences in personality traits or other qualities. There is some indication that such differences do exist, although again serious difficulties in interpretation arise.[7] There is the danger, as before, that the findings merely show the stereotype-images of what the respondents think a person in their group should be like. We do not know whether the qualities revealed by these studies are those which an individual must possess to attain a given position or whether they are or can be developed as a result of holding a given position.

Further discussion of these methodological problems would carry us too far afield. In general, the literature we have examined suggests the following general conclusions.[8] No single set of personal traits essential to the performance of managerial jobs has yet been established to the general satisfaction of psychologists and personnel experts. Different combinations of qualities may carry different men equally far. The qualities needed depend to some extent on the nature of the job and of the organizational environment in which the job is placed. Even more important, we are handicapped in not having clearcut criteria of successful performance to which to relate personal attributes.[9]

So much for the negative evidence. It does seem possible to say something on the positive side, provided this is done with appropriate qualifications and with full recognition of the fact that no list of managerial qualities can be expected to hold universally, for all successful businessmen or for all types of positions.

One reviewer of the literature in this field has concluded that, despite the contradictory evidence, the studies available do suggest that certain qualities are important for executive or managerial success. Thus, something better than average intelligence is required of persons in leadership positions. They tend to be well rounded in terms of interests and aptitudes; they have better than average facility in communication; they display mental and emotional maturity; they appreciate the value of cooperative effort and seem to know how to deal effectively with people and, more generally, to make effective use of the so-called executive

[7] Cf. L. W. Porter and E. E. Ghiselli, "The Self Perceptions of Top and Middle Management Personnel," *Personnel Psychology*, x (Winter, 1957), 397–406; also, H. D. Meyer and G. L. Pressel, "Personality Test Scores in the Management Hierarchy," *Journal of Applied Psychology*, xxxviii (April, 1954), 73–80; and C. G. Browne and R. P. Shore, "Leadership and Predictive Abstracting," *Journal of Applied Psychology*, xl (April, 1956), 112–16.

[8] See, for example, Mace, *The Growth and Development of Executives*, chap. 2.

[9] The measurement of what constitutes effective performance in various types of jobs is a major objective of a study now being conducted by the Educational Testing Service in cooperation with a group of companies.

skills. Perhaps most clearly of all, they possess a strong inner drive that impels them to strive for accomplishment and recognition.[10]

These qualities supposedly characterize leaders in general and therefore cover a broader area than administrative and staff positions in business. Nonetheless, this list of qualities provides a suggestive starting point.

If we turn now to some of the studies concerned exclusively with the qualities presumably required for success in business, we find that certain personal qualities tend to be mentioned more often than others, and that the list usually includes the leadership traits mentioned above. Examination of a number of such studies indicates that the following traits tend to be emphasized most often: mental ability, skill in human relations, the ability to assume responsibility and make decisions, judgment, general administrative skills, character, imagination, breadth and flexibility of mind, and loyalty to the organization. Two others mentioned earlier, personal motivation and ability to communicate, were listed less often but probably should also be included as conditions which all managers should meet.[11]

To this we can add some firsthand evidence of our own. In the course of the present study, intensive interviews were held with the officials of a sample of some ninety companies, chiefly large concerns but with a sprinkling of smaller ones. While the sample was neither random nor strictly representative of all American business, we did attempt to secure a broad representation by industry and by geographical area. Within each company, questions in an eight-page interview form were put to a group of executives ranging from the president to the personnel director

---

[10] C. E. Goode, "Significant Research on Leadership," *Personnel*, XXVII (March, 1951), 342–50.

[11] The literature summarized in this paragraph is described in Appendix A. It should be said here that the too brief discussion in the text, just because it is brief, suffers from a certain ambiguity. Some of the personal qualities listed need to be described more fully if the meaning we attach to the words used is to be perfectly clear. This same semantic problem arises elsewhere in this section. As an illustration, "motivation" can be directed toward different ends, and some kinds of motivation, which tend to be of a self-destructive character, can make for failure rather than success as an executive. This has been brought out in studies by Gardner and Henry. (See Appendix A.) Perrin Stryker has emphasized this semantic problem in a recent article in *Fortune*, going so far as to say that the terms used to denote executive qualities "have no generally accepted meanings." ("On the Meaning of Executive Qualities," *Fortune*, June, 1958, p. 116.) While we recognize these difficulties of definition and interpretation, we think that the problem of communication is not insuperable, given the problem to which we are addressing ourselves. Sufficient agreement on the meaning of the qualities listed is possible so that we can proceed to consider what they imply for the kind of education likely to be most useful to the businessman. The problem would be more difficult if, in a particular organizational context, we were asking a group of executives to use this (or any other) list of traits in order to identify the particular individuals most likely to succeed in their companies.

and members of his staff. The titles and duties of those interviewed varied from company to company but usually included at least the top officials concerned with personnel and management development.[12]

In each company, we asked the respondents to specify, on the basis of their firm's experience, the personal qualities (including technical training) that were most important for success in business management. The qualities that were given the greatest weight were motivation and personal drive, skill in interpersonal relations, moral character, and superior (although not necessarily extremely high) mental ability. Other qualities that tended to be stressed were breadth and imagination, judgment, willingness to accept responsibility and to take risks, ability to communicate, and command of general administrative skills.[13] Except for certain types of jobs, possession of specialized knowledge and technical skills was considered of only moderate or minor importance. This lack of emphasis on the need for specialized knowledge and technical skills, at least above the lower levels of supervision and except for some specialized staff positions, is in general confirmed by the other literature we have considered.[14]

We have examined the evaluation criteria actually used by a number of companies for selecting and promoting management personnel. The lists of qualities used vary from company to company, and not infrequently a particular company will have different sets of criteria for different types of positions. While it would be easy to add to the qualities we have already chosen to emphasize, there would be no great advantage in doing so. The more detailed the list, the easier it is to challenge any particular trait that is included.

We might, however, take a brief look at the qualities companies seem to stress when they recruit on the college campus. In one study by the National Industrial Conference Board, the personal characteristics most emphasized by a sample of 195 companies in their college recruiting were, in order: character, growth potential, personality, attitude toward work and company, intelligence, and appearance and health.[15] This

[12] The sample and questionnaire are described further in Appendix B.

[13] Despite our interviews and the examination of evaluation forms and the like, we cannot say how much reliance these companies actually placed on such lists of personal traits in selecting men for promotion—or how effective the use of such lists turned out to be.

[14] J. H. S. Bossard and J. F. Dewhurst reported that this same lack of emphasis on specialized knowledge prevailed among employers at the end of the 1920s. Cf. *University Education for Business*, (1931), p. 108.

[15] *Employment of the College Graduate* (Studies in Personnel Policy No. 152, 1956), p. 24. The evidence that was most emphasized in judging these characteristics was, in order of importance: impression made during the interview, personal history and background, grades, extracurricular activities, work experience, opinion of college authorities, and psychological test scores (p. 21).

study did not indicate the kinds of knowledge and training that were emphasized.

Another survey asked each of a group of companies to select from the college graduates recruited five years earlier the one who now seemed to show the greatest promise for advancement to the higher levels of management. Of the ninety-seven men selected, forty-eight had majored in engineering, twenty-eight in business administration, and twenty-one in liberal arts. The qualities most often cited as making these men outstanding were, in order of frequency of response: ability to work with people, ability to get things done, intelligence, initiative, leadership and administrative ability, capacity for hard work, judgment, adaptability, dependability, loyalty, and vision and imagination.[16] Again, the qualities are not greatly different from those we have derived from other sources.

In their college recruiting, the companies we interviewed seem to place the greatest emphasis on the evidence provided by student activities, personal impression, scholarship record, and psychological tests—in roughly that order. Specific courses were emphasized only for technical positions. As was to be expected, in recruiting for sales positions, these companies put the emphasis on personality and extracurricular activities more, and on grades and specific courses less, than for other types of positions.

One final piece of evidence may be cited. C. W. Randle recently reported on a study of executive qualities based on an intensive appraisal of some 1,400 executives.[17] This study, while subject to the limitations characteristic of all work of this sort, has a number of advantages, including differentiation among the executives studied by level of authority and type of functions performed. For all executives combined, Randle found that the following characteristics, in addition to performance on the job, tended to differentiate the best from the poorest executives: motivation and personal drive, intelligence, leadership, administrative skills, initiative, creativeness, human relations skills, judgment, and flexibility.[18] Certain other qualities, though possibly important, did not discriminate between good and poor executives.

Again, the same qualities we have found mentioned in other studies tend to be repeated. Let us repeat what was said earlier. No list of traits has universal validity in identifying managerial talent, and different combinations of qualities may carry men equally far, depending on a variety of circumstances. It is highly probable that, to some extent, the qualities

[16] F. S. Endicott, "Employment Trends in 1955," *Journal of College Placement*, March, 1955, p. 48.

[17] "How to Identify Promotable Executives," *Harvard Business Review*, xxxiv (May-June, 1956), 122–34.

[18] We have combined a few of Randle's categories.

needed for success in particular positions may emerge out of the demands of the job rather than represent traits which the individual previously possessed.[19] As one study has put it, success as an executive depends not merely on the possession of a list of qualities, but on "*the proper organization of abilities, knowledge, and personality traits.*"[20] Nonetheless, there seem to be certain basic abilities and skills which are generally required in business. The most important of these seem to be above average intelligence, including analytical ability and judgment; skill in interpersonal relations; the ability to accept responsibility and to make decisions in the face of uncertainty; general administrative skills, including the capacity to lead others, to plan, to organize and delegate, to develop subordinates, etc.; breadth and flexibility of mind as well as imagination; some facility in verbal communication; and strong personal motivation. Clearly, also, companies want loyalty and the ability to think in terms of the organization as a whole, even though this may make for the conformity of the Organization Man and may to some extent conflict with the more dynamic aspects of some of the other qualities mentioned.

No doubt, other observers could prepare lists of personal qualities that would differ in some respects from the list we have presented. Any list, as a set of criteria for predicting success in business, would suffer from all of the limitations of the "personality" approach we have discussed. Nonetheless, it is difficult to believe that other types of evidence would change radically the general picture of the kind of person business needs for responsible administrative and staff positions. The evidence available is reasonably convincing that, in a rough and general way, the characteristics we have emphasized are those which the business schools should be seeking to develop. But we should like to point out again that potentially successful businessmen may possess these traits in varying combinations, and that the quality of performance depends not merely on a particular bundle of traits but on their interaction with the particular environment in which the performance takes place.

Responsibility As Well As Competence

Most businessmen and educators agree that the business practitioner should have a well developed sense of social responsibility. This is a subject endowed with more than its share of clichés, but the abundance of platitudes does not diminish the importance of the problem.

---

[19] For some discussion of the ways in which different managerial jobs may require different combinations of qualities, see the discussion by M. M. Mandell in M. J. Dooher and Elizabeth Marting, *Selection of Management Personnel*, vol. 1 (1957), pp. 207–24.

[20] G. U. Cleeton and C. W. Mason, *Executive Ability* (1946), p. 26. Italics added.

The problem arises out of two facts. First, the businessman's decisions affect both his "external" and "internal" environment. What he does is of consequence to all those outside his firm who are directly or indirectly affected by his firm's activities; and what he does is of obvious concern to the groups within the firm. Organizational health depends upon an appropriate reconciliation of the company's objectives and of the goals of the formal and informal groups of which the organization is composed. This is now almost universally recognized, and statements by corporation executives regarding their obligations to employees, customers, stockholders, and other groups tend to be made in all seriousness, however banal these statements may sometimes sound to the listening skeptic.

The second fact is that businessmen make up an elite group in our kind of society. Even outside their business activities, they are expected to assume a leadership role—in local, regional, and national affairs. As a matter of fact, the welfare of their firms requires that they assume a leadership role. Otherwise they lose the opportunity to influence the way in which their environment impinges upon their purely business activities.[21]

While the situation is far better than it was even a generation ago, it is probably fair to say that businessmen as a group are still not meeting the responsibilities that inevitably go with their position of authority in a private enterprise and democratic society which faces the kinds of changes that lie ahead of us. The threat to the free world imposes upon businessmen the obligation to exercise their leadership in ways that will contribute to the stability and rapid growth of the American economy and that will also contribute to international harmony. They must adjust smoothly to the enormous technological changes that are in progress. They need to show the wisdom of Solomon in reconciling the conflicting pressures to which they are subjected, pressures which become stronger as we try to make democracy work in an increasingly pluralistic society. And the continuing health of American society requires that they play an active and enlightened role in local and national affairs generally.[22]

These facts create a twofold need: for awareness and for a particular set of attitudes. The businessman needs to be aware of his external environment, even when it does not immediately affect the profitability of

[21] Recognition of this fact is the basis of much that is both good and bad in modern public relations. A very recent development has been the attempt in some large companies to encourage their executives to take an active role in politics. See *The Wall Street Journal*, July 23, 1958. See also, on this range of issues, C. Wright Mills, *The Power Elite* (1956).

[22] Yet, as one study points out, "There exists a frightening lack of interest in the business community for participation in government service." Harvard Business School Club of Washington, D. C., *Businessmen in Government* (Harvard Business School, 1958), p. 36.

his enterprise, and he needs to be sensitive to the nature of the goals of all those groups which are affected by his firm's activities. He needs a set of attitudes to go with this awareness—a willingness to be concerned with the welfare of others, a sense of responsibility that leads him to accept a leadership role in the wider society of which his firm is a part, and a philosophy (which is the product of something more than unthinking prejudice) to provide a guiding line in the exercise of this leadership role.

Awareness is both broadened and sharpened by knowledge. In Chapter 4 we referred to the kinds of knowledge that help to develop the businessman's understanding both of the conditions of his nonmarket environment and of the goals within his organization that must in some way be reconciled. Businessmen are recognizing the need for such knowledge, as is evidenced not only by the statements and speeches of leading executives but also by the kind of material included in many executive development programs, by the publications and other activities of such business groups as the Committee for Economic Development, and by the subjects dealt with in business conferences and the annual reports of corporations.

It is easier to develop awareness than an appropriate set of attitudes. Even awareness depends in part upon the prior existence of a particular kind of attitude—the desire to become aware of what is going on around one. To some extent, businessmen have been forced into an awareness of their changing environment because of the way in which it has affected their business problems. Here is an important role for the colleges, including the business schools. They can widen the mental horizons of the students who will be future businessmen and develop in them both a sense of need and a desire to keep broadly informed about the world around them.

For some reason, this seems easier to do at the national than at the local level. Many businessmen, as well as other citizens, may know a great deal about the workings of their national government and at the same time be largely ignorant of what goes on in their local city halls and county courthouses.[23] Most firms are probably more directly affected in their daily operations by local than national regulations. Yet few businessmen have much of an idea of how well or badly their local governments are run. They frequently are only dimly aware of the nature of the

[23] As *Fortune* puts it, "until only a few years ago it was still regarded as somewhat disreputable for a businessman to get very close to City Hall." ("The Businessman's City," February, 1958, p. 94.) It has been suggested to us that this lack of familiarity with local governmental affairs is less true of businessmen in the smaller communities than in the larger cities. It is probably also less true of small businessmen who are native to a town than of the executives of large concerns.

political, economic, demographic, and other forces which shape their local communities and influence the actions of local government officials.[24]

As we use the term "attitudes," it means the whole set of values by which a person governs his conscious behavior. Every person has a more or less consciously formulated philosophy, a scale of values, with which to weigh the alternatives that are open to him. In a private enterprise system, no group needs more to have a carefully thought out philosophy than do businessmen, and it is vitally important to society as a whole that their philosophy contribute to the viability of an economic and political system that depends on the unplanned cooperation of groups with partially conflicting goals. As we said in Chapter 1, society requires of to-day's businessman a "broad knowledge and sensitive perception, with a well developed philosophy and set of ethical values, and with the ungrudging willingness to accept the responsibilities inevitably associated with the possession of power."

Heterogeneity in Business Careers: Its Influence on the Kinds of Qualities Required

As we have noted before, business is not one but a wide variety of occupations. What difference does this diversity make with respect to the kinds of knowledge and skills required for different kinds of business positions?

In considering this question, we have to take account of four kinds of diversity in careers. Businessmen may differ as to the nature of the function they perform within a company, the kind of industry in which they operate, the degree of authority they possess, and the size of firm with which they are associated.

DIVERSITY IN KINDS OF JOBS

Let us consider functional specialization first.[25] Most college graduates

---

[24] The situation has been improving; and, for reasons of self-interest that merge with the public interest, a number of national concerns have active programs of civic participation at the local level; for example, Ford, General Electric, General Motors, Sears Roebuck, and a number of others. *Fortune*, however, cites the complaint of some civic leaders that, in the case of the large corporations, "their community-relations effort is apt to be on the innocuous level of open-house days at the plant, children's tours, and free use of the company's baseball diamond." ("The Businessman's City," February, 1958, p. 94.) Obviously there are important exceptions, but the statement also contains a large grain of truth.

[25] Research now being conducted at the Educational Testing Service by J. K. Hemphill aims at providing a more useful classification of management positions (in terms of the kinds of work, responsibilities, etc. involved) than is now available. The results thus far obtained

begin as either salesmen, staff specialists, or possibly first-line supervisors. In the latter two cases, and sometimes in selling jobs also, some specialized skill and knowledge are required. The amount of technical competence required tends to diminish as the degree of administrative responsibility increases. In general, also, it seems to be true that the kind of mental ability measured by intelligence tests is highest among staff specialists and lowest among salesmen.

Randle, in the study previously cited, divided his executives into four groups: sales, manufacturing, engineering and research, and finance and accounting. In only the latter two did technical knowledge seem to be a critical factor. Planning, flexibility, and analytical ability and judgment were "discriminating" factors in manufacturing but not in the other functional areas (except that planning was important in engineering and research).[26] Ability to gain the confidence of others was important in all categories except accounting and finance. Accuracy and thoroughness were most important in accounting and finance, but creativeness was not a discriminating factor in this area. Personal leadership was more important in sales management and manufacturing than in the other two areas. Administrative skill was most important in manufacturing and in accounting and finance. Initiative was most important in manufacturing.[27]

None of these differences is very surprising. They must be interpreted in light of the fact that, as we noted earlier, the same study found a list of general abilities and skills that were common to all the functional areas.

Our own survey of companies yielded somewhat similar results. The majority of companies responding to this question thought that there were differences in the qualities needed for line and staff jobs. Thus line and staff positions call for somewhat different sorts of human relations skills. The former require the ability to inspire others to do what is needed; the latter require the capacity to "sell one's ideas" to those with the authority to put them into effect.[28] Line positions, naturally, call for administrative skills much more than do staff positions, but imagination, breadth, and ability to handle abstract ideas were considered to be more important for staff than for line positions.

The great majority of those who responded did not think that staff and

suggest that positions in different functional areas may be quite similar in terms of the basic job elements involved.

[26] A characteristic was discriminating if it tended to differentiate between more and less successful executives.

[27] Randle, "How to Identify Promotable Executives."

[28] A similar distinction is made by Perrin Stryker in "Which Route Is Up?" *Fortune*, June, 1955, p. 158.

line positions called for materially different kinds of college training, although exceptions were made for accounting and sometimes for other specialties. This may be due in part to the very considerable amount of horizontal movement between line and staff positions that we discovered, in addition to the availability of company training programs. Only about 25 per cent of our companies reported little or no movement between administrative and nonadministrative positions. There was more movement from staff to line jobs than in the opposite direction, although half the companies reported moderate to considerable movement in both directions.

With some exceptions, our companies had no strong preferences for any particular kind of college training for line supervisors. When specialized training was mentioned, it was usually in connection with various types of staff positions, and the preference was somewhat greater for engineering students than for those with specialized business training. But the prevailing view was that it was not necessary to specify different kinds of college training for most line and staff positions, that much specialization within business administration was not necessary, that even in nontechnical jobs, engineering and science provide a desirable training for a business career, and that specialized knowledge makes the least difference in sales positions, for which a liberal arts education may be as valuable as a major in business administration.

Some further evidence is available from the replies to a questionnaire we sent to a representative sample of forty-eight college and university placement offices.[29] As is to be expected, the latter reported that company recruiters, in recruiting for particular functional jobs, tended to show a preference for students who had majored in the corresponding functional area. The desire to secure students with specialized training was strongest in accounting and least strong in sales and sales management, with finance, personnel, and production falling in an intermediate position.

There has been an increasing tendency for business firms, particularly the larger ones, to recruit for general training programs. In recruiting for such programs, much the strongest preference seems to be for business majors without regard to the field of concentration within business administration. According to the placement officers who responded to our questionnaire, companies are frequently willing to take liberal arts students into these training programs.

The reports of college placement offices partly confirm and partly contradict the information we secured directly from company officials.

[29] See Appendix C for a description of this survey.

The nature of the contradiction has been the subject of many wry comments by college officials, who contrast the public statements of the company president praising the value of a liberal education and the practice of his recruiters who seek specialized training for particular jobs.

We frequently encountered this conflict within a business organization in our company interviews. The antagonists are top management and the central personnel department, on the one side, and the lower-level operating supervisors, on the other. It is the latter primarily who look to the colleges for specialized training.[30] When, with particular job specifications in hand, company recruiters visit a campus with a business school, they show a preference, *all other things being equal*, for a student with special training in the functional area for which he is being considered.

Business schools are giving in much too easily to pressure from company recruiters; to some extent they are using this pressure as a rationalization for too much proliferation of special courses and fields of concentration within their institutions. It is important that they resist this pressure for a number of reasons. American business is beginning to put more emphasis on its long-range needs in the field of management development and less on the requirements of the first job. The shift involves a growing emphasis on the more general types of knowledge, abilities, and skills required for advancement to positions of administrative responsibility.[31] Both our company interviews and the replies of the college placement officers indicate that for many, if not most types of jobs, a general business education is considered entirely satisfactory. At the same time, our company interviews suggest that, even for nonengineering jobs, there

[30] In a sample of 240 companies, the Conference Board found that in one-third of the cases the final selection decision was made by a department head, in 18 per cent of the cases by a committee, in 17 per cent by a personnel department specialist, in 8 per cent by the head of the personnel department, and in 8 per cent by a plant or branch manager. A vice president or the president made the decision in 9 per cent of the cases. Thus, in 41 per cent of the companies the hiring was made by operating supervisors below the vice president level, and these officials presumably had an important if not the dominating voice in the 18 per cent of the cases representing selection by a committee. Cf. National Industrial Conference Board, *Employment of the College Graduate*, p. 25. For some further discussion of this conflict between top management and first-line supervisors on the issue of specialized versus general training, see Herrymon Maurer, "The Worst Shortage in Business," *Fortune*, April, 1956, p. 204.

[31] In our company interviews, we asked if the firm emphasized primarily the first job or its long-term management needs in recruiting college graduates. Something less than a third did put the emphasis on the first job; about three-fifths said they emphasized long-term needs; and the remainder said they emphasized both. Among those emphasizing the first job, only a few thought this involved any serious conflict with their long-term needs; a slightly larger number thought there might be some but not a serious conflict between short-run and long-run recruiting objectives. For the sample as a whole, about one-third thought there was some conflict between their short-run and long-term recruiting objectives.

is a widespread belief in business that an engineering education equips a student for a business career as well as or better than a major in business administration. While recruiters may state a preference for particular types of business training, they will also take students with other kinds of training if the latter meet the companies' standards with respect to personal qualities, academic record, and other criteria.[32] It is worth noting that while the placement offices on campuses having a business school reported some difficulty in placing liberal arts students in other than selling jobs, the liberal arts colleges without business schools generally reported that ample opportunities in business were available to their graduates, and that it was possible to place their students in a number of functional areas other than sales, including production, personnel, and finance, as well as with companies having general training programs.

Bossard and Dewhurst pointed out nearly thirty years ago that business school graduates do not necessarily settle down in the particular fields in which they concentrate in college. Thus they found that only 38 per cent of the Wharton School alumni they surveyed had specialized in the field in which they were then working.[33]

Comparable data for all business school alumni are no' available. It is well known, however, that a significant fraction of business school graduates take their first job in a field other than that in which they concentrated, and that a significant fraction also experience one or more changes in the type of work they do during their business careers.[34] Excluding the accountants, perhaps half of the business school graduates in recent years have taken their first jobs in a field other than that in which they majored.[35] Further changes occur as the years go by. In particular, the

[32] The placement officer in the business school of a large state university offered the following estimate of the situation on his campus. About 25 per cent of the company recruiters come with fixed specifications as to the training desired; 25 per cent have few or no specifications; the remaining 50 per cent announce specifications but frequently hire men without the training originally specified.

[33] *University Education for Business*, p. 171.

[34] A survey of Stanford Business School alumni in 1953 asked for the first and present jobs of respondents. For graduates of 1927–41, a comparison of present jobs and first jobs showed a significant movement out of the fields of public accounting, industrial accounting, financial research, production management and industrial engineering, sales, and retail merchandising, among others. The fields into which there was the greatest movement were general management (by far the most important), financial administration, sales management, industrial relations and personnel management, management consulting, and teaching. Stanford Business School *Alumni Bulletin* (July, 1953).

[35] This statement is based on conversations with college placement officers and some actual data supplied by a number of schools. The more a school and its students emphasize preparation for the first job, the more likely are the latter to take their first job in the field in which they concentrated in college.

more successful move out of special areas into positions involving general administrative responsibility.

It seems reasonable to conclude that the business schools have gone too far in emphasizing specialized training for particular kinds of jobs, especially at the undergraduate level. Although company recruiters still favor the specialist, the trend in business is toward greater emphasis on the more general types of competence, and it is clearly the broader types of qualities which are needed for the higher positions of administrative responsibility. A very slight degree of specialization beyond the basic core of business subjects is ordinarily enough to help the college graduate make his start in business.

THE SPECIAL NEEDS OF PARTICULAR INDUSTRIES

So much for specialization by function or kind of position. Businessmen also vary as to the industry with which they are associated. Does this make any difference? Many business schools allege that it does, and specialized training in preparation for careers in particular areas of industry—for example, real estate, insurance, retailing, banking, transportation, or construction—is fairly common.

Although there is very little evidence to support the need for this sort of specialized training, there is a good deal of evidence that points in the opposite direction. As we have already indicated, the personnel departments and top executives of the companies we interviewed did not place heavy emphasis on specialized business training except for some of the more technical jobs. We examined particularly the replies of the companies in fields for which the business schools tend to offer specialized training. With a few exceptions, these companies did not emphasize the need for specialization in the problems of their industry, although most wanted special training in particular functional areas such as accounting.

The four railroads in our sample were interested in getting engineers but evidenced no special desire for railroad or transportation majors. The airline displayed no great interest in specialized training in its field; this was also true of the four public utilities. The latter, like the railroads, had a strong preference for engineers. Three of the four banks wanted broadly trained recruits; the fourth wanted graduates who had taken "practical courses," although not necessarily in the details of bank operations. None of the four insurance companies emphasized college training in insurance, although one admitted that its branch offices took a different attitude. (In all these cases, we are reporting the views of personnel and other officers in the "home office.") In a number of cases, campus recruiters from these companies may have asked for special training in their particular fields.

Two of the three real estate firms we interviewed expressed an interest in recruiting graduates with a major in the field of real estate. Our two large construction companies wanted chiefly engineers, or those with an adequate background in science and mathematics; one hired practically no business school graduates.

The field of retailing calls for special comment. Most business schools offer one or more specialized courses in retailing; a large number permit it as a field of specialization; and a few universities have special schools of retailing. Yet there is considerable evidence, in addition to that supplied by our own company survey, that a specialized major in retailing is of limited value for students planning a career in the retail field.

Among the companies we interviewed, three of five retail firms did not want specialization in retailing, one wanted a moderate amount, and one wanted a good deal. Our survey of college placement offices suggested that recruiters in this field did not express a strong preference for retailing majors. Something of a paradox is involved. Retailing firms seek out retailing majors but, for the most part, do not seem to value very highly the training the latter have received. The answer to this paradox is not hard to find. In recent years, retailing has not been a popular field with college graduates; the department stores and merchandising chains have had difficulty in securing an adequate supply of qualified recruits. Retailers want the colleges to offer retailing programs in order to interest students in retailing as a career. A student with a major in retailing is presumably motivated toward a career in retailing. He is eagerly sought by retailers because of that motivation and not because of the virtues of his training.

This situation also occurs in other fields. Some business schools, in effect, permit themselves to be used as service agencies for particular industries, offering specialized programs more to interest students in particular fields than because such training is essential for personally successful and socially constructive careers in those fields. It is our impression that local pressure for such service programs tends to come from industries that college graduates find particularly unattractive because of low starting salaries, for example, or unattractive working conditions. We have serious doubts that such an attempt to offset the competitive disadvantages of particular industries in the market for college graduates is a legitimate function of the business school.

Our survey of college placement offices suggests that even company recruiters do not strongly emphasize the desirability of specialization in particular industry fields. We asked the placement offices at universities that had business schools to indicate, for a given list of fields, whether recruiters showed a "strong preference," "some preference," or "little or no preference" for students having a major in the field in question. In *no* field did the majority of replies indicate a "strong preference." The fields in which recruiters showed a "strong preference" most often were transportation, advertising (both a "functional" and an "industry" field), and, to a less extent, banking. The largest number of replies indicating

TABLE 7

REPORTS BY COLLEGE PLACEMENT OFFICES REGARDING PREFERENCES EXPRESSED BY COMPANY RECRUITERS FOR SPECIAL TRAINING IN PARTICULAR INDUSTRY FIELDS

	Number of Placement Offices Reporting		
Industry Field	*"Strong Preference"*	*"Some Preference"*	*"Little or No Preference"*
Transportation	12	15	4
Utilities, excluding transportation	0	17	11
Insurance	2	12	21
Banking	9	15	11
Real estate	3	15	14
Retail trade	0	13	22
Advertising	16	15	2

Source: Tabulated from 37 replies to a questionnaire sent to a sample of college placement offices, but not all respondents completely answered this question. See Appendix C. This question was asked only of placement offices in universities having business schools. A few scattered replies referring to some industry area other than those included in this table have been omitted.

"little or no preference" were in retail trade and insurance. There were no cases of "strong preference" reported in the case of the utilities (excluding transportation) and retail trade. In the utilities, real estate, and banking, there were a substantial number of replies indicating "little or no preference," but the number of replies indicating "some preference" was somewhat greater. In insurance and retail trade, for both of which there was very little indication of "strong preference," the number of replies indicating "little or no preference" substantially exceeded those indicating "some preference." These replies are summarized in Table 7.

On the whole, the replies suggest less pressure from recruiters for specialized training in particular industry areas than we had expected. This is not to argue that pressure for specialized training from particular industries does not exist. While it does exist and creates a serious problem for some schools, the pressure is applied less at the recruiting level than at the level of the dean and the faculty. The pressure is exerted for a number of reasons: to increase the "prestige" of the industry, particularly in the case of some "low prestige" fields, to generate interest in the field among students, and sometimes because of a sincere belief that the field in question does require special knowledge and skills.

So far as we can determine, the basic abilities and skills emphasized earlier in this chapter are needed in much the same degree in all industries, and the similarities among industries in the qualifications needed are a great deal more important than the differences. The differences have to do with the technical and institutional peculiarities of particular industries and are learned more thoroughly and with greater economy through experience and training programs in the industry than through formal courses in college. However, a better understanding of the peculiarities of a particular industry's market and nonmarket environment can be developed by an occasional course which is truly analytical and which attempts to get at the underlying forces creating particular kinds of problems for particular sectors of the economy. These sectors should in general be broadly defined, and the courses should be at a high analytical level. Some courses in the "principles" of real estate, transportation, insurance, or banking may occasionally meet these criteria. Courses in real estate brokerage, how to operate a hotel or restaurant, or how to run a radio or television station obviously do not.

DIFFERENTIATION BY LEVEL OF AUTHORITY

In addition to operating in different functional areas and industries, businessmen vary in the degree of authority they possess and the magnitude of the administrative problems they confront. There is fairly wide agreement as to how this sort of diversity is related to the qualities businessmen should have.

It is at the lower levels that specialized knowledge and technical skill may be important. Ability to fit into an organization and to get along well with associates, willingness to take orders and follow instructions, and qualities of thoroughness and dependability are particularly needed at the lower levels. At the higher levels, qualities of personal leadership, the general administrative skills, the ability to accept responsibility and to make decisions in the face of uncertainty, and strong personal motivation become particularly important. It is at the higher levels, also, that

he businessman finds it necessary to give considerable thought to what
n Chapter 4 we called the firm's nonmarket environment.[36]

This sort of distinction between the qualities required at the lower and
upper levels of management must, at best, be very crude and obviously
subject to a variety of exceptions. Some of the qualities required of top
level managers are frequently needed at the lower levels also. Of course,
the promise of these qualities must be present if a person is to advance
to the higher ranks. One question we asked in our company interviews
was: "For the higher levels of management, which of the qualities considered important are in shortest supply?" The qualities mentioned most
often were human relations and general management skills, followed by
"organization-mindedness" and willingness to accept responsibility and
to take risks.

Randle, in his study of some 1,400 executives, attempted to distinguish
the qualities that are particularly important at the top, middle, and lower
levels of management. All of his general management qualities (see page
30, above) showed up more strongly in successful top executives than at
the lower levels. The quality that showed up most strongly was motivation. At the middle level, flexibility and analysis and judgment were discriminating characteristics between more and less successful executives.[37]
Mental capacity was a particularly discriminating factor in the lower
level of management (where we should expect the range of mental ability
to be fairly wide).

The larger business firms are today becoming increasingly concerned
with the problem of "management development," i.e., of developing a
supply of men with the qualities needed for the higher levels of management. The recent rapid growth in "executive development" programs of
various sorts is examined in Chapter 12. These programs vary among
themselves, and not all companies look for the same things in sending
their executives to them. But it is fair to say that, taking these programs

---

[36] For a forceful statement of the difference in qualities required by top and middle management, see R. N. McMurry, "Man-Hunt for Top Executives," *Harvard Business Review*,
January-February, 1954, especially pp. 49-50. He emphasizes particularly "the magnitude
of the risks which the two classes of executives are called upon to take." R. L. Katz emphasizes three kinds of skills needed by administrators: technical, human, and conceptual. The
first is most important in the lower levels, and the last is most important at the top levels of
management. "Skills of an Effective Administrator," *Harvard Business Review*, January-February, 1955, pp. 33-42.

[37] The fact that these qualities were 'discriminating" at the middle but not the top level
suggests that executives must have these qualities to rise to the top at all. Dependability was
a discriminating characteristic at the top level but not at the middle or lower levels, suggesting that this was a fairly general quality below the top level. On all of this, see Randle, "How
to Identify Promotable Executives," pp. 129-30.

as a whole, American corporations are seeking ways of developing in their executives some or all of the following qualities: breadth of outlook (ability to view the company as a whole, to assess its place in the industry, and to appreciate the significance of changes in the nonmarket environment), flexibility of mind, a more rational approach to problem-solving and decision-making, improved human relations and communication skills, greater administrative proficiency, and greater capacity for self-analysis and self-development.

DIVERSITY IN SIZE OF FIRM

The ingredients of business competence stressed in the early pages of this chapter hold for business firms of any size. The same qualifications can make a man successful in both a large and a small business. Such is the testimony provided by the careers of many businessmen.

There are, however, some differences in the problems posed by large and small business that should be noted. It is well to remember that a substantial fraction of business school graduates eventually settle down in firms of small or moderate size, and that a significant number take their first job with relatively small concerns.[38] Against this background, the business schools (particularly the graduate ones) have sometimes been criticized for teaching their students as if all of them would spend their entire business lives in large firms. While a minimum set of qualities are essential for success in large or small business, does small business have special needs of which the business schools should take account? To a limited extent, the answer is "yes." Some schools have been recognizing this by setting up courses with titles such as Problems of Small Business.[39]

Subject to some qualifications, we suggest that small firms present the following special problems. Their organizational problems are less difficult than in the larger firms. On the other hand, there is less specialization of function and considerably less use of specialized experts within the organization. As a corollary, there is less opportunity for staff research and greater difficulty in keeping up with the latest developments that

[38] According to a survey of Harvard Business School alumni published in 1956, more than one-third of those graduating during 1922–25 had become owner-managers, and more than one-half of all reporting alumni were associated with firms having fewer than 1,000 employees. Harvard Business School *Alumni Bulletin*, Summer, 1956. In 1958, about 44 per cent of Stanford Business School alumni were with firms having fewer than 1,000 employees. About a quarter were associated with firms having 100 or fewer employees. Stanford Business School *Alumni Bulletin*, January, 1959.

[39] There is no single dividing line between small and large business. A firm with less than 100 employees is today small by nearly any standard; for some purposes, a firm with two or three thousand employees may be small. Not long ago, *Fortune* considered the special management problems of "middle-sized" companies, defined as having from 500 to 2,500 employees. See Daniel Seligman, " 'Middle-Sized' Management," *Fortune*, May, 1955.

ffect the company's operations. Small firms cannot afford the kinds of internal training programs utilized by the larger companies, and only with some difficulty can they spare men to attend programs of any length conducted by other institutions. To the extent that small firms are also new and rapidly expanding, they raise special problems such as the need to secure adequate capital funds, the difficulty of maintaining working capital, and the need to develop a satisfactory distribution system for their products.[40]

Small firms cannot afford to rely on college recruitment as a source for management personnel. It is not merely that such recruiting involves more immediate expense than these firms can afford. More important, they cannot afford the training (including the ripening through experience) that is necessary. The chief means of entry of college graduates into small firms seem to be the following: entry into a family business immediately after graduation, going into business for themselves (usually after some work experience), or moving into the management of a small firm after some years with a larger company. In addition, small firms hire some inexperienced college graduates "over the counter."

In our company survey, we found that the smaller companies tended to place somewhat greater weight on the importance of mental ability and human relations skills than did the larger companies. It was the largest companies that placed the greatest weight on skill in communication. General management skills were stressed more by the moderately large companies than by either the very large or by the smaller firms. We are not sure how significant these differences are. Such other differences as showed up in our respondents' replies when classified by size of company were not important enough to warrant reporting them.

Our survey of college placement offices yields some additional information. Smaller companies, when they use the college placement office, tend to hire for specific jobs rather than for long-run management needs. The smaller companies show a somewhat greater interest in business administration majors than the larger firms, and are more likely to be interested in a field of specialization within business administration. On the other hand, interest in holders of master's degrees comes almost exclusively from the large companies. All of this reflects the small firm's inability or unwillingness to provide as much training as the large firm. It also indicates that small firms tend to hire on an *ad hoc* basis as particular openings arise and to neglect their longer-run needs for upper-level management personnel (which they may satisfy by eventually bringing in ex-

---

[40] "There is wide agreement, amounting to doctrine, that taxation, management, and finance together form an interrelated triumvirate of small-business problems." ("Does 'Small Business' Get a Fair Shake?" *Fortune*, October, 1953, p. 164.)

perienced men from other firms). To the extent that small firms do emphasize college training for particular jobs, they also neglect the fact that
being small and without elaborate staff departments, they particularly
need men with broad business training. However, the smaller firms frequently act as if such broad training, to be really valuable to them, can
be acquired only by experience with some other (and usually larger)
company.

All this suggests that the opportunities for the business schools to meet
the special needs of small business in their regular degree programs are
rather limited. Certainly there is no strong argument for emphasis on
specialized business fields because small firms occasionally look for specialists in these areas.[41] To the extent that small firms do emphasize
special knowledge in their recruiting, they are ignoring their needs for
the more general and fundamental kinds of business knowledge and
skills, and increasing their dependence on other firms for the more
broadly developed men they may need later for their top positions. However, it does appear that there is a need for an interesting "problems"
type of course which the business schools might offer as an elective. There
is also clear need for special institutes and conferences that seek to help
businessmen deal with both the general problems of small business and
with the special problems of particular industries.

Business Competence in the Face of Rapid Change

The outstanding fact about the problems with which today's businessman must cope is the rapidity with which they are changing. We took a
look at the more important of these changes in Chapter 1: the increase
in size and organizational complexity of business enterprise, the expansion and changing character of markets, the accelerating tempo of scientific and technological change, the development of new analytical tools
as a basis of rational decision-making, the changing role of government,
and so on.

As Dean G. L. Bach has recently pointed out:[42]

It will be 1970 before most of our undergraduate business students of today
really begin to assume significant managerial responsibility, as they enter their

[41] The fact that a small company may not have the resources to provide extended training
for the few college graduates it hires "should not cause a school of business to conclude that
it must give more specialized training at the expense of a broad education. Small companies
can almost always procure more experienced executives from larger companies." *Business
Looks at Business Education* (published by the School of Business Administration, University of
North Carolina, 1958), p. 9.

[42] In *Management Science*, IV (July, 1958), 351–64.

30's. It will be 1980 before they begin to reach general management responsibility, in their early 40's. And it will be perhaps 1990 before those few who finally reach the top as presidents and general executives have much chance of getting there, in their early 50's. It is thus primarily to the 1970's, the 1980's, and even to 1990 that we should be looking as we plan our curricula and do our teaching.

Thus the business schools are attempting to train young men and women for a business world the nature of which can be but imperfectly foreseen but which will differ radically from that in which we have been living. Some of the implications for business education are obvious.

Clearly the business schools should do all they can to develop those qualities of mind that are most needed in times of rapid change. These include a sense of historical perspective, breadth and flexibility of mind, scientific curiosity, and generalized analytical ability and judgment which are not tied down to methods and procedures that will soon be obsolete.[43]

In addition to these qualities of mind, tomorrow's businessmen will need the kinds of fundamental knowledge and analytical tools that will most help them to cope with the kinds of change that as yet can be only imperfectly foreseen. This almost certainly means that today's business students should acquire a sound working knowledge in the natural sciences and mathematics and in economics and the other social sciences, as well as some idea as to how the expanding knowledge in these areas has already influenced and in the future will influence even more the course of business. Such knowledge is needed so that these future businessmen can assess the significance of future changes in science and technology, in economic and political affairs, in the place of business in society, and in international relations. They will need this knowledge also in order to know how to communicate with and make effective use of staff specialists.

In addition to emphasizing certain qualities of mind and those underlying disciplines in which advancing knowledge will have a profound effect on the course of business, the business schools should also do what they can to keep abreast of and to teach the most important of the newer developments in business administration that have general applicability, particularly those whose greatest importance still lies in the future. Among these newer developments in business management are new quantitative methods to provide a more rational basis for decision-mak-

---

[43] The need for historical perspective and flexibility of mind has been well stated by James C. Worthy. See "Education for Business Leadership," *Journal of Business*, xxviii (January, 1955), 78–79.

ing (as applied, for example, in inventory control, production planning, quality control, market research, capital budgeting, and the like), more rational methods for personnel selection and management development, and greater emphasis on organizational planning and administration (including the element of human relations and the improvement of communication systems).

It would be dangerous to try to spell out in much detail the new kinds of skills and knowledge that will be needed in the years ahead. One question we asked in our company interviews was: "Which types of management (including staff) jobs are likely to become more important in the future?" The answers varied widely, depending on the company and the individual respondent's background. The replies were far from startling and seemed largely to represent a projection of such trends as had impressed themselves on the men being interviewed. The trends most often stressed were the growing importance of general administration, the new developments in data processing and mathematical programming, more emphasis on research in various business functions, and still greater emphasis on the human relations aspect of management.

It has been suggested to us that the technological revolution now taking place in data processing and the array of new quantitative techniques being developed to provide a more rational basis for decision-making will have the following effects upon the structure of business management.[44]

1   The line between planning and performance will shift upward in the management hierarchy. The present trend toward decentralization will to some extent be reversed, and the amount of centralized planning and coordination will increase.

2   In line with this, there will be an accelerating interest in research as companies seek to make the world in which they operate more predictable, and as they seek a more rational basis for decision-making. More specialized areas of research will develop in fields other than process and product development, utilizing mathematics, statistics, and the basic social science disciplines.

3   More research, creative, and programming jobs will develop in the higher levels of management, and many lower- and middle-management positions will tend to take on more of a programmed character.

[44] The following numbered paragraphs are based on part of a memorandum prepared for this study by Thomas L. Whisler of the University of Chicago, and rests on some research conducted by Professor Whisler and Professor Harold J. Leavitt of Carnegie Institute of Technology. See also their article "Management in the 1980's," *Harvard Business Review*, XXXVI (November-December, 1958), 41-48.

4 More jobs will require creative and innovative abilities together with an understanding of the interactions between the firm and its environment.

5 There will be some shift in concern with human relations from the supervisor-worker level to the top levels of management.

In general, current trends seem to point toward more centralized planning and coordination, more emphasis on nonengineering types of research, a greater role for staff specialists in the higher levels of management, a wider use of analytical tools taken from a variety of scientific disciplines, and lessened reliance on the initiative and judgment of line officials in the lower and middle levels of management. The need for a high order of mental ability seems to be increasing. At the same time, the old needs will continue for the qualities we have previously emphasized: skill in human relations, ability to accept responsibility, breadth and flexibility of mind, integrity. And however much progress we may make in the next generation toward a more rational basis of managerial decision-making, the need for judgment and for the ability to reach decisions on the basis of incomplete information will continue to be crucial.[45]

Conclusions

The conclusions reached deductively in Chapter 4 both amplify and provide a logical framework for the findings of the present chapter. In the earlier chapter, we emphasized the broad areas regarding which knowledge was needed; we also emphasized certain abilities and skills.

The present chapter has contributed a little more to our impressions as to the kinds of knowledge required. Business is coming to place greater emphasis on the kinds of knowledge that contribute to analytical capacity, to breadth and flexibility of mind, and to the ability to cope with a technological, social, economic, and political environment that changes

[45] Forrest H. Kirkpatrick refers to "eight major trends that will affect business management over the next twenty-five years and will, in some measure, influence any educational program pointed toward preparing young men and young women for business careers:" "increased attention to the human equation," increased emphasis on long-range planning, the "fast rate at which developments in the physical and social sciences are being applied to business administration," growing acceptance by management "of responsibility outside the business enterprise," greater acceptance of women in all levels of management, "acceptance by individuals of more than one career plan and career pattern," greater recognition of the limitations of training in specific job techniques "coupled with marked recognition of the importance of actual competence in a particular field of knowledge or activity," and the greater use of educational and training resources in business itself. See his remarks in "Collegiate Business Education in the Next Quarter Century," *West Virginia University Business and Economic Studies*, v, No. 4 (February, 1958).

with bewildering rapidity. Business still has a demand for specialized knowledge, but the demand for specialized training for the lower positions in management is tending to diminish, and the demand for a higher order of specialized knowledge and technical skill—derived from the physical and social sciences and from mathematics and statistics—is tending to increase. Beyond this, the need is for some knowledge of business and economic "fundamentals," of the art of communication, and of the problems created by organizational relationships, as well as for the kind of broad background that contributes to the basic abilities mentioned a moment ago.

What this chapter has brought out most clearly are the basic skills and abilities—however they may be acquired—which are most needed in the business world. The most important of these are analytical ability, judgment, skill in interpersonal relations, the ability to accept responsibility and to make decisions, general administrative skills (including the capacity to lead others, to plan, to organize and delegate), breadth and flexibility of mind, imagination, facility in personal communication, and strong personal motivation. These qualities are not needed in precisely the same combination for every type of position and for all kinds of careers in business. But, particularly for the higher administrative positions, they seem to be the qualities that need most to be emphasized.

Because of the diversity of business occupations and the need for specialized knowledge and skills, these conclusions require some, but not a great deal of modification. So far as their resources and the caliber of their students permit, the business schools would be well advised to concentrate on the kinds of basic knowledge and skill development suggested in this and the preceding chapter.

This conclusion is subject to the following qualifications. With the increasing complexity of business operations, the need for staff specialists is increasing, at the same time that there continues to be an insistent demand for able administrators. Many students will find that they can make their most significant contribution in staff positions. However, the growing need will be for men with a high level of analytical ability and with a sophisticated command of analytical and research tools derived from the fundamental disciplines. Sound training in the physical and social sciences and in mathematics and statistics, combined with the ability to apply these tools to business problems, is becoming much more important than detailed knowledge of current practice or the acquisition of routine skills. These conclusions gain added strength from the fact that similar findings are being applied in other branches of education. A closely related illustration is the movement of some of the leading engineering schools toward an "engineering-science" approach and away from an emphasis on specialized techniques.

The second qualification arises out of the wide variation in the abilities of those who seek a business education. Unfortunately, many who are admitted to business schools do not have the kinds of qualifications emphasized in this chapter, and many do not have the mental ability to acquire the analytical tools that are increasingly necessary. These students will never rise far in the business world. But even these students will benefit most from an emphasis in college on the basic analytical tools, on the fundamentals of business administration and economics, and on a good general education. We shall have more to say about the problem of the poor student in later chapters.

The analysis in this and the preceding chapters has put almost exclusive emphasis on the student's future career as a whole, and has deprecated attempts to train a student in college for his first job. Most thoughtful educators and the more articulate businessmen support this position. But it is also true that at the recruiting level there is still a fair amount of emphasis on specialization, and the student's entry into business is undoubtedly made easier if he has some familiarity with the kind of business he is entering and the kind of job with which he begins. To some extent, this need can be met by personal counseling, by outside reading, and by work experience during the college years. But it also lends some support to those who argue for some specialization within business administration. However, it does not seem to us that this argument can justify more than a small amount of specialization at best. The long-term needs of business and the career needs of the student require that emphasis be placed on the kinds of fundamental knowledge and basic skill development described in this and the preceding chapter. Special training for the first job is justified only if it can be done without interfering with this more important objective. Since the time a student has in college, even if a graduate year or two are added, is scarcely sufficient for this broader objective, the opportunities for preparing the student for his first job are severely restricted. This will become a less serious problem as business increasingly accepts the responsibility for this initial training. We make the urgent plea, both here and elsewhere in this report, that the business schools make more of an effort to educate businessmen as to their responsibilities (and long-term interests) in this regard instead of, as is too often the case today, capitulating to the pressures exerted by some company recruiters and some local business interests.

There is one final qualification to make. Our analysis has emphasized basic skills and the more fundamental kinds of knowledge. While this is clearly the trend of the future in business education, it does present at least one danger against which business schools need to be on guard. A broad curriculum emphasizing general principles, fundamental knowledge, and breadth of view does not prepare the student for the routine and detail that are likely to characterize his early years in business. He must learn to accept the routine and to benefit from it. What he has learned must be elaborated by experience before he is ready for the higher levels of management. A frequent complaint by businessmen against the products of particularly the best known graduate schools is that "they all want to be vice-presidents tomorrow." More and wiser counseling can help with this problem. A more plentiful use of cases and problems taken from the lower levels of management can also help.

chapter 6

THE ROLE OF EDUCATION
IN THE DEVELOPMENT
OF BUSINESS COMPETENCE

PUT IN the briefest possible terms, competence in any field is the product of some combination of education, experience, and personal traits. This is true of any kind of professional competence, including competence in business.

Knowledge is the chief product of education, although it can be acquired in other ways also—for example, through reflective observation and experience. Experience, in addition, develops an ability to apply knowledge previously acquired, in good part by a process not inaccurately described as "feedback." Experience in concrete situations "edits, disciplines, and evaluates knowledge" acquired in other ways—for example, by formal education—and thus shapes knowledge into particular skills.[1]

Competence, in business or any other field, depends not only on education and experience but also on the possession of personal traits. These traits can be considered to be of three types: mental, physical, and those concerned with personality. These qualities not only contribute directly to the development of competence but also interact with education and experience. They help to determine the individual's ability to learn from education and experience, and they in turn may be influenced by the latter. Thus education can sharpen analytical ability or help to develop or inhibit particular personality traits.

The Nature of Business Competence

In Chapter 5 we examined the "qualities" which presumably make for business competence. These qualities turned out to be a combination

[1] Cf. David Krech and R. S. Crutchfield, *Elements of Psychology* (1958), p. 450, from which the quoted phrase is taken.

of skills and of mental and other personal traits which contribute to the possession of certain skills.

This is not surprising since, when we speak of business competence, what we mean in effect is a bundle of skills. Chapters 4 and 5 suggest that the practice of business involves the following basic sets of skills: skill in recognizing, anticipating, and solving problems, including the ability to make decisions; skill in developing and maintaining effective organizational relationships; skill in interpersonal relations; and skill in communication. While the last three could be lumped together as one interrelated set of skills, it is more convenient to treat them separately.

The "qualities" emphasized in Chapter 5 relate to this set of "basic skills" in the following ways. Analytical ability, judgment, ability to accept responsibility and make decisions in the face of uncertainty, breadth and flexibility of mind, and imagination all contribute to skill in problem-solving and decision-making. The other "qualities" mentioned in the list on page 81 are, with one exception, simply the other "basic skills" listed here: organizational skill, skill in human relations, and skill in communication. The one exception is strong personal motivation, which we consider under the heading of "attitudes," although it undoubtedly also contributes indirectly to skill.

Today's businessmen must be not only competent but also responsible. Hence to the aforementioned skills we must add a set of attitudes, which can be summed up as a concern for more than personal gain and a philosophy with which to make this concern effective. Actually, another and narrower set of attitudes is also necessary. This has to do with the individual's attitudes toward his work and his own career. Here we include personal motivation, organizational loyalty, and the like.

THE BASIC SKILLS

Problem-solving consists of determining (and anticipating) the need for action, searching for alternative lines of action and evaluating the probable consequences of the alternatives, and making rational choices among the alternatives in the light of a complex of organizational objectives. All this must be done in an environment which is continually changing, without full knowledge of all the relevant variables and of their interrelationships, and in the face of partially conflicting organizational objectives.

Organizational skill implies the ability to devise administrative arrangements which contribute to effective decision-making: arrangements that generate needed information, that provide for a fruitful division of labor, and that facilitate translation of decisions into action. Organizational skill also implies ability both to maintain and to make use of these arrangements: to plan, coordinate, delegate, and so on—in short, to be an administrator.

Skill in interpersonal relationships is an element of organizational skill, but it is so important that it needs to be treated separately. For the administrator it involves the ability to exercise personal leadership. For anyone concerned with organizational behavior, it implies the ability to work harmoniously with others, and this, to some extent, implies skill in persuasion—which in different forms is a skill that is needed by the salesman, by the line supervisor, and by the staff specialist seeking to induce a line department to try a new idea.[2]

This brings us to *skill in communication*. Communication is a two-way process; it involves receiving and interpreting as well as transmitting information. This information may be in either verbal or numerical form, and verbal communication may be either written or oral. The problem of effective communication in business organizations involves three kinds of skills: skill in formulating one's ideas and in transmitting them either orally or in writing, skill in receiving and interpreting nonquantitative information, and skill in generating, transmitting, and interpreting the flow of data needed for making and implementing decisions. The latter kind of skill may be specialized, as in the case of the accountant or statistician. But a more general kind of ability—to understand and to interpret information in quantitative form—is required of all businessmen.

Businessmen apply these skills in the four problem areas described in Chapter 4: the market and nonmarket environments in which their firms operate, the internal organizational environment of the firm, and the economic management involved in acquiring inputs and converting them into goods and services for sale.

The educational issue for the business schools, then, resolves itself into this question: How can they make their maximum contribution to the development of the basic skills (and attitudes) required for dealing with problems in some or all of the four areas just mentioned? A related question is: Should they attempt to develop "generalists" who can apply a set of basic (and particularly administrative) skills in a variety of situations, or should they concentrate on the particular bundles of skills required by the specialists within particular problem areas, such as accounting systems, market research, or some phase of production management? Or should they try to do some of both?

---

[2] Compare Chester Barnard's comments on "the importance of persuasion in human affairs" in "Education for Executives," *Journal of Business*, XVIII (October, 1945), 179–80.

The Role of the Business Schools in Developing Business Competence

Of the three foundation stones on which the development of business competence must rest—formally transmitted knowledge, experience, and personal traits—clearly the first presents the greatest opportunity to the business schools.

THE KINDS OF KNOWLEDGE NEEDED

Chapter 4 suggested the kinds of knowledge which, at least ideally, the businessman should have. We stressed there the need for knowledge that would aid the businessman in dealing with several different aspects of the structure and functioning of business: the fact that the business firm is an organization, the complex and changing market and nonmarket environments within which business must operate, and the problems of economic management with which any business organization must be concerned.[3]

As we noted in this earlier discussion, the kinds of knowledge needed include not only the field of business administration proper, but also the physical and particularly the social sciences, some mathematics and statistics, and even the humanities. Systematic knowledge derived from these different areas, if the student can learn how to use it, contributes to business competence in several ways. General knowledge of facts and principles provides the background for a rational approach to business problems. To paraphrase Chester Barnard, it sharpens observation, prevents the neglect of important factors, gives the advantages of a more general language, and reduces the inconsistencies between behavior and its verbal description.[4] In addition, knowledge develops particular personal qualities and adapts them to particular needs. Thus some kinds of knowledge develop and sharpen analytical capacity so that it can better cope with business problems. A better understanding of human behavior reinforces those personal traits that contribute to an individual's ability to elicit cooperation from others.

A knowledge of principles and a command of analytical tools in the areas described in Chapter 4 also contribute to the businessman's ability to cope with the kinds of change that the future is certain to bring. He will have a better appreciation of the forces making for change, in the

[3] See pp. 61–69, above.
[4] See Barnard's foreword to H. A. Simon, *Administrative Behavior* (2nd ed., 1957), p. xliii. Barnard was talking about knowledge of a science of organization and administration, but his comment also applies to systematic knowledge in other areas.

economy at large and in his own business. Such knowledge will give him the kinds of analytical equipment that will not only aid him in his own decision-making, but will also help him to make effective use of more highly trained staff specialists in dealing with particular kinds of problems. The businessman needs some grounding in, for example, the physical sciences, statistics, and the social sciences so that he can communicate with specialists in these areas and so that he will have an appreciation of what he can and cannot expect of them.

What is needed at the level of the university is a broad foundation on which the businessman can then build through a process of self-development that includes observation, experience, and possibly further formal training. Even for those planning specialized careers, this broad educational base is necessary. Specialized training at a high analytical level needs to be solidly based on the relevant underlying disciplines and thus should ordinarily be deferred to the graduate years. Specialized training of a more routine sort can be obtained on the job, in various sorts of nonuniversity technical institutes, and in other ways. Even students of limited ability who will not rise very far in the business world need the broadening, mental discipline, and exposure to principles that we suggest. Their education may have to be less rigorous than that which the more able students can absorb; but they, no less than their abler colleagues, require a broad educational foundation on which to build. If they cannot benefit from the kind of broad and reasonably rigorous training which a university can and should provide, less demanding and more specialized programs should be available to them elsewhere, as, for example, in technical institutes and junior colleges.[5]

LEARNING TO UTILIZE KNOWLEDGE

Formally acquired knowledge will not be very useful to the future businessman unless he learns how to apply it. This is the function of what we call "experience." Formal education can never be a substitute for experience, but to a limited extent it can approximate experience and thus contribute to the student's ability to use in real-life situations the knowledge he has acquired. In this respect, collegiate business education, if well done, can contribute to each of the kinds of skills on which business competence is based. The business school can train the student in the use of analytical tools (statistics, accounting, economic analysis, etc.) and give him experience in using these tools in situations that resemble

---

[5] The problem of developing an adequately differentiated program for students of different levels and kinds of ability is dealt with at several places in this report. See, for example, Chapters 7 and 13.

those he will encounter in the business world. (Rigorous intellectual discipline in itself contributes to problem-solving ability.) Real-life cases, role-playing, and other types of assignments can give the student limited experience in analyzing and solving some of the kinds of problems with which he will have to deal later on. Through practice in the classroom he can make a start on learning how to combine innate intelligence, a command of analytical tools, and judgment in the solution of various kinds of business problems.

Skill in human relations is partly the product of the understanding that comes from education and experience and partly a matter of personality. Education can help the student to realize that problems do arise out of the fact that organizations are made up of human beings. It can contribute some understanding of the determinants of human behavior. And it can, through role-playing and the like, give the student some experience in handling interpersonal relations.

Opportunities also exist for developing general administrative skills through simulated experience, particularly through the use of business cases that illustrate various types of administrative problems. Of all the types of skills included in business competence, however, the one which the colleges are best equipped to develop through simulated experience is skill in verbal communication. Through the use of problems and cases, there is also considerable opportunity for developing skill in using and interpreting quantitative data.

The business schools have probably done less than they could to integrate formal teaching with relevant experience outside the classroom, for example, with the students' extracurricular and noncampus activities. Opportunities also exist to combine work experience with formal instruction, and some schools now do a limited amount in this direction.[6]

The main point to be made here is that business education is more than a matter of didactic teaching, more than a matter of "book learning," more than a matter of knowledge acquired without the ability to use it. Formal education for business is one in a sequence of steps which lead to the development of a set of basic skills (and attitudes) that constitute business competence.[7]

Let us try to avoid misunderstanding. Although we emphasize the need for skill development, we are concerned with the general or basic skills previously enumerated. We are not concerned with the more routine

[6] The whole subject of teaching methods is discussed in some detail in Chapter 15.

[7] L. F. Urwick has argued strongly that business and the colleges need to cooperate to bring about a better integration of education and experience, instead of treating them as entirely separate stages in the student's development. (*Management Education in American Business*, American Management Association, 1954.)

vocational skills, although we are interested in those specialized but "higher-order" skills which require the mastery of rigorous analytical tools.

It should be clearly understood, also, that we do not minimize the importance of systematic knowledge or the need to teach subject matter. As we emphasized in Chapter 4, not one but a number of systematic bodies of knowledge underlie the practice of business. Systematic knowledge is the first ingredient of professional competence. The medical student must learn his anatomy and physiology (and before that some biology and chemistry) before he is ready for clinical medicine. The engineer must know his mathematics and mechanics before he is given problems in machine design or airport construction. The same is true of business administration. Systematic knowledge in as many as possible of the relevant areas should be taught at as high a level as the student can handle. The generalizations and theory derived from systematized bodies of knowledge—for example, in economics and the other social sciences and in the basic fields of business administration—should, so far as possible, be the foundations on which "clinical teaching" is then built.

At the same time, to come back to the point originally made, didactic teaching by itself is not enough. The passive absorption of knowledge by the student can hardly be called education.[8] Even in the liberal arts the student needs to participate actively in the learning process. To paraphrase Whitehead, all education is the acquisition of the art of utilizing knowledge. It is a process of self-development, in which the student develops the capacity to see the relevance of what is being learned and to build on this knowledge an ability to deal with problems that he will meet in later years. Professional education in general and business education in particular must rest on this idea. "Education for business competence" should seek to develop in the student a capacity for dealing with the kinds of problems he will face in later life. This implies a set of basic skills. The development of these skills requires that the business schools not merely transmit knowledge, but give the student practice in utilizing this knowledge in the kinds of situations he will encounter in his business career. As a group of businessmen have put it, the business school grad-

---

[8] "Much of American education is plagued with an affliction I would call subjectmatteritis. The most pervasive and insidious educational fallacy I know of is that education is achieved by merely learning subject matter; that the more ground covered in class—the more pages assigned in the book—the greater the education. And what is equally bad and makes educational reform almost impossible is the corollary that the way to improve education is merely to change subject matters in the curriculum. This theory overlooks the fact that the ability to think straight and constructively has to be learned by actually doing such thinking." R. E. Doherty, *The Development of Professional Education* (1950), p. 5.

uate "should not be simply an ambulant handbook of accumulated data."[9]

DEVELOPMENT OF PERSONAL QUALITIES

The third leg of the tripod that supports professional competence is the sum of an individual's personal qualities. These also can be affected by education, and here the business schools do much less than they might. We have already mentioned that analytical ability can be sharpened in the business school. Teaching by the case method may, as many business educators believe, help to develop judgment and give the student courage to make decisions in the face of incomplete information. Both general education and business courses broadly taught should contribute to breadth and flexibility of mind and possibly stimulate the imagination. The personal qualities that contribute to skill in human relations can probably be affected by education and particularly by personal counseling. More problematical is the business school's ability to influence motivation and personal drive.[10]

It is fair to say that few schools or instructors take such considerations into account in curriculum planning, course content, and the development of teaching methods.[11] The schools have been particularly deficient in two respects. Virtually nowhere have we found the amount and kind of personal counseling which, in our view, is required. Nor are the schools doing much to screen students on the basis of the more obvious personal qualities that are required for business competence.[12] This is a difficult thing to do, particularly at the undergraduate level, and the problem is

[9] *Business Looks at Business Education*, a study sponsored by the School of Business Administration, University of North Carolina (1958), p. 8. This is a thoughtful document by a group of North Carolina businessmen.

[10] This is perhaps too pessimistic a comment. Business schools inevitably serve as a screening device with respect to motivation. Students who are repelled by business find this out in a business program and tend to drop out. A well taught and stimulating business program probably can arouse interest in students and motivate them toward useful business careers, although it may not be able to generate the personal drive and ambition that business firms want. On the negative side, also, it should be mentioned that liberal arts graduates who go into business are frequently dissatisfied because they were not originally motivated toward or psychologically prepared for a business career.

[11] But awareness of this problem is not new. See J. H. S. Bossard and J. F. Dewhurst, *University Education for Business* (1931), p. 12. For another earlier study that emphasized the role that business education should play in developing personal qualities, see J. A. Bowie, *Education for Business Management* (1930), pp. 50–51.

[12] A few of the graduate schools give weight to evidence bearing on qualities other than mental ability in their admission procedures. The case for screening business students at both the undergraduate and graduate levels on the basis of motivation and personality traits as well as mental ability is put forward vigorously in *Business Looks at Business Education*, pp. 20–21.

made much more difficult by the known weaknesses of available testing procedures.

As we have seen, business education must be concerned not only with competence but also with responsibility, not only with skills but also with the attitudes of businessmen. This means that business schools have an obligation to do what they can to develop a "sense of social responsibility" and a high standard of business ethics in their graduates.

There is general agreement among business educators that the needed attitudes are not likely to be developed by formal courses in "business ethics," and few such courses are now given. There is a widespread belief, based as much on hope as on fact, that students are exposed to ethical considerations in most business courses. Probably the schools should give somewhat more explicit consideration to ethical issues and introduce problems having strong ethical overtones into various business courses. We agree, however, that formal courses in business ethics accomplish little and are likely, if anything, to repel the student.

The business schools can make a contribution in the somewhat broader (and vaguer) area sometimes designated as "the social responsibilities of business." Awareness can be developed through courses in history and various of the social sciences. Special courses can be designed bearing such titles as "Business Responsibilities in the American Society," "Ideas and Social Change," and "Business Activity and Public Welfare." These deal with aspects of the changing nonmarket environment of business and with the role of business and the businessman in our kind of society. In addition, other courses dealing with organization and human relations can make the student aware of the interaction of individual and group goals within the firm. Out of such courses, if well taught, can come awareness and also the reflection from which socially constructive attitudes may emerge. Such courses do not lend themselves to lecture and textbook, and "objective" examinations pervert their very purpose.

Graduate versus Undergraduate Business Education

As we emphasized in Chapter 4, collegiate business education is only a small part of the total education of the businessman. It is the function of the colleges to lay the basic groundwork, to provide the foundations on which the student can later build through experience on the job and further formal training. Business education, like college education generally, should provide the basis for continuing self-development.

The following statement by a group of businessmen is worth quoting in this connection:[13]

In view of the widely diverse types and phases of business and industry into which graduates go, it is apparent to us that a school of business cannot prepare all of its graduates to be competent in all respects. It is more feasible and logical for business itself to train the graduate in the characteristics, attributes, and limitations of its products, the nature and degree of competition in its field, the technical knowledge necessary with regard to equipment and processes, and the organization of the business itself. We in business can do almost all types of *training* better than a school of business. The job of a school of business is education. Industry can train more effectively, more economically, and with greater skill than can a university or school of business. We look to the school for graduates who understand the fundamentals of business principles, rather than graduates who specialize in detailed practices.

While the case seems overwhelming for emphasizing in the business schools breadth and the sort of training that will develop the basic problem-solving, organizational, and communication skills, a good many observers doubt that the kind of training needed can be satisfactorily provided at the undergraduate level. The grounds for this skepticism are several.

First of all, it is argued, undergraduates do not have the intellectual maturity and judgment that rigorous training aimed at developing the problem-solving and organizational skills requires. These basic skills are of a high order and call not only for mental ability, but also for mature judgment and particular personal qualities. It has also been suggested that undergraduates as a group lack the necessary seriousness of purpose and are too much concerned with the social and extracurricular aspects of college life. More generally, it is claimed, high-level professional training of any sort should be at the graduate level, so that the training can fully absorb the student's time and energy and because this training should build on a foundation of general education and preprofessional courses which it is the function of the undergraduate years to provide.

A final argument against undergraduate business training is of a different sort and leads to the conclusion that formal business education should be preceded by responsible, full-time work experience as well as by an undergraduate program in nonbusiness subjects.[14] The argument for deferring formal training until the student has had several years of business experience rests not only on the additional maturity of the stu-

---

[13] *Business Looks at Business Education*, p. 13. Italics are in the original.
[14] Cf. Stanley F. Teele and John F. Chapman, "Education for Business," *University of Toronto Quarterly*, xxvi (July, 1957), 542–43.

dent, but also on the fact that, with this background, the formal training he then receives will be much more meaningful to him. The systematic knowledge he acquires then will illuminate his past experience, which thus will help to shape new knowledge into the basic skills and attitudes the business school is seeking to develop.

The leading graduate schools report that, in general, their students do better work if they have already had some business experience or at least military service. A number of businessmen have also expressed to us the view that business training is best obtained at the graduate level, and preferably after some business experience. University executive development programs for "middle management" reflect essentially the same point of view.

We are inclined to believe that this view is correct, but only in the following limited sense. The additional benefit from a combination of work experience and a good graduate program is worth the additional time and expense for those students who are in a position to undertake such a program without heavy financial sacrifice by themselves and their families, and who have the mental ability and other qualities that make them likely candidates for the higher positions in management.

It is obvious that, in the words of Teele and Chapman, this kind of program represents "an ideal which few students can afford, and many do not yet seek."[15] Interpolating several years of business experience between a bachelor's degree and graduate training is not feasible for most students who might benefit from it. However, we share the view that, for most students with the motivation, ability, and other qualities which promise a successful career in business, graduate training in business is better than undergraduate. We also agree that the undergraduate years should be devoted to a broad education with emphasis on English, natural science, mathematics, history, and economics and the other social sciences.

While the ideal education for the most able of tomorrow's businessmen would be of the sort just described, the less desirable alternative of an undergraduate program in business administration will for a long time be the course taken by the majority of students seeking a business education in college. Although the four undergraduate years are not really enough to provide the basic background and training the future business-man and citizen should have, we do not recommend that the colleges and universities eliminate their undergraduate programs in business administration. Undergraduate business instruction can, if improved, serve a useful purpose for those students strongly motivated toward a business

[15] *University of Toronto Quarterly*, xxvi (July, 1957), 543.

career who are unable or unwilling to take the better but longer and more expensive route. It is wiser for the undergraduate business schools to concentrate on improving their programs than to face all the problems (which would be insoluble for many) of converting themselves into exclusively graduate institutions. However, some schools, particularly in the better and wealthier universities, are already beginning to think in terms of eventually dropping their undergraduate programs.

A desirable compromise might be a five-year program in which three years would be devoted to general education, including "preprofessional" subjects, and two years to a business program that would take advantage of the added maturity and background of the student. The Amos Tuck School at Dartmouth College has conducted such a "three-two" program for many years, and the wider adoption of this plan has been urged by others.[16] The advantages and disadvantages of this compromise arrangement are discussed in some detail in Chapter 11.

The Elements in a Business Administration Curriculum

The formal education of the businessman, before he begins the practice of business, falls naturally into several parts. In this respect it resembles professional training in a number of other fields.

Of primary importance is the requirement of a general or liberal education. This general education must serve two purposes. It must provide the basis for the development of what we think of as an educated man, including the liberal values, the perspective, the flexibility of mind, the analytical ability, and the moral values that we associate with liberal education. In the case of business, as in some other professions, parts of general education must also serve a preprofessional purpose. As medicine and engineering are rooted in the natural sciences, so business is rooted in the social sciences (including history), in science and technology, and in the analytical tools of mathematics and statistics.

A broad education, with appropriate attention to the fields we have emphasized, gives the future businessman a background with which to cope with his nonmarket environment, provides a start toward an understanding of organizational behavior, and offers a basis on which to build an understanding of the functioning of economic markets and the prob-

[16] For example, the businessmen authors of *Business Looks at Business Education* state (p. 20) that: "Most of us . . . would prefer a graduate of a five year program, consisting of three years of liberal arts and two years of business, leading to a Master's degree." A similar recommendation has been made by Thomas H. Carroll. See, for example, *Business Education for Competence and Responsibility*, a paper delivered at the 1956 Conference on Professional Education for Business and published by the American Association of Collegiate Schools of Business.

lems to be met in economic management. It also starts the student on the development of his ability to make rational decisions, to appraise personal and organizational goals, and to deal with other people.

The general educational base then needs to be followed by what we may call the "professional core." This should consist of a systematic body of knowledge which is specialized in the sense that it attempts to say what is known about the functioning of business in its environment, but which is general in the sense that it does not concentrate on any particular kind of business or on any particular type of job in business. This core program should seek not only to acquaint the student with a body of fundamental knowledge about business, but also to develop in him the ability to use this knowledge in actual business situations. There is little disagreement about the need for such a core of general business courses.

Most business schools require another step beyond the core of business subjects, namely, a field of concentration in some particular aspect of business operations. We have already expressed our objection to much specialization in an undergraduate business program. Our findings in Chapter 5 led to the conclusion that the business schools have gone too far in emphasizing specialized training, particularly at the undergraduate level. This is true of "functional" specialization and even more true of specialization in particular industry areas. Specialization, we believe, belongs at the graduate level, and then only if the specialized field has a high analytical content. Otherwise specialized training is best obtained in conjunction with work experience.

The kinds of undergraduate and graduate curricula that these considerations suggest will be described briefly in Chapter 7 and then elaborated in considerable detail in Chapters 8, 9, and 11.

Additional Evidence on the Role of Education in Developing Business Competence

The kind of business education proposed in the preceding pages finds wide support from both businessmen and educators, although relatively few business schools fully carry out the sort of program that we are here advocating. And as we saw in Chapter 5 and as many business school deans are quick to point out, businessmen frequently do not practice what they preach, particularly on the issue of broad vs. specialized training. (Nor, for that matter, do all business school deans.)

EVIDENCE FROM COMPANY INTERVIEWS

Our own explorations into the business world suggest strongly that business needs the kind of education that has been described. The companies we interviewed tended to stress the need for acquiring in college a general understanding of business operations, a knowledge of economics, a grounding in the basic engineering subjects, and whatever kind of training would contribute to analytical ability, skill in verbal communication, and skill in human relations. Specialized training in college was, in general, not emphasized except for "technical" jobs that called for a specialized background in engineering, accounting, or one of the physical sciences.

Turning to the "qualities" (discussed in Chapter 5) a businessman should possess, we can report that there was general agreement among our respondents that analytical ability could be sharpened in college. There was also a more cautious opinion that perhaps judgment could be developed somewhat by the effective use of cases, although it was generally believed that judgment was primarily a product of experience. Some also believed that a college education helped to stimulate the imagination.

There was considerable agreement that the colleges could and should do something to develop human relations skills, but opinions varied as to how this might be done. As a minimum, the student should be made aware of the importance of the problem. Some thought that more could be done, for instance, by teaching something about the principles of human behavior and by developing a more sensitive awareness to interpersonal relationships through role playing and other techniques. Some thought that extracurricular and social activities could do more in this direction than classroom instruction. Indeed, there was widespread agreement that one of the main benefits of college, regardless of the course of study, is the development of poise, self-confidence, and the ability to deal with others.

There was, of course, no disagreement that the colleges should try to develop skill in verbal communication. We received the expected complaints regarding the inability of the typical business school product to write and speak effectively. However much the colleges are now doing in this regard, it is clearly not yet enough.

As for the development of administrative skills, the general feeling seemed to be that this came more from experience than from formal education. However, a not uncommon view was that the business schools could make some modest contribution in this area.

Our respondents believed that the schools could (and do) help to develop breadth and flexibility of mind through both business and non-business courses. A number of respondents felt that the business schools could do something to influence motivation, for example, by stressing the importance of business as a calling and by giving students a realistic picture of what was involved in business as a career.

There is one respect in which apparent practice in the companies we interviewed does not support our recommendations in this chapter. If we take the answers we received at face value, the companies we visited did not place a high value on graduate training in business. The great majority either stated that their companies preferred the products of undergraduate schools or else were indifferent as between the holders of bachelor's and master's degrees. There were, of course, some companies that expressed a strong preference for recruits with graduate training, for either all or some types of jobs. And some companies wanted a few men with graduate training, even though they hired chiefly graduates with only bachelor's degrees.

A certain schizophrenic tendency was apparent in a number of our respondents. A good many stated that ideally the best preparation for business was that which we have recommended—an undergraduate program in liberal arts or engineering followed by graduate business training. Yet the recruiting policies of their companies reflected this view to only a very limited extent.

A number of explanations suggest themselves. Our respondents had only limited control over the recruiting practices of their companies, which favored the holders of bachelor's degrees for several reasons. The number of graduate school products available was, of course, small compared to the number with only bachelor's degrees. A considerable number of the graduate degree holders were from schools of only indifferent reputation. Some companies shied away from recruits with graduate training because of the fear that the latter had exalted ideas regarding salary and promotion. And a good many companies undoubtedly believed that, given the jobs to be filled and the great importance attached to personal qualities, it was sufficient to concentrate their recruiting at the undergraduate schools.

We do not think that these findings warrant any serious modification of our previous recommendations. We still believe that business would get a better trained product if the student had the combination of undergraduate and graduate education that we recommend for those able to benefit from such a program. We believe that the advantages of the program would quickly be recognized by the larger business concerns in particular. There is evidence of this in the past success of the products of the better graduate business programs.

Whatever the merits of the argument about delaying business training to the graduate years, our company survey casts no doubt on another of our recommendations: the need for a broad and rigorous type of business training which emphasizes the more fundamental kinds of knowledge and the development of the basic problem-solving, organizational, and communication skills.

SOME OTHER EVIDENCE

Our survey of college placement offices confirms the results of our company survey regarding the lack of a strong preference for graduates with master's degrees.[17] When such students are sought, recruiters seem to be seeking both specialized and general business training in about equal proportions. Graduate training is desired for research-type positions (such as economic and market research), for some positions in accounting and finance, for some positions in personnel and industrial relations, and for various types of management training programs. Our college placement offices also report that large companies tend to show a greater interest in students with graduate training than do the smaller concerns.

The attitudes of recruiters toward specialized training in particular business fields was discussed in Chapter 5. Recruiting for general training programs is quite widespread and is increasing. Typically, recruiters do not specify any particular specialization within business in hiring for general training programs and frequently will take liberal arts graduates.

Table 8 provides some indication of the main fields for which college graduates are being recruited. Several features of the table deserve comment. More than 40 per cent of the total number of the college graduates hired by this particular group of companies were in engineering; if we add chemistry and physics, the total comes to 50 per cent. Of the nonengineering fields listed, the largest was in sales followed by accounting and general business trainees. It must be remembered that this is a sample for only one year and covers only 200 companies which actively seek college and university graduates. More important, the sample is biased in that it is largely confined to companies that recruit on college campuses. This bias leads to some exaggeration of the relative importance of engineering.

[17] Of the twenty-nine university placement offices giving a definite reply to this question, twenty-three reported that companies did not prefer a master's degree and six reported that such a preference did exist. In his annual survey of recruiting trends, Frank Endicott asked over a hundred companies whether they considered the M.B.A. "a special asset in qualifying for positions which normally required only a Bachelor's degree." Eighty-seven gave "no" as an answer; thirty-six replied affirmatively. "Employment Trends in 1955," *Journal of College Placement*, March, 1955, p. 44.

TABLE 8

THE EMPLOYMENT OF INEXPERIENCED COLLEGE MEN DURING 1956
AS REPORTED BY 192 COMPANIES

Field	Number of Companies	Number of Men
Total engineering, all types	—	7,419
Total nonengineering	—	9,766
Accounting	108	1,533
Advertising	35	93
Chemistry	71	947
Economics	18	63
Finance	29	182
General business trainees	85	1,379
Insurance	9	249
Law	21	43
Market research	27	61
Marketing	20	194
Merchandising	10	43
Office management	9	31
Personnel	56	168
Physics	27	186
Production management	44	385
Sales	79	2,065
Secretarial	10	74
Statistics	26	87
Time and motion study	29	131
Other fields	49	807
Reported totals only	3	1,045
Grand total		17,185

Source: Frank S. Endicott, *Trends in the Employment of College and University Graduates in Business and Industry*, 1957 (mimeographed). The figures refer approximately to the year 1956. This study is also summarized in National Industrial Conference Board, *Management Record*, January, 1957.

In view of the current interest in the value of a liberal arts education for businessmen, another aspect of the survey which yielded the figures in Table 8 should be mentioned. The responding companies were asked to indicate what percentage of the college men hired could have qualified by graduating from a liberal arts college. The replies indicated that "men from Liberal Arts colleges could have qualified for about 37 per cent of all jobs for which college graduates were employed last year by these companies. The percentage who *were* graduates of Liberal Arts colleges was about 27. Half of the companies indicated that they hired about as many such men as could qualify."[18] It should be noted that the men

[18] See the source cited for Table 8.

actually hired from liberal arts colleges might have had some background in business or economics and indeed might even have majored in business administration, since many liberal arts colleges offer a business major which may include virtually all the courses in the required core of the typical undergraduate business school.

We have not been able to make our own survey of college graduates in business to ascertain either how they now evaluate the education they received in college or whether any relationships can be discerned between kinds of education and training and career patterns. The evidence that is available is only of the most fragmentary sort.[19]

One of the first careful questionnaire surveys of the alumni of a business school was that which Bossard and Dewhurst made of the graduates of the Wharton School. This was nearly thirty years ago and throws light only on the training provided by the Wharton School before 1930. Wharton alumni rated the importance of eight specified fields of knowledge in the following order: English, "descriptive analysis of business activities," "social setting of business life," "administration of business activities," methods of measurement, "studies broadly interpretive," physical sciences, and, bringing up the rear, foreign languages.[20] The relative importance attached to English and to foreign languages by business school alumni today would undoubtedly not be greatly different. For obvious reasons, the physical sciences would probably be valued more highly today than they were by Wharton alumni thirty years ago.[21]

Pending the kind of comprehensive study of the relation between education and business success which badly needs to be done, the following additional generalizations seem to be worth making on the basis of the spotty evidence available.

1) The importance of a college degree of some sort in business has been steadily increasing; so has the percentage of businessmen who are

[19] We spent considerable time and thought investigating the possibility of a mail survey of a carefully designed sample of business school alumni. We finally concluded that we did not have the time to do the kind of thorough, detailed study that was needed. This is a project which we hope some other group will undertake. It would also be desirable to combine this with a study of a large sample of businessmen regardless of education in order to be able to compare the career patterns of businessmen with various kinds of educational background. The latter project presents more serious sampling problems than does a study of only business school alumni.

[20] See *University Education for Business*, Chapter 8.

[21] Nonengineering college graduates in General Electric ranked foreign languages, followed by miscellaneous sciences and history, as the courses least valuable in their careers. English was considered the most valuable course, followed by economics and general business. Interestingly, those who had graduated in business administration also gave a low rating to "Miscellaneous Business" courses. *What They Think of Their Higher Education*, General Electric Educational Relations Service (1957), pp. 7, 17.

college graduates. For success in business a "college degree has become more important than great wealth, and easier to obtain."[22]

Apparently business firms seek a number of things in pursuing the college graduate. College serves as a minimum screening device and implies at least that its graduates have the intelligence, motivation, self-discipline, and educational background necessary to finish college.[23] Our company interviews suggest that business also looks on the colleges as helping to develop certain general qualities: breadth and some intellectual awareness, on the one hand, and poise, self-confidence, and some ability in interpersonal relationships, on the other. As one group of reflective observers has put it, "industry places a high value on the college degree, not because it is convinced that the four years of schooling insure that individuals acquire maturity and technical competence, but rather because it provides an initial point of division between those more trained and those less trained; those better motivated and those less motivated; those with more social experience and those with less."[24] In addition, business seeks the knowledge and skills developed by special curricula such as those in engineering, science, and business administration.

2)   The proportion of businessmen who received some business training in college has also been steadily increasing, and a large number of others have felt compelled to obtain some formal business training in other ways.[25]

3)   Businessmen who majored in business administration in college have, on the whole, found their professional training in college useful, but not as useful as have those in some other professions.[26] One of the

---

[22] Mabel Newcomer, *The Big Business Executive* (1955), p. 146. Cf. also Herrymon Maurer, "The Worst Shortage in Business," *Fortune*, April, 1956. For further data on the increasing proportion of businessmen who have gone to college, see: "The Nine Hundred," *Fortune*, November, 1952, p. 135; W. L. Warner and J. C. Abegglen, *Occupational Mobility in American Business and Industry* (1955), p. 108; Dael Wolfle, *America's Resources of Specialized Talent* (1954), p. 309.

[23] Cf. National Industrial Conference Board, *Employment of the College Graduate*, Studies in Personnel Policy No. 152 (1956), p. 4.

[24] *What Makes an Executive*, Report of a Round Table on Executive Potential and Performance (1955), p. 64.

[25] For their samples of business leaders, Warner and Abegglen (*Occupational Mobility in American Business and Industry*, p. 112) report that 7 per cent of the 1928 group had some business training in college compared to 33 per cent of the 1952 sample. Seventy-one per cent of the 1928 group had had no formal business training of any kind, compared to 42 per cent of the 1952 sample of executives.

[26] This is the clear implication of the findings by Ernest Havemann and Patricia West. See *They Went to College* (1952) especially pp. 128, 130. General Electric's business school graduates were more satisfied with their educational choice than were other nonengineering graduates but not as much so as the engineers. See *What They Think of Their Higher Education*, p. 12.

strongest complaints of business school graduates is that they had insufficient training in verbal communication.[27] Some wish that they had
had more in science and technology.[28] It is not clear whether business
school graduates feel, on net balance, that their college business training
was or was not too specialized. This would depend, among other things,
on how specialized a program they had taken in college. There is a bit
of evidence that some feel that their business education was not too helpful during their first few years out of college, and some wish that their
business training had been more "practical."[29] While in some cases this
may mean a desire for more narrowly specialized training within business, we suspect that for a good many the basis of this complaint is that
their business courses, whether broad or narrow, placed too much emphasis on merely imparting knowledge and not enough on the development
of the basic skills that would have permitted them more effectively to use
what they had learned.

4)   A recent study of its college graduates made by General Electric
Company calls for special comment. While confined to employees of
one company with a specialized range of technologically centered activities, the study was based on 14,000 replies to a carefully devised questionnaire. Forty-five per cent of the replies were from nonengineering graduates; and, of these, 38 per cent had majored in business administration.[30]

The college courses most recommended by the nonengineering graduates for those planning management careers were, in order: English,
economics, general business, mathematics, engineering and science,
psychology, and humanities. The emphasis generally was on the need
for a broad program, and the nonengineering graduates reported that
various "business courses of a specialized nature had little career value,
since the information contained in them could have been achieved in a
much more practical fashion in the business world."[31] Those who had

[27] Cf. Bossard and Dewhurst, *University Education for Business*, Chapter 8; *Wall Street Journal*,
November 3, 1948, reporting a study by the Society for the Advancement of Management;
General Electric Educational Relations Service, *What They Think of Their Higher Education*.

[28] See, for example, Havemann and West, *They Went to College*, p. 128.

[29] Cf., for example, *Report to Tuck Alumni* (Dartmouth College), May, 1956, pp. 1–2;
Boston University Business Review, Spring, 1956, p. 31; Harvard Business School *Alumni Bulletin*,
Spring, 1949, p. 21. In general, one would suppose that those who found their business school
training of limited value during the first few years in business would have come from schools
that emphasized general rather than specialized training.

[30] The questionnaire was distributed in 1955 and the findings were published in January,
1957, by the Educational Relations Service of General Electric under the title of *What They
Think of Their Higher Education*.

[31] *What They Think of Their Higher Education*, p. 7.

majored in business administration and were in nontechnical jobs listed the five types of courses that had been most valuable to them as being, in order: English, mathematics, economics, accounting, and business. (Those in technical positions merely reversed the order of mathematics and economics.)

In general, this survey lends strong support to the kind of program in business education that we have proposed, with one important exception. Neither the group of college graduates as a whole nor those who had majored in business considered that history or the social sciences other than economics had much value as background for a career in business. The one possible exception was psychology, and this was highly valued only by those with degrees in liberal arts and education. We suspect that this finding reflects both on the breadth of view of the respondents (the great bulk of whom were in junior positions) and on the kinds of courses in history and social sciences that they had had in college.[32]

5)   Engineering graduates in business are increasingly turning to business courses to help them qualify for managerial positions. What they seem to find most helpful are the "core" courses in the fundamental subjects, including economics and human relations, especially as presented in the better graduate programs in business administration.

6)   In this connection, it is worth mentioning again that employers place a high value on engineering training, even for nontechnical jobs. What seem to be particularly valued as a result of such training are analytical ability, the capacity to deal with problems in quantitative terms, and familiarity with scientific and technological developments. At the same time, engineers are frequently found to be too narrow when placed in managerial positions. They are unaccustomed to dealing with problems that cannot be completely formulated in quantitative terms; they are frequently disturbed by the need to make decisions promptly on the basis of incomplete information; they tend to ignore the "human" aspects of a problem and generally to fail to appreciate the importance of interpersonal relationships; and they have an insufficient command of economics and the main functional fields of business. It is to correct these deficiencies in their background that so many engineers seek additional

---

[32] It might be added that the three areas of study which the nonengineering graduates felt had contributed most to their use of leisure time were general business, literature, and history. On this the authors of the report remark: "Apparently college graduates within the Company have a lively interest in business activities not directly associated with their own work. In some instances, local government activity was cited as a leisure-time application of knowledge gained through business courses." *What They Think of Their Higher Education*, p. 8.

training in business administration. In this case the right kind of business training clearly broadens the individual.[33]

7)   While many college graduates with only a liberal education succeed in business careers and are happy with both their educational and occupational choices, this is not universally true. Of the sample of college graduates studied by Havemann and West, the group that was most dissatisfied with their choice of college courses consisted of those with majors in the humanities and social sciences who had gone into business.[34] The authors conclude as follows:[35]

The facts, obviously, are these: the graduates who had a general education are quite satisfied if they have gone on to take specialized training and have ended up in a high-paid profession. They are also satisfied, despite finances, if they have gone into one of the low-paid "learned" professions where a general education provides a suitable and useful background. The large proportion of generally-educated graduates who regret their college choice is accounted for almost entirely by those who have wound up in business jobs. The business field is not what the generally educated graduates foresaw, and in it they have little opportunity to use their knowledge of literature, history, sociology, or Latin conjugations. Moreover they find themselves, by and large, passed by men who have had more technical training. Some of them console themselves with the thought that college taught them how to enjoy living, even though they are somewhat dislocated jobwise and have less financial success than their college competitors from the specialized fields. But a great many come to the conclusion that a broad cultural background is simply not worth the price that it seems to exact in terms of workaday failure. . . . Among the generally educated graduates who now hold business jobs, fully half wish that they had taken more specialized training.

At the same time, these and other studies suggest that business and professional people who were able to secure a broad education in college tend in later life to read more books, to engage in more community activities, and on the whole to hold more progressive opinions than do those who concentrated entirely on specialized training or did not go to college at all.[36]

---

[33] The strengths and weaknesses of engineers as business managers are analyzed by W. B. Given, Jr., in "The Engineer Goes into Management," *Harvard Business Review*, January-February, 1955, pp. 43–52. See also J. A. Bowie, *Education for Business Management* (1930), pp. 52ff.; W. B. Donham, *Education for Responsible Living* (1944), chap. 2 and p. 61; and George S. Odiorne, "The Trouble with Engineers," *Harper's Magazine*, January, 1955, pp. 41–46.

[34] Some of these graduates, because of a lack of clear-cut goals, would undoubtedly have been dissatisfied in almost any kind of career.

[35] *They Went to College*, pp. 153–54.

[36] Cf. Havemann and West, *They Went to College*, pp. 152–53. Stouffer's findings clearly show that tolerance of unpopular political views varies directly with the amount of education,

We think we see a moral in these findings. The world needs broadly educated men and women, but the business world needs also men and women with some modicum of business training, particularly of the sort that we have recommended. This training serves two purposes: it helps to develop business competence, and it provides an orientation which helps some students in moving from the leisurely and intellectually oriented college years into the more prosaic and exacting world of business.

Hence we believe that the business schools have an extremely important service function to perform for the rest of the university community—particularly for the students in liberal arts but also for those in other curricula. Every undergraduate business school should offer an integrated sequence of a few carefully planned business courses for non-business students who are looking forward to business careers. Such courses, while broad in nature and avoiding detail, would give the student an introduction to the analytical tools, institutions, and vocabulary of business, and also some understanding of the mutual interaction between business and its environment. This suggestion is considered further in Chapters 10 and 18.

THE OPINIONS OF LEADING BUSINESSMEN

Thus far we have not referred extensively to the opinions of the more articulate leaders of the business community. Their views have been so widely quoted that to do so again here would be superfluous. Increasingly, these opinions have come to stress the values of a liberal education and the need for "the range of interests and the mental disciplines that education in the liberal arts or humanities is peculiarly well fitted to give."[37] Less attention is paid to the possible need for more technical educational requirements. When they are mentioned, the stress tends to be on a broad knowledge of business, an ability to deal with people, some familiarity with science and technology, the capacity to think clearly, a broad understanding of the nonmarket environment of business, and an appreciation of the role of business in our kind of society.[38]

but he does not attempt to distinguish among kinds of education. Also community leaders, including businessmen, are more tolerant than the population at large. S. A. Stouffer, *Communism, Conformity, and Civil Liberties* (1955).

[37] The quoted phrase is from *Fortune*, April, 1953, p. 113. For a sampling of views along these lines, see R. A. Goldwin, ed., *Toward the Liberally Educated Executive* (1957), and *The Randall Lectures*, given at Harvard in 1956, both published by the Fund for Adult Education.

[38] Of course there are many businessmen—particularly in smaller companies and those associated with various kinds of trade association groups—who would argue for specialized and vocational training in college; but these are not the views that appear in the national journals and are expressed in public addresses.

The tenor of the argument in this and earlier chapters of this report is enough to indicate that we are not disposed to argue with these views. However, a caveat is necessary regarding the recent fashion among many business leaders and educators to put exclusive emphasis on the values of a liberal education, interpreted as referring more to the humanities than to the social or physical sciences. This attitude, we suspect, frequently reflects an incomplete evaluation of the needs of business for educated manpower and something less than accurate knowledge of the more promising recent developments in collegiate business education. (It also, of course, represents a laudable effort to redress a balance which had been badly upset by rapid advances in science and technology.) William H. Whyte, Jr. is undoubtedly correct when he says that today's business leaders "graduated while the straight A.B. was still the fashion, and many have at least a sentimental attachment to the humanities."[39] (It is also our impression that a good many have a prejudice that comes close to snobbishness regarding the products of business schools other than those of a few of the leading graduate institutions—even though their recruiters may eagerly seek the graduates of these schools at commencement time.)

The issue, as we see it, is not a simple choice between liberal education and business education. The issue is how to combine both, and how to insure that the business part of the combined education adequately develops the basic skills we have emphasized and avoids the narrow and low-level kind of vocational training that has brought discredit on particularly the undergraduate business schools. As management tends to become steadily more rational in its approach and thereby takes on more of the attributes of a profession, the need will grow for men who have not merely a "liberal" education but an education which is liberal (in the sense of a concern with the humanities) and also scientific and professional.[40]

[39] *The Organization Man* (1956), p. 79.

[40] Theodore Yntema, vice-president of Ford Motor Company, has a conception of liberal education which comes close to providing this kind of combined education. He defines liberal education as the acquisition and development of a sense of values, a set of basic abilities and skills that are widely transferable, a "judiciously selected knowledge of classified facts and relationships," and satisfaction in participating in all the various aspects of life. The basic skills and abilities concern recognizing and solving problems, working with people, communicating, organizing, persistence of effort, and memory. "Transferable Skills and Abilities," *Journal of Business*, XXXI (April, 1958), 91–95.

chapter 7

IMPROVING THE QUALITY
OF BUSINESS EDUCATION:
SUMMARY AND PREVIEW

IT IS time to draw together the findings of the preceding chapters and to translate them into more specific recommendations regarding the kinds of education and training the business schools should seek to provide. In attempting to do this, the present chapter can be considered both a summary of the conclusions reached in Chapters 3–6 and a preview of the detailed recommendations and of the critical review of business curricula which follow in Part III. Or, to put it another way, the present chapter, by drawing on our findings in the earlier chapters, seeks to formulate a set of benchmarks by which we can evaluate the existing programs of the business schools and suggest the kinds of improvement most needed.

We can begin by restating a series of propositions that flow logically from the preceding analysis. Collegiate business education should educate for the whole career and not primarily for the first job. It should view the practice of business professionally in the sense of relating it to what we have in the way of relevant systematic bodies of knowledge. It should emphasize the development of basic problem-solving and organizational skills and socially constructive attitudes rather than memory of facts or training in routine skills.

It should recognize that businessmen in the decades ahead will need a higher order of analytical ability, a more sophisticated command of analytical tools, a greater degree of organizational skill, a greater capacity to deal with the external environment of business, and more of an ability to cope with rapid change than has been true in the past. Not only are these propositions supported by the analysis of earlier chapters, but they are also accepted by the more thoughtful leaders in both the business and educational worlds. Yet there are relatively few business schools that adhere consistently to these principles in the details of their educational programs.

The Need for Flexibility

The general direction in which the business schools need to move is clear. But while the general direction is clear, we need a flexible approach in attempting to bring about improvements in current practice. No single "ideal" program should be imposed on all students and all business schools for a number of reasons. We do not yet know enough to be able to say that one kind of program is best under all circumstances; this is particularly true when we begin to spell out the details of curriculum, course content, and teaching methods. And then there are the elements of diversity with which business education must cope: the wide range in the kinds of careers that can be followed; the variation among students in ability, motivation, and resources to finance their education; and, last but far from least, the tremendous variation in the human, financial, and physical endowments of the business schools themselves.

Hence, a flexible approach is needed. There has to be not one but several educational routes to a business career. The "problem of business education" has not one but several facets. Stated in terms of schools and students, they include: What is a workable approximation to an "ideal" program for the best qualified students toward which the better schools should move? What can be done to raise standards and improve educational programs in the poorer schools? What can be done for the less well qualified students who may not be able to meet the minimum standards for an adequate education for business, but who will go into business nonetheless? The problem of how to achieve a compromise between quality and quantity faces all but a select few of the undergraduate schools in the United States, and the problem will become more severe as the democratization of higher education continues. This issue is most acute for those institutions which must compete actively for students or are vulnerable to pressure from parents, alumni, taxpayers, and local business groups.

There is yet another facet of the problem of business education which concerns the student who, while planning a business career, prefers not to enroll in a business school. Alternative educational routes must be left open, and the business schools have an obligation to perform a minimum service function for these students. This is an obligation which, at least so far, the business schools have largely failed to meet. It is probably also fair to say that, by and large, it is an obligation which the liberal arts departments have not been anxious to have the business schools assume.

Because of this need for flexibility, we believe that each of the following types of programs can serve a useful function in the education of businessmen, depending on the circumstances.

1 A broad two-year business program at the graduate level is best for those students who have the qualifications to secure the maximum benefit from it. This should be preceded by undergraduate work in the arts and sciences or in a very broad type of engineering program. It is helpful, also, if two or more years of work experience, or at least military service, intervene between the undergraduate years and graduate business training.

2 A five-year program, with the first three years being devoted to nonbusiness courses, is a somewhat less desirable alternative but one which, for many schools and students, would be preferable to a conventional four-year curriculum. The two years of business administration should be at the same high professional level as that implied under our first alternative.

3 The most widely used alternative will continue to be a terminal undergraduate program in business, with something like half the total work being in business and related subjects. The great need is not to eliminate the undergraduate curriculum in business administration (which it is impossible to do in any event) but to improve its quality: to raise standards of admission and performance, to introduce greater breadth and rigor, to move away from a narrow kind of vocational specialization, to emphasize more the development of the basic analytical and organizational skills, and to reduce the emphasis on factual detail and the learning of routine procedures.

4 Some considerable number of poorer students who now receive bachelor's degrees in business administration would be excluded from the kind of undergraduate program that we propose. The worst of these students should not be in college at all, and the lowering of standards in some public and private institutions to accommodate such students makes a travesty of the notion of "higher education." Such students should move from secondary school to a one- or two-year terminal program in a junior college or similar type of institution, if they pursue their formal education further at all.

5 There are two other categories of students who might want to go into business but would not attend a business school in a university or four-year college: able students who prefer to major in something other than business and students who can meet the standards

of another college on the campus but not those of the business school. The business schools should make available as electives to both of these groups a carefully planned sequence of a few broad business courses.

These alternative educational routes to a business career provide the basis for a flexible program, geared both to the wide range of needs among students and to the unequal distribution of resources among schools. Business education also needs to be flexible in another respect. Every school should keep its program under continuous study; experimentation and willingness to change should be the rule at every institution. Even the best curriculum soon becomes out-of-date. As knowledge accumulates—regarding what to teach and how to teach—and as needs change, educational programs should change accordingly.

The Graduate Program in Business Administration

Business schools today offer two basically different kinds of master's programs in business administration.[1] The exclusively graduate schools (and a few of the "comprehensive" schools) tend to concentrate upon a two-year program which assumes no previous work in business administration, is built around a fairly broad core of business subjects, and emphasizes preparation for a general management career. A number of schools which offer both graduate and undergraduate work tend to concentrate on a one-year master's program which presumes the equivalent of an undergraduate major in business administration, does not emphasize in the graduate year a common core that all students must take, is essentially a year of specialization, and implicitly stresses preparation for a staff career or teaching rather than general management. A number of schools with one-year master's programs have developed several variants that fall between the two types of graduate programs just described.

THE TWO-YEAR MASTER'S PROGRAM

While the consensus is not perfect, the leading graduate schools of business agree on the main outlines of a desirable two-year program leading to the master's degree. Building on our earlier analysis and the substantial consensus that already exists, we recommend a core that would cover, in one way or another, the following areas: administration, organization, and human relations; managerial economics; accounting and statistics; some or all of the functional fields (finance, marketing,

[1] The detailed review of master's programs appears in Chapter 11.

etc.); national income, business fluctuations, economic growth, and forecasting; the legal, political, and social framework of business, with considerable emphasis on historical developments; and business policy.

Beyond the core, it should be possible for the student to proceed in either of two directions. He may wish to concentrate in some particular area, or he may spread his efforts more broadly, taking additional work in several fields.

We cannot afford to ignore the undergraduate education of students seeking graduate business training. Graduate business students need a "preprofessional" background (for example, in the social and physical sciences and in mathematics and statistics) as well as the elements of a liberal education. We believe that the business schools with graduate programs should do more than they are now doing to specify, or at least suggest, the kinds of undergraduate (nonbusiness) courses which students should have before undertaking graduate work in business.

THE ONE-YEAR MASTER'S PROGRAM

The blunt fact is that the majority of students currently studying for the master's degree in business are enrolled in makeshift programs which are generally unsatisfactory. This unhappy situation arises from the fact that most graduate business curricula (except in a number of the exclusively graduate and a very few comprehensive schools) were originally conceived as merely another year of specialization and electives for students whose undergraduate major was in business.

With the growing number of applications for graduate business training from students without an undergraduate background in business administration, many schools are now offering a hybrid kind of master's program which requires from one to two years to complete. If the student does not have the necessary business prerequisites, he spends up to half of his two years making up undergraduate requirements, frequently in the same sections taken by undergraduates but occasionally in special graduate sections.

This situation is clearly unsatisfactory. We believe that every master's program which seeks to train for general management careers should have a solid core of required graduate courses, designed for graduate students, and that students should not be permitted to satisfy more than a moderate fraction of this core by courses previously taken. This proposal is expounded in greater detail in Chapter 11. The aim is to establish the standard of a two-year graduate program, oriented toward managerial decision-making, and to permit only limited departures from this standard for the student with previous training in business administration.

The one area in which we are prepared to accept a one-year program that builds on an undergraduate business major is accounting. Many business schools now try to prepare their undergraduates for the C.P.A. examinations by the time they receive the bachelor's degree. In doing so, they inevitably act as trade schools, sacrificing breadth to cram into their students all the specialized knowledge and skills needed to pass the certifying examinations—even to the extent of offering and giving credit for "cram" courses.

A slowly increasing number of undergraduate schools are refusing to serve this trade school function, and some, to their credit, have never done so. The answer to this problem is clearly a fifth year, assuming that the student begins his training in accounting as an undergraduate. This is in keeping with the recommendations of the Commission on Standards of Education and Experience for Certified Public Accountants, published in 1956. We shall have more to say later about the training of accountants.

Undergraduate Education for Business

Current dissatisfaction with the quality of undergraduate business education is widespread and acute. It is virtually inevitable that this should be so. We have already seen that it is practically impossible to do in the four undergraduate years what the undergraduate business schools try to do: to provide both a general and a professional education of satisfactory quality. In fact, the situation is much worse than this implies. The undergraduate schools are plagued with more than their share of poor students with inadequate backgrounds; curricula have not been planned to meet the kinds of needs we have described; teaching is frequently at a superficial level, emphasizing description and procedural detail and failing to provide a true intellectual challenge to the student; both general education and business fundamentals are too often sacrificed for the sake of specialized knowledge and skills that may soon be obsolete; and faculties are frequently inadequately trained and too immersed in their own specialties.

The insistent demand by students and parents for some form of business training in the undergraduate years cannot be wished away. It is the inevitable result of the dominating role which business plays in American society, the continuing democratization of higher education, and the inability or unwillingness of most students to defer their professional training until after a sound general education has been obtained. Eventually, we anticipate, the pressure for business training at the under-graduate level will subside somewhat. Even so, it can be assumed that for the indefinite future most college students seeking a business educa-tion will receive it at the undergraduate rather than the graduate level. But if we are to meet the future needs of American business and of the broader society it serves, widespread and fairly drastic reform is neces-sary. Change is called for in curriculum, in teaching methods and course content, and in academic standards. These, in turn, imply other im-provements—in quality and training of the faculty, in research, and so on—to which we shall give some attention in Part IV.

GENERAL EDUCATION

The analysis of Chapters 3–6 suggests the kind of curriculum that is needed if we are to have undergraduate business education at all. The primary emphasis should be on a broad general education, with due at-tention to the "preprofessional" aspects of that education, and on a rationally planned and integrated "core" of business subjects that will provide the student with an introduction to the various kinds of knowl-edge described in Chapter 4 and start the process of developing the *basic* skills described in Chapters 5 and 6. The emphasis should be on develop-ing a foundation on which the student can then continue to build in a world of rapid change.

We recommend that not less than half of the four-year undergraduate program be devoted to general education and believe that considerably more would be desirable. This minimum of 50 per cent is higher than what most under-graduate schools now require, and higher also than the minimum (40 per cent) specified by the American Association of Collegiate Schools of Business.

While the precise figure of 50 per cent is obviously arbitrary, it is easy to demonstrate that less than this is clearly too little. Our case for at least this much of general education rests not on some vague notion of a total amount of liberal education that is ideal, but on an actual inventory of the cultural and preprofessional subjects that a competent and respon-sible businessman in a democratic society should have. This inventory is listed in detail in Chapter 8 and adds up to about two full years of col-lege work or a bit more. Even this presumes a better secondary school preparation than that with which many students now enter college. In our opinion, anything less than this is unacceptable, not only because the student as a future citizen needs this much of a cultural background *but also because at least this much is necessary to provide the base of cultural and preprofessional subjects on which his business training should be built.*

THE BUSINESS CURRICULUM

The professional part of the undergraduate curriculum should consist primarily of a large core of required courses that will provide an introduction to each of the main aspects of the structure and functioning of business: managerial accounting and statistics; advanced economics, including both internal economic management and the external economic environment of the firm; organization and administration; a series of courses in the functional fields (marketing, finance, etc.); some work on the legal, political, and social environment of business; and a capstone course in business policy. This required core, depending on the particular arrangement of courses, should comprise between a third and 40 per cent of the total four-year program. The details are presented in Chapter 9.

Now we come to the question of a field of specialization within business. We start from the basic position that, particularly at the undergraduate level, business itself is enough specialization. The arguments against much specialization have been elaborated in the preceding chapters and need be only summarized here. First, there is the opportunity cost; the more time spent in concentrating on a special field, the less time there is for a minimum of general education and the necessary core of basic business courses. Second, specialization at a truly professional level belongs in the graduate school and must rest on an undergraduate foundation in the basic "tool" disciplines, on which skill in specialized business applications can then be built. Third, we believe that the preceding chapters have demonstrated fairly clearly that the extent of the demand by business for specialized training at the undergraduate level has been greatly exaggerated. Indeed, it is fair to say that the pressure for undergraduate specialization comes as much or more from business school faculties than from businessmen.

Business does need two types of specialized training, but neither of these can be easily provided at the undergraduate level. There is, first, the need in the lower ranks of management for the kind of special knowledge and skills that can best be obtained on the job or in special training programs related to particular jobs. There is, second, a growing need for high-level staff specialists with the kinds of technical competence in one or more of the basic disciplines and analytical tool fields which is best obtained at the graduate level. Beyond this, the major need of business is for general business knowledge and the basic problem-solving and organizational skills emphasized in earlier chapters.

We suggest, therefore, that the undergraduate schools require no "field of concentration" at all, although it is desirable to permit the student to have a few business electives, to be chosen from a modest array of broad courses and seminars made available beyond the core. The number of business electives should be small and would depend in part on the amount of time that is absorbed by the core of required subjects.

As a less desirable alternative, schools might require a field of concentration, but we shall suggest in Chapter 9 that this be limited to a maximum of twelve semester units, of which half should be taken in a nonbusiness but related field. This would, among other desirable results, eliminate the demand for a large number of highly specialized courses which should not be in the curriculum at all. During some transitional period, all twelve semester units might be used for business courses. This would be particularly necessary for students majoring in public accounting.

The curriculum proposed here is designed for the conventional type of separately organized school of business. In addition, several hundred colleges have departments of business, frequently combined with economics, which attempt to offer degree programs in business administration. The special problems of these departments are considered in Chapter 10, in which we shall also review the undergraduate business training offered by the engineering schools.

Teaching Methods and Course Content

In general, business courses can be taught with any one of three kinds of emphasis, which can be called the descriptive, the analytical, and the managerial-clinical. Present practice in the undergraduate schools is to concentrate too much on a purely descriptive approach, in which fairly detailed subject matter is presented to the student, who passively absorbs and then regurgitates it on examinations.

The analysis in earlier chapters suggests that what is needed is a combination of the analytical and the managerial-clinical, although some descriptive material cannot be avoided. The student needs to acquire a command of systematic knowledge at as high an analytical level as he can handle and then be made to put this knowledge to use in problem-solving situations that will help him develop the basic skills that he will need as a businessman. In other words, the business schools should emphasize both "principles" and clinical teaching. By clinical teaching we mean the use of cases, problems, role-playing, and other types of assignments that will give the student some limited experience in dealing with the kinds of problems he will encounter in the business world. However, schools should be careful not to overdo the use of cases, particularly at the undergraduate level and especially in the introductory courses.

There are some other obvious things to be said about teaching methods. In *no* course should a student's reading be confined exclusively to a single textbook. Written work should be continuously and heavily stressed, and students should be given the opportunity to communicate on tests and examination by means other than check marks.

In short, the business schools need to stress more than they now do the simple educational verities—above all, that of making the student participate actively in the learning process and of helping him to develop for himself the basic analytical, organizational, and communication skills he will need all his life. Through counseling as well as teaching, the effort should be made to develop so far as possible the personal qualities stressed in the preceding chapters, including breadth of mind and sensitivity to the social implications of individual and business behavior.

These and other suggestions for improving teaching methods, including making use of the student's organizational experience outside the classroom, will be considered further in Chapter 15.

The Question of Standards

The simple fact of the matter is that academic standards are too low in most of the business schools in the United States. The undergraduate schools and the business departments not organized as schools are particularly serious offenders. The problem is a twofold one. Admission standards are too low, with the result that too many students are accepted who do not have either the background or the innate ability to survive a rigorous college program.[2] On top of this, most schools do not attempt to offer a rigorous program, in part because of the high attrition rate that would result, in part because the faculty is not motivated to insist on high standards.[3]

The facts are clear. Business administration gets a much larger fraction of poor students and a smaller percentage of the best students than do the traditional professional fields. The mental ability of undergraduate

[2] While this is correct as a generalization, schools do differ in their admissions standards—from a few with highly selective screening procedures to some which are willing or are legally bound to accept virtually all high school graduates who apply. A trend toward higher admission standards has become apparent in the last few years.

[3] We are glad to report that there seems to be a growing number of exceptions to this generalization. A number of deans have spoken to us with pride of their high attrition rates, particularly among lower division students in universities that have low admission standards.

business students averages somewhat lower than for all college under-graduates. This contrast also stands out at the graduate level.[4]

Clearly, this situation needs correcting. Truly professional training implies standards which are presumably higher than those applied to the college population as a whole. Few would deny that at least the upper and middle levels of business call for a high order of competence, al-though this competence is the product of a number of factors in addition to those measured by intelligence tests. And as we know, the need for a high order of business competence grows *pari passu* with the increasing complexity of business operations and of the environment to which busi-nessmen must adjust. If business programs are geared to the pace of the poorest students, the needs of society for adequately trained businessmen are not being met. If standards are raised, we exclude some range of students who now qualify. And, to face an unpleasant but very real fact, some universities rely on their business schools for an important source of revenue. In the case of the tax-supported institutions, taxpayers may demand that their children be offered collegiate training for business, which is an occupation assumed to be open to all in a private enterprise economy.

The answer, we think, lies both in higher standards and in differen-tiation among educational programs. Standards should be raised, either through more selective admissions or through higher attrition rates or both. The excluded students will have access to the other departments of the university, if the standards of the latter can be met, or to the grow-ing number of junior and community colleges. The time has come to put an end to an all too common situation in which the undergraduate busi-ness school is the repository for the rejects from engineering, the natural sciences, and other curricula in liberal arts—and is viewed by both stu-dents and faculty as resting near the bottom of the academic hierarchy, slightly above the colleges of agriculture and education.

In view of the wide disparity among schools and the student popula-tions they serve, some variation in standards is inevitable. But the mini-mum level of acceptability—in admission standards and in quality of work—should clearly be raised. For the undergraduate schools we sug-gest a simple and flexible guide: *standards should if possible be moderately higher and in no case lower than for the liberal arts college on the same campus.* This is a flexible operating rule that permits a business school to have stand-ards which are realistic, given the kinds of students its university seeks to serve, and yet also reflects the view that professional training for business calls for a level of competence and for standards of performance fully as

---

[4] Cf. Chapter 13.

high as, and perhaps higher than, those expected on the average of students who major in one or another of the arts and sciences. It is less easy to apply a comparable rule at the graduate level. Here, all except the very best schools need to screen applicants more selectively and to raise the standards of what is considered acceptable work by those who are admitted.

The years ahead present an ideal time in which to bring about a general raising of standards. With the rapid increase in college enrollments that is in prospect, admission requirements and standards of work can be raised without a serious decline in business school enrollments and the attendant problems of adjustment that this would entail. Some moves in this direction are already taking place, and the "mounting tide" of college applications will force further steps in this direction.

The analysis in this and the preceding chapter implies a series of alternative educational routes to a business career, tailored to the capabilities, motivation, and financial resources of the student: graduate training preceded by undergraduate work in liberal arts or engineering; a fairly high level undergraduate business program, the quality of which will vary among schools but which in general will meet a set of standards much higher than those now prevailing; undergraduate majors in nonbusiness fields, but with the student having the opportunity to take a few elementary business courses; and terminal programs at a lower level in junior and community colleges and in other types of adult education programs for those unable to attend a four-year college. We believe that the undergraduate business schools should welcome a division of labor whereby the last route named is increasingly used by students who have difficulty in meeting the kinds of standards that we suggest.

The Issue of Specialization Once More

Instead of emphasizing the basic skills that make for business competence, too many business schools have been concentrating on a narrow and vocational kind of training which, though it may help the student to land his first job, is likely to handicap him in adjusting to new situations and in demonstrating his capacity to advance to more responsible positions. We have already taken the position that this type of narrow and low-level skill development does not belong in college at all.

A high degree of specialization implies too much concern with the details of the way things are now being done or have been done in the past. The business schools need to focus their attention on the fact that the working lives of today's students will stretch forward to the end of the twentieth century. Detailed familiarity with current and past procedures will be of very limited help to these students. Command of the important analytical tools and basic skills, ability to think for themselves, and some historical perspective and breadth and flexibility of mind will stand them in far better stead.

THE PROLIFERATION OF COURSES

While there are exceptions to this as to most generalizations, it is fair to say that, other things being equal, the quality of a business school tends to vary in *inverse* proportion to the number of business courses it offers. One sign of the low state of collegiate business education is the fact that most business schools, particularly at the undergraduate but also at the graduate level, are both offering and requiring too many business courses. Many of these courses are not only too narrow and specialized, but, more important, they contain little real substance and provide little or no intellectual challenge to the student. Thirty years ago, Bossard and Dewhurst strongly criticized the business schools for the amount of course proliferation then prevalent. The situation is, if anything, worse today than it was then, although within the last few years some signs of improvement have begun to appear.

We have yet to see or hear a satisfactory defense of the degree of course proliferation that exists in many (if not most) of the undergraduate business schools. It is not merely that too many courses are being offered, although this in itself implies a wasteful use of scarce resources. More serious, course proliferation means narrowness and, as it is practiced in many business schools, also routine learning of unimportant detail. If it is the function of a collegiate business school to sharpen and broaden the mind and to develop in the student "professional competence and responsibility," it is not likely to do so by multiplying courses in everything from Advanced Credits and Collections to Specialized Secretarial Work.

We hear a great deal about the critical faculty shortage that confronts collegiate business education. But one wonders how serious this faculty shortage really is when the schools have the resources to offer not only marketing principles and marketing management, but also a string of courses on various aspects of advertising, retailing, wholesaling, purchasing, salesmanship (perhaps both "elementary" and "advanced"), and the like; not only principles of insurance, but also separate courses on life, property, fire, casualty, and other types of insurance, not to mention claims procedure, agency management, and the tax and legal aspects of insurance; and similarly in other fields. Examination of a sample of course announcements reveals such further examples as elementary and advanced typewriting, radio station management, trade associations, real estate brokerage, hotel front office procedure, materials handling, closing real estate transactions, airport management, public relations correspondence, operating a small store, and freight claims procedure.[5]

As we have already noted, not only are there too many courses in most business fields, but also there are too many fields of specialization and typically too many courses are required within the field of concentration. Our detailed recommendations in Part III call for a drastic streamlining, both in the number of special fields made available to the student and in the number of courses required within any particular major field, particularly at the undergraduate level. Even at the graduate level we question the value of much specialization in most of the conventional business fields.

As for public accounting, where the need for some degree of specialized training is unquestioned, the answer clearly lies in a five-year program, with much of the specialized work in accounting deferred to the fifth year.

Here the business schools face a great challenge, and the opportunities for substantially improving the quality of collegiate business education depend in part on how they meet this challenge. A drastic streamlining of specialized course offerings and elimination of heavy concentration requirements will permit more time for the essential ingredients of general education and professional training; some contribution would be made toward alleviation of the faculty shortage; both faculty and students would benefit from the improvement in the intellectual atmosphere; it should be easier to insist on higher academic standards in the basic courses and to concentrate on the development of the basic skills that we have emphasized; and it would be easier to enforce higher admission requirements since many of the poorest students would no longer be attracted by the prospect of concentrating on narrow and superficial vocational courses. We do not mean to imply, however, that *only* poor students take such courses.

THE PROBLEM OF FACULTY ADJUSTMENT

A school is no better than the abilities and interests of its faculty. If the more specialized business school teachers are forced to broaden their horizons, to look for underlying principles that govern the procedures and factual detail they have been teaching, to develop new teaching ma-

---

[5] Let us say here that this wasteful course proliferation is not peculiar to business administration. It exists in other professional schools and also in the liberal arts colleges. The tendency to teach "more and more about less and less" is almost a universal failing in American higher education.

erial in broader areas than those in which they have been working, a significant improvement in the quality of both teaching and research should result.

We do not wish to minimize the difficulties in bringing about such a change. All instructors in the more specialized areas will find the adjustment a difficult one; some will find it impossible. The change cannot be effected overnight. Many will need to be retrained to teach in a broader area and with the use of more rigorous analytical tools. Faculty members will certainly fight to keep their favorite courses. For some schools, undoubtedly, the opportunity for important change along the lines we propose will be governed by actuarial considerations and must wait on the resignation, death, or retirement of key faculty members.

We do not mean to suggest that a business school automatically enters into educational Utopia as soon as it halves the number of its course offerings and eliminates the more specialized fields of concentration. There are business schools today that avoid the evils of course proliferation and overspecialization but which must be rated poor by almost any set of standards: inadequately trained faculty, low academic standards, and courses taught out of textbooks with a maximum of description and a minimum of analysis. Nonetheless, there can be no doubt that the state of collegiate business education will be much healthier if the virus of overspecialization can be removed.

SOME OTHER ARGUMENTS

It is sometimes argued that the student of indifferent ability and poor educational background needs specialized training to secure a job and to prepare him for the specialized career in the lower levels of business in which he will spend his working life. The excuse of mediocre students is utilized to justify a mediocre educational program.

This argument is almost completely without merit, a view which we share with many leaders in both general and business education. Throughout this study we have remained sensitive to the issues raised by the diversity in student abilities, interests, and career objectives. It is partly because of the less gifted student that we have argued for reform rather than abolition of the undergraduate program. But if the less well qualified student belongs in college at all, he needs the broader type of program we propose as much as—perhaps more than—his more talented classmates. In the long run, he suffers rather than benefits from a narrowly specialized training that unfits him for a world of rapid change and for a society that prides itself on its occupational and social mobility. Our recommendations permit a slight degree of specialization that will

be of some help with the first job; a variety of courses and programs wil.
be available to help him after college if he settles down in a particular
specialty. Indeed, as schools of business move toward broader programs,
they might well investigate how they can cooperate even more than they
are now doing with their extension divisions and evening colleges in
making available the special and technical courses needed by the local
business community.

The needs of small business and the specialized character of certain
industries have also been used to justify specialized business training. We
believe that we largely disposed of these arguments in Chapter 5. Ownership and management of a small business does not call for a different
kind of training than that required by future managers of large corporations. If anything, the small businessman's background should be
broader, since he will not have a battery of staff specialists to help him.
As for retailing, insurance, real estate, banking, etc., we saw in Chapter
5 that the need for special training in college for students entering these
fields has been greatly exaggerated.

Business Administration and Liberal Arts

It is not difficult to make a strong case for the liberal values of a well
conceived business program. Given sufficient intellectual content and
taught in such a way as to reveal the broad implications of how business
functions, many business courses could be made to offer the liberalizing
values that we associate with courses in the humanities and physical and
social sciences.[6] Indeed, a well planned and well taught course in administration or finance can provide more of an intellectual challenge
than many of the courses offered in the humanities. And a high-level
course in managerial economics can be as challenging and as rigorous as
many of the courses in the physical sciences. Rigor does not require that
there be single and demonstrably correct solutions to problem situations.
It should be a main purpose of the business schools to introduce a high
level of rigor in this broader sense into all of their courses.

This leads us back to a suggestion made briefly earlier, on which we
shall elaborate in Chapter 10. The business schools and departments have

[6] However, this does not provide any argument for reducing the amount of general education required of business students below what we are proposing. If business courses are to
have the liberal values that we suggest are possible, they must in general assume that the
student has the background provided by a good general education. In addition, general education provides the basis for certain types of knowledge and skills which the educated person
must in any event have (English, history, science, etc.) and which cannot be provided by
business courses.

an obligation to make available to nonbusiness students on the campus a small and select list of business courses that the latter will find useful, whether they eventually go into business or not. These would be courses not ordinarily taken by students in the business school. These courses would deal with some of the basic analytic tools and broadly consider the functioning of business within its market and nonmarket environment. If these courses are properly planned and well taught, no liberal arts college should be reluctant to accept them in partial fulfillment of the requirements for a liberal arts degree.

Other Issues Affecting the Business Schools

So far in this chapter we have been concerned only with the kind of education that should be offered to future businessmen—and, to some extent, with the quality of students who should receive this education. It is on these matters that the analysis of Part II has the most direct bearing. But these are not the only issues facing the business schools. To improve the quality of their educational programs, the business schools must cope with some other problems, for example, insuring an adequate supply of properly qualified teachers and improving the quality of the staff they already have.

In addition, schools of business administration, in common with other professional schools, have three other functions to perform: to advance knowledge in their field through research, to train future teachers and research workers, and to provide a variety of service activities for government, business, and the community at large. Each of these functions presents special problems for the business schools; we took a brief look at some of the issues involved in Chapter 3.

The two most critical questions concern ways of increasing the supply of adequately trained teachers (including additional training where needed for those now teaching) and, even more important in the long run, how to accelerate the growth of a verified body of knowledge which can be both taught to students and used as a basis for policy by businessmen and others who are concerned with the functioning of business.

At this stage we are ready to proceed with a detailed survey of undergraduate and graduate curricula. This will be undertaken in Part III. There we shall describe in some detail what the business schools and departments of business are currently offering in the way of undergraduate and master's programs in business administration, and we shall evaluate what the schools are now doing against the standards suggested in this and earlier chapters. In Chapter 12 we shall pay attention to the nondegree offerings of the business schools—particularly so-called manage-ment development programs but also evening and extension courses and special conferences and institutes for businessmen. Then in Part IV we shall consider the quality of students and faculty (Chapters 13 and 14), ways of improving teaching and research (Chapters 15 and 16), and the kinds of doctoral programs needed, particularly in order to train future teachers and research workers (Chapter 17).

PART III

A Critical Survey
of Business Curricula

chapter 8

THE UNDERGRADUATE

CURRICULUM:

GENERAL EDUCATION

WHILE an educational institution ultimately stands or falls not on its curriculum but on the quality of its students and faculty, the curriculum is not unimportant. As the structure through which education is accomplished, it becomes a partial determinant of the quality of that education. It also reflects the educational philosophy of the faculty which framed it. Thus, although secondary to students and faculties, curricula have an important influence on the extent to which educational objectives are achieved. Or, as it has been stated elsewhere:[1]

A college curriculum is significant chiefly for two things: it reveals the educated community's conception of what knowledge is most worth transmitting to the cream of its youth, and it reveals what kind of mind and character an education is expected to produce. The curriculum is a barometer by which we may measure the cultural pressures that operate upon the school.

Part II of this report culminated in a set of conclusions regarding the kind of education for business which, in our opinion, the colleges and universities should provide. In this and the following chapter, these criteria will be expanded and applied to the problem of the undergraduate curriculum.

While we shall offer some quite specific recommendations regarding desirable changes in curriculum in this and later chapters, these recommendations are to be interpreted primarily as indicating the directions in which we believe the business schools need to move. We have no desire to impose a straitjacket on the business schools. To make our points clear, we shall suggest specific types of courses and the approximate amount of time which, in our judgment, should be devoted to each. But there is undoubtedly room for legitimate disagreement with the nature of some of our recommendations; faculty resources vary widely among

---

[1] Richard Hofstadter and C. DeWitt Hardy, *The Development and Scope of Higher Education in the United States* (1952), p. 11.

schools; even the best curriculum must change as new needs develop and knowledge accumulates; self-study, experimentation, and willingness to change are more important than the particular courses a school chooses to require at any particular time.

Thus, we do not expect that any school will want to accept all of our curriculum recommendations literally and without modifications. While our specific recommendations offer one possible way of improving present practices in most schools, there are other ways of achieving the same educational objectives. The important thing is that the curriculum seek to meet the kinds of needs emphasized in this report in the most effective way that the resources of the business school permit—and that study and experimentation looking forward to further improvement be a continuing part of each school's activities.

The Balance Between Professional and General Education

As we pointed out earlier, undergraduate schools of business clearly have a responsibility for general (or "liberal") as well as for professional education. The school of business cannot avoid this responsibility by confining its jurisdiction to the last two years, leaving the first two years for whatever the student wishes to study or for whatever the liberal arts college chooses to require. In addition, we accept as axiomatic that in the undergraduate years the goal of general education must take precedence over the goal of professional and business education. We must, therefore, turn first to the role of general education in the undergraduate business curriculum.

WHAT IS GENERAL EDUCATION?

It is necessary to digress briefly in order to settle a few terminological difficulties arising from the dichotomy of "general" and "professional" education. It has often been argued that business courses—for example, principles of marketing—have some of the same liberalizing values associated with courses in, say, Boswell, modern European history, or Etruscan art. If the business courses are broadly conceived and properly taught, we are inclined to agree, just as we should agree that not all courses offered in the sacrosanct areas of literature, arts, and sciences are wholly and fully "liberalizing." One observer has written:[2]

[2] Daniel Borth, "The Principles That Should Guide Professional Training for Business," *Collegiate Education for Business* (A Conference sponsored by Alpha of Alabama Chapter, Beta Gamma Sigma and University of Alabama Extension Division, April 8 and 9, 1954, in Uni-

Just as we need a thorough rethinking of what constitutes business courses, so we need a complete rethinking of what are liberal arts courses. Nothing is more *illiberal* than a course in an arts college in ancient history which devotes itself to memorization of dates, recital of uncoordinated events, and over-devotion to the scandals of the kings and queens of the day. Some courses in advanced English literature so often bear the imprint of the interests of the particular English instructor in the inconsequential minutiae and the techniques of a single author that the placement of such a course in an arts college should not characterize the course as broadening or balanced. On the other hand, nothing is more unthinking than a business school curriculum which considers business advertising to be liberal arts if taught in a college of arts and business if taught in a college of commerce. (In one school the same textbook is prescribed.)

We do not believe that most business courses, as they are now taught, have the liberalizing values which their proponents claim for them. In the case of some, it is largely a matter of how they are taught and what is expected of the student. There are other courses in which it would be difficult to find any liberal content, no matter how they were taught. It is chiefly (although not exclusively) the basic courses entering into the "core" of the business curriculum that permit of broad and "liberal" treatment.

Although recognizing that some business courses may contribute some of the same values that we hope to find in a liberal arts curriculum, we shall adhere to a conventional if somewhat arbitrary distinction between general education and professional business courses. This is partly a matter of convenience. But more important, we believe that there are some educational values which suffer when considered only from the viewpoint of business, and business courses are almost inevitably taught from such a viewpoint.

We shall, therefore, consider as professional courses those which have as their primary purpose the preparation of students for a business career. All other courses will be included under the heading of general education. From the viewpoint of the business student, then, courses in the departments of mathematics, English, history, political science, and sociology are nearly always "general education" courses, just as courses in accounting, marketing, management, and statistics are primarily "professional."

Obviously this distinction works better in some cases than in others. The most troublesome field is economics. Here we shall have to be some-

versity, Alabama), p. 43. See also Michael McPhelin, S.J., "The Humanities and Education for Business," *Collegiate News and Views*, VIII (October, 1954), 1-4.

what arbitrary, although there is some logic in our procedure. We shall include courses in elementary economics and economic history in general education. All other economics courses, if required as part of the program in business administration, will be considered professional courses. While this division sometimes leads to results that are open to question, the line has to be drawn somewhere, and we think that this is as good a place to draw it as any other. The other social sciences will not be treated in this way. They are not as intimately related to business as is economics; and there is less opportunity for the business or professional viewpoint to dominate.

A COMMENT ON LIBERAL ARTS COURSES

While we have stressed repeatedly the need for the business student to have a sound background in general education, we recognize all too well that the recommendations we make in this chapter regarding liberal arts requirements are not likely to serve fully the objectives we have in mind, given the well recognized limitations of undergraduate offerings in the arts and sciences in many, if not most, institutions. It is far beyond the purpose of this report to attempt to reform the teaching of the liberal arts in our undergraduate colleges; in addition, we are obviously not competent to make such an attempt. We can only urge that the faculties of the business schools work with their colleagues in the arts and sciences to improve the kinds of courses and teaching which business (and other) students need to have. The emphasis should not be, as many in the humanities would probably put it, on an "appreciation" of the liberal arts. Rather, the stress should be on developing in the student the capacity to appreciate, understand, enlarge upon, and use in his daily life what he learns in his liberal arts courses. This should be the goal of general education in the humanities and also in the physical and social sciences.

THE MINIMUM GENERAL EDUCATION REQUIREMENT

In Part II of this report we emphasized the importance to the business student of academic work in the natural and social sciences and the humanities, both for their "cultural" or "liberal" value and for professional reasons. In Chapter 7 we strongly recommended that at least half of the four-year undergraduate curriculum should be nonprofessional in character. This recommendation follows from general considerations of balance as between professional and general education as well as from our evaluation of the minimum required in each of the several nonprofessional areas of study.

This recommendation of "at least half" differs only moderately from the official position of the American Association of Collegiate Schools of Business:[3]

At least forty per cent of the total hours required for the bachelor's degree must be taken in subjects other than business and economics provided that economic principles and economic history may be counted in either the business or non-business groups.

Few business faculties would openly deny the desirability of the Association's requirement of 40 per cent, even though a considerable number of faculties do not follow it in practice. On the other hand, some faculties encourage or require their students to take more than 50 per cent of their work in nonprofessional areas.

The Carnegie Corporation Survey of Business Education found that half of the schools of business answering its questionnaire reported that they required *less* than 40 per cent "liberal arts and other nonbusiness courses" in their curriculum[4] (Table 9). Thirty-six per cent of the schools required more than 40 but less than 50 per cent nonbusiness, while a scant 14 per cent required half or more of the four years' work in nonprofessional areas.[5] Apparently more than half of the schools replying to this questionnaire were members of the American Association of Collegiate Schools of Business.

Our analysis of the undergraduate curricula of a sample of thirty-seven Association members revealed that 38 per cent were violating the "forty per cent rule," even if economic principles and economic history were

[3] *The Constitution and the Standards for Membership in the American Association of Collegiate Schools of Business* (1958). The Standards Rating Committee of the American Accounting Association recommended in a report published in 1954 that "liberal, cultural, and general non-business studies" should account for "approximately 50 per cent of the total curriculum." "Report of Standards Rating Committee," *Accounting Review*, XXIX (January, 1954), 43.

[4] The survey covered "all accredited four-year undergraduate and all accredited graduate institutions of higher education offering programs in business administration" in 1957. Two questionnaires, one for departments or divisions of business, and the other for schools or colleges, were sent to 585 institutions. Responses for 422 schools and departments were tabulated and reported in *Summary of Preliminary Findings* (revised August 1, 1958). Henceforth, this set of findings will be referred to as "Carnegie Survey of Business Education, *Summary of Preliminary Findings*." We are indebted to Professor Frank C. Pierson, director of the survey, for making the results available to us.

[5] The reader is referred to the Carnegie Survey of Business Education, *Summary of Preliminary Findings*, p. 21, for the detail of these summary totals. See also the next footnote. The tabulation summarizes the replies as given by the responding schools, without any adjustments, and involves some inconsistencies. Thus some schools included elementary economics as a required nonbusiness course, and others did not. Similar inconsistencies arose in the treatment of business English, business mathematics, R.O.T.C., physical education, etc.

always counted as nonprofessional.[6] (See Table 9.) Only one-sixth of the schools required 50 per cent or more nonbusiness work. Investigation of a sample of nonmember curricula revealed about the same thing, for 37 per cent of the schools required that students have less than 40 per cent of their work in nonbusiness courses.[7]

It is striking that the Association schools as a group differ so little from nonmember schools in this respect. The reason for this similarity lies as much in the fact that many member schools are in violation of Association standards as in the fact that nonmember schools are meeting Association curriculum standards in anticipation of making application for membership. We visited every one of the institutions included in our sample of Association schools, and there is no doubt that many member deans are aware of the fact that member schools often violate with apparent immunity both the letter and the spirit of the Association's curriculum standards.

In spite of the frequency with which the present standard of the Association is being ignored, we strongly recommend a minimum requirement of sixty semester units of nonbusiness courses, exclusive of both R.O.T.C. and physical education. These 60 semester units would be 50 per cent of a standard four-year program which required 120 semester units of academic subjects.

Undoubtedly, many schools, both in and out of the AACSB, will resist this proposal. We are convinced, however, that the arguments presented in Part II and summarized in Chapter 7 require no less. It might even be urged that the undergraduate curriculum should contain a maximum of

---

[6] Our calculations were based on the definition of "nonprofessional" stated earlier in this chapter. The important characteristics of that definition are that a) economic principles and economic history were counted as nonprofessional; b) business English, business mathematics, etc., were counted as professional; and c) physical education and R.O.T.C. were counted neither as professional nor nonprofessional. Of course, the total number of semester or quarter hours required for the degree was adjusted to reflect the exclusion of physical education and R.O.T.C.

We computed the nonprofessional proportion of the undergraduate curriculum for each of the sample schools (all members of the AACSB) by two methods: 1) the total number of required nonprofessional semester units divided by 120 semester units, and 2) the same numerator divided by the actual total number of semester units required for an undergraduate degree less units required in R.O.T.C., physical education, and hygiene. The statements in the text are based on the first method of computation which, as can be seen in Table 9, gives the larger proportion of nonprofessional semester units.

[7] We found it necessary to develop a sample of seventy-four schools whose requirements and course offerings could be examined in detail. The sample is described in greater detail in Appendix E. The results of this detailed examination of the curricula of these schools will be frequently referred to in this and subsequent chapters. We are quite confident that this sample of seventy-four is reasonably representative, for our purposes, of the population from which it was drawn.

TABLE 9

PROPORTION OF TOTAL UNDERGRADUATE UNITS
REQUIRED IN NONBUSINESS COURSES

| | Percentage Distribution of Schools | | |
| | Computational Method[a] | | As Reported to Carnegie Survey |
Percentage of Total Units Required in Nonbusiness Courses	(1)	(2)	
Under 40%	38%	43%	50%
40% through 49%	46	46	36
50% and over	16	11	14
	100%	100%	100%
(No. of Schools in the Sample)	(37)	(37)	(170)

[a] For thirty-seven schools, all members of the AACSB. For a description of the two methods of computation, see footnote 6 on page 152.
Source: See footnotes 4, 5, and 6 on pages 151–52.

40 per cent business and economics, i.e., 60 per cent general education. We do not see how the minimum of general education can be less than 50 per cent unless the school wishes to expand its total degree requirement. In that case, the recommendation could be worded so as to read: "at least the equivalent of two full years' work in areas other than business and economics," i.e., sixty semester units. Our discussion in this chapter assumes that the student has only the four undergraduate years for both general and business education. We have already indicated the limitations of such a program and the reasons for believing that a student's general education could well be extended over three or four years.

The General Education of the Business Student: the Humanities

In Part II we suggested the subject matter areas which should be included in any undergraduate business curriculum. Each of these areas will be briefly considered, with emphasis on the amount, kind, and approximate level of instruction which would seem to serve best the career needs of undergraduate students.

The comments to follow are not intended as a statement of rigid requirements. We realize not only the variety and diversity of needs to be served and resources available, but also the desirability of experimentation. However, significant departures from the broad recommendations to be presented should be based on clearly enunciated educational objectives.[8] In our view, these objectives should conform to those which emerged from the analysis in Part II of this report. We do not think that practices which are radically at variance with the following recommendations can often be defended on the basis of experimentation. At least the burden of proof should rest on the faculty concerned.

Throughout this chapter, but especially in the sections to follow, we use the terms "courses" and "semester hours" only in order to give concreteness to our recommendations. Our objective is to indicate the areas which should be covered, the general nature of the emphasis that is needed, and the time that might appropriately be devoted to each area. No reader should look upon our recommendations as constituting a curriculum *per se;* rather, they should be interpreted as guidelines to be used by those who do have the responsibility for curriculum construction. These guidelines are those suggested by the analysis of earlier chapters, and, so far as we can judge, they also reflect the views of the more progressive leaders in American higher education, both in and out of the business schools.

ENGLISH COMPOSITION, LITERATURE, AND SPEECH

Of all the areas of student competence, the one concerning which educators—and employers—are in most agreement is that of "communication." Complaints about the ability of students to write, read, and speak effectively are not new nor are they limited to business students. But we cannot ignore this problem simply because it is a chronic one of which everyone is aware.

There is, of course, no general standard saying what is the optimum amount of composition, literature, and speech for college students, much less for business students. Of the seventy-four undergraduate curricula which we analyzed in detail, twenty-one required approximately two semester courses in this area, thirty-three required three or four courses, and seventeen required more than four.[9] A source of underestimation may come from the fact that courses in business English or business speech

---

[8] This was also the general position adopted by the Committee on Evaluation of Engineering Education of the American Society for Engineering Education when it presented its curriculum recommendations. Cf. *Report on Evaluation of Engineering Education, 1952–1955* (1955), pp. 11 ff.

[9] For the seventy-four schools in our sample:

	Semester Units Required in English Composition, Literature, and Speech						
	0	1–4	5–7	8–10	11–13	14–	Total
No. of AACSB schools	2	1	13	10	5	6	37
No. of non-AACSB schools	0	0	8	8	10	11	37
Total	2	1	21	18	15	17	74

given in the business school are not included. However, only about one-third of the Association members and one-seventh of the non-Association schools require either business English or business speech.

We recommend that schools require that their students take four or five semester courses (twelve to fifteen semester units) in English composition, literature, and speech. We suggest a year of composition, a year of English literature, and a half-year of speech, although we fully recognize that literature and composition need not and perhaps should not be taught in isolation. Local alternatives will, of course, determine the manner in which this requirement will be spelled out. The minimum is put at four or five courses, since many schools have proficiency systems whereby the first of two courses in composition can be met by examination.[10]

Schools should not include in this requirement "adapted" courses such as business English, letter writing, or business report writing. In our view, none of these is a satisfactory substitute for a standard sequence in composition and literature given by the English department. We are convinced that courses in business English and letter writing as such have no place in the university curriculum.[11] Businessmen speak and write the same language as the rest of us. If such courses are offered, we recommend that they be on a noncredit or elective basis. They should not be used as a means of meeting—or subventing—the basic English requirement.

The report writing course is of a somewhat different character, usually being offered after students have had some basic training in the English department. If offered, it should be considered a part of the professional curriculum and not used to reduce the standard English requirement. A separate report writing course is probably not necessary if extensive writing assignments are required in virtually all courses, and this clearly should be the case. Language can be mastered only by continuous use. Report writing should play an important role particularly in the course on business policy. Where possible, reports should be read for organization, style, grammar, and spelling by specially qualified readers; and in

[10] Possibly the speech requirement might also be met with a proficiency examination.

[11] We are not alone in this conviction: "It is especially harmful to degrade a fundamental college course in reading, speaking, and writing by including concepts implied by such topics as 'business correspondence,' 'case recording,' 'oral presentation to professional groups,' 'engineering English,' and 'writing for professional publication.'" (Ernest V. Hollis and Alice L. Taylor, *Social Work Education in the United States* [1951], p. 193.) And: "If English composition is degraded to teaching such topics as 'business correspondence' and 'report writing,' for example, it becomes a trade course which regiments thought, cramps originality, and ceases to be a subject of college level at all." Elliott D. Smith, "The Education of Professional Students for Citizenship," in *Education for Professional Responsibility* (1948), p. 201.

this case, form as well as substance should be a factor in grading.[12] This is not, of course, to deny a possible place for a report writing course in schools whose students need or desire work beyond the core requirement recommended here.

About two out of five schools of business in our sample had specific speech requirements, and a non-Association school was much more likely to have such a requirement than a member school. This considerably understates the frequency with which speech is taken by business students, since a number of schools have group requirements, in which a certain number of units must be chosen from, for example, speech, English composition, literature, and foreign languages. Some of these schools, as well as others, recommend that students include a course in speech as an elective.

Concern with the problem of effective communication has by now extended to all parts of the college campus. Given the degree and generality of dissatisfaction with present results, it is both surprising and disconcerting to find that departments of English have not taken the lead in attempting reform. However, as others have also noted, other departments and particularly the professional schools have had to take the initiative. This has been particularly true in the case of the business schools.[13] This is unfortunate, since the business schools already have more than enough problems without assuming the additional burden of attempting to offer instruction in English composition and literature. The basic training in English should be the responsibility of the English department, although professional schools have the responsibility as well as the right to join other departments of the university in a common attack on this common problem.

Literature has been included in this section since it bears directly on competence in communication. It also is inseparably linked with composition as a matter of pedagogy on many campuses. We recognize, however, that it has implications that go beyond effective communication, and thus we will consider it again in our discussion of the humanities.

These few comments on the problem of effective writing and speaking for undergraduates cannot be complete without including the familiar injunction that even the best formal training in the English language will not alone produce graduates who are skilled in verbal, particularly

[12] We would also urge that students be required to *rewrite* their papers until they are judged to be satisfactory. Only if they are required to do this will "learning by doing" have its maximum effect.

[13] Cf. Richard L. Kozelka, *Professional Education for Business* (AACSB, 1954), p. 66. A few schools employ special assistants to read papers in business courses from the point of view of grammar, clarity, spelling, etc.

written, communication. Few of the skills which undergraduate faculties in general and business schools in particular seek to develop in their students are composed of such a large proportion of "experience" or "practice" relative to "knowledge." Skill in written communication can be developed in undergraduates *only* if students are continuously required to use the knowledge acquired in their English courses—that is, only if the faculty provides opportunity for active and creative types of educational experience throughout the remainder of the students' college careers.[14] Thus the professional faculty should assume explicit responsibility for the development of skill in communication once the period of formal training is over. A faculty which has not assumed such responsibility is hardly in a position to criticize its students and their secondary preparation or their own colleagues in the department of English.

HUMANITIES AND FINE ARTS

We include here those areas of human knowledge and understanding which are encompassed by the terms literature, language, fine arts, and philosophy. (History might also be included here, but we prefer to consider it at a later point.) Since it is the function of the undergraduate years to educate the whole man and not merely provide technical training for the businessman, these are fields in which the undergraduate student of business administration should also have some work.

Literature and written and oral communication have been considered in the preceding paragraphs from a professional point of view: undergraduate professional schools must see to it that their students attain some level of proficiency in the use of the English language. There is, of course, a more general argument for including a study of the English language in any undergraduate curriculum. But this latter consideration merely strengthens our earlier recommendation.

In addition to English literature, nonprofessional considerations suggest that the student should take other courses in the area of the humanities and fine arts. We cannot, as in the preceding case, rationalize any specific requirement. We suggest four semester courses as a minimum; local preferences and student choice should be allowed, within limits, to determine the particular courses.

We should, however, like to make a plea in favor of exposing the student to some foreign culture. The traditional way of accomplishing this

[14] Hollis and Taylor have this in mind when they comment: "Not all the blame for the fact that a majority of professional practitioners are poor listeners, readers, writers, and speakers should be placed on the undergraduate college. Professional school educators generally fail to build on the primary contribution of language and other 'tool' subjects that may have been made by liberal education." *Social Work Education in the United States*, p. 193.

has been through a foreign language requirement. Considering, however, the way that foreign languages are too often taught, the manner in which they have tended to disappear from the secondary curriculum, and the all-too-real resistance on the part of students, it seems that a superior way of achieving the same goal would be through a concentration requirement whereby the student would be obliged to integrate a few courses around one foreign culture. These courses could be chosen from offerings in language, literature, history, and geography, although first-year foreign language courses should perhaps not be included. Considering the changing nature of the world in which a business firm must operate, we feel that there is also considerable justification for this suggestion on professional grounds.

Both Bossard and Dewhurst and the more recent General Electric study found that college graduates in business look back on their foreign language courses as among the least useful taken in college. Although we can only guess, we suspect that the reaction to a "foreign culture" requirement of the sort proposed here would be much less negative. The need for exposure to some such "foreign culture" sequence as we suggest is confirmed by views expressed to us by businessmen as well as by the obvious fact that the United States is now more closely bound to the rest of the world than ever before.

Combining the two recommendations thus far made—four or five courses in English literature and language and at least four additional semester courses in the humanities and fine arts generally—we have a total of eight or nine semester courses (twenty-four to twenty-seven semester hours). This is a little more than most schools of business are currently requiring in the humanities, although it is certainly less than some schools specify, particularly those in Roman Catholic institutions. Almost one out of four schools of business requires no more than three courses in the humanities and fine arts (including English language, literature, and speech); nearly half of all schools, members and nonmembers, require from five to eight courses; and one in twelve requires more than eight.[15] Nonmember schools tend to require more work in the humanities than do member schools.

[15] For the seventy-four schools in our sample:

| | Semester Units Required in Humanities (including English, Speech, and Fine Arts) | | | | | | | |
	0–4	5–7	8–10	11–13	14–16	17–25	26–	Total
No. of AACSB schools	0	5	5	11	8	5	3	37
No. of non-AACSB schools	0	3	4	5	10	12	3	37
Total	0	8	9	16	18	17	6	74

The Natural Sciences and Mathematics

MATHEMATICS

After competence in English, the area of greatest concern is probably mathematics. As with the English requirement, the problem is not unique to the business school or even to the undergraduate college. The cry for better preparation in mathematics is echoed by the graduate departments in an increasing number of fields, and the same echo can be heard from employers who recruit directly from the secondary schools. The mathematical preparation of the college student is notoriously inadequate for the kind of world in which he will live in the decades ahead; this is becoming particularly true of the student planning a business career.

Slowly the business schools are beginning to recognize this. Spurred by the public outcry brought forth by belated recognition of Russian scientific achievements, the secondary schools are now beginning to recognize the need for wider and better preparation in mathematics. Reluctantly and all too slowly, teachers of mathematics in the colleges and secondary schools are coming to admit that the subject must be taught in new ways to meet new needs and that far more students than in the past must be exposed to a range of mathematics considerably beyond elementary arithmetic and ninth grade algebra.

It is beyond the province of this report to review all the reasons for the sorry state of training in mathematics in American schools and colleges. One point in particular, however, impresses us, as it has many other observers. As a field of knowledge, mathematics is as living and dynamic as, say, physics, chemistry, or psychology. The theory and applications of mathematics are continually changing, and never more dramatically than at the present time.[16] Yet the teaching of mathematics has remained static. The same subjects have been taught in the same ways for decades, in the elementary and secondary schools and also (except to advanced students in mathematics) in the colleges.[17]

Thus the college preparatory student typically studies one or two years of algebra and a year of plane geometry, and, as often as not, no more mathematics than this. None of the newer concepts of modern mathe-

[16] Cf. a recent series by George A. W. Boehm, "The New Mathematics," *Fortune*, June and July, 1958.
[17] Cf. "Teaching Math in the Twentieth Century," *Carnegie Corporation of New York Quarterly*, April, 1958, pp. 6–8.

matics, no matter how elementary, is introduced, and the courses are usually so taught that they remain alien to the student's experience and mode of thinking. Standards of performance are often low, and many students resist the mental discipline imposed on them. Only a few schools are exceptions to this indictment, although their number is fortunately increasing.

Let us turn now to the college student in a school of business administration. Typically, he is required to take no mathematics worthy of the name. He may have to take business mathematics or mathematics of finance, in which he devotes many hours to eighth-grade arithmetic, to nineteenth-century arithmetic shortcuts which deny the existence of desk calculators, to problems in compound interest, annuities, etc., which deny the existence of prepared tables and handbooks as well as the principle of division of labor, and to other esoterica which are embarrassingly sub-collegiate or which will be of value only to one graduate in a hundred. Some schools offer remedial-type courses in which high school deficiencies are more or less repaired. College algebra, which reviews the second year of high school algebra and then perhaps proceeds to modern algebra, is a frequent requirement. A few business schools are beginning to require the traditional courses in analytic geometry and introduction to the differential calculus. And occasionally one finds a school of business requiring a course entitled Modern Mathematics or Elementary Mathematical Analysis, covering a wide range of topics from college algebra and trigonometry to an introductory treatment of a number of more advanced topics.

Currently about 85 per cent of all schools of business, as measured in our sample, require *some* mathematics in college, although in a number of cases this requirement can be met by proficiency examination or a superior secondary preparation. Of those schools in our sample which did have some sort of mathematics requirement, slightly less than half required one semester's work, and about half required a year's work. Very few require more than one year.[18] Nonmember schools are more likely to have a mathematics requirement than are Association schools. However, if they have a mathematics requirement at all, the latter will typically specify more mathematics than nonmembers, although the difference is not great. Of the schools with some kind of mathematics in the curriculum, nearly three-fourths specified some sort of general course in mathematics.[19]

[18] For our sample of 74 schools, 11 had no requirement; 32 required two to five semester units; 27, from six to eight; and 4, from nine to twelve. These counts include all kinds of offerings, whether offered by the mathematics department or by the school, and regardless of level or content (except that statistics is excluded).

[19] We distinguished between "mathematics" and "business mathematics" by examining

The standards of mathematical competence implied by these requirements are inadequate for the kind of world in which tomorrow's businessmen will work and live. In recommending a prompt and significant raising of these standards, we are being guided by our own analysis of needs in Part II, by the testimony of businessmen and business school alumni, by recent developments which have greatly widened the applications of mathematics in the social sciences and in business, and by the more advanced thinking of the educators, social scientists, and mathematicians who have concerned themselves with how to teach mathematics to those who will not themselves be professional mathematicians, physical scientists, or engineers. The need to raise the standard of mathematical competence is now being recognized by the better business schools, and some have introduced new requirements just within the last few years.

Schools of business generally need to take three steps. *First*, the schools' catalogues should encourage students who plan on majoring in business administration to acquire a sound secondary-school preparation of from three to four years of mathematics.[20] *Second*, degree credit should no longer be granted for courses which are designed to remedy secondary-school deficiencies. Students should, depending on local conditions, be required to remedy such deficiencies either before matriculation or else on a noncredit basis. Certainly, if the business schools continue to permit the use of valuable undergraduate time for secondary-level work, professional education must be delayed into the fifth year—or perhaps shifted altogether to the graduate years.

As a *third* step, the schools should require appropriate college-level

course descriptions in catalogues and bulletins. Often we had notes taken during our visits to schools to supplement official descriptions. The results for our sample of 74 schools are as follows:

	Require None	Math Only	Business Math Only	Require Both
AACSB schools	8	19	5	5
Non-AACSB schools	3	19	11	4

Clearly, nonmember schools are more likely to require "business mathematics" than are Association schools. Only five of the twenty-five schools requiring "business mathematics" required more than one semester of it.

[20] Increasing numbers of secondary schools are likely to move away from the standard bill-of-fare described a few paragraphs back. If we take the recent recommendations of the Commission on Mathematics of the College Entrance Examination Board as a reasonable approximation of what will come to prevail within the foreseeable future in the better high schools, well-prepared students will arrive at the university having completed at least three and preferably four years of secondary mathematics. This would include one year each of standard secondary algebra, geometry (including analytic), intermediate algebra and trigonometry, and what the Commission calls "elementary analysis"—functions, probability theory, and statistical inference. Cf. Commission on Mathematics of the College Entrance Examination Board, *Modernizing the Mathematics Curriculum* (1958); for a summary of this, see "Teaching Math in the Twentieth Century," especially pp. 6–8.

work in mathematics. We suggest a minimum of one year. More might be urged for better students, and indeed more is necessary for those interested in careers in certain fields of business. These courses should presume something close to the first three years' work in the secondary-school sequence described above. As a minimum, the required year in college should presume two years of high school algebra. As mathematics teaching in the secondary schools improves, the prerequisites should be extended to include a brief introduction to trigonometry and analytical geometry, the essential concepts of which can readily be absorbed in high school even by students who are "not mathematically inclined." In no case should the college requirement include introductory algebra or what is usually taught in courses on business mathematics or mathematics of finance.

The college requirement should include, however, what might be termed modern mathematical analysis. By this we mean the kinds of mathematics recently suggested by the Committee on the Undergraduate Program of the Mathematical Association of America, the Committee on Mathematical Training of Social Scientists of the Social Science Research Council, and by many others.[21] This is the kind of mathematics that is of growing importance in the social sciences and in a wide range of business applications.[22]

A year's course along these lines would be appropriate for freshmen and sophomores anticipating work not only in business administration but in many of the biological and social sciences as well. The only prerequisites would be two years of secondary school algebra and one year of geometry.[23]

[21] See *Universal Mathematics*, 2 vols. (1954), *Elementary Mathematics of Sets with Applications* (1958), and *Modern Mathematical Methods and Models*, 2 vols. (1958), issued by the Committee on the Undergraduate Program of the Mathematical Association of America; the report of the Committee on Mathematical Training of Social Scientists of the Social Science Research Council, *SSRC Items*, June, 1955 (reprinted in *Econometrica*, xxiv [January, 1956]); and the new texts that have recently appeared to meet the need of nonmathematicians for sophisticated introductions to the major areas of mathematics. One example of the latter is *Introduction to Finite Mathematics* (1956) by John G. Kemeny, J. Laurie Snell, and Gerald L. Thompson.

[22] For a discussion of the kinds of mathematics needed by businessmen, see R. K. Gaumnitz and O. H. Brownlee, "Mathematics for Decision Makers," *Harvard Business Review*, May–June, 1956, pp. 48–56; also Boehm, *Fortune*, June and July, 1958, and Michael Verhulst, "Mathematics for Managers," *Impact of Science on Society*, vii (March, 1957), 16–31.

[23] Following this first course, a second course of either one or two semesters could continue the calculus into integration, perhaps elaborate on matrix theory or probability, and then move into new topics such as partial differentiation and multiple integration, differential and difference equations, linear programming and game theory, and special applications. While few schools would feel free to impose such a second course as a general requirement on all students, such additional work should be recommended as an elective to all and might be required of majors in some fields—for example, production management or business statistics.

The course suggested here would stress mathematics as a means of dealing with problems rather than as an end in itself. It would recognize that the traditional undergraduate curriculum in mathematics does not provide a satisfactory background for students in business administration and a number of other fields. Many mathematicians are aware of the weaknesses of the traditional curriculum, and the recommendations prepared by a committee of the Mathematical Association of America for revision of the undergraduate curriculum correspond closely to the program outlined here.

It is obvious that formidable obstacles stand in the way of significant reform in the business school mathematics requirement. Students come with inadequate backgrounds, and they often seem to have insufficient ability for, say, the calculus. We suspect, however, that the stress on the inadequate background of the students has been overdone; in any event this consideration will become less important in the future as the teaching of mathematics in the secondary schools improves. Experiments in several universities suggest that a course in what we have called modern mathematical analysis can be handled by the average student with two to three years of conventional secondary school mathematics. Students who, apart from deficiencies in their backgrounds, cannot master the elementary, albeit sophisticated, program outlined here may well be unsuited for successful and responsible careers in business. Indeed, we suggest that they are unsuited for truly college-level work.

Another objection that can be raised to our program is that the mathematics department may be unwilling to cooperate. This is sometimes a difficult problem. As previously noted, however, mathematicians themselves have begun to review their attitudes toward the undergraduate curriculum, and business schools will undoubtedly have less difficulty in the future than they might have had in the past.[24] Even so, local conditions may seriously limit what any particular school can accomplish. It will always be the case, however, that some significant improvement can be made over a situation in which the existing requirement is college algebra, mathematics of finance, or business mathematics. And certainly in today's world, schools cannot justify failure to require *any* mathematics at a truly college level. Thus, in our opinion, the minimum should be a year beyond what can reasonably be expected in high school, and with a coverage of topics along the lines indicated.

[24] Indiana (with the help of a mathematician on the business school staff) and Santa Clara are recent examples of places where cooperation between mathematics and business faculties has resulted in more substantial fare being made available to business undergraduates. Tulane and others are also experimenting, apparently with satisfactory results, with courses in modern mathematics.

THE NATURAL SCIENCES

As in the case of mathematics, it is becoming increasingly important that the businessman have some background in science and technology.[25] It is equally important that he obtain an appreciation of the scientific method and of the spirit of inquiry that motivates science. He needs it as part of his general education as well as for professional reasons. In view of the kind of world we live in, and to which business must adapt itself, this is hardly a debatable issue.

Ideally, the student should have at least an introduction to each of the main branches of science, both physical and biological; he should have a laboratory course in at least one and preferably two sciences; and he would benefit greatly from a survey of the history of science and an introduction to engineering technology.

It is, of course, not practical to suggest such a program. The cost in terms of time is too high; the undergraduate business student has other subjects to conquer if he is to be properly prepared. It is necessary, therefore, to look for ways of compressing and compromising the ideal into the practical.

Fortunately it is possible to look to the student's preparatory years for help. The requirement of at least one course in each area, physical and biological, can be retained, with the stipulation that high school work in biology, chemistry, or physics will count toward this distributional requirement. Weak though many high schools may be in the natural sciences, it still is reasonable for the undergraduate curriculum to presuppose at least one year in one science.

The science requirement should call for some laboratory work and for a modest amount of study in depth. Both could be achieved through a one-year laboratory science course in college. The laboratory requirement might be met, on the other hand, by offering two years of high school laboratory science upon matriculation. The depth requirement could then be met by any year's sequence in science at the college level.[26]

We also urge that business schools attempt to arrange suitable courses in technology and history of science, to supplement the more conventional courses. The schools should also support experiments by the sci-

[25] Cf. Alexander King, "Management as a Technology," *Impact of Science on Society*, VIII (June, 1957), 82.

[26] Business students, like other undergraduates, are notorious for subventing science requirements by avoiding chemistry, biology, and physics, and taking geography, rural biology, psychology, meteorology, etc. The requirement should therefore be written so as to prevent this sort of evasion.

nce departments which seek to find new ways of combining or presenting natural science materials for nonscientists.

In effect, we are recommending the the school of business require from one to two years' work in the natural sciences, depending on local offerings and previous background. The requirement could be set at two years, and then one semester's credit be given for each year of high school science, except that each student should be required to take at least one year of standard science work in college. Properly prepared students would then have two semesters free for electives in nonbusiness subjects. The poorly prepared student would find it necessary to take two full years' work in the science departments. But such students should be exceptions if the school has a proper statement of admissions in its catalogue.

The above recommendations probably do not differ greatly, so far as amount is concerned, from present practice. Our sample suggests that two out of three member schools and nearly four of five non-Association schools require some natural science, with the great majority of these specifying one year's work or more. Only 17 per cent of the schools having science requirements seem to be requiring less science than we propose here.[27] Again, Association schools are more likely not to require any science than are nonmembers.

Since some schools specify "natural science *or* mathematics," it may be useful to compare our recommendations in these two areas with present practice. Our recommendations call for from two to four semesters of natural science and for two or more of mathematics, or a total of from twelve to perhaps twenty-four semester units. The range comes from providing some allowance for secondary school preparation and for local restrictions. About 20 per cent of the schools are requiring far too little (i.e., less than a year's work) in the areas of mathematics and natural science combined. On the other hand, over half of the schools require three or more semester courses, and over a third require two or more years' work.[28]

[27] A caveat is necessary here. Our recommendation is for two years of natural science, hoping that half will be anticipated before matriculation but requiring that at least half be taken in college. Thus our recommendation is similar to present practices depending on the way colleges and universities are currently relating secondary level work to undergraduate requirements in science.

[28] For the seventy-four schools in our sample:

| | Semester Units Required in Natural Science and Mathematics (excluding "Business Mathematics") | | | | | | |
	0	1–4	5–7	8–10	11–13	14–	Total
No. of AACSB schools	3	5	10	5	8	6	37
No. of non-AACSB schools	2	6	7	9	7	6	37
Total	5	11	17	14	15	12	74

The Social Sciences

THE "BEHAVIORAL SCIENCES"

Of all the subjects which he might undertake to study formally, none is more appropriate for the businessman-to-be than human behavior. It is not the general or liberal values alone that justify the inclusion of this topic in the business curriculum. The very nature of the firm and of the manager's role in the firm suggests that every person anticipating a responsible position in a modern business enterprise needs a substantial amount of knowledge about human behavior. Thus, we stress human behavior as an element in the undergraduate business curriculum more for its professional implications than for its general educational significance, although the latter is far from unimportant. Chester Barnard has stated the argument succinctly:

The need of understanding in the field of human relations would justify long discussion. I shall confine myself to three points, all of which I think are susceptible, at the initial stages at least, of treatment in educational institutions. The first I would stress is the need of inculcating an appreciation of the importance and of the inevitability of nonlogical behavior on the part of human beings.

Next, I think an adequate understanding in the field of human relations involves instruction as to the nature of general social systems. I am aware that, in their present state, sociology, social anthropology, and social psychology, particularly as sciences as distinct from philosophic disciplines, have been subject to much criticism.

There is in my opinion much that is valuable to be taught about general social systems; but for the present, at least, it might well be presented to the young student not so much as science but rather as something much better than any common-sense understanding of the world he lives in can be.

My last suggestion with respect to understanding in the field of human relations is that there should be instruction about formal organizations as organic and evolving systems.

In this connection I should like to make clear my reason for emphasis upon formal organizations as *organic* and *evolving* social systems. It is that we persistently think about such systems in terms of mechanical, rather than biological, analogy. Our widespread use of mechanical and electrical systems makes this convenient. It results in regarding an organization as static and fixed, like a machine, instead of something that is living, that has to grow up, and that is ever progressing or regressing with changing states of equilibrium of the human forces involved.[29]

[29] Chester I. Barnard, "Education for Executives," *The Journal of Business*, XVIII (October 1945), 177–78.

By human behavior we mean most of the subject matter of the fields of psychology, sociology, and (cultural) anthropology. Essentially, this is the concern of what has come to be called "the behavioral sciences," which in turn may be defined as "the scientific study of human behavior." We also accept the view which holds that the behavioral sciences should be broadly enough defined to "embrace the study of man at the level of the individual, the primary or intermediate group, or the mass society or civilization. . . ."[30] It will be convenient, however, to discuss in this section only the three fields mentioned and to leave for later the fact that other fields, such as economics, political science, and history, have behavioral aspects.

Our present concern about human behavior implies the view that business administration is the enlightened application of the behavioral sciences, *inter alia*, to business problems.[31] But to what extent do schools of business accept this view?

Except for some of the graduate schools of business, they hardly accept it at all, if undergraduate curricula are to be the evidence. Only an eighth of the seventy-four schools in our sample required a course in sociology, about a fourth required psychology, and none required anthropology.[32] Of the twenty-three schools requiring any behavioral science, only eight were members of the AACSB, although our sample is divided evenly between Association and non-Association schools.[33]

[30] From *A Report on the Behavioral Sciences at the University of Chicago* (October 1, 1954), p. 5. For further discussion, cf. The Ford Foundation, *Annual Report for 1953*, p. 64; *The Behavioral Sciences at Harvard* (June, 1954); and *Survey of the Behavioral Sciences at the University of Michigan* (July 1, 1954), pp. 3f.

[31] Although this implies that business administration is neither an intellectually and scientifically detached "art" nor merely applied economics, we do not subscribe to the idea which has wide acceptance among some business educators that the behavioral—or social—sciences include essentially all the important learning experiences that should constitute an undergraduate business program. Cf. Hollis and Taylor, *Social Work Education in the United States*, p. 202, for a discussion of the same issue but in the context of another profession; Donald K. David, "The Tasks of Business Education," in Thomas H. Carroll, ed., *Business Education for Competence and Responsibility* (1954), p. 21; W. Lloyd Warner, "Social Science in Business Education," in *The Challenge of Business Education* (1949), pp. 20–29; and J. H. S. Bossard and J. F. Dewhurst, *University Education for Business* (1931), p. 103.

[32] The detail for our seventy-four school sample is as follows:

| | Number of Schools Having Requirements in Psychology and Sociology | | | | | |
	Psychology Only	Sociology Only	Both	Either	Neither	Total
AACSB schools	6	1	1	8	29	37
Non-AACSB schools	8	2	5	15	22	37
Total	14	3	6	23	51	74

[33] Representatives from over a dozen schools of business gathered in a two-day conference at the School of Business of the University of Chicago in May, 1958, to discuss the role of the behavioral sciences in the school of business. This is one of several recent indications of a growing interest in this subject by the more progressive business schools.

This apparent lack of concern at the undergraduate level is somewhat perplexing, particularly since, in our discussions with deans and faculty members, we heard repeatedly the refrain that business administration draws heavily on, and is to some extent a synthesis of, a number of basic fields, including economics, psychology, and sociology.

It is quite possible, of course, that there is some significant lag between the acceptance of an idea and its implementation, and that the present idea is a fairly recent one. This can be accepted as a partial explanation, but only as a partial one. While interest in the "behavioral sciences" has grown rapidly in recent years, recognition of the relevance of psychology and sociology for business administration is of long standing and was emphasized by Bossard and Dewhurst nearly thirty years ago.[34] Another factor has been the trend over several decades toward more technical and specialized training in the business schools, with an associated neglect of the basic preprofessional areas. Unfortunately, the view of many business school faculty members is so narrow and vocational that they display little interest in anything other than their own specialties. There is also a certain provincialism on the part of some social science departments, which may evince little interest in cooperating with the business schools or in serving any students other than their own majors.

Finally, the essential fundamentals of the behavioral sciences may be included in the course offerings of the business school in such fashion that the need for separate, formal work is partially removed. It is indeed often the case that some psychology or sociology finds its way into such courses as advertising, market research, management principles, personnel management, or human relations. It could hardly be otherwise. The question then becomes not *whether* but *how* the relevant and significant contributions of the behavioral sciences can best be integrated into the undergraduate business curriculum.

This statement of the issue makes explicit an important problem faced by every professional department—a problem which involves much more than the behavioral sciences. But it implies other problems also, particularly the general issue of the relations between the professional school and the liberal arts departments. It seems to us that the basic work in the social or behavioral sciences should be offered by instructors trained in these fields, and not as byproducts in business courses staffed by persons whose primary training and interests are probably inadequate for the job that is required. If psychology or any other discipline is indispensable for the proper preparation of business graduates, the principles of that field should be taught by someone trained in the field, and not by a marketing

---

[34] Cf. *University Education for Business*, pp. 359ff.

or management instructor. This is entirely apart from the question as to whether these courses should be offered within the business school or not. This should be a matter for local determination.

Our recommendation is that the undergraduate business curriculum include a minimum of one year's work in the behavioral sciences at an introductory level, stressing concepts, problems, principles, and methods.[35] Local conditions will usually severely limit the alternatives available. It is likely that one semester each of General Psychology and Introduction to Sociology will be the only sequence which can quickly be included in the curriculum in many cases. Most of the schools now having requirements in this area specify one-semester courses.[36] Various types of introductory survey courses, if well designed and taught, are also appropriate. However, survey courses should be approached with care. While they can be very useful if well done, they run the danger of failing to give the student sufficient command of the separate bodies of knowledge that he is required to integrate. There is also the problem that introductory courses designed chiefly for psychology or sociology majors are not necessarily appropriate for business and other students not intending to major in these fields. This problem is likely to be more acute in a university than in a college atmosphere. Where this is a serious problem and suitable introductory courses are not available, the business school either can embark upon what may be a long-term campaign to gain cooperation from the social science departments involved, or it can offer the necessary work itself.

Business schools need also to be beware of special interests, within both the social science and business departments. Courses in industrial sociology, motivation research, personnel testing, and human relations are not suitable vehicles for meeting the present need. Our recommendation has as its goal the exposure of prospective business leaders to the *fundamentals* of the behavioral sciences. Intermediate level or special-topic courses such as those listed should come *after* the introductory sequence

[35] We are not qualified to indicate what topics should be covered by this requirement. However, as a purely suggestive device we do offer the following list of the kinds of topics from psychology, sociology, and cultural anthropology which might well be considered in the naming or specifying of such a requirement: perception and perceptual organization; motivation, emotion, and frustration; adaptive behavior, particularly creative problem-solving and learning; measurement and abilities, growth and behavior, and personality and conflict; social psychology generally; social organization, including large- and small-scale organizations and social stratification; population and human ecology; collective behavior; social change; and culture and personality.

[36] Number of schools in our sample requiring varying amounts of "behavioral science:"

Semester units required	None	1-4	5-7	8-10	Total
Number of schools	51	13	8*	2	74

Five of these require one semester each of two different fields.

and be recognized for what they are—important elements of various applied fields in business.

OTHER SOCIAL SCIENCES (EXCEPT ECONOMICS)

In addition to the "behavioral sciences"—and aside from economic
principles, which will be considered separately—there are a number of
other fields which the analysis of Part II suggests might be included in an
undergraduate business curriculum, particularly history (including economic history), political science, and geography.

Clearly, an adequate general education should include some work in
these fields. Many schools recognize this by requiring that students use
part of their electives for work in the social sciences, or by actually specifying requirements in history or political science. Nearly 70 per cent of
the schools specify courses in history (including economic history) or
political science, while about 40 per cent have a requirement of social
science electives. When schools do specify history or political science,
they typically require between one and two years' work.[37] The schools
that state their requirements in terms of social science electives also tend
to require from one to two years' work.

Our recommendation in the area of history and political science is for
the inclusion of at least twelve semester units in these two fields. This
would normally cover at least one year of history, with the remainder
being additional history, economic history, political science or government, etc. Local conditions—for example, state or university requirements in American history and government—must, of course, be taken
into account. General social science or "western civilization" courses
could easily be fitted into this category.[38]

We have no illusions that this suggested requirement is anything more
than a bare minimum. More would be desirable for professional reason
alone, entirely apart from arguments based on considerations of good
citizenship and general culture. We have stressed repeatedly the im-

[37] For the seventy-four schools in our sample:

	Semester Units Required in History (including Economic History) and Political Science						
	0	1–4	5–7	8–10	11–13	14–	Total
No. of AACSB schools	12	8	7	5	4	1	37
No. of non-AACSB schools	11	1	7	11	7	0	37
Total	23	9	14	16	11	1	74

[38] Courses like Business History, The Role of Business in Modern Society, and Competitive
Ideas in an Industrial Society, on the one hand, and History of Science on the other, could
conceivably be counted, although they might as easily go toward the fulfillment of, respectively,
the professional and natural science requirements.

portance to the businessman of historical perspective, breadth and flexibility of mind, and awareness of and ability to adjust to a continuously changing environment. Our suggested requirements in history and political science will certainly not achieve this objective by themselves. But they can make a start, on which other courses and the student's own reading can further build.

THE TOTAL REQUIREMENT IN SOCIAL SCIENCES
OTHER THAN ECONOMICS

The preceding two sections have dealt with undergraduate requirements in psychology, sociology, anthropology, history, and political sci-

TABLE 10

SEMESTER UNITS REQUIRED IN SOCIAL SCIENCES
IN SEVENTY-FOUR SELECTED BUSINESS SCHOOLS

Type of School	Number of Schools Requiring Indicated Number of Semester Units								
	0	1–4	5–7	8–10	11–13	14–16	17–19	20+	Total
AACSB schools	3	4	6	10	5	6	1	2	37
Non-AACSB schools	2	1	7	6	12	6	2	1	37
Total	5	5	13	16	17	12	3	3	74

ence, and excluded all economics except economic history. Our recommendations add up to about eighteen semester units—six in the behavioral sciences and twelve in history and political science.

It would appear that in each of these areas we recommend somewhat more than business schools are currently requiring. In each case, however, there is some understatement of existing requirements because of the variety of ways undergraduate curricula are constructed. It is useful, therefore, to compare our combined recommendations of eighteen semester units in all social sciences (except economics) with combined requirements in our sample of business schools. Table 10 summarizes information previously presented in this chapter, although the totals are shown for the first time.

The figures still understate conditions at schools which, as a matter of school or university policy, rely on students' judgment or the faculty's advising effectiveness instead of detailed statements of distributional requirements. It is hardly likely that the five schools apparently requiring no course work in the social sciences certify for the undergraduate degree

students with absolutely no social science except elementary economics
And yet it may be that some students are graduated from these (and
other) institutions with woefully inadequate amounts and kinds of social
science training. This is part of the problem of "specification" versus
"election." The information presented in this section can be interpreted
as being approximately indicative of current practices, with the distor-
tion being mainly on the side of underestimation.[39]

Even if we allow for some understatement, Table 10 suggests that our
minimum recommendation of eighteen semester units is met or exceeded
by only a minority of business schools. If we allow a tolerance of a one
semester course for the kind of problem discussed in the preceding paragraph, we can conclude that well over half of the schools have requirements in the social sciences which are inadequate as to amount. Needless
to say, even fewer schools have satisfactory requirements when content is
also considered.

ECONOMICS

Economics encompasses subject matter which, from the point of view
of the business school, is essential for both general and professional education. In a real sense it occupies a pivotal position in the business curriculum. At the beginning of this chapter, we decided to include economic
principles and economic history under the heading of general education
and to treat all other economics offerings under the heading of professional education. Arbitrary though this decision is, it still seems to be the
most expedient of the several alternatives.

Since we have dealt with economic history in connection with the discussion of the other social sciences, it is necessary here to consider only
the question of the introductory economics course, which, though going
under several slightly different labels, is omnipresent in business school
curricula. In fact, not only did elementary economics appear in every
curriculum examined, but it nearly always appeared as a year's course.[40]

The present practice of offering a year's sequence in elementary economics is one with which we concur. We also agree with the implication
of the words "elementary" and "principles" which occur so often in the
titles of such courses. Although we agree with this implied emphasis on

---

[39] Another warning is necessary regarding geography, usually considered as one of the
social sciences. Our tallies exclude courses in commercial, business, and economic geography
on the grounds that they are essentially professional courses. The social science totals here
would be slightly higher if the offerings of the nine AACSB and seven nonmember schools in
our sample requiring such courses were included.

[40] There is some variation as to exact number of credit hours (e.g., six or eight semester
units, eight or ten quarter units), but this seems to be insignificant.

analysis or theory, we urge strongly that business and economics faculties cooperate in experimenting with alternative ways of organizing and
presenting economics at the elementary level.

General Education: A Summary of Recommendations

In the preceding pages a number of recommendations have been made
regarding the desirable distribution of the nonprofessional portion of the
undergraduate business student's four years. It may be desirable to summarize these recommendations before proceeding in the next chapter to

TABLE 11

SUGGESTED MINIMUM GENERAL EDUCATION PROGRAM

FOR UNDERGRADUATE BUSINESS STUDENTS

Subject	Semester Courses	Semester Units or Hours
Humanities and fine arts	8-9	24-27
English language and literature	4-5	12-15
Humanities and fine arts electives	4	12
Natural sciences and mathematics	4-8	12-24
Mathematics	2-4	6-12
Natural sciences	2-4	6-12
Behavioral—social sciences	8	24
Behavioral sciences	2	6
Economics—elementary	2	6
Other social sciences	4	12
Total general education component	20-25	60-75

consider the professional component of the undergraduate's training and
education.

Our first recommendation was that at least half of the four years' undergraduate curriculum should be nonprofessional. This compares with
the requirement of the AACSB of "at least 40 per cent." Current practice
falls considerably short of what we propose, with roughly five out of six
schools falling below our standard of two years of nonprofessional work.

We have recommended further that these sixty semester hours be specified in some detail rather than be left largely to the student's discretion.
We do this on the grounds that the content of the general education part
of a student's undergraduate work is as important as the content of the
professional portion.

Our suggestions for a minimum program in general education for undergraduate business students is summarized in Table 11. In terms of the usual three-unit courses, our recommendations call for two years or more in English composition, speech, and literature; two additional years in the humanities; one year or more of college-level mathematics; one to two years of natural science, depending on secondary school preparation; a year each in the behavioral sciences and elementary economics; and two years in history and political science.

All of this adds up to about half of a four-year program—or more if the student is deficient in English language, mathematics, or science. Such students, of course, must expect to take a little longer to secure a degree. R.O.T.C. and physical education would also increase the degree requirement beyond 120 semester units. We have assumed that 120 semester units of academic work, exclusive of R.O.T.C. and physical education, constitute a full undergraduate program.[41]

The nonprofessional curriculum proposed here should be interpreted as a minimum. Students should be encouraged or required to take more work in some areas, depending on particular interests and local conditions. It should also be noted that our recommendations exclude advanced economics (which will be considered in Chapter 9), vocational skill courses in shorthand and typing (which should not be offered for degree credit), and nonuniversity level courses such as are frequently offered in business mathematics and arithmetic, business letter-writing and English, commercial geography, etc.

And finally, it cannot be emphasized too strongly that our recommendations are intended to imply something regarding the *kind* or *content* of the courses to be offered. For example, it should not be possible to meet the behavioral science requirement by a year's course in industrial psychology, or the requirement in mathematics by work in elementary algebra and mathematics of finance. The English requirement should mean composition, literature, and speech; the mathematics requirement should mean college-level instruction in "modern mathematical analysis"; the natural science requirement should involve an introduction to the physical and biological sciences, including a year's laboratory work in college; the behavioral science requirement should introduce the student to the concepts, problems, principles, and methods of psychology, sociology, and, perhaps, anthropology; and the "other social sciences" requirement should include work in history, political science, and related areas.

[41] Undergraduate professional curricula tend to require more than 120 semester units. The typical, four-year engineering curriculum requires about 140 semester units. (See Chapter 10). Business curricula may have to move in this direction.

On the other hand, it must be recognized that local conditions vary, and hence some flexibility is necessary. There should also be room for experimentation. But we repeat a position taken earlier. Significant departures from these broad recommendations should be encouraged only if they are based on clearly enunciated educational objectives that in general conform to those presented in Part II of this report. Unfortunately, present practices which fall considerably short of our suggested standards can seldom be justified on these grounds. The business school that permits its students to graduate with even less than 40 per cent of their work in nonbusiness courses, with little or no college-level work in science and mathematics, and with their preparation in English confined to business letter-writing, is not experimenting in an attempt to implement better the desirable educational goals. It is simply offering a poor grade of education which inadequately prepares the student either for life or for a responsible business career.

We turn now to consider the purely professional part of the curriculum.

chapter 9

THE UNDERGRADUATE

CURRICULUM:

PROFESSIONAL EDUCATION

IN CONSIDERING the professional component of the undergraduate curriculum, we shall, as in Chapter 8, begin with the conclusions of Part II and proceed to translate them into specific recommendations. The reader should remember that our recommendations are to be interpreted merely as providing guidelines, within which considerable variation and opportunity for experimentation are possible. The important thing is that the business schools move in the general direction that has been indicated. The detailed curriculum suggested here offers one way of doing this, but the same objective can be achieved through a number of variants of the particular program that we suggest. Whatever the particular curriculum adopted, it should, in our opinion, satisfy two criteria. It should seek to meet the educational needs described in Part II, and it should be subject to frequent revision in the light of increased knowledge.

The bulk of this chapter is concerned with the business core, that is, those courses required of all business students regardless of the particular area within business administration in which they may choose to specialize. This concept of a core as an indispensable body of courses is a common one in education and has been a part of some business curricula for many years. It was not until 1949, however, that the AACSB specified a core to which all member schools were to be held. Although the content of that core continues to change, and although we shall have to criticize the Association's present requirements on a number of counts, this step in 1949 was an important one. It has had a significant and continuing impact on both member and nonmember schools. It has led to greater uniformity in requirements and to some raising of standards, particularly among the poorer schools.

After the core concept, the growing emphasis on "management" has probably been the most important curriculum development in business education since the Second World War. This interest in management has taken two forms. First, it has now become fairly common to stress a "managerial approach" in many courses, with an increased emphasis on managerial problem-solving, particularly through the use of cases. Second, there has been, especially in the last few years, a growing number of attempts to identify and to develop a field of study which might be called management or administration.

We shall later discuss the increasing emphasis on management problems in the teaching of the functional fields. First, however, we need to examine one of the most perplexing curriculum problems that the business schools are currently facing. What should be taught in the field variously called "management," "administration," or "organization?"

At present, there is no generally agreed answer to this question. We shall begin, therefore, by considering the various ways in which the field of management or administration can be interpreted and follow this with our suggestions as to what should be required in this area. Then in subsequent sections we shall deal with the other parts of the business core: the functional fields (marketing, finance, personnel and industrial relations, and production), information and control systems (chiefly accounting and statistics), advanced economics, the legal framework of business, and business policy.

Most business schools require a field of specialization beyond the core, and in many schools this requirement is quite substantial. In the latter part of this chapter, we shall review prevailing practices in this regard and suggest some ways in which we think these practices need to be improved.

Alternative Approaches to The Field of Management

In Part II we stressed the importance of the administrative aspects of business from a number of points of view. The businessman's decision-making is done in an organizational context and is affected by that context. Hence, as was pointed out in Chapter 4, the businessman needs to know something about how human beings function in organizations, what conditions are necessary to secure effective action within organizations, and what problems arise when one attempts to make and to implement decisions within organizations. In addition, Chapters 5 and 6 cited a large body of evidence regarding the need to develop in future businessmen the various organizational skills—skill in handling administrative relationships, skill in interpersonal relations, and skill in communication.

All this is by now generally recognized. But how do we define the bodies of knowledge that are relevant, and what should the business schools teach in order to develop an understanding of organizational behavior and some modicum of organizational skill?

It seems to us that there are at least four different aspects of the field of "administration and organization" that need to be distinguished. Failure to make these (or similar) distinctions, we suspect, is one important reason why many schools have had so much difficulty in deciding what should be taught in this field. The four aspects that need to be distinguished are: 1) methods of managerial problem-solving, an area which for brevity we shall call management analysis, 2) organization theory, 3) management principles, and 4) human relations.[1]

By *management analysis* we mean an explicitly rational approach to the making of decisions about the allocation of resources within the firm. What is involved is a study of the methods available for the analysis and solution of the substantive problems which are the concern of economic management. The scientific approach to managerial decision-making has had its greatest development within the area of production management, beginning with Frederick Taylor and his disciples and extending up to the latest developments in operations analysis. Since the Second World War, quantitative and, more broadly, scientific methods of analysis have been applied to a steadily widening area of management problems.

The methods available for a scientific or rational approach to managerial decision-making can be viewed broadly or narrowly. Broadly considered, they include any techniques that help the decision-maker to discover and evaluate alternatives and to make that choice which seems, in the light of given objectives, to be most rational. In this broad sense, management analysis includes all analytical and informational tools that contribute to a scientific approach to any management problem. The methods used may be quite crude, and little in the way of rigorous quantitative analysis may be involved. In this broad sense, a considerable part of the business curriculum may be concerned with management analysis.[2]

In a narrower and more technical sense, management analysis can refer to those more sophisticated quantitative techniques that have been developed to aid in rational decision-making. These methods have found

---

[1] We are not completely satisfied with this classification, and, as we note later, there is considerable overlapping among the categories. Despite this, we have found this sort of differentiation useful in our own thinking and hope it will prove useful to others. Although the classification is our own, we do not think it is inconsistent with the literature on management. Cf. H. Koontz and C. O'Donnell, *Principles of Management* (2nd ed., 1959), chap. 2; and J. G. March and H. A. Simon, *Organizations* (1958). Cf. also the contents of such journals as *Administrative Science Quarterly* and *Management Science*—particularly Gifford H. Symonds, "The Institute of Management Sciences: Progress Report," *Management Science*, III (January, 1957), 119–28.

[2] If we take this broad point of view, then much of what is involved in a good course in business policy, oriented toward developing skill (including judgment) in decision-making, might be subsumed under the heading of "management analysis."

their greatest use in the solving of production problems but have also been used to deal with problems in, for example, marketing, transportation, and finance. Management analysis in this more technical sense draws on such fields as statistical decision theory, mathematical programming, inventory theory, and motion economy, and includes much of what goes under the heading of operations analysis. It is sometimes referred to as "management science."[3] In the rest of this chapter, we shall, unless otherwise stated, use the term "management analysis" in this narrow and more technical sense.

Organization theory, or "theory of administration," is concerned with the scientific study of human behavior in organizations. It deals with how human beings function in organizations, with what conditions are necessary to secure effective action within organizations, and with the problems that arise in connection with making and implementing decisions in an organizational context. It might also be described as dealing with the internal organizational "environment" of the business firm (and other types of organizations).[4]

As management analysis has its roots in microeconomics, mathematics, statistics, and accounting, so organization theory draws heavily on the behavioral sciences; in addition, it also can draw on such disciplines as mathematics, statistics, and biology. Organization theory does not, as some have assumed, center around the economic theory of the firm, decision theory, or game theory; nor is it concerned primarily with spelling out "management principles" regarding such matters as span of control, delegation of authority and responsibility, and the basic elements of the management function. It is a (synthesized) discipline rather than an applied field, and as such it is not concerned with problems from the normative point of view. That is, it seeks to develop testable generalizations about certain aspects of human behavior but does not set out to prescribe what should be done to achieve particular goals. Being concerned in good part with the interactions between individuals and their organizational environment, it substantially overlaps the more scientific parts of human relations. But it is more than human relations, because it is concerned with the total organizational context and the ways in which this affects decision-making.

In the last few years there has been a sharpened interest in this field of

---

[3] See, for example, the journal, *Management Science*, published by The Institute of Management Sciences.

[4] Cf. the discussion in Chapter 4. Clearly this definition does not limit organization theory to the study of business organizations. Another definition has been offered to us by Professor Mason Haire of the University of California: Organization theory is the collection of an integrated set of abstract generalizations about the interrelations of people and processes in groups with productive objectives. (In a letter to the authors.)

organization theory, and a few schools have been groping toward the development of a teachable and useful course in this area.

In contrast to the first two, that part of the field of management which we would label *principles of management* is concerned with describing and distilling the best of current management practices into a set of generalizations which workers in this area call principles.[5] It differs from organization theory, also, in terms of methodology (more pragmatic), level of abstraction (less theoretical), the viewpoint from which problems are considered (more the viewpoint of higher management officials), and emphasis placed on individual attitudes and motivation (less emphasis on the individual as a variable). On the other hand, the more scientifically based portion of management principles can be derived from organization theory, just as some of the hypotheses the organizational theorist might wish to test might originate as "principles" of management. The two fields overlap and supplement each other.

The area of management principles has been playing an increasingly important role in business school curricula since the Second World War. Several textbooks in the field have been widely used, and in addition there is a considerable body of journal and monographic writings.[6]

The fourth aspect of management is the familiar one of *human relations.*[7] A fair number of schools require work in human relations, either in a separate course or as part of some kind of course in management.[8] Clearly human relations can be close to management principles in its methodol-

---

[5] The use of this latter term would seem to the organizational theorist to be a euphemism, for the "principles" are not generated by the hypothesis-and-test route. But in the sense that a principle is a settled rule or law of action or conduct, students of management principles are justified in using the term.

[6] Relevant writings include those of Fayol, Gulick, Urwick, White, R. C. Davis, Dimock, Holden, Mooney, Sheldon, Drucker, and Newman. Cf. Koontz and O'Donnell, *Principles of Management*, p. ix and chap. 2. For some critical comments on the "proverbs of administration" that pass as principles of management, see H. A. Simon, *Administrative Behavior* (2nd ed., 1957), pp. xxxiii–xxxiv and chap. 2.

[7] This is an area which, in its normative aspects, overlaps management principles and also the functional field of personnel administration. As a body of generalizations it overlaps organization theory as well as social and industrial psychology and several branches of sociology. The literature on human relations, in both its positive and its normative (human engineering) aspects, is too vast to cite here. Courses on human relations seem to rely on special textbooks written for the purpose, on casebooks and books of readings, on texts in social and industrial psychology, and on a variety of journal and monographic literature. As examples, see B. B. Gardner and D. G. Moore, *Human Relations in Industry* (3rd ed., 1955); Mason Haire, *Psychology in Management* (1956); and Robert Dubin, *Human Relations in Administration* (1951).

[8] Instruction in human relations is taught not only under this title but also under such labels as principles of administration or management, administrative practices, personnel management, introduction to management, etc. For examples of present practice, cf. C. E. Summer, Jr., *Factors in Effective Administration* (1956) and the separately published "Appendix III: The Development of Administrative Effectiveness."

ogy and normative orientation, since, as human relations is usually taught, it is concerned with "practical" considerations and situations. Although theory derived from the behavioral sciences may be utilized, the emphasis is usually on the development of rules and principles which can be applied readily to situations that managers are likely to encounter. On the other hand, a theoretical course without normative prescriptions, deeply rooted in psychology and sociology, can be devised and is so taught in some schools.

The undergraduate business curriculum should probably include instruction in each of these four aspects of management. "Methods of managerial decision-making" or management analysis can enter into the curriculum in a number of places: in a fourth semester of quantitative controls as suggested later, in the kind of course on production management that we shall describe, in the other functional courses, or in the course on business policy. Human relations can also be taught in several places: as a separate course, in connection with organization theory or management principles, or possibly, if one is given, in a course on personnel administration. These possibilities will be investigated as we proceed. But now we wish to consider the place of "organization theory" and "management principles" in the curriculum.

The Place of Organization Theory and Principles of Management

Repeatedly in Part II we emphasized the need to develop the student's organizational skills and his understanding of the organizational problems with which the business manager must deal. This suggests that the business curriculum should contain materials on the organizational context of business decision-making. More specifically, we recommend that some work be required in the area of "administration-organization" which would combine the second and third aspects of management described in the preceding section. The first of these is based on a body of generalizations that we referred to as *organization theory;* the second, the pragmatically derived body of knowledge which was labeled *management principles.* Although their origins and methodologies are quite different, they deal, to a considerable extent, with a common set of problems.

The accumulation of knowledge in both these areas is meager, although writers from Fayol to the author of the latest textbook have produced a considerable body of literature on "the principles of management." In fact, serious doubt exists in some quarters that a systematic body of knowledge which can be called organization theory does in fact yet exist.

Nonetheless, we think that the following conclusions are valid: organizational skill is a necessary concomitant of effective business operation; formal instruction can make a significant contribution to the development of such skill; sufficient knowledge presently exists for formal university-level courses to be offered; and, finally, the amount of knowledge about organizations, business and otherwise, will increase greatly in amount, relevance, and importance in the years to come.

CURRENT PRACTICE

Courses in management or administration are by now quite common, and some business schools have set up departments of management or organization. But these labels cover a wide variety of practices as well as, in some cases, considerable confusion as to the meaning of the labels themselves.[9]

A good illustration of this confusion regarding management as a field and its place in the curriculum can be found in the standards of the AACSB and in the ways in which member schools interpret these standards. The 1958 "Standards for Membership" of the Association lists management as one of seven fields in which "candidates for the undergraduate degree shall receive basic instruction." Management is interpreted "to denote Industrial or Production Management, or an integrating course in organization and management or a business policy course." Apparently, factory management, human relations (if properly labeled), "pure" organization theory, and principles of management all satisfy this requirement equally well, as does a case course in business policy that offers practice in solving any kind of business problem. Each of these courses is actually used to satisfy this requirement by one or another member school. The only thing that can be said for this confusion is that it perhaps represents a better situation than the earlier standards of the Association which limited management to production or personnel management.[10]

One important reason for this confusion is the failure to distinguish

[9] For a useful survey of current practice and thinking in the business schools, see Summer, *Factors in Effective Administration.*

[10] The initial, 1949 standards of the Association identified seven core fields, one being "production or industrial management." The Executive Committee at the same time issued an interpretation: "Production or Industrial Management is used as a generic term to describe courses in Industrial Management, Production Management, Industrial Relations, and Personnel Management, Production Planning and Control, as well as courses in manufacturing or production." Cf. "The Development of Curricular Standards of the American Association of Collegiate Schools of Business, with Particular Reference to the Business Base," a paper delivered by Thomas L. Norton at the annual meeting of the Middle Atlantic Association of Collegiate Schools of Business, October 11, 1957 (mimeographed).

among the different approaches to "management" that we have tried to delineate. This failure, in turn, reflects the long lag between developments in the scientific literature, refinements in business practice, and experiments of the most progressive schools, on the one hand, and standard educational practice, on the other.

The kinds of developments which many business schools have not yet absorbed and translated into their curriculum planning include: 1) the broadening of the concept of "scientific management" from its original narrow sense so that it now applies to all aspects of management; 2) the spread of interest in the field of human relations—including increasing emphasis on the notion that management or administration is "getting things done through people;" 3) the growing concern with problems of internal organization as increasing size has multiplied administrative problems; 4) the increasing attention being paid to problems of organization and group behavior by social scientists; 5) the recent dramatic applications of electronic means of storing and processing information; and 6) the beginning of a stream of successful efforts to solve business problems through the use of mathematical and statistical techniques utilizing hypotheses borrowed from various of the social and natural sciences.[11] Attempts by various schools to reflect some or all of these developments in their teaching have not been helped by the prevalence of the idea that all courses should reflect a managerial viewpoint and should utilize the "case" method of teaching.

Another source of difficulty is the fact that present management offerings in many schools are administered by the department which has long offered the work in production management. This has not made for fresh thinking or for mastery of the most recent literature. The problem can be seen in the extent to which elements of obsolete courses in production or industrial management find their way into new courses presumably dealing with the broader aspects of management.

From what has been said, it is clear that a tabulation of course offerings or requirements in management is not likely to reveal very much about the realities of current practice. Still, such a count is not without some interest. For our sample of seventy-four schools, we tabulated the required courses having titles such as organization, administration, and principles of management—hopefully what we have termed organization theory and management principles. While "management" in this sense is not unequivocally a requirement of the AACSB, somewhat more than half the schools in the Association apparently require one or more "manage-

[11] We do not imply that all of these developments should be treated in the same course. To do so would be to fall victim to just the sort of confusion we are criticizing.

ment" courses.[12] The same is true of schools of business which are not members of the AACSB. Courses with still other labels may occasionally contain material on management in the sense intended here, although it is rash to place much confidence in course titles. The same caution applies to departments of "management," which are likely to administer the school's offerings in the field of production and personnel and possibly also in office management and other special areas.[13]

A SUGGESTED REQUIREMENT

Our own recommendation is that schools include in their degree requirements a specification of three to six semester hours in the general area of organization theory and management principles, possibly including human relations. Schools will need to experiment to determine how instruction in these areas should be organized.

We can do no more than suggest in the most general way the kinds of topics that should be included in a course or sequence in organization-management. The field is still in too inchoate a form for us to do more than this, and, to repeat, each school needs to experiment and to share its experiences with others.

On the side of organization theory, there is a not inconsiderable literature by sociologists, psychologists, political scientists, and economists.[14] The material on management principles is more widely known and, unlike that on organization theory, has already been synthesized in some widely used texts. We suspect that, for the time being, the wisest procedure at the undergraduate level is to plan a course that will combine

[12] For the seventy-four schools in our sample:

	Number of Schools Requiring Courses in Fields Indicated	
	AACSB Schools	*Non-AACSB Schools*
Organization and Administration	4	10
General management	17	13
Either one	21	20
Neither one	16	17
(Production or industrial management)	(16)	(12)

[13] See, for example, a survey of management departments conducted by the Ohio State management faculty, *A Survey of Administrative Policies, Plans, and Practices of Management Departments and Divisions in Leading Universities in the United States* (1954, mimeographed). Our thanks are due to Professor K. D. Reyer of Louisiana State University for calling our attention to this report.

[14] In addition to the widely cited volumes by Chester Barnard (*The Functions of the Executive* [1938]) and Simon (*Administrative Behavior*), see also the journal, *Administrative Science Quarterly*, and the very useful survey of the literature entitled *Organizations*, by March and Simon. Among the topics that are critically reviewed in the latter volume are "classical" organization theory (including the contributions of the scientific management movement), the need to treat the individual as a variable in studying organizational structure and behavior, the way in which conflict in organizations affects decision-making, and the cognitive aspects of decision-making in organizations.

in some proportions not only organization theory and management principles but also some human relations, particularly since the significant generalizations in the last named area are really a part of the broader area of organization theory. One possibility is a two semester sequence, the first of which would provide a general orientation in the interrelated areas of organization theory, human relations, and management principles, and the second of which would concentrate on the development of organizational (including human relations) skills through the use of cases and various types of role-playing techniques. This, however, is only one of a number of alternatives and not necessarily the best one.

The Market Environment and Functional Management: The Functional Fields

In Chapter 4 we emphasized that the business firm is concerned with problems of *economic management* and that such management is strongly conditioned by the *market environment* within which it operates. The firm acquires men, money, and materials, and combines them in order to offer something for sale.

Thus firms operate in commodity, labor, and financial markets, and have problems of economic management which can be considered under the headings of marketing, production, employee relations, and finance. In other words, the traditional functional fields of the business curriculum have both an internal-managerial and an external-market aspect. Thus we have both marketing and marketing management, finance and financial management, and, on a slightly different basis, industrial relations and personnel management. The field of production, on the other hand, has chiefly only a managerial aspect, although it can also include consideration of the environmental factors (science, technology, and the like, as well as relative factor prices) that affect the purely managerial aspects of production.

The business student needs some understanding of each of the kinds of markets within which the business firm must operate. This entails some study of the structure and functioning of commodity, financial, and labor markets. This work should for the most part be at a high, analytical level, although a certain amount of institutional description cannot be avoided. Students should be asked to probe fairly deeply into the underlying market forces that help to create the kinds of marketing, financial, and personnel (including wage) problems with which the business firm must deal. This inevitably means going to the underlying disciplines—to economics and the other social sciences, including psychology and sociology—and it should also necessitate making use of the quantitative tools of statistics and accounting.

The more competent instructors in these business fields have always drawn, openly or implicitly, on the social sciences—something that social scientists and others have not always realized. The *better* courses in marketing use a fair amount of economic analysis and also draw some material from sociology and psychology. The same is true of industrial relations when it is well taught. A thorough course in finance must of necessity rest on an economic analysis of money and capital markets, although here as in the other functional fields the *typical* instructor and textbook tend to sacrifice analytical substance for descriptive detail.

But while some instructors do provide their students with challenging intellectual fare, introductory courses in the functional fields typically contain little real analysis. (We have the impression that the situation has improved slightly in the last few years.) The prevalence of low-level courses which emphasize superficial description and memory work is to be explained by a variety of factors: inadequate training of teachers and inadequate background of students, the poor intellectual atmosphere in many schools, the lack of communication with social scientists, the slow progress of research in developing significant bodies of generalizations in some of these areas, and, related to all these factors, the poor quality of many of the textbooks on which undergraduate instruction relies all too heavily.[15]

We are not competent to suggest in detail the topics that should be treated in the various functional areas. We would emphasize, however, that teaching in these fields needs to include considerable emphasis on what might be called the "external-analytical" aspects of each area and not confine itself either to pure description or to an exclusively "internal-managerial" approach. Whether it is marketing, finance, or industrial relations, the student needs to be exposed to what exists in the way of a verified body of knowledge regarding the underlying forces which shape and change the market environment within which the firm operates.

Although we emphasize an analytical approach to marketing, finance, and industrial relations, we recognize that students must also be introduced to a significant amount of descriptive material—terminology, institutions, and procedures. But this kind of teaching should be held to some irreducible minimum, a minimum very much below that which now seems to be prevalent.

We now come to the internal, managerial aspects of the functional

---

[15] For further discussion of some of these matters, see Chapters 14 (on the quality of faculty) and 15 and 16 (on teaching and research).

fields. To an increasing extent, and particularly in the schools with a strong management orientation, a managerial, problem-solving, and clinical emphasis is being given to the first, core course in each of the functional areas. This has meant, among other things, an increasing use of the case method in these courses.

This trend has been generally viewed with approval. Clearly, a problem-solving type of course, which forces students to analyze more or less complex business decisions and reach answers for themselves, is an attractive alternative to the older descriptive type of course. Within limits, it helps to develop problem-solving skill, including that intangible quality called judgment. More generally, it is important that students be exposed to the way in which problems in the functional areas present themselves to businessmen and get some practice in the ways in which solutions to these problems might be found.

But having said all this, we must now voice a note of caution. While granting that the student should not be confined to the external-analytical aspects of the functional fields, we do not think that students can begin solving the businessman's problems until they first have some analytical tools and principles with which to work—both those that concern the firm's market environment *and* those which bear on the firm's internal operations. Thus problem-solving in, for example, marketing needs to rest on an understanding of the functioning of product markets, the psychology of consumer behavior, etc.; and it needs to be based also on the economic, organizational, and other aspects of the theory of the firm.

There is a contradiction here that must be faced. The first course in a functional field is a part of the required core because in some sense it is considered to be basic. This presumably means that here the student will be exposed to a range of principles and analytical tools that he needs both for subsequent courses and for his later work in the business world. But the student cannot begin solving problems *via* real-life cases without the necessary tools and other substantive knowledge. If systematic bodies of knowledge relevant to these functional fields exist, then this knowledge belongs in the first or core courses in these fields.

We offer this caution not because we oppose the new managerial and clinical emphasis in the functional fields but because we favor what we consider to be its proper use. Particularly for undergraduates, a problem-solving and clinical treatment should rest upon a solid command of the substantive knowledge and analytical tools which are needed to make this approach a fruitful learning experience for the student. The problem-solving approach, whether at a high or low analytical level, is still too much neglected in most schools. In the weaker schools, little more than a descriptive treatment is offered. There is little emphasis either on problem-solving or on a broader kind of analytic treatment.

In the case of marketing and finance, the simplest procedure is to require a semester's work in each field, as is now the general practice.[16] The important need is to reduce the amount of descriptive detail and to increase the emphasis on both analysis and managerial problem-solving. To do this would involve a major change in course content and teaching methods in many, perhaps most, institutions. Most of the introductory courses in marketing that we examined spent too much time on descriptive detail; on the whole, this was also true of the first course in finance. For reasons we shall elaborate later, money and banking is not an adequate substitute for a course in finance, and we strongly recommend a change in the Association's standards in this respect.

We are not at all sure how the field of personnel and industrial relations can best be handled. To only a limited extent is "personnel" the managerial analogue of industrial relations. Personnel as a field is concerned more with what is called "human relations," but too often courses in personnel involve little more than a description of routine administrative procedures. On the whole, we favor having in the core a course that would concentrate on industrial relations, although some material on personnel management might be included.[17] We doubt that there is need for a second course concerned exclusively with personnel management. In any event, the teaching of personnel management, whatever the course in which it is included, should be at a high, analytical level. Next to the course in production, perhaps more educational sins have been committeed in the name of personnel management than in any other required course in the business curriculum. Personnel management is a field which has had a particularly small base of significant generalizations with which to work (beyond what is important in the area of human relations), and, partly for this reason, it is an area which has not been held in high regard in the better schools.

There is certainly no need to require a separate course in personnel if the core also includes a course in human relations. We have already suggested that material on human relations should be included in the ad-

---

[16] All Association schools in our sample required marketing, but about a fifth did not require finance. Roughly a fifth of the nonmember schools had no marketing requirement; more than a fourth did not require finance. See Table 13. For additional information on marketing, see H. E. Hardy, "Collegiate Marketing Education Since 1930," *The Journal of Marketing*. XIX (April, 1955), 327–28.

[17] About 50 per cent of the member schools in our sample and about 40 per cent of the nonmember schools require a course in either industrial relations or personnel-human relations. Among the member schools, the former is required more often than the latter.

ministration-organization sequence, where the subject of human be-havior in groups must in any event be treated. Teaching in the field of human relations, wherever it is offered, should emphasize both significant generalizations that can be drawn from psychology and sociology as well as the kind of human-relations problem-solving that has been made familiar by such courses as Harvard's "Administrative Practices."

Other ways of treating the functional areas will occur to the more imaginative schools, and experimentation should be encouraged. We should, however, like to re-emphasize one point. While a managerial emphasis and the use of cases have their place in the first courses in the functional areas, they should be subordinated to a thorough grounding in the functioning of the markets concerned and to the development of a command of the substantive knowledge and analytical tools that are needed for rational decision-making. To some extent, this analytical equipment can be put to use in problems and cases in the basic functional courses. Skill in its use can be further developed later in the "policy" course and possibly in other courses that might be designed for this purpose.

THE SPECIAL CASE OF PRODUCTION

The first course in production management raises particular problems of its own. It was originally included as a core subject by the AACSB and is still accepted as satisfying the present requirement in "management." Many schools feel obligated to offer it, although it was a part of the re-quired core in only about a fourth of the member schools and in only about an eighth of the nonmember schools in our sample. Yet there are few courses in the curriculum that have caused more problems, and it is doubtful whether any course in the core has been more poorly taught. Production management courses are often the repository for some of the most inappropriate and intellectually stultifying materials to be found in the business curriculum. Not only do many faculty members have little respect for such courses, but students in a number of schools complained more strongly to us about the pointlessness of the production requirement than of any other.[18]

The introductory course in production management typically covers such material as a description of standard machine tools, types of factory buildings and plant layouts, systems of lighting, methods of job evaluation and time and motion study, methods of handling and storing materials,

---

[18] Actually, they complained most often about statistics. But they seldom questioned, as they did in the case of production, the need for the requirement and the relevance of the materials presented.

the details of production scheduling, and so on in interminable detail. It also is likely to include some introductory material on "management organization and principles" and a bit on personnel management. The typical first course in production tends to be almost entirely descriptive and to be taught out of a textbook which, like the usual textbook on "introduction to business," has a high ratio of pictures to text. In a number of schools which have found it impossible to obtain adequately qualified staff, the course may be taught by an instructor who knows little more than his students and whose background is largely confined to reading a few standard texts.

At the other extreme, the instructor may be a manufacturing specialist, usually an engineer, who is likely to be preoccupied with problems of plant engineering. Where this is the case, the course, while at a reasonably challenging level, may be more in the field of industrial engineering than production management. Hence it is likely to be too narrow and slanted too much in the direction of engineering, given the needs which the core curriculum in business administration is supposed to serve. In addition, business undergraduates are unlikely to have the background needed for a good course in industrial engineering.

This suggests part of the problem which schools have encountered in the production field. Without some engineering background, students are not equipped for a rigorous course that deals with the kinds of topics traditionally included in the introductory course in production management. The result is that, if the course is required of all students, they get the kind of low-level and purely descriptive course we have described.

There is another problem about the way the production field is treated to which schools have given insufficient attention. Virtually all production courses concern themselves almost exclusively with *factory* production. As important as manufacturing is in the American economy, it is after all only one sector of the business world. Other types of business enterprise also have what can be called production problems, since all firms must in some way combine labor and some form of capital equipment to produce some kind of product. Thus, from the point of view of strict logic, there is no more reason for requiring a course in manufacturing production than there is for requiring a course in retail store management or bank operations.

There can be no doubt that there is a need here which is not now being met. The basic need is to give the student some understanding of the place of "production" in the totality of business operations and to teach him something about the kinds of problems that arise in production and about the tools which are available for meeting these problems.

Production problems in a firm may be classified as to whether they are essentially "technological," "human," or "economic" in nature.[19] The technological or physical problems are the domain of the engineer. His tools are primarily the engineering and natural sciences. To deal with the human aspects of production, on the other hand, we must resort to the behavioral and related sciences and the business disciplines which have been partially derived from them. Such problems are the concern both of personnel specialists and general management. Human problems are not confined to the production line and are best studied in a broader context.[20] Hence it is better to deal with them elsewhere in the curriculum, for example, in a course in management or in human relations.

The third area of production problems is the economic. It is this third range of topics, the economic problems of production (or operating) management, which should be included in the undergraduate business curriculum under the heading of production management. Such a course would introduce students to the application of *analytical techniques* to problems of allocating resources within the firm. As the engineering, natural, and social sciences have prime relevance for the technological and human problems of production, so microeconomics and the quantitative disciplines of mathematics, statistics, and accounting are most relevant for the analysis and solution of economic production problems.[21]

We suggest strongly that existing requirements in production management be reviewed in light of the considerations presented here, and that inappropriate courses—the usual case, unfortunately—be abandoned or revised. Undoubtedly, most schools will need to spend considerable time in study and experimentation before a satisfactory course can be devised. Where, for one reason or another, a satisfactory course along the lines suggested cannot be developed, production management should be excluded from the core of required courses.[22]

[19] E. H. Bowman and R. B. Fetter, among others, have recognized this distinction. Cf. their *Analysis for Production Management* (1957), p. 6. Our discussion owes much to this text.

[20] There are, of course, varieties of problems involving *people* which are more or less unique to the production process. But this is not a strong argument for teaching them under the heading of production.

[21] In this connection, see Alexander King's comments regarding the range of problems which "tend to be dismissed by the engineer as being the province of the economist, and by the economist as being the province of the technologist." "Management as a Technology," *Impact of Science on Society*, VIII (June, 1957), esp. pp. 83–84.

[22] For examples of some of the topics which might be included in the kind of course we propose, see Bowman and Fetter, *Analysis for Production Management*. This book, written for juniors and others in the School of Industrial Management at M.I.T., may assume too much mathematics for some business undergraduates, although schools following our recommendations as regards mathematics would not find this a problem. For other schools, unwilling to adopt realistic quantitative requirements, the alternatives would seem to be a) to drop pro-

Several additional comments need to be made about the kind of course in production management that we suggest. Inevitably, such a course will, to a considerable extent, be concerned with manufacturing production. But by no means should it stop there. There are ample opportunities for dealing with the economic problems of managing physical resources in other types of business: equipment and routing problems in transportation; warehousing, inventory, and store layout problems in retailing; management of the physical aspects of bank operations; a variety of problems that come under the general heading of office management; and so on. Also, while we have emphasized the need for developing in this course the more precise types of analytical tools used in modern management science, we do not suggest that the course be confined to this alone. There is room for consideration of such broader problems as long-range production planning and product development, which do not necessarily lend themselves to precise analysis and quantitative solutions. No more here than in any business course should the student be left with the idea that mathematical or statistical techniques can eliminate the need for the weighing of nonquantifiable evidence and the exercise of the semi-intuitive faculty of judgment.

THE FUNCTIONAL FIELDS: SUMMARY

What should be the total requirement in the functional fields? We have suggested that both the managerial and the external aspects can be dealt with in the same course in the case both of marketing and finance. We have recommended a course in industrial relations (with a minimum of the conventional material on personnel management) and a new type of course in production management. We have also suggested a course in human relations, which might more properly be considered a part of the administration-organization sequence. This makes a total of four or five semester courses.[23] In recommending such courses, we hope that some schools will take the initiative in doing a considerable amount of experimentation—and in making the results of their experiments known to business educators generally.

Our suggested total requirement for the functional fields (excluding

duction management from the core curriculum, b) to replace production management with a more general course, "introduction to engineering" or "survey of technology," or c) to design a course similar in purpose to the one represented by the Bowman and Fetter text, but requiring a different kind or level of mathematical competence.

[23] In addition to the tool subjects of accounting, statistics, economics, and business law, the Association requires that the undergraduate student receive instruction in marketing, finance (for which money and banking is an acceptable substitute), and "management" (which can be anything from production management to business policy).

administration-organization) is not very far from present practice. Most Association schools require one course each in marketing and finance; a little less than half specify a semester or more of production or industrial management; and slightly more require a semester's work in the area of personnel-industrial relations. For all of these fields combined, about one-fourth of the schools in our sample had a total requirement of one or two courses; somewhat more than one-half required a total of three or four courses; and the remainder required five or more semester courses. Nonmember schools, which follow about the same pattern, are less likely to require production, industrial relations, and marketing, but more likely to require a course in personnel management.

Clearly, our recommended total requirements can be fitted into the curriculum framework of most schools without difficulty.[24] Here as elsewhere the question is what and how to teach rather than how much.

Information and Control Systems

ACCOUNTING

The importance of accounting as a system of information and control has long been accepted by businessmen and business educators. Statements to the effect that "accounting is the language of business" are commonplace but nonetheless true. It is not surprising, therefore that accounting is a required field of study in every undergraduate business curriculum that we have examined. This, of course, is as it should be.

The amount of accounting typically required today is about the same as it was thirty years ago: one year or six semester units. Forty of the seventy-four schools in our sample reported such a requirement, with thirty-three reporting more. About 10 per cent of the institutions specified four or more semester courses. There was little difference in practice between member and nonmember schools.[25]

Despite universal acceptance of the need for accounting in business curricula, there is considerable dissatisfaction with the content of the accounting requirement. On this issue no consensus as yet exists, although a start seems to have been made on the road to eventual agreement.

The principal conflict concerns the extent to which students should be

[24] Cf. Tables 12 and 13.
[25] For the seventy-four schools in our sample:

| | Semester Units Required in Accounting | | | | | |
	o	1–4	5–7	8–10	11–13	Total
No. of AACSB schools	o	1	19	13	4	37
No. of non-AACSB schools	o	o	21	12	4	37
Total	o	1	40	25	8	74

able to omit the procedural detail in the introductory course and move on to what is called managerial or interpretive accounting. This issue quickly becomes entwined with another. Should students majoring in accounting and other business students both take the same introductory course, or should the two groups be segregated?

The typical situation is for both types of students to take the same course in elementary accounting, a large part of which deals with procedural and descriptive detail. The student who is not an accounting major gets in his two required semesters of accounting a great deal of what can fairly be called bookkeeping, some introduction to specialized accounting forms for which he will seldom if ever have any use, some information that duplicates what is taught in other courses, a modest amount of "accounting theory"—and very little training in how to interpret and use accounting data.

We have the impression that, for both the accounting major and the general business student, there is a good deal of waste motion in the elementary course. Even more important, the general business student does not get the training he so badly needs in how to use accounting as a managerial tool. A good deal of what he needs is to be found only in the more advanced accounting courses.[26]

Clearly some change needs to be made in the accounting requirement that now exists in most schools. Experimentation is needed, and it is probable that different schools will find different but equally acceptable answers. In general, the answers should conform to the following three criteria:

1) The nonaccounting student should not be required to take more than a one-year course in accounting.

2) The introductory course taken by nonaccounting majors should minimize the time spent on procedural detail, emphasizing instead basic principles and theory and the use of accounting as a managerial tool.[27]

---

[26] Although we are critical of the usual accounting requirement for general business students, in all fairness we should also say a word in defense of teachers of accounting. Accounting departments typically have the highest standards in the business school, their students typically work harder than other students, and accounting is often if not usually the most rigorous field of study offered. While we are not sure that students planning to be public or private accountants need to get in college all of the technical detail that they are expected to master, they are often subjected to a more rigorous educational experience than are other business students.

[27] "A clear-cut distinction should be drawn between basic accounting principles and accounting procedures. Basic principles can be learned in the classroom. The student can be introduced to accounting procedures at an elementary level, through the academic process, but detailed and elaborate procedures, forms, records, and techniques can be learned more quickly and thoroughly by exposure to actual operating conditions and practices." The Commission on Standards of Education and Experience for Certified Public Accountants, *Standards of Education and Experience for Certified Public Accountants* (1956), p. 54.

3) As part of his training in the informational and control uses of accounting, the business student should have some exposure to the subject matter now included in courses in cost accounting, budgeting, and analysis of financial statements.

We are loath to suggest an answer to the question as to whether accounting majors and other business students should take the same introductory course. A possible answer is integration for one semester only, after which the nonaccounting majors would take a semester of managerial accounting while the accounting specialists would go on to their sequence of more technical courses. But this is only one of several possible alternatives.

We should make it clear that by no means are all schools as backward in revising their accounting requirements as the preceding discussion may have implied. Actually, the views expressed here are based on suggestions made to us by thoughtful accountants and other faculty members and businessmen. And a number of schools have been experimenting with ways of meeting the very problem that we raise here. Our comments are meant to apply only to those schools which have not yet awakened to the needs of their students for sophisticated training in the use of accounting. Of these, unfortunately, the number is still too large.

STATISTICS

Closely related to accounting as an information-control device is statistics. As in the case of accounting, statistics is part of the core of the AACSB and is thus required by nearly every school of business. Thus all of the member schools in our sample required a course in statistics, and so did over 80 per cent of the non-Association schools. Typically a one-semester course is required.[28]

While there is general agreement that statistics should be required of business students, the problem of *what* and *how* to teach has long plagued the business schools.[29] A useful parallel can be drawn here with the problem of what kind of accounting is best for students who do not plan to be professional accountants. As in the case of accounting, we think

[28] For the seventy-four schools in our sample:

| | *Semester Units Required in Statistics* | | | |
	0	*1–4*	*5–7*	*Total*
No. of AACSB schools	0	32	5	37
No. of non-AACSB schools	6	23	8	37
Total	6	55	13	74

[29] See, for example, J. H. S. Bossard and J. F. Dewhurst, *University Education for Business* (1931), pp. 442–43.

that a particular kind of introductory course in statistics is most appropriate for business students who do not expect to become specialists in the subject.

It will be helpful if we distinguish three different kinds of emphasis in teaching statistics and other tool courses: the descriptive (or procedural), the analytical, and the interpretive. We have already suggested that the required course in accounting should be oriented toward the interpretive rather than emphasize procedural detail. Some non-interpretive work is necessary, of course, but the amount should be minimized. In the case of statistics, similarly, the procedural content should be held to a minimum. Also, although there is a great deal of analytical content in modern statistics, we suggest that the analytical be subordinated to the interpretive.

Thus it seems to us that the most satisfactory approach to statistics for business students—as with accounting—would be to attempt to train students to be interpreters or users of statistics rather than statistical analysts or producers. Let it be added quickly, however, that the required statistics course must also include certain procedural (or descriptive) and analytical materials if it is to serve its intended purpose. But the primary orientation of the course should be neither descriptive nor analytical in the special way that we use these words here.

To be more explicit, we do not think it necessary or useful to emphasize the construction and detailed characteristics of index numbers, graphs and charts, measures of central tendency and dispersion, correlation and regression coefficients, and time series; nor the development and involutions of sampling concepts, the theory of significant differences, "t-" and other distributions, etc. In other words, we think inappropriate both the many old-fashioned, descriptive and the many modern, inference courses that are now required by schools of business. On the other hand, we do think appropriate a course which, while minimizing derivation and technical complexities, would utilize a considerable number of these topics in considering the use and great power of statistics in organizing and handling the quantitative aspects of the real world, particularly but not solely that part of the world in which a businessman must operate and make decisions.

There are a few other issues regarding the statistics requirement that need to be treated briefly. One is whether statistics should be offered by the business school or by someone else, for example, by the mathematics or economics department. Instances can be found of dissatisfaction and satisfaction with both arrangements, as well as with the compromise that has an all-university first course in elementary statistics followed by a second course offered by the applied department itself. Although the case for a course emphasizing business and economic applications is strong, alternative arrangements might also be acceptable to the business faculty.

Another debated issue has to do with how much mathematics should be used in the course and, as a consequence, what kind and how much mathematics should be a prerequisite. In our opinion, the kind of interpretive course that is needed can be taught to students with as little as a good secondary-school background in mathematics as well as to those with bachelor's degrees in that subject; that is, interpretive statistics can be taught using as little or as much mathematical and symbolic language as students' backgrounds permit. There is ample evidence from a number of schools that students with no more than secondary-school algebra and geometry can grasp statistical concepts, although they are naturally prevented from exploring the means by which statisticians build, test, and elaborate these concepts.

Another problem is suggested by the common complaint that, even after students have had a course in statistics, they are unable to use even the simplest statistical tools in the courses they then take in the various business fields. There is no doubt that the complaint is justified. One explanation is that many students are *not* exposed to statistics in the way we have suggested. Class descriptions and instructors' protestations to the contrary, statistics continues to be taught descriptively or analytically, but seldom interpretively. In the one case there is an undue emphasis on dull descriptive material; in the other, there is too much concern with a mathematical approach which tends to obscure the powerful uses of statistics behind an algebraic veil which the student is unable (or is unwilling to try) to pierce.

Another important explanation for the apparent ineffectiveness of the statistics course is related to the level of statistical literacy of the faculty. Paraphrasing a generalization usually applied to language skills, we can say that the level of statistical sophistication of students will inevitably be limited by the statistical sophistication of the faculty. The mere taking of a course in statistics, no matter how good that course is, will not carry students very far in developing the ability to use statistics unless in subsequent courses they are required to use their newly acquired knowledge under the tutelage of faculty members who are themselves statistically literate.

INFORMATION AND CONTROLS: THE WHOLE AREA

We recommend that schools have a total requirement in quantitative information and controls of three or (preferably) four semester courses. Not more than one year of this would represent accounting; at least one semester would be statistics. Schools wishing to experiment with courses in quantitative controls which combine statistics and accounting would fit easily within this recommendation.

Beyond the work in accounting and statistics as management tools, there is room for some further exposure to information and control systems and their role in business analysis and operations. Given that basic accounting should not take up more than one year, additional work might be taken in advanced statistics, sampling and survey methods, statistical quality control, the use of statistics in accounting, business information systems *per se*, data processing, business decision theory, or operations analysis. Local needs, interests, and resources will necessarily set limits on what can and should be offered.

We envision the total requirement as one which introduces the student to the whole range of quantitative tools that will be important to management. (From this point of view, the requirement includes also the minimum amount of mathematics recommended in Chapter 8.) Accounting should loom large in this requirement, as should modern statistics; but great care must be exercised that these subjects be treated as a set of information and control devices to be used by the businessman— not as routine procedures to be learned by bookkeepers and statistical clerks or, at a higher level, a set of esoteric techniques to be utilized by the professional accountant or statistician. The requirement should also reach beyond traditional accounting and statistics and introduce the student to newer developments in the application of logical systems and scientific methods to the solution of business problems. This part of the business core can play an important role in developing an attitude, a way of looking at the problems and issues which businessmen must face, and in introducing the student to the use of formal systems in organizing information for the analysis and solution of business problems.

There is no doubt that some schools will find it difficult to staff the full program we suggest. A year of accounting and a semester of statistics will be all they can manage. While we think that a two-year requirement is the goal toward which schools should probably work, it is more important that the typical school concentrate upon improving its present elementary courses in accounting and statistics than that it rush to introduce a fourth semester of quantitative analysis before the necessary foundations have been properly strengthened.

The Place of Advanced Economics in the Business Program

We saw in Chapter 8 that it is virtually universal practice for schools of business to require a one-year course in elementary economics, usually in the sophomore year. There is, however, much less uniformity with respect to an economics requirement beyond the elementary course, and only a handful of schools require the amount and kind of additional work in economics that we shall recommend. The membership standards of the AACSB do not specify any advanced work in economics.

This is not to say that an additional course or two is not frequently required. According to our sample, about 80 per cent of the schools in the AACSB and about 70 per cent of nonmember schools require some work in economics other than elementary economics and economic history. Schools differ in the amount they require, but most frequently they specify only one semester's work. Usually this is a course in money and banking, although some schools require courses in business fluctuations or cycles, economics of the firm, public finance, government regulation of business, or general economic theory.[30]

AGGREGATIVE ECONOMICS

Money and banking, public finance, and business cycles (or fluctuations) may be considered together since, as usually taught, they overlap considerably. Of the forty-eight schools in our sample requiring any one of this group of courses, forty-six specified money and banking. (Some of the forty-six also specified one of the other two courses.)

We endorse the inclusion of "aggregative economics" in the business curriculum. The analysis of Part II suggested strongly that the businessman needs to be familiar with the aggregative aspects of the firm's economic environment. This goal cannot be achieved, however, by requiring a conventional course in money and banking. Such courses usually ignore or give insufficient coverage to national income accounting and measurement, the role of nonmonetary factors in economic fluctuations, economic growth, forecasting, fiscal policy, problems of economic choice associated with the goals of stability and growth, and so forth. On the other hand, an excessive emphasis is typically placed on the banking system and its history, on the technical complexities of the money market, and on the particular characteristics and operational problems of the banking industry. Public finance courses likewise represent an unsatis-

[30] For the seventy-four schools in our sample:

	Money & Banking	Fluctu- ations	Economics of the Firm	Public Finance	Other	None
No. of AACSB schools	27	5	7	5	7	7
No. of non-AACSB schools	19	7	1	1	9	11
Total	46	12	8	6	16	18

Required Courses in Advanced Economics

factory way of giving the business student the background he needs in aggregative economics.

The popularity of money and banking is largely due either to inertia or to confused and unsuccessful attempts, which the standards of the AACSB have encouraged, to meet two needs with the same course. The Association explicitly accepts money and banking in satisfaction of its core requirement in the field of finance. In addition, many business schools avoid facing up to the need for training in modern aggregative economics by falling back on the same course in money and banking that they have been offering for years. The result is that more than half of the schools of business require a course which serves neither of its ostensible purposes, although it undoubtedly does serve to swell the enrollment in one of the staple courses in the economics department.

Some schools supplement or replace money and banking with courses in "business conditions," "cycles," or "intermediate economic theory." The content of such offerings is so varied that an evaluation is difficult, particularly in the last-named instance. But to the extent that it is a conventional course in macrotheory for economists, it does not adequately meet the needs of the business school. On the other hand, courses dealing with business cycles and forecasting probably come close to providing satisfactory fare for the business student. This is particularly true if the course includes, in addition to the usual topics, material on economic growth, forecasting, and policy issues, and if it excludes or de-emphasizes the usual sort of history and critique of alternative business-cycle theories.

The course that we recommend would correspond more or less to the better courses currently being taught under the title Business Cycles and Forecasting or Business Fluctuations. Its objective would be to develop in the student an awareness of the impact of dynamic forces on economic activity in general and specifically on the decisions which must be made by and within firms, by individual savers and investors, and by society as a whole.[31] Courses in money and banking, public finance, and economic theory alone would not be sufficient, although the course we describe would cover some of the same ground.

MANAGERIAL ECONOMICS

Only eight schools of the seventy-four in our sample had requirements in "economics of the firm," "managerial economics," or "business eco-

---

[31] Topics would presumably include some or all of the following: national income accounting and analysis; economic indicators and measures; aggregative economic analysis, including both fluctuations and growth and with due consideration to the role of money in a dynamic economy; forecasting for the economy and the firm; and problems of public policy concerned with stability and growth.

nomics." In addition, a small number of schools had an undergraduate requirement in "general economic theory" or some sort of a "government and business" requirement.[32] These figures strongly suggest that the vast majority of business schools do not expose their undergraduates to any economic analysis, after the elementary course, which is directed toward the problems of the business firm in the areas of price and output decision, investment planning, factor utilization, and so on.

Some part of the explanation undoubtedly lies in the unwillingness of many departments of economics—particularly when independent of the business school—to provide the kind of courses which would be appropriate for business students. But much of the fault also rests with the business faculty itself, for many schools have made no effort to introduce an appropriate course for their students. The reason usually given is either that "managerial economics" is not necessary or else that it is too difficult if correctly done. Such arguments are frequently used to justify faculty resistance to the modern trend toward the use of sharper analytical tools in business decision-making.

The findings in Part II of this report leave no doubt in our minds that potential business managers and their staff consultants need to be able to use the tools of economic analysis. We recommend, therefore, that schools require a course in what might be described as managerial economics. This course would have as its primary objective the introduction of the student to the use of the tools of economic analysis in formulating and solving management problems and thus in the development of appropriate business policy. While the orientation of the course should be toward the development of analytical tools, it should not be a conventional course in economic theory as typically taught in the economics department. Joel Dean has put the distinction and problem in the following way:

The purpose of this book [*Managerial Economics*] is to show how economic analysis can be used in formulating business policies. It is therefore a departure from the main stream of economic writings on the theory of the firm, much of which is too simple in its assumptions and too complicated in its logical development to be managerially useful. The big gap between the problems of logic that intrigue economic theorists and the problems of policy that plague practical management needs to be bridged in order to give executives access to the practical contributions that economic thinking can make to top-management policies.[33]

---

[32] Of course, the schools which had requirements in "general economic theory" were exposing their students to some of the topics which we have denoted by the terms aggregative and managerial economics. There were eight schools in the group of seventy-four for which this would be true. Two had requirements in macrotheory and one in microtheory, while five required courses in both.

[33] *Managerial Economics* (1951), p. vii. The recent text by Spencer and Siegelman (1959) has

Appropriate topics for such a course would include elements of decision theory and criteria for decision-making by the firm, output and "scale" decisions, a brief introduction to linear programming, concepts of profits, production and cost functions, equilibrium (industry and firm), competition and its many variations, demand theory, pricing policies, capital budgeting and investment decisions, analysis of uncertainty, and inventory management.

A FINAL COMMENT

In recommending work in aggregative and managerial economics, we are seeking to develop in the student both an awareness of the interaction of the firm with its economic environment and some familiarity with the use of modern economic analysis in rational decision-making. But this is not to be interpreted as necessarily meaning that all schools should require two courses in advanced economics, one in each of these two fields. It is highly desirable that faculties experiment with alternative ways of introducing advanced economics into the curriculum so as to achieve the two stated objectives.

On the other hand, schools would be wise to abandon requirements in economics which do not fully meet the needs of their students. Courses in conventional intermediate economic theory, money and banking, and public finance are examples. It is to be expected that any effort to drop such courses from the required curriculum will generate opposition from vested interests, just as the proposals for new courses along the lines suggested will meet some resistance. Business schools will need to overcome such obstacles if they are to meet legitimate student needs. Whether this means that the schools which do not include economics departments should offer their own "business economics" is something on which we need not take a stand. While it can be argued that, as long as courses are staffed with competent people, it should not make much difference whether they are offered in the economics department or not, a strong argument can be made for offering them in the business school on grounds of "favorable climate."[34]

the same title and essentially the same objective as Dean's book. There are also a few other text- and casebooks which seek to serve the same purpose.

[34] Several recommendations of the Subcommittee on the Study of Economics in Schools of Business of the Committee on Undergraduate Teaching of Economics and the Training of Economists of the American Economic Association coincide with our own conclusions. See "The Teaching of Undergraduate Economics," *American Economic Review*, XL (December, 1950, Part 2, Supplement), 107ff. The reader is also referred to the following: Howard R. Bowen, *The Business Enterprise as a Subject for Research* (Social Science Research Council Pamphlet No. 11, May, 1955), particularly pp. 19ff.; and Neil H. Jacoby et al., "Economics in the Curricula of Schools of Business," *American Economic Review*, XLVI (*Papers and Proceedings*, May, 1956), 551–77.

Law and Business Enterprise

Business law, like economics and accounting, is found in practically every business curriculum. Typically, students are required to take a year's work. Many schools offer additional courses on an elective basis, and a few require more than the equivalent of a year's course.[35]

It will be recalled that in Part II we emphasized the importance of the nonmarket environment of business. Legal and political institutions loom large in this environment.[36] Recognition of this fact is one reason for the almost universal inclusion of one or more law courses in the business curriculum. But this is not the full explanation, and it is even less an explanation of what is taught in these courses. The growing criticism of the content of the conventional courses in business law implies no denial of the importance of the legal framework within which business must operate.

To understand fully the role which business law typically plays in the business curriculum, we must turn back to the early development of collegiate education for business. Schools of business as we know them today had their origins in schools of commerce, beginning roughly around the turn of the century. The early emphasis on commerce stemmed from the fact that the major market for business school graduates was in trade, finance, and transportation—and, for the most part, in small concerns. Manufacturing firms normally sought business-school graduates only for positions in accounting or finance, if they sought college graduates at all. In short, the emphasis was on "commerce, accounts, and finance." It was only natural, therefore, that business law should have been an essential ingredient of the curriculum, focusing as it did on the commercial and financial problems of business and emphasizing the legal aspects of ordinary business dealings, business forms, forms of business organization, and points of litigation which commercial and financial firms were likely to encounter.[37]

[35] For the seventy-four schools in our sample:

	Semester Units Required in Business Law				
	0	1–4	5–7	8–	Total
No. of AACSB schools	1	15	19	2	37
No. of non-AACSB schools	0	10	23	4	37
Total	1	25	42	6	74

[36] Cf. also *A Symposium on the Place of Business Law in Higher Education* (American Business Law Association Bulletin, Vol. 3, No. 1, May, 1958).

[37] Cf. any early text or casebook; also Bossard and Dewhurst, *University Education for Business*, p. 405.

Educational practices are slow to change. The same kind of business law is still being required as a "tool" course, supplying information about and familiarity with the law of negotiable instruments, contracts, bankruptcy, etc., and paying relatively little attention to the environmental role of the law.

This is clearly *not* the kind of legal background that the typical businessman, particularly the more responsible business managers, will need in the closing decades of the twentieth century. The nature of business and the role of the business schools have changed dramatically in the last fifty or seventy-five years. This is the age of the large firm, of specialized staff services, of a growing emphasis on administration and on a scientific approach to management problems, and of an increasingly complex environment that impinges on business operations in ever new ways. It is an age, also, that cries for broad and farsighted business leadership that comprehends how the present evolved out of the past and is evolving into the future.

The businessman who will operate in this kind of world has little need for the kind of course in business law that is a standard requirement in most undergraduate business schools. We therefore recommend that this particular course (or combination of courses) be dropped as a requirement—although it may have to be retained as an elective, perhaps in modified form, for accountants and others who may have special need for it. A movement in this direction has already begun, and in 1957 the AACSB relaxed its requirements in order to make it possible.

In the place of "business law," we suggest the inclusion of a course on "the legal framework of business"—although obviously this need not be the title. Such a course might seek to familiarize the student with the fact that all business must be conducted within the framework of the law, that such a legal environment forms the basis for rules of conduct among businessmen, and that a broad comprehension of the law is essential in setting business policy. In other words, such a course would seek to give students an appreciation of the workings and origins of legal institutions and the functions of the law as a system of social thought and social action.[38] Such a course might include topics such as the following: the background, importance, and role of law in our society; the legal system of the United States and its workings; private property and contract as basic concepts of a free enterprise system; and the evolution of legal attitudes toward business, including the changing relations between business and government.

[38] Paraphrased from a mimeographed description of a new course supplied to us by the School of Commerce, Accounts, and Finance, New York University.

Some schools may prefer to develop a "framework" course that is even broader than this, that would deal with the social, political, and other aspects of the environment of business—including the changing intellectual climate—as well as with the legal framework. Such a course, in effect, would consider the nature of the changing interactions between business and a wide range of other institutions and social attitudes that comprise the changing environment within which business must operate.[39]

A number of schools require—and many more offer—courses with such titles as "government and business" or "public policy toward business." Such offerings cover some of the topics which we believe should be treated in the kind of "framework" course that we propose. Exactly how "government regulation," "business law," and "government" (as offered by the political science department) should be related is something schools will have to work out on an individual basis, perhaps after some experimentation. However it is done, the sort of broad requirement we propose will be far more valuable to today's business students than most of the courses in business law that are now required. And it should also provide the basis for a more fruitful working relationship between the business and law faculties on the same campus.

We have discussed the possibilities of reform in the business curriculum with a number of deans and faculty members. Proposals to drop or change long established courses in any field will, of course, encounter resistance. We have been impressed, however, by the fact that one objection in particular has been raised so many times to any drastic change in the law requirement. "If we adopt this suggestion," we have been asked repeatedly, "what will we do with our teachers of business law?" Perhaps too naively, we find it difficult to accept the implication of this question—that the faculty members concerned, all trained in the law, cannot widen their mental horizons enough to give the kind of course proposed here.

The Integrating Course in Business Policy

The capstone of the core curriculum should be a course in "business policy" which will give students an opportunity to pull together what they have learned in the separate business fields and utilize this knowledge in the analysis of complex business problems.

[39] For a quite different view of how business law should be treated in the curriculum, see the American Business Law Association symposium on *The Place of Business Law in Higher Education*, previously cited.

The business policy course can offer the student something he will find nowhere else in the curriculum: consideration of business problems which are not prejudged as being marketing problems, finance problems, etc.; emphasis on the development of skill in identifying, analyzing, and solving problems in a situation which is as close as the classroom can ever be to the real business world; opportunity to consider problems which draw on a wide range of substantive areas in business; opportunity to consider the external, nonmarket implications of problems at the same time that internal decisions must be made; situations which enable the student to exercise qualities of judgment and of mind which were not explicitly called for in any prior course. Questions of social responsibility and of personal attitudes can be brought in as a regular aspect of this kind of problem-solving practice. Without the responsibility of having to transmit some specific body of knowledge, the business policy course can concentrate on integrating what already has been acquired and on developing further the student's skill in using that knowledge.[40] The course can range over the entire curriculum and beyond.

Clearly a policy course must come in the senior year—preferably in the last term. It just as obviously must be a case course; we can imagine no other way of achieving the same objectives. The continued development of communication skills should clearly be included an as objective. Schools with the appropriate business contacts can experiment with "live cases" in which businessmen come and present problems from the experiences of their own firms.

If the argument for a policy course is so strong, why do so few schools require it?[41] First, some faculties have a bias against the use of cases—a *sine qua non* of a policy course. While we have stressed the need to teach principles, there is no doubt that the development of problem-solving skill requires the use of cases, particularly in the latter part of the student's program. Second, some deans report that their requirements already are "too tight"—there is no room. This argument also can be brushed aside. Reduction of the excessive amount of specialization required by virtually every school using this argument would provide room for several policy courses.

The next two arguments are somewhat more serious. The first of these concerns staffing. Some deans have argued that policy courses require instructors who are well-trained in all areas of business and have a sub-

---

[40] Some schools have also found that comprehensive examinations can perform a useful integrating function.

[41] Of the seventy-four schools of business whose undergraduate curricula we studied, four AACSB and eight nonmember schools had required courses in business policy.

stantial amount of business experience. We cannot agree with this description of what is needed, although we admit that such courses do pose staffing problems if they must be offered on a multi-section basis. The instructor in a policy course should have a technical background at least equal to what most of his students possess; this surely is not a restrictive condition. In addition (and this is the major difficulty), he must have the maturity, sophistication, and mental poise so that he can approach problems in a variety of ways and not merely from the viewpoint of the particular area in which he may be a specialist. He must be able to admit he does not always or even usually know "the" answer and that he can think of problems as having indeterminate and conditional solutions —i.e., he does not think in terms of "black and white." This prescription should not be too restrictive for most faculties.

The last objection to a requirement in business policy is that its role can be played equally well by other courses in the curriculum, perhaps after some slight modifications in the latter. We do not believe that this is true, for reasons which are summarized in the list of advantages of a policy course presented earlier. In addition, as we have already noted, there is some hazard involved in relying heavily on cases in the basic functional fields.

While this evidence is not conclusive, we should also cite our conversations with students in a large number of schools. Students are unqualifiedly in favor of such courses, even in schools where we suspect they were only moderately well taught. Student opinion, of course, is an insufficient reason for including a new course in the curriculum; but it is not without weight when added to the other evidence that has been presented.

The Professional Base:
Summary of Recommended Core Requirements

Table 12 presents a summary of our recommendations for the core of required professional courses.[42] In considering this table, the reader should keep in mind that course titles are simply labels for empty boxes until we know what course content these labels are intended to signify. The labels used in Table 12 refer to boxes which have the course content described in the preceding sections. A school may now have virtually all

[42] With a moderate amount of change, the core we suggest could be used for students planning on careers in government rather than business. Some schools, as we noted earlier in this report, offer programs in both business and public administration. The kinds of modifications needed to meet the needs of the future government administrator are fairly obvious and need not be spelled out here.

TABLE 12

SUGGESTED PROFESSIONAL BASE OR "CORE" FOR

UNDERGRADUATE BUSINESS STUDENTS

Subject	Semester Courses	Semester Units or Hours
Organization theory and management principles (pp. 182–86)[a]	2	6
The market environment and functional management (pp. 186–94)[b] Finance Marketing Industrial relations Human relations Production or operations management[c]	3–5	9–15
Information and control systems (pp. 194–99)[b] Managerial accounting Statistical analysis and related topics	3–4	9–12
Advanced economics (pp. 199–203)[d] Aggregative economics Managerial economics	2	6
Legal environment of business (pp. 204–06)[e]	1	3
Integrating the management viewpoint Business policy (pp. 206–08)	1	3
Totals	12–15	36–45

[a] Treatment of human relations is to be included either here or as a separate course.
[b] Experiments in integration and coordination are to be encouraged.
[c] Production management should not be required if staff resources permit only the kind of course which is now common. See pp. 190–93.
[d] This is in addition to elementary economics, for which provision was made in the general education base described in Chapter 8.
[e] Including possibly other aspects of the business environment.

of the labels listed in the table but yet may fail to meet most of the standards that we have proposed in this chapter. Hence the table should be used only in conjunction with the detailed discussion that has gone before. To facilitate doing this, we have indicated in the body of the table the pages on which each suggested requirement has been described.

The total core requirement adds up to between twelve and fifteen semester courses, or between thirty-six and forty-five semester units (excluding elementary economics). This represents a range of from 30 to nearly 40 per cent of four years' work (120 semester units).

This requirement falls well within the range of what is now current in undergraduate business schools, although details vary from school to school. This is evident from Tables 13 and 14. While we have proposed

TABLE 13

SUMMARY OF CORE REQUIREMENTS BY FIELDS,
SEVENTY-FOUR SELECTED BUSINESS SCHOOLS

Field	Number of Schools Requiring Indicated Number of Semester Units										Total Requiring Some Work
	AACSB Members					Nonmembers					
	0	1–4	5–7	8–10	11+	0	1–4	5–7	8–10	11+	
Accounting	0	2	19	12	4	0	0	13	21	3	74
Marketing	0	28	8	1	0	8	25	2	0	2	66
Management[a]	1	14	14	7	1	6	16	12	1	2	67
Finance	9	25	3	0	0	10	22	3	1	1	55
Economics[b]	7	12	8	8	2	11	15	9	2	0	56
Statistics	0	31	5	1	0	6	23	8	0	0	68
Business law	1	15	19	2	0	0	10	23	3	1	73
Business policy	33	4	0	0	0	29	7	1	0	0	12
All other core[c]	7	12	10	3	5	5	11	10	8	3	62

[a] Includes general management, organization and administration, production and industrial management, personnel management, and human and industrial relations.
[b] Excludes elementary economics, economic geography, and economic history, but includes all other required courses in economics (including money and banking).
[c] Includes transportation, insurance, real estate, introduction to business, business mathematics, business communication, and economic geography.
Source: See Appendix E.

some courses that are not now generally required, we have omitted others; and even the upper limit of the range we recommend is well within the bounds of what is feasible, particularly in light of our later recommendation that schools reduce their present emphasis on a field of specialization beyond the core. The maximum of our recommended range would be nearly 40 per cent of the four years' work, leaving fifteen semester units for electives in business subjects if our "50 per cent" rule is to be observed.

The reader should note carefully what has been excluded from the recommended business base. First, there are the courses which are excluded because something else has been put in their place; for example, no money and banking or public finance and no business law of the conventional sort. We also argued against including the conventional kind of production management.

Secondly, there are a number of subject areas which have been omitted because we feel there is little or no justification for their inclusion. Conventional business mathematics, business English, and letter writing fall

TABLE 14

DISTRIBUTION OF BUSINESS SCHOOLS BY SEMESTER UNITS REQUIRED IN BUSINESS CORE, SEVENTY-FOUR SAMPLE SCHOOLS

Semester Units in Business Core	37 AACSB Schools	37 Non-AACSB Schools	Total
11–15	—	—	—
16–20	—	2	2
21–25	1	6	7
26–30	5	5	10
31–35	8	6	14
36–40	11	8	19
41–45	8	4	12
46–50	—	2	2
51–55	3	2	5
56–60	1	1	2
61–65	—	1	1
Total	37	37	74

Note: Business core excludes elementary economics and economic history but includes all other required courses in economics.

Source: See Appendix E.

under this heading. We believe that the general education recommendations presented earlier better provide for the needs which these courses attempt to serve. In addition, we have excluded the sort of freshman survey course usually entitled Introduction to Business. There seems to be little excuse for such courses, regardless of title. They are largely descriptive and contain little analysis of any sort. They emphasize memory work; and they lend themselves all too readily to true-false or other kinds of examinations which contribute little to the intellectual development of the student. In short, by attempting to cover everything, they cover nothing.[43] We also can find no justification for requiring and giving credit for typing and other courses which aim to give the student command of routine, albeit useful techniques.[44]

A third category of exclusions covers courses (for example, transporta-

[43] Several deans have advanced the argument that the course is necessary for purposes of orientation. We grant the desirability of some orientation and counseling but do not see why it cannot be done through a few lectures and by personal advising. It is hardly necessary to require and give credit for a full course.

[44] It may be desirable to require each student to obtain some minimum proficiency in typing, but it is difficult to justify college credit for satisfying such a requirement.

tion or insurance) which may have a legitimate claim to be in the catalogue, but which we do not think need to be included in the core. It is possible that some of these areas are important enough to be required of students with certain career goals, but the business base is not the place to treat these special needs.

The Issue of Specialization

The evidence presented in Part II argues overwhelmingly against the degree of specialized business training that now prevails in most undergraduate business schools. The argument against such specialization is both positive and negative. On the positive side, we found that the primary need is for a broad business and general education. Where special training is required, it is likely to be of a kind which is better obtained either in connection with work experience or at the graduate level. Even more important, there is the negative argument that any considerable investment of time in specialized training in the undergraduate years reduces below the minimum acceptable level the time available for general education and the basic business subjects.

We therefore concluded in Chapter 7 that, if undergraduate programs in business are to exist at all, they should give priority to the general education base and the professional core. Our recommendations in these areas indicate that there is little room left for specialization, even if one believes it can make a positive contribution at the undergraduate level. In fact, assuming a four-year program of 120 semester units (net of R.O.T.C. and physical education), our recommended requirements in general education and the professional core claim 80 per cent or more of the time available before any provision is made for electives.

THE FIELD OF CONCENTRATION

We have already expressed the view that at the undergraduate level business itself is enough specialization for most students. It may be desirable, however, to permit students to take in the senior year one or two advanced courses or seminars in business in addition to what is available in the core. The offerings beyond the core would depend on the interests of faculty and students. If any further room remains in the student's program, he should elect additional nonbusiness courses—although it would often be desirable for these electives to be coordinated with and complementary to the advanced work in business.

Thus, against the present all too common pattern of perhaps 30 to 40 per cent in nonbusiness subjects and a "concentration" of eighteen or more semester hours in advertising, finance, etc., our recommendations call for a strong nonbusiness base of at least 50 per cent, a high-level, analytically oriented professional core of from 30 to 40 per cent, and either no field of concentration at all or a field of concentration limited to a maximum of twelve semester units, of which six would be in a nonbusiness but complementary field.

Assuming for the moment a reasonable secondary preparation and adherence to our recommendations, a student would have twelve or more semester units available for elective use after the general education and core requirements had been met. If his interests were in personnel management and industrial relations, it would seem not unreasonable for him to take an advanced course in some aspect of that field, followed perhaps by a field seminar. The remaining time could then be used for additional work in some nonbusiness field, perhaps industrial psychology or sociology—or perhaps in some nonbusiness area in which he had a nonvocational interest. The student interested in marketing or insurance could follow a similar pattern—two courses or seminars in the field, supplemented outside the school by whatever interested him professionally or personally.

These elective courses beyond the core should emphasize breadth and analytical depth, not narrowness and superficial vocational skills. In the limited amount of concentration that we envisage there would be no room for courses in window display advertising, real estate brokerage, airport management, advertising copy, hotel front office procedure, public relations correspondence, and similar examples of low-level vocational training. There would be room for courses and seminars, with a strong analytical and managerial emphasis, in such fields as marketing management, market research, advertising, security analysis and investments, insurance, and real estate.

While we believe that this limitation of the field of concentration to six semester units of business and six units of complementary nonbusiness courses is not only feasible but necessary, its general adoption would probably create some transitional problems. Many schools may find it necessary to move toward the recommended goal in two steps. As a first step, to be adopted immediately, schools might forbid the taking of more than twelve semester units of business subjects beyond the professional core. In other words, in the first stage the field of concentration would be limited to twelve units but these might all be in business subjects. This could then be followed within a reasonable time by the second stage, in which only six units of the field of concentration could be in purely business subjects; or, better, no major field would be specified.

The most difficult problem exists in accounting, and it is this field that would probably require the longest transitional period. We would, for the time being, permit students who contemplate careers in accounting to take twelve semester hours in that one field. But under no circumstances should the work in accounting constitute more than twelve hours beyond the elementary course.[45] There is growing recognition that the necessary business fundamentals and general education and also the needed accounting training cannot both be crammed into the "four-year box." *To attempt to do so is to deny the justification for the privileged professional status which public accounting otherwise has the right to claim for itself.* Preparation for a career in public accounting should require a minimum of five years, under either a "three-two" or the more conventional "four-one" arrangement. Under no circumstances should an undergraduate business school undertake to prepare students for the c.p.a. examinations by the time they receive their bachelor's degree. Fortunately, the leaders in the profession have already arrived at this conclusion and are presently engaged in the necessary missionary work.[46]

CURRENT PRACTICE

If the business schools are truly to abjure excessive specialization, it will be necessary for them to reduce the number of major fields which they now make available. Five or six fields should ordinarily be enough. Ordinarily, also, it should not be necessary to offer more than two or three courses in any one field (beyond the basic course that may be required in the core). This rule would eliminate half or more of the present course offerings in a number of schools, in itself an outcome profoundly to be desired.[47]

What we are proposing is not significantly different from what a few schools of business are presently requiring of their undergraduate stu-

---

[45] In this respect we differ with the Committee on Standards Rating of the American Accounting Association, which recommended that 25 per cent of the student's total work be in accounting—with another 25 per cent in general business. (Cf. *The Accounting Review*, XXIX, January, 1954, cited in *Standards of Education and Experience for Certified Public Accountants*, p. 46.) We do not argue that the additional work in accounting may not be necessary for professional accountants. We simply do not believe it should be obtained in the undergraduate years with a consequent sacrifice of more general subjects.

[46] See, in particular, *Standards of Education and Experience for Certified Public Accountants;* also S. M. Woolsey, "The Bachelor of Accounting Degree," *Collegiate News and Views*, XII (December, 1958), 1–3.

[47] In addition to two or three semester courses in each of a few major fields, a school may well want to offer an occasional course in some other area in which a faculty member wants to teach or for which there is a strong local demand. But three rules should be observed. The student should ordinarily be limited to two business courses beyond the core. The course should have considerable analytical content. And the instructor should be well qualified.

dents. There are a few that now require no concentration beyond the core. The loophole in most of these cases, however, is that, although the school does not *require* any major field other than business itself, the student is permitted to take elective work in business so that a fairly conventional field of specialization is possible.

Nonetheless, these schools are much less to be censured than are those which frankly require excessive specialization for the bachelor's degree. Nearly half of the member schools in our sample *required* fields of specialization which contained *as a minimum seven or more semester courses.* This represented one-sixth or more of the total requirements for the degree.[48] Two-thirds of the schools required more than four semester courses (twelve semester units). It should be emphasized that these figures refer to minimum requirements, whereas in fact many students utilize available electives to take more business courses than are required, usually in their field of concentration.

There has been a significant tendency for students to major in "management" or "general business," when that option is available to them. These two fields are frequently not genuine areas of concentration since they usually require fewer courses and give more freedom than the more conventional majors in accounting, marketing, and the like.[49] Our tabulation in Table 15 of the actual number of students majoring in various fields puts management-general business first with 27 per cent of all students. Accounting was second with 22 per cent, and marketing and retailing was third with 17 per cent.

Table 15 strongly supports the conclusion that five or six fields of

[48] The results in detail for our sample were as follows:

Number of AACSB Schools Having Fields of Specialization
Containing as a Minimum the Semester Units Shown

	0	9–12	15–18	20–21	24–25	28–	Total
No. of AACSB schools	3	8	9	6	6	4	36

Determining major requirements is a difficult task. We used official bulletins and announcements, supplemented by printed materials obtained during our visits to the schools. As closely as was possible, the number of semester units required as a minimum beyond the core was determined for each major or field of concentration. The one having the smallest requirement was entered in the summary tally (unless it was a general business major). Thus there is a significant degree of underestimation in the figures we report. (N.B. The entries above sum to thirty-six rather than thirty-seven, since even after a personal visit to one school we were unable to understand completely its degree requirements.)

[49] Bossard and Dewhurst, after noting that the general business curriculum was the choice of about half of all business school undergraduates at the end of the 1920s, remarked as follows: "This situation seems highly significant, and one cannot but wonder whether its implications have been grasped fully by the leaders who are shaping collegiate education for business. Its fundamental meaning seems to be that a large proportion of students find business *per se* enough by way of specialization for their college education." *University Education for Business,* p. 316.

concentration are usually enough. Nearly 50 per cent of the students in our sample majored in two fields, management-general business and accounting. These two areas plus the four standard fields of marketing, production, finance, and personnel-industrial relations accounted for no less than 80 per cent of all students. Some part of the remainder were economics majors in schools that had their own economics departments.

TABLE 15

DISTRIBUTION OF UNDERGRADUATE BUSINESS STUDENTS
BY MAJOR FIELDS

Field	At AACSB Schools	At Non-AACSB Schools	At All Schools in the Sample[a]
Management and general business	26%	29%	27%
Accounting	21	26	22
Marketing and retailing	16	19	17
Production and management	5	4	5
Finance	4	5	5
Secretarial studies	4	6	5
Personnel and industrial relations	6	2	5
Insurance	3	2	3
Real estate	2	0	2
Economics	1	5	2
Miscellaneous	13	2	7
Total	100%	100%	100%

[a] Schools included in our two samples are listed in Appendix E.
Source: Information is taken from the questionnaires returned to the Carnegie Survey of Business Education. We are grateful to Professor Frank C. Pierson, the director of that survey, for making the returned schedules available.

Thus fewer than 20 per cent of all business students would be affected by the recommended reduction in the number of major fields. The problems of adjustment would be much greater for business school faculties than for students. Formidable vested interests have been built up in various of these minor fields, and quite understandably the faculty members concerned will hardly view with equanimity the suggestion that undergraduate students not be permitted to specialize in these areas and that the number of courses offered be drastically reduced.

Nonetheless, it seems to us that the time has come to face up to the fact that "specialization has been running riot" in American business schools. Dozens of minor fields of specialization have been permitted to develop that never should have been introduced at all. Many of these involve specialization in the problems of some industry, and we saw in Part II that there is little evidence that business itself needs this kind of specialized training at the undergraduate level.

A part of the problem lies in the way that the main fields of business have been divided and subdivided in the process of proliferating fields of concentration and course offerings. We examined the offerings of the seventy-four schools of business in our sample and were able to derive a list of 191 different titles for fields of specialization, including professional selling, cotton marketing, property insurance, air and surface transportation, resort and club management, industrial journalism, executive secretaryship, aeronautical administration, extractive industries, and light building. Naturally, many of the items in our list were simply different labels for only slightly different areas. To cite a few cases, a large urban school had twenty-seven fields of specialization within business; several had from twenty to twenty-five; and a dozen or so additional schools had more than twelve separate fields of concentration for undergraduates.[50]

While our proposals may sound radical to the more specialized members of business school faculties, neither our evaluation nor our recommendations regarding specialization are new. Nearly thirty years ago, Bossard and Dewhurst wrote:

It must be clear from the foregoing analysis that many of the specialized curricula announced by colleges of commerce are but expressions of a wish or professions of faith. One wonders whether much of the purported specialization in the collegiate business schools, most of it perhaps, is not mere window dressing, designed to impress students and businessmen. It may be that it does serve these purposes. Conceivably it has a value in making concrete the different aspects of business activity. Undoubtedly, the announcement of these various specialized curricula has been thought necessary to satisfy the ambitions of members of business school faculties. This factor has been particularly important at certain institutions. For the most part, the real reasons for the development of any extensive specialization have to do with matters other than that of the educational interests of the students.[51]

What they said then is true now. The only difference is that, if anything, the situation is worse now than it was then.

[50] We have not included in this enumeration such nonbusiness fields as journalism and public administration when such fields are offered by a business school.

[51] *University Education for Business*, p. 313.

The reference to "window dressing" raises a further question about many of the fields of specialization now inflicted on business students. If the justification for a major field within business is study in depth, then the field needs to be viewed as a whole, and successive courses in the field should build up the student's understanding in a logical and cumulative way. The current practice is to chop a field into a number of relatively small pieces—in the case of marketing, for example, into retailing, wholesaling, purchasing, advertising, salesmanship, etc.—and, with some restrictions, to let the student choose a selection from the available pieces. Even when the field is completely prescribed, there is usually not a logical and cumulative development of the subject. Fortunately, a few schools are attempting to develop an integrated approach to some of the standard fields of specialization.

THE SPECIAL PROBLEM OF SECRETARIAL AND RELATED MAJORS

It is time for schools which have not yet done so to divest themselves of their secretarial programs and to stop giving degree credit for typing, shorthand, office filing, and similar courses.[52] It is not the function of a college to turn out stenographers, and to speak of secretarial training as a part of professional business education is to engage in a semantic exercise that deceives no one. Virtually without exception, secretarial majors tend to weaken the business school. The secretarial courses are not of college level;[53] the students in them have no great interest in or facility for the more substantial business courses; the instructors are generally uninformed regarding the important business fields and can make little

[52] Secretarial majors are still found in many schools and departments of business. Of our sample of thirty-seven member schools, twenty-five listed courses in typing, shorthand, office procedures, etc. Of the some 250 departments of business which supplied information to the Carnegie Corporation Survey of Business Education, directed by Professor Pierson, something over 60 per cent offered a curriculum in secretarial studies. (*Summary of Preliminary Findings* [revised August 1, 1958], Table VI.) The number of secretarial majors in a business school offering the field is likely to be small, but we found some schools in which a hundred or more students were majoring in the field. Of the business schools replying to Professor Pierson's questionnaire, about 15 per cent reported that secretarial work was one of the four major fields most often chosen. (*Summary of Preliminary Findings*, Table XXXV.) As shown in Table 15, 4 per cent of undergraduate majors in our sample of member schools, and 6 per cent in non-member schools, were in secretarial studies. An additional number are in business education. Probably, also, some additional secretarial majors are concealed in the "general business" programs of some schools.

[53] This is true not only of the familiar courses in typing and shorthand. Consider the following catalogue description of a frequently offered course, examples of which we have visited: "*Principles and Practices of Filing*. Fundamentals of indexing and filing, combining theory and practice by the use of miniature letters, filing boxes and guides. Alphabetic, Numeric, Triple Check Automatic, Geographic and Subject filing."

contribution to the school's educational planning; and, by the nature of the case, no significant research can come from this section of the faculty, however conscientious and able they may be.

Similar considerations hold for programs in "business education," i.e., the training of future teachers of commercial subjects in the secondary schools. Such programs are frequently shared with the school of education on the campus. In our view, they should be shifted completely to the schools of education, which can send their students to the business school for the needed basic courses.

Business school deans seldom defend these secretarial and "business education" programs, and some have tried, not always successfully, to get rid of them. Where they continue in the business school, they are tolerated as stepchildren; and like the stepchild of the fairy tale, they are likely to be hidden in a dark corner—or, more typically, in the basement where the practice typewriters and office machines are kept.

THE EXTENT OF COURSE PROLIFERATION

If the recommendations in the preceding sections were adopted, many schools would find it necessary to drop a substantial number of the overly specialized courses now in their lists of offerings. It should not be necessary to offer more than two, three, or at the larger schools, four advanced courses in each of a few broad fields, with one of the courses in each area being a seminar or a course with a general title (such as "Current Problems in . . .") which would cover different topics each year. Another desirable move would be to institute a senior seminar which would not be restricted to any particular field or set of topics. We hope also that more schools will see fit to institute honors programs involving special seminars; such programs are now rare. Perhaps some of the faculty manpower that would be released by the abolition of much of the specialization currently blighting collegiate business education could be channeled in this direction. For most schools a total offering of forty to fifty semester courses would provide for all of our minimal recommendations, as well as allow for advanced work including seminars in each of six fields.

An examination of the catalogues of member schools suggests that even schools acknowledged to be relatively free of the curse of specialization are guilty of undue proliferation of courses. Counting undergraduate courses only and using the semester course meeting three hours a week as the standard, we found that the thirty-seven member schools in our sample were distributed as follows: one had less than forty courses; twenty had between forty and eighty courses; nine had between eighty and 120; and five had between 120 and 160.[54] One school had 188 under-graduate courses listed in its catalogue.

If transportation, real estate, utilities, and insurance are lumped into a conglomerate field, "industry," then we can say that this field is the worst offender in terms of proliferation. If industry is too heterogeneous a category, then first place goes to the field of marketing: eleven of the thirty-seven schools offered more than twenty semester courses, and three offered more than thirty. But, of course, every field offers opportunities for proliferation, even such fields as business English, in which one school offered thirteen courses, and business law, in which two schools offered twelve courses. At the other extreme, a few schools in our sample had the equivalent of fifty or fewer courses listed in a recent catalogue.[55] But even these schools, which deserve praise for resisting the urge to slice sometimes thin subject matter even thinner, are not exemplary in every field. One of them had fourteen industry courses and eight courses in marketing; and all of them had excessive undergraduate offerings in ac-counting.

The Timing of Professional and General Education

The order in which we have dealt with the curriculum in this and the preceding chapter may have suggested that we believe that the four undergraduate years should be neatly divided in half: general education in the first two years and professional education in the last two. Some schools do subscribe substantially to this view, but current opinion leans generally toward the idea that there should be some general education in all four years, although the amount will necessarily have to decline sharply between the first two and the last two years. Putting some general education in the junior and senior years may imply that there must be some business courses in the first two years. This creates something of

[54] We do not know, of course, if these courses were given every year. Such evidence as we have leads us to believe that most courses are given at least once a year. Courses in economics and in other nonbusiness areas were excluded unless they had a specific business orientation. The tallies in more detail were as follows:

No. of Semester Courses	No. of Schools	No. of Semester Courses	No. of Schools
Under 40	1	100–119	3
40–59	10	120–139	1
60–79	10	140–159	4
80–99	6	Over 159	2

In converting quarter hours to semester units, one quarter hour was counted as equal to two-thirds of a semester unit. If graduate courses are added to undergraduate offerings, the totals exceed 200 courses for several schools.

[55] It should be added that showing restraint in course offerings is most difficult for the large schools with substantial budgets. The small school with a few faculty members and a small student body does not have to try hard to hold down the number of courses offered.

a conflict because of the growing opinion that not many of the required business courses are suitable for lower division students. A number of schools have recently moved some of their core courses from the sophomore to the junior year.

These issues are related to the question of whether or not the business school should assume jurisdiction over all four years. The common arrangement is for the business school to admit students either at the beginning of the freshman year (four-year school) or at the beginning of the junior year (two-year school). A small number admit students at the beginning of the sophomore year. The difference, however, is often only one of formal organization. In many four-year schools, the bulk of the professional work is delayed until the junior year, while in most two-year schools the professional prerequisites—e.g., accounting, statistics, and business law—are taken in the first two years.

While, on the whole, we lean somewhat toward the two-year type of school, the few suggestions we have to make regarding the timing of courses can be implemented by a school that takes its students for two, three, or four years.[56]

General and professional courses should be scheduled in such a way as to maximize the transference from "principles" to "application" and from the general to the more specific. As an example, consider the different roles of the behavioral sciences and of history in the curriculum. The former requirement is meant to provide a basic understanding of human behavior which students will find helpful in their professional studies, and thus should be met before these professional studies begin, presumably in the junior year. Mathematics, elementary economics, and the English language requirements are similar to the behavioral sciences in this respect. The history requirement, on the other hand, while relevant to a number of professional courses, is not so directly a foundation for the business curriculum and, therefore, need not come at a particular place in the curriculum. With respect to the professional courses, the same rule is valid: basic and tool courses should come first, then clinical and integrating courses.

The Need for Flexibility and Experimentation

As we warned at the beginning of both this and the preceding chapter, the curriculum recommendations presented here suffer from a major weakness. They are too detailed and specific and, if taken literally, allow

[56] For a discussion of this issue, see Meeri Marjatta Saarsalmi, *Some Aspects of the Thought Underlying Higher Education for Business in the United States* (Indiana Readings in Business, 1955), pp. 266–69.

too little for legitimate differences of opinion and for experimentation.

The implied rigidity in our recommendations is in one sense intended, and in another sense not. We have thought it desirable to spell out our suggestions in considerable detail so that the nature of what we were proposing would be perfectly clear. We felt it mandatory to show in some detail in what ways current practice fails to meet what we consider to be acceptable standards. We also wanted to provide detailed guidelines for those schools which are seeking help in improving the quality of their curricula.

It is probably in the area of general education that our recommendations are particularly open to criticism on the grounds of too much specificity and too little flexibility. While recognizing that there must be room for variation among schools, we had yet another reason for spelling out our recommendations in what must seem like unseemly detail. As we have suggested several times, the undergraduate business schools are attempting in effect to do the impossible, to provide a satisfactory general *and* professional education in four years. From most points of view, the verdict must be that it cannot be done. Yet it is clear that the attempt will continue to be made. We share the view of many others that, if the attempt is to be made, primacy must be given to the objective of general education. Yet the majority of business schools have been doing just the opposite. By making our recommendations quite specific, we have sought to emphasize how little time there is for all the things that need to be done in providing a general education foundation *even when the minimum requirement in general education is set at 50 per cent of the total required for the undergraduate degree.* Thus we look on the detailed recommendations as providing proof that not more than half the undergraduate's four years should be devoted to professional education. They also help to show how skimpy a student's education will be in a number of areas even if 50 per cent of the four years' work is devoted to general education.

While, for these reasons, we have felt it necessary to spell out our proposals in considerable detail, we should be the first to grant that there are alternative ways of reaching the educational objectives we seek—and that in particular areas other alternatives may well be better than those that we propose.

Indeed, continued improvement implies the willingness to experiment, and throughout this chapter we have urged the need for experimentation—and for publicizing the results of experiments that seem promising. But while it is clear that not every business school will want to or should adopt all of our detailed recommendations, we are prepared to argue that every business curriculum should be based on clearly stated educational objectives. And we think that these objectives should not differ significantly from those which were presented in Part II of this report. While differences in practice are to be encouraged, the need for flexibility should not be permitted to become an excuse for low standards and a poor educational program.

A more difficult and pervasive problem arises from the fact that a variety of local conditions may make it difficult for particular schools to adopt our proposals, even when a substantial part of the faculty may wish to do so. The first of these local conditions involves students. The large metropolitan schools, for example, provide education on a part-time basis for thousands of young people who insist on curricula which are "practical" and as immediately applicable to their jobs as possible. Many schools, particularly in the South but also in other parts of the country, must provide an education for large numbers of youngsters who come from small high schools and are woefully unprepared for the kind of professional program we have proposed. The problems faced by these schools are serious, and radical improvement will not come overnight. It is unfortunate but inevitable that there will continue to be some undergraduate business schools which simply cannot offer first-class, professional education for business. It is not inevitable, however, that they should be full members of the Association, which acts as the accrediting agency for collegiate business education.

Other kinds of local restrictions may include pressures from local business interests, an unsympathetic administration, and inability to secure cooperation from other departments on the campus. But the most serious obstacle of all is likely to be a substantial segment of the business school faculty itself. Opposition to our suggestions must be expected from faculty members who give the kinds of courses that we think should be eliminated, as well as from all those who are content with things as they are.

In such schools, change will probably have to come more gradually than we should like. We hope that this report will provide some of the stimulus needed to start and accelerate the kind of change that is necessary. The most effective spur would be an overhauling of the standards of the American Association of Collegiate Schools of Business. While some of our recommendations may be too detailed to be spelled out in the Association's standards, collegiate business education would benefit substantially if these standards were brought in line with the general tenor of our proposals. In particular, the Association might: 1) set a minimum of 50 per cent for the amount of general education, 2) put a low maximum limit on the amount of work permitted in the field of concentration, 3) revise its core requirements along the lines suggested in this chapter, and 4) consider whether it wishes to specify the kind and amount of those parts of the general education base which are most directly preprofessional in character. It would help also if the Association were more effectively to implement its standards (even the inadequate ones that it now has).

In ending this overly long discussion of curriculum problems, we should repeat the note of caution with which we began Chapter 8. Important as curricula are, the best curriculum in the world cannot make up for a lack of proper objectives, an inadequate faculty, a poor student body, and the resulting lack of a stimulating intellectual atmosphere. These are matters to be discussed in later chapters. But given the teachers and students and an appropriate set of objectives, the curriculum then does become important, for it is the medium through which educational goals are implemented.

chapter 10

OTHER UNDERGRADUATE

PROGRAMS IN BUSINESS

THIS REPORT has as its major focus the degree programs of schools of business in colleges and universities. Instruction in business, however, is offered in a number of different forms and in a variety of organizational settings. This chapter is concerned with several of the more important of these "minor" programs, namely:

1) "Service" programs in business administration for students majoring in nonbusiness fields.

2) Degree programs in business in colleges and universities not having separately organized business schools—i.e., degree programs administered by departments of business and economics.

3) Business curricula in engineering schools.

4) Business programs in community or junior colleges.

Programs for Nonbusiness Students

We suggested in Part II that the business schools have a responsibility to provide some instruction in business for undergraduates majoring in nonbusiness areas. Liberal arts graduates (and engineers) will continue to be an important source of managerial talent. A modest amount of formal instruction in business administration will enable such students to embark more quickly and more successfully on a business career and ease the problem of adjustment, particularly for the liberal arts graduate.[1] This is a service function which the business schools are not now adequately performing.

We suggest a modest program of four or five semester courses geared especially to the needs of students who are not majoring in business administration. A wide range of possibilities suggest themselves, and schools will need to experiment to find what best fits their own resources and the interests of their potential audience.

[1] Cf. our earlier comments on the adjustment problems of the liberal arts graduate in Chapter 6. Other students—for example, in law and engineering—might also profit from service courses of the sort described here.

Certainly such a program would include a semester of accounting, perhaps with an admixture of statistics. Procedural detail would be almost completely omitted. Other courses might cover the nature and functions of economic management (combining some "managerial economics" and illustrative material from the functional fields); the firm as an organization; the market environment of business; problems of economic instability and growth; and the social, legal, and political framework of business.[2] These or similar courses would undoubtedly require some elementary economics as a prerequiste. No doubt many students would have room in their programs for only a part of this or some similar sequence. Cooperation with some departments might lead to combined majors into which such courses could be fitted.

Properly designed and taught, these service courses could be as respectable a part of a liberal arts curriculum as anything presently offered under that often misleading label. A sequence of four or five semester courses, constituting about 10 per cent of a four-year program, would be useful for any undergraduate anticipating a career in private or public management but not matriculated in a business program. Difficulties would undoubtedly arise in implementing this proposal. But the opportunities and need for this kind of program are such that the effort necessary to overcome these obstacles is almost certain to pay large dividends. So far, the efforts of the business schools in this direction have been largely limited to an occasional "survey" course in accounting for nonbusiness majors and perhaps a course or two specifically designed for engineers.

Degree Programs in Departments of Business

In addition to the 160 schools and colleges of business with which we are primarily concerned, some 400-odd departments have programs leading to degrees in business.[3] The latter confer about one-third of the bachelor's degrees awarded annually in business in the United States and therefore are important enough to justify some comment at this point.[4]

As the preceding figures suggest, departments tend to be much smaller than schools. Nearly 90 per cent of the business departments awarded

[2] Some of these might be regularly chosen by economics majors.

[3] See Table 3. Perhaps half of these departments are actually departments of economics and business, awarding degrees in both areas. Some of the others are largely oriented toward the preparation of high school business teachers, but purport also to train students for managerial positions in business. Our remarks, and our data, apply only to the business administration side of these combined departments.

[4] See also the chapter on the teaching of business administration in liberal arts colleges by Joseph Coppock in Frank Pierson *et al., The Education of American Businessmen* (1959).

fifty or fewer degrees in 1956.[5] Several other differences are also worth noting. Departments usually have less autonomy than schools and apparently for this reason have not been eligible for full membership in the AACSB.[6] Departments tend to be affiliated with colleges; schools are usually components of universities. Thus, the business faculty may find itself in the one case in an environment which is oriented toward undergraduate education and the arts and sciences, whereas in the other case the orientation may be more in the direction of professional and graduate training. It is also worth mentioning that departments are more heavily concentrated in the Central and Southwest regions than are schools.

THE FACULTIES

How small these departments typically are is indicated by the fact that about half of them have three or fewer regular, full-time faculty members, excluding those in economics. And only one-fifth had more than six. Faculties of business schools, by contrast, seldom number as few as ten members, and half have more than twenty on a regular full-time basis, excluding those in economics.[7]

Faculty members in business departments typically have had less graduate training than those teaching in business schools. Only 20 per cent of the faculty members in the departments of business covered by the Carnegie survey held doctor's degrees. Nearly 40 per cent of those in schools of business, on the other hand, possessed doctorates.

Teachers in business departments tend to be paid less and teach more hours per week than do their colleagues in business schools. Nearly 60

[5] The following table classifies 386 departments (omitting departments affiliated with technical institutes and universities rather than colleges) and 160 schools (counting the University of California at Berkeley and U.C.L.A. and New York University's graduate and undergraduate schools separately) according to number of degrees in business conferred in 1955-56.

Number of Degrees Conferred

	1–50	51–100	101–150	151–200	201–250	More than 250	Total
No. of depts.	335	37	10	1	2	1	386
No. of schools	18	37	29	19	11	46	160

Source: U.S. Office of Education, *Earned Degrees Conferred by Higher Educational Institutions 1955-56* (Circular No. 499, 1957), Table 17.

[6] The *Standards for Membership* of the Association, as of May, 1958, reads as follows: "To be eligible for membership . . . a school or college shall be a distinct and independent degree-recommending unit responsible directly to the central administrative authority of an institution of higher learning to which other independent degree-recommending units are similarly responsible." However, in 1959 two divisions of business were admitted to full membership.

[7] The best evidence available on faculties of departments of business is that obtained in 1957 by the Carnegie Corporation Survey of Business Education under the direction of Professor Frank Pierson. Cf. *Summary of Preliminary Findings* (revised August 1, 1958). This is the source unless otherwise noted for all quantitative information on faculties in this section.

per cent of the former teach fifteen or more hours per week, while only one-ninth of the latter teach as much as this. More than 80 per cent of the teaching staff in schools teach twelve or fewer hours; the fraction is only one-fifth for those in business departments.

The picture that emerges of the typical business department is not a reassuring one: usually fewer than five faculty members, poorly paid and frequently not well trained, with heavy teaching loads and instructing in a variety of courses for many of which they are not well prepared. Under these conditions, there is heavy reliance on textbooks; teaching is not apt to be at a very high analytical level; case teaching is relatively rare, and there is likely not to be much emphasis on problem-solving. The faculty usually fails to keep up with recent developments, either in the scientific and professional literature or in business practice. No research comes out of these departments, and few services are offered to the business community. The sole task in these departments is undergraduate teaching in the narrow sense of the term, and the quality of that teaching frequently leaves much to be desired.

CURRICULA IN DEPARTMENTS OF BUSINESS

In order to get some idea of the kinds of programs offered by departments of business, we selected a sample of thirty-seven business departments for detailed analysis. The method of selection is described in Appendix E. Our remarks in this section are based largely on this sample and on a comparison with the sample of thirty-seven member schools studied in Chapters 8 and 9.

Departments of business have curricula which differ significantly from those of the AACSB schools mainly in the amount of work in business administration that is required. Association schools typically require both a larger business core and a greater amount of specialization and elective work in business. In the one case, the total requirement in business is about 50 per cent of the total for the degree; in the other, about one-third of the four years' work is typically in business subjects.

Nearly every school belonging to the AACSB requires work in accounting, business law, statistics, marketing, and some sort of advanced economics. Only accounting is required to the same degree by business departments. In fact, fewer than half of our sample departments required any advanced economics (money and banking in every case), and only about one-fourth required a course in marketing.[8]

Unlike most schools of business, departments often do not require work

[8] The numbers of schools and departments requiring at least one course in the areas indicated are as follows (from two samples of thirty-seven curricula each): accounting, 37 schools, 36 departments; statistics, 37 and 21; marketing, 37 and 10; business law, 36 and 24; any

in a special field within business administration. Of the thirty-seven departments studied, twenty-one had no fields of specialization other than business itself, and ten had only two fields (nearly always general business and accounting). Of course, it may be possible for students to use their electives so as to have a *de facto* field of specialization even if their departments do not require one. As we should expect, however, the opportunities for specialization, in terms of course offerings, are much more meager in business departments than in business schools.[9] And even when a field of specialization within business is required, the specification of courses tends to be moderate, with twelve hours being the typical requirement. The departments of business are clearly less guilty of the sins of specialization than are the business schools. One important reason, obviously, is that these departments usually have too few faculty members to permit very much specialization.

Although the required amount of professional education in departments of business tends to be significantly smaller than in business schools, the requirement in general education is only slightly larger. About the same amount and kind of social science is required and only a trifle more natural science and mathematics. In the area of the humanities and fine arts, however, the difference is substantial, chiefly because the departments tend to have much larger requirements in English composition, speech, and literature. Usually, also, students in departments are free to take somewhat more electives than their counterparts in the business schools.

OBJECTIVES OF BUSINESS EDUCATION IN A LIBERAL ARTS SETTING

Departments of business, despite their more limited resources, stress the same objectives as the full-fledged business schools: preparation for a general career in business, training in some business specialty, and giving the student an advantage in finding his first job.[10] Of these, only the first seems appropriate for the business department in a liberal arts college, and then only with some qualifications. The same is true of those "general" colleges which are more diversified in character than the strictly liberal arts colleges—not only because the resources of most college de-

kind of advanced economics (usually money and banking), 30 and 15; organization-general management, 21 and 9; finance, 28 and 13; personnel-industrial relations, 19 and 6; business communications, 18 and 10; production-industrial management, 16 and 3; business mathematics, 10 and 14; business policy, 4 and 4; and "miscellaneous" courses (mainly "industry" courses, introduction to business, and economic geography), 19 and 18.

[9] The departments in our sample typically had about twenty-five courses listed in their bulletins, as against something like seventy-five courses for schools.

[10] See the discussion of objectives in Chapter 3.

partments are wholly inadequate for highly specialized curricula, but also because the provision of a solid foundation in general education and a grounding in the basic tools and concepts of business leave no room for the development of competence in one of the business specialties.

A general or liberal arts college, however, may properly offer its students some preparation for a nonspecialized career in business. If it does so, it will then need to pay some attention to the same broad professional skills as does the school of business. Even more than the business school, however, it has an obligation to stress breadth of knowledge and perspective and to give its students some understanding of the way in which business functions within a changing social, political, and economic environment. The department of business in a liberal arts college should emphasize an "external-analytical" approach more and a managerial approach less than the professionally oriented business school. A department in a general college might possibly take an intermediate position.

In short, the teaching of business administration in a college should have a strong orientation toward general education. On this basis, the colleges can meet an important need by offering imaginative, high-level, and liberally oriented programs in business. These might be limited "service" programs for students concentrating in other fields, or they might be full-fledged majors for those who want to concentrate on the study of business.

So far as we can ascertain, few colleges are offering this kind of program, either on a limited service basis or as a field of concentration.[11] Some of the best liberal arts colleges will have nothing to do with business courses at all (except for a course in accounting and possibly corporation finance). But much more typically, colleges offer programs in business which are no more than poor imitations of what is available in the full-fledged schools of business. When the original being imitated is not very good to begin with, when the original's narrow professional objectives have little place in an undergraduate setting, and when the imitators' resources are obviously inadequate, it is not surprising that not much good can be said for the imitation.

SOME POSSIBLE ALTERNATIVES

To make the most effective use of their limited resources, departments of business need to try a fresh approach. Three alternatives are open to them. The first alternative is not one that we recommend and in any

[11] Claremont Men's College ("A Liberal Arts College Emphasizing Business and Public Administration") represents an interesting attempt to combine general and professional education in a liberal arts context.

event is available only to the relatively few departments of business that are already quite large. This is to become a full-fledged business school, if the department insists on offering a full-blown degree program in business. If this alternative is chosen, the faculty concerned should not only become a school and offer its own degree but it should also be prepared as a minimum to meet in full the prevailing standards of the American Association of Collegiate Schools of Business.

Only a few of the larger departments are in a position to elect this first alternative. These might include the dozen or so business departments that confer more than a hundred degrees each year. Most of the other collegiate business departments would be well advised not to try to offer regular, professional programs in business. We do not profess to know exactly what is the minimum size for an undergraduate school of business, but it is obvious that respectable training in the variety of core courses described in Chapter 9 cannot be offered by a faculty of three or four or even five—the number of faculty members that most colleges have in their departments of business.

The second alternative is the obvious one for the smaller departments of business, particularly in colleges which stress the values of liberal education. This would be to abandon their degree programs in business and to concentrate on offering a service program within the framework of the liberal arts degree. We have already indicated why we think this kind of program is important and needs to be offered much more widely than it now is.

We have already explained what we mean by a service program, but, to repeat briefly, it might include four or five semester courses in business offered for students who already are majoring in another field. These courses should be planned as an integrated sequence, thus constituting what many colleges term a "minor," but at least some of them should be available individually on an elective basis. Presumably the courses would cover some or all of the core areas of the business curriculum, although a substantial amount of integration would be required. The teaching should stress breadth and analytical content, with less of a managerial emphasis than one would expect in a good business school. Grinnell College has been experimenting with a program along precisely these lines.

For those departments not strong enough to adopt our first alternative (to become full-fledged schools) and unwilling or unable to put the second into effect, the only remaining alternative is to continue to offer degree programs in business. But these programs, reflecting their academic setting, should differ somewhat from the program offered by the professional school of business.

It seems reasonable that the minimum requirement in general education should be larger than that which we proposed for the business schools —say, 60 instead of 50 per cent. The business core might be smaller, covering the same areas as would a full-fledged business school but with more integration of subject matter and perhaps more emphasis on the market and nonmarket environment of business. There should be no field of concentration within business at all.

Although the argument for requiring more general education of the student in a general or liberal arts college scarcely needs justification, one very practical point should be stressed. The resources of the kind of business department that we are now discussing are by definition very limited. The substitution of additional general education, particularly of a preprofessional character, permits the few faculty members in the business department to concentrate on what they can do best and enlists the resources of other departments in providing challenging courses for the student.

The business core described in Chapter 9 might be condensed in various ways to meet the limited resources of a small department of business. The requirement in accounting and statistics, with emphasis entirely on managerial or interpretive aspects, could be held to one year. The functional fields might be integrated in various ways. In any event, the production course might be dropped, and there is certainly no need for a course in personnel management. There should be at least a semester of administration and human relations. The course in business conditions and forecasting might be given by the economics department.

There should be a fair amount of emphasis on managerial problem-solving and a moderate use of cases, but probably less than in a full-fledged business school. If possible, the business policy course should be required. In place of the policy course, if it is not required (or possibly in addition to it), we suggest the inclusion of a senior problems seminar or an honors course. With the help of the economics, history, and political science departments, even more stress might be put on the legal, social, and political framework of business than would be the case in a conventional business school.

In all, such a program might include a general education base of about seventy-two semester hours (60 per cent of the total), a broad business core of thirty to thirty-six units, and twelve to eighteen units of electives. Including electives, the total of business and closely related subjects should not exceed about forty units (one-third of the total for the degree). This is a little less than most departments of business are now requiring.

For the small department, with only a few faculty members and somewhat isolated from the main stream of developments in collegiate business education, the kind of program we suggest would constitute a substantial improvement over what now frequently passes as a major program in business. What are most needed to improve matters are initiative and imagination, a respect for the liberal tradition in higher education, and recognition that the small business department can offer a reasonably challenging program tailored to its own resources and educational setting without slavishly imitating the full-fledged business schools.[12]

Business Education in an Engineering Setting

Collegiate education for business is not confined to schools and departments of business administration. An increasing amount of training for business goes on in the engineering schools and technical institutes. A combination of technical and business training is highly prized by many companies, and this sort of combined training is available today at both the graduate and undergraduate level. As we shall see, it varies widely in quality—but the best is indeed quite good.

THREE WAYS OF COMBINING ENGINEERING AND BUSINESS EDUCATION

Business and engineering subjects can be offered to the student in various combinations, and the program as a whole can be administered by either the engineering or business school. For our purposes, it is important to distinguish among three types of programs, which can be given the designations "industrial engineering," "industrial administration," and "production management."[13] The last is a conventional field of concentration in the business school. The first is at least a first cousin

---

[12] Professor Coppock, in his chapter previously cited, suggests an interesting fourth alternative for liberal arts colleges—no major in business administration and no business courses but a variety of "prebusiness" programs of study composed of different combinations of available courses in the fields likely to be most useful to businessmen: economics, mathematics, English, history, etc. This suggestion implies that there would be no department of business administration, that the student would major in some other field, and that faculty counseling would help him to choose a useful combination of "prebusiness" courses—in much the same fashion as is now done with premedical or prelegal students. There is much to be said for this proposal. It is not incompatible with our second alternative, which does provide for a few broad "service" courses in business. All three of our alternatives, it might be added, assume that a college has and wishes to retain some sort of program in business administration.

[13] A number of institutions have joint programs in engineering and business whereby students meet the requirements of both curricula and receive both degrees. Usually both are bachelor's degrees, although sometimes the business degree is the M.B.A. The text discussion is concerned only with curricula which lead to a single degree.

of the standard program in mechanical engineering. The second, industrial administration, is the most interesting and promising from our point of view.

Let us consider industrial engineering first. Engineering curricula have three standard elements: a base in the arts and sciences, with a heavy emphasis on mathematics and science; a core of what are often called the basic engineering studies; and a collection of courses in a special field of engineering.[14] Industrial engineering has been one of these special fields, so that we can identify a curriculum in industrial engineering as a regular engineering program which has a base in the arts and sciences (about 45 per cent) and an engineering core (about 30 per cent), followed by a group of courses (about 25 per cent) in industrial engineering and business.[15] (See Table 16.) This last group may include courses that have traditionally overlapped engineering and production management (such as time and motion study, plant layout, etc.), the newer courses in such areas as statistical quality control, data processing, and operations research, as well as some of the standard business school requirements in economics, accounting, and one or more of the functional fields. Understandably, jurisdictional disputes between the engineering and business school faculties are not infrequent. Sometimes the same course, with a different emphasis, is offered in both schools.

"Industrial engineering" is an accurate title for this kind of program. It *is* a program in engineering, and only incidentally in business administration. The time spent on *general* business subjects is very small. Beyond the science and general engineering requirements which it has in common with other engineering curricula, its primary focus is on the technical aspects of production.

The production management major offered by the business school has one important characteristic in common with the conventional program in industrial engineering. While it requires much less work in mathematics, science, and engineering and much more in strictly business subjects, it also is concerned with the technical problems of (chiefly manufacturing) production. While there are a few programs which attempt to require an adequate technical base for this sort of specialized training,

[14] For information (and further references) on engineering curricula, see American Society for Engineering Education, *Report on Evaluation of Engineering Education, 1952–1955* (1955), and J. B. Sanders, *General and Liberal Educational Content of Professional Curricula: Engineering* (U.S. Office of Education, Pamphlet No. 114, 1954). We have supplemented published analyses by a personal examination of a small number of programs in each of the fields discussed in the text. See Table 16.

[15] These percentages are only approximate. The actual percentages within each category vary considerably among schools.

TABLE 16

A COMPARISON OF UNDERGRADUATE ENGINEERING, INDUSTRIAL
ADMINISTRATION, AND BUSINESS CURRICULA: TYPICAL AND
RECOMMENDED

(*Semester Units*)

Curricula	General Education				Engineering			Business and Economics			
	Total	Science and Mathematics	Humanities	Social Sciences	Total	Engineering	Production Engineering	Total	Advanced Economics	Business Core	Total Requirements
Typical curriculum in:											
Engineering	61	36	9	12	80	—	—	0	—	—	141
Industrial engineering	60	30	9	9	54	39	15	12	0	12	140
Industrial administration	60	24	9	12	36	30	6	40	0	33	144
Production management	48	9	15	18	12	0	12	54	3	39	120
Recommended curriculum in:											
Industrial administration	72	24	24	24	33	—	—	36	6	30	141
Business	60	12	24	24	0	—	—	36-45	6	30-39	120

Note: The detailed figures often fail to add to totals because elective units are not included.
Source: Information on engineering curricula is from J. B. Sanders, *General and Liberal Educational Content of Professional Curricula: Engineering*, U. S. Office of Education Pamphlet No. 114 (1954). The typical industrial engineering and industrial administration curricula are derived from an analysis of the catalogue descriptions of programs at the following institutions: Alabama Polytechnic Institute, University of California (Berkeley), Carnegie Institute of Technology, Case Institute of Technology, University of Connecticut, Georgia Institute of Technology, Illinois Institute of Technology, Massachusetts Institute of Technology, North Dakota Agricultural College, Ohio State University, Purdue University, Rensselaer Polytechnic Institute, Stanford University, Texas Agricultural and Mechanical College, Yale University. The typical production management curriculum is from Chapter 9, as is the recommended business curriculum.

not much can be said for the conventional undergraduate concentration in production management. Not only is this much undergraduate specialization a poor route to a management career, but it seems to us to be an equally bad route to a high-level technical career. First of all, the base in science and mathematics in such curricula is nearly always inadequate. We encountered no program which required as much in these areas as the recommendation—about thirty-six semester hours—of the American Society for Engineering Education. Second, production programs usually have such a small engineering content, perhaps twelve semester hours, that the whole endeavor seems somewhat futile. In addition, of course, the lack of a sound background in science and mathematics often reduces the technical courses to a highly superficial level.

We come now to programs in what we have called industrial administration. They also bear other labels such as industrial management and engineering administration. Unlike the two types just discussed, the industrial administration program attempts to combine a *general* background in science-engineering with a *general* business training. The heavy emphasis on production is missing.

The distinguishing feature of industrial administration programs is that they are genuine hybrids, combining engineering and business studies on a base of general education. By contrast, a production management curriculum is a business program with a few engineering courses, while the industrial engineering program emphasizes engineering but includes a few business and management-oriented, engineering-type courses. The industrial administration programs tend to have a conventional general education requirement (about 45 per cent) which includes more mathematics and science courses than business students normally take, but fewer than engineers are required to have. (See Table 16.) Then there is a core in engineering, which usually covers the engineering sciences in a somewhat more condensed form than in the engineering programs. There is a substantial amount of variation, however, and some schools confer degrees in industrial administration that require almost no work in conventional engineering courses. Where this occurs, we have what amounts to a program in business administration built on a base of general education which contains more science and mathematics than the business student usually gets.

The third part of the curriculum in industrial administration is devoted to economics and business subjects. This typically occupies about 30 per cent of the curriculum and corresponds fairly well to a regular business core—economics, accounting, statistics, law, management, and the functional fields. There is usually no field of specialization, although some schools do distinguish between "operations" (or "processing") and "organization" (or "administration"), the difference lying in whether the student's elective work is primarily on machine and system operations or on individual and group behavior.

THE CASE FOR A TECHNICAL APPROACH TO BUSINESS

How important is formal training in engineering for students planning on management careers? As we saw earlier, many employers place a high value on engineering training. What seems to be valued, however, is not the engineering knowledge itself. Rather, employers find that engineering graduates as a group have been more carefully screened in terms of ability than have liberal arts or business students. They are generally familiar with scientific and technological developments; they are trained to deal with problems in quantitative terms; and they are skilled in the analytical, problem-solving approach to situations. In short, engineers have been subjected to a reasonably rigorous training which stresses the development of analytical and quantitative skills based on a strong foundation in mathematics and science.[16]

On the other hand, the weaknesses of the engineer's training are serious. They involve particularly the difficulties that engineers have in dealing with qualitative problems, in making decisions on the basis of incomplete information, in coping with the broader aspects of the external environment, and in appreciating the importance of interpersonal relations. Engineers are handicapped by their ignorance of economics and the functional fields of business and by their lack of background in the other social sciences. On balance, engineering training is far from being an ideal preparation for business, although it often is superior to many business programs as now constituted.

Industrial engineering programs are not an exception to this conclusion. The industrial engineering and business courses in such curricula usually center on the engineering problems of manufacturing processes. The graduate in industrial engineering seldom receives an adequate training in the important business subjects described in Chapter 9. Thus, industrial engineering is not a satisfactory preparation for a career in management unless—and this is becoming increasingly common—it is followed by a graduate program in business or industrial administration. Even then, it would be better if the undergraduate years included more in the humanities and social sciences and fewer courses on the technical aspects of production management.

The typical undergraduate program in industrial administration, having a full core in business, suffers less from the weaknesses of the conventional engineering curriculum. But industrial administration still falls short of the ideal arrangement under which training in business is postponed to the graduate level.

A good program in industrial administration calls for a sound base in general education, a solid core of business subjects, and a thorough introduction to the engineering sciences. In Chapter 8 we suggested that the general education base should total at least sixty semester units. This

[16] Alexander King has put the matter as follows: "It is not argued here that scientists and engineers make better managers than men trained in other disciplines, but rather that some science and engineering is a necessary ingredient in the training of most managers of the future." "Management as a Technology," *Impact of Science on Society*, VIII (June, 1957), 71.

should probably be raised to seventy units or more because of the additional mathematics and science which the student in industrial administration needs. To this would be added thirty-six units for the minimum business core of Chapter 9 and, say, thirty-three units for the engineering core.[17]

This produces a curriculum totaling about 140 semester units, compared to the typical program in liberal arts or business of about 120 units. The bachelor's degree in engineering typically requires more than the degree in liberal arts or business, 140 units being about the national average. The curricula in industrial administration that we examined also tended to stipulate about 140 units of work, although the range was substantial, from 120 to 170 units. A good program in industrial administration would thus require a total amount of work no greater than engineering students are accustomed to, although it might mean more than four years of study for some students.

Many programs of sufficient length, however, are deficient in terms of content. The social sciences and humanities often receive inadequate attention. And some programs are even short in mathematics, science, or basic engineering courses because they have been diluted to accommodate students who are unable to meet the usual standards in engineering. It is not uncommon for students who do not perform well in freshman mathematics and physics to be shunted in their sophomore year to the program in industrial administration. Some programs in industrial administration contain too many business courses; others suffer from the opposite weakness.

While an undergraduate program in industrial administration can offer a good preparation for a career in business, the conditions necessary for this to be so are not easy to meet. It must be a heavy program, totaling more than four years at the pace college students typically observe; there needs to be more work in the humanities and social sciences than engineering students ordinarily take; there must be a substantial core in both general engineering and the basic business subjects; and the work should be at a rigorously high level and not watered down to meet the needs of students rejected by the other engineering curricula. While hardly any undergraduate programs in industrial administration fully meet all of these standards, a few come close to doing so. It seems to us that this is clearly the direction in which the engineering schools should be encouraged to move if they wish to offer undergraduate business training.

[17] There is little consensus as to what should be included in the engineering core. Those we examined required from 15 to 52 semester units. The American Society of Engineering Education describes a core in "engineering sciences" which implies about 36 units. Our figure of 33 probably represents a minimum.

The preceding comments apply only to the undergraduate level. The better graduate programs in industrial administration are simply good programs in business administration catering to students with an undergraduate background in science or engineering. Hence they will be considered along with other master's programs in Chapter 11.

Business Education in the Junior Colleges

Junior colleges are playing an increasingly important role in education beyond the high school, and they will certainly be even more important in the future than they have been in the past.[18] Already they have an important place in the scheme of business education, serving both as terminal-vocational schools and as preparatory institutions from which students transfer to the business programs in the four-year colleges and universities. In both of these capacities the junior college meets important social needs.

Business education in the junior colleges deserves more space than we can give to it in this study. Even a brief review, however, may serve a useful purpose, since the essential facts are less well known than they should be.

Programs preparing students for positions in business are offered in most of the six hundred junior colleges in the United States, although these programs do not culminate in baccalaureate degrees unless students transfer to senior colleges for additional work.[19] Conceptually, the structured junior college programs are either terminal or transfer ("uni-

[18] This section is based on a memorandum prepared by Frederick C. Schadrack, a member of our staff now on the faculty of San Francisco State College. For a substantially similar analysis, see the chapter by L. G. Medsker in Pierson *et al.*, *The Education of American Businessmen*.

[19] The junior college is defined as an institution of higher education which confers certificates, diplomas, and associate's degrees for up to two years of instruction beyond the high school. The American Association of Junior Colleges (AAJC) reported that in the 1955–56 school year 628 junior colleges in the United States and its possessions enrolled 763,075 students. ("Junior College Directory, 1957," *Junior College Journal*, XXVII [January, 1957], 280.) Unless otherwise noted, this is the source of statistical data cited in this section. The number of institutions reported here differs markedly from the 505 reported for the fall of 1955 by the U.S. Office of Education. The U.S.O.E. data are presented in W. A. Jaracz, "1955 Opening (Fall) College Enrollment," *Higher Education*, XII (January, 1956), 66. The difference between the two figures is primarily due to the fact that the U.S.O.E. included only accredited institutions while the AAJC included nonaccredited institutions as well. Part of the difference may also be attributed to differences in definitions; the AAJC includes some "separately organized junior colleges, general colleges, or lower-divisions of four-year colleges and universities" and university extension centers. (See "Junior College Directory, 1957," p. 278.) The American Council on Education's *American Junior Colleges* (4th ed., 1956), using the AAJC definition, lists 531 accredited junior colleges in 1955.

versity-parallel"); in practice the distinction is often obscured. Students not infrequently transfer to senior colleges after completing terminal curricula, and many students in transfer curricula do not.[20]

TERMINAL PROGRAMS IN BUSINESS

Terminal-vocational education in junior colleges covers a wide variety of areas in business, from general business to specialties such as apparel merchandising. A description of the offerings of the Metropolitan Junior College of Los Angeles illustrates the range and philosophy of terminal business education in the junior college:

Not only can students secure education in business in many fields such as accounting, secretarial science, merchandising, business management, and salesmanship for job entrance, but there are available many highly specialized areas. These include medical secretarial training, legal secretarial, court reporting, Spanish shorthand, school office management, school plant management, apartment house management, and practice with instruction on practically every type of business machine manufactured and used today. When newer machines are installed in a business concern, employees may return to the college for short courses of instruction. In short, the functions of the colleges are built directly into the functions of progressive business practices. . . . students may take instruction in no less than 14 specified fields in accounting. Among some of these are accounting for attorneys, insurance, service stations, radio shops, medical offices, auto dealers, income tax, etc.[21]

Naturally, not all junior colleges offer such extensive programs. The smaller the college and the less varied are employment opportunities in the community being served, the less extensive will be the vocational offerings. Among terminal business-type curricula, the most frequently offered are "secretarial-business" and "general business." Among the others frequently offered are salesmanship and merchandising. Accounting or bookkeeping is another popular offering.[22]

The least specialized of the programs, the general business curriculum,

[20] Cf. L. J. Bethel, "Types of Junior Colleges," in *American Junior Colleges* (3d ed., 1952), p. 7; also Grace V. Bird, "Preparation for Advanced Study," in Nelson B. Henry, ed., *The Public Junior College* (1956), p. 85.

[21] Jesse P. Bogue, "Junior Colleges," in *Education for Business Beyond High School* (The American Business Education Yearbook, vol. XIV, 1957), pp. 306–307. For an illustrative list of such programs, see California State Department of Education, *Business Education Curriculums and Subjects in California Junior Colleges* (Business Education Publication No. 69, 1953), pp. 3–5.

[22] See Nelson B. Henry, ed., *The Public Junior College*, p. 100; also W. C. Himstreet, *A Study of Business Education in the Public Junior Colleges of California* (unpublished doctoral dissertation, University of Southern California, 1955), p. 177; and Henry H. Armsby, Walter C. Eells, and S. V. Martorana, *Organized Occupational Curriculums, Enrollments, and Graduates, 1956* (U.S. Office of Education Circular No. 512, 1958), p. 121.

generally includes such courses as English, economic principles, accounting, bookkeeping, American history and government, use of business machines, commercial law, selling, typing, and business arithmetic. Usually only two or three general education courses are required and perhaps two more can be selected. It is common to require adapted general education courses such as business English, business mathematics, and business psychology.[23]

We have made no attempt to investigate how well the junior colleges are performing this terminal, vocational-training function. The training is job oriented and reflects an evaluation of employers' needs. At the same time, an effort is made to provide the student with some general elementary skills (in English and mathematics) and a small amount of general education that will serve him as a citizen and in his problems of personal adjustment.

All this, we think, is to the good. While undoubtedly there is substantial room for improvement, the junior colleges are rendering an essential service in providing these terminal programs in business. *It is in the junior colleges and not in the business schools of the four-year colleges that these vocational programs belong.* The obstacles to eliminating vocational training in the four-year colleges should become less as the junior college movement continues to spread. Business educators have much to gain from lending their support to the establishment and expansion of junior and community colleges, both because of the important needs the latter can serve and because of the opportunity it offers to improve the quality of education and professional training in the senior colleges and universities.

We have one uneasiness about these terminal programs, assuming that they are well taught to meet their limited objectives. There is some danger that the junior colleges, in their enthusiasm, may claim too much for what they are doing and thus mislead their students into thinking that they are being adequately prepared for careers in management or in one of the professional specialties, for example, accounting.

There is also some danger that a too narrow approach may sometimes be taken in these vocational curricula. While there is no argument about the vocational objective, too much emphasis may be placed on learning current procedures, which indeed may vary considerably among individual employers; and too little attention may be paid to the more general types of knowledge and skills required for a particular occupation. The problem is similar to that which, at a higher level, the four-year

---

[23] The thinness of the general education component of the terminal general business programs suggests that if graduates of these programs are admitted to senior colleges, they will spend some time repairing deficiencies.

colleges also face. It has been suggested, in this connection, that some of the present vocational programs in the junior colleges might be broadened, although retaining their vocational orientation, and that some of the more specialized instruction might be deferred until the student is already at work.[24]

TRANSFER PROGRAMS

About half of the regular students in junior colleges are in transfer programs. Many of these, perhaps half, never go on to advanced study.[25] But a good many do make the transfer, and to this extent the junior colleges provide up to two years of college work for students who will eventually receive bachelor's degrees and go on to careers in business or one of the professions. This transfer function of the junior colleges is almost certain to grow, and, as college enrollments mount, it may be increasingly necessary for the senior colleges to turn over a substantial part of the responsibility for the first two years' work to the junior colleges.[26]

A problem exists here which we can only note in passing. As we have mentioned, half or so of the students in these junior college transfer programs will not do advanced work. In effect, they are in a terminal program, although, for some time after graduation from high school, they "cling tenaciously to the less attainable professional goal which they think has greater social prestige."[27] It does not necessarily follow that such students—whose failure to transfer to a four-year college may be due to a variety of factors, including lack of mental ability, problems of psychological adjustment, lack of financial resources, etc.—are worse off than if they had taken an avowedly vocational curriculum. But some of them, at least, would probably be better off in a more vocational type of program.

The "transfer" program in the junior colleges is much more important as a *de facto* terminal program than as a source of students who eventually receive a degree in business from a four-year college or university. There were perhaps 75,000 regular students enrolled in junior college business programs in 1955–56. This was probably between a fifth and a fourth of the total business enrollment in all colleges. However, probably

[24] For a discussion of this and other problems presented by vocational education in the junior colleges, see L. L. Bethel, "Vocational Education," *The Public Junior College*, pp. 94–117; and J. P. Bogue, in *American Junior Colleges* (1952), pp. 33–38.

[25] Cf. Bird, "Preparation for Advanced Study," *The Public Junior College*, p. 80.

[26] Cf. *The Public Junior College*, particularly chap. 15; also The Joint Staff of the Liaison Committee of the Regents of the University of California and the State Board of Education, *A Restudy of the Needs of California in Higher Education* (1955).

[27] Bird, "Preparation for Advanced Study," *The Public Junior College*, p. 80.

not more than 15,000 eventually transferred, and probably not more than 10,000 eventually graduated. Allowing for normal attrition, perhaps around 10 to 12 per cent of the business degrees awarded in 1957 and 1958 went to students who had started out in a junior college.[28] This proportion, however, is likely to grow as the junior college movement continues to expand.

About 60 per cent of the junior colleges have transfer programs in business.[29] The rest no doubt prepare some students for transfer to schools or departments of business without having formal prebusiness programs. The composition of the transfer curricula in business is largely governed by the requirements of the colleges or universities to which the students intend to transfer. By their admission policies the senior colleges have a virtual veto over the junior college transfer curricula; and, in so far as the latter are inadequate, the senior colleges must accept a good share of the blame. The situation can be complex; there may be several senior colleges with different programs served by one junior college. In this case, the junior college will generally work out a core in general education and prebusiness comprising the courses required in common by all the senior institutions in its area, and then make available and guide the student into the other courses required by the school of his choice. If the junior-senior college system is to function effectively, the senior colleges need to coordinate their business programs and work more closely with the junior colleges.

A limited review of transfer business curricula in the junior colleges indicates little deviation from a standard lower division collegiate business school curriculum. At least two semester courses are generally re-

---

[28] These estimates are derived as follows. About 20 per cent of the students enrolled in California public junior colleges were business majors. (W. C. Himstreet, *A Study of Business Education in the Public Junior College*, p. 240.) From data for 342 junior colleges in 1955 Medsker estimated the median percentage of regular business enrollments to total regular enrollments by states as 23 per cent. (See his chapter in *The Education of American Businessmen*.) An estimate of 20 per cent appears conservative and reasonable. Applying this percentage to the 379,000 freshman-sophomore enrollment in all junior colleges in 1955–56 yields the estimate of about 75,000. Using Himstreet's finding that about 20 per cent of the business students in California junior colleges transferred to a four-year college, we derive the figure of 15,000 as the number transferring from all junior colleges (over approximately a two-year period). (We also are forced to assume that the number of transfers from junior college business programs who chose another curriculum after transferring was offset by those from nonbusiness curricula who chose to major in business after transferring.) About 45,000 bachelor's degrees in business were awarded in 1956–57. The total was probably around 90,000 over a two-year period, of which perhaps ten thousand were junior college transfers. Needless to say, these estimates are subject to a very wide margin of error. We have assumed an attrition rate of 33 per cent after junior college students enter a four-year institution. In the business schools at the University of California (Berkeley and Los Angeles) it has ranged between 30 and 40 per cent.

[29] *American Junior Colleges* (1956), pp. 528–55.

quired in English and speech, in physical and biological science, in economics (introductory or American economic history), in the humanities, and in accounting. At least one course is generally required in mathematics, history and government, and psychology and sociology. Other than accounting, the business courses that appear with some frequency in the junior college transfer programs are business law, statistics, business mathematics, and economic geography. The variations that exist among these programs normally reflect the varying requirements of senior business schools served by the junior colleges.

Apparently junior college students who transfer to schools of business have no sounder base in general studies than do students who enter a four-year school as freshmen. The same need for improvement exists here as in the four-year colleges. The transfer students have an additional handicap, however, to the extent that they take "professional" courses before they transfer. Some junior college courses in business have no senior college counterparts, so that the student cannot receive degree credit for them. This is the result of the blurred line separating transfer and terminal offerings in many junior colleges. An additional complication is that business courses which are university-parallel (e.g., elementary accounting and business statistics) often are of inferior quality or unsatisfactory orientation, due both to the sometimes limited qualifications of the instructor and, more generally, to the fact that such courses must serve a diverse student body.

The qualifications of the business faculties in the junior colleges frequently leave much to be desired. A recent study suggests that 70 per cent of the instructors in business have master's degrees as their highest degree, most of the others having only a bachelor's degree.[30] Fewer than a third of the degrees were in business or economics, including secretarial studies. In fact, none of the doctor's and only 28 per cent of the master's degrees were in business. Education was the most common background, particularly among the holders of graduate degrees. In other words, a large proportion of those who teach business subjects in the junior colleges were probably trained to teach commercial subjects at the secondary school level.

The situation is probably made less serious by the fact that most transfer students receive the bulk of their professional work after leaving the junior college. This is as it should be, for the junior colleges are better

---

[30] One and one-half per cent held doctorates, and nearly two per cent held no academic degree. These results are based on a sample of 417 business instructors in California public junior colleges. Himstreet, *A Study of Business Education in the Public Junior Colleges of California*, p. 367. Other studies tend to show the same pattern; cf. L. L. Jarvie, "Making Teaching More Effective," *The Public Junior College*, p. 218.

equipped to offer general (or vocational) than professional education. Schools of business might well consider how they can encourage the postponement of professional work until the student reaches the junior year. They should also encourage the junior colleges to improve their general education and preprofessional requirements along the lines suggested in Chapter 8. By their admissions and degree requirements, the senior colleges help to shape the transfer curricula of the junior colleges. With this power goes the responsibility to work closely with the junior colleges in planning an improved program for prebusiness students. A concomitant responsibility of the senior business schools is to train instructors for the junior colleges.

Unfortunately, limitations of time and space prevent our carrying further this all too brief survey of the role of the junior colleges in collegiate business education. So far this role has been chiefly that of vocational training. But, we suspect, the "transfer function" of the junior colleges will also grow rapidly. In the performance of this function, the junior colleges should maintain the same standards, and govern their teaching by the same philosophy, that we expect in the first two years of the senior colleges and universities. This will not be easy to do, both because of the greater diversity and lower average quality of students in the junior college transfer programs and because of the limited background of many junior college teachers. The business schools of the universities have a responsibility, in part based on self-interest, to work closely with the junior colleges toward a workable solution to these problems.

chapter 11

THE MASTER'S PROGRAM IN

BUSINESS ADMINISTRATION

IN 1957–58, about a fifth of the approximately 600 colleges and universities with degree programs in business administration offered the master's degree in business. The total number of master's degrees awarded in that year, however, was less than 10 per cent of all business degrees.[1] As we pointed out in Chapter 2, collegiate business education in the United States is overwhelmingly an undergraduate operation. While many others share our view that business education is best deferred to the graduate years, the vast majority of students continue to get their business training at the undergraduate level.

This phenomenon is not to be explained by the fact that graduate business programs are new or that few schools offer such programs. Forty years ago, at the end of the First World War, the ratio of graduate to bachelor's degrees in business was about two-thirds of what it is now. While the number of schools offering graduate degrees has steadily increased during the last twenty or thirty years, particularly since the Second World War, graduate enrollments have not grown much faster than undergraduate.

While approximately 125 institutions confer master's degrees in business, graduate training is heavily concentrated in a small number of the larger business schools. Nine schools accounted for more than half of all the master's degrees awarded in 1955–56. About 25 per cent of the total was awarded by two institutions, Harvard and New York University.

The Main Issues in Graduate Business Education

Graduate business education presents a number of issues with which the business schools are still struggling. While these issues can be separately stated, they are in fact closely interrelated.[2]

---

[1] See Tables 1 and 3.

[2] Some of these issues are briefly treated in R. L. Kozelka, *Professional Education for Business* (American Association of Collegiate Schools of Business, 1954), chap. 5.

1) There is still uncertainty as to how much effort should be put into expanding graduate training at the expense of the undergraduate program. The exclusively graduate schools have reached one answer, but one that most business schools are not prepared to accept and which is beyond the reach of most departments (as distinct from schools) of business.

2) There is some uncertainty as to the kinds of careers which should be emphasized in planning the master's program. The exclusively graduate schools tend to emphasize preparation for general management careers that do not depend on mastery of a body of specialized subject matter. A few of the schools that also have undergraduate programs explicitly take this view. Most schools, however, either implicitly stress preparation for specialized staff careers (including accounting) or are torn between a desire to emphasize a broad managerial approach and their inheritance from the past that leads them to put the main stress on command of specialized subject matter. Further uncertainty exists as to the extent to which the master's program should also seek to train teachers and research workers.

3) Because of these uncertainties, the majority of schools have not yet decided whether the master's degree in business should be considered a *graduate* or a *professional* degree. Many business schools, regardless of the kind of program they offer, are likely to aver that their master's degree is a professional degree.[3] A professional degree prepares for practice rather than teaching or research, and the program leading to the degree does not build on an undergraduate base in the same field, although some "preprofessional" work in related areas may be desirable. Law is one of the best examples of a postbaccalaureate professional program. In contrast, the traditional master's degree in most of the academic disciplines (Master of Arts or Master of Science) is a graduate degree, for which undergraduate work in the same field is a prerequisite. This type of master's program is designed to train students chiefly for teaching and for research, whether in the universities or elsewhere.

The exclusively graduate schools and a few of those also having undergraduate programs clearly look on their master's degree as a professional degree. Some other schools act as if they considered the master's degree a graduate degree and emphasize the undergraduate prerequisites. Still

[3] This is suggested not only by the statements in their catalogues but also by the extent to which they use the designation M.B.A. rather than M.A. or M.S. We were not infrequently told that a school's M.B.A. was intended as a professional degree although in all respects (undergraduate prerequisites, emphasis on specialized subject matter, and even the requirement of a thesis) it was clearly a graduate degree. See also Kozelka, *Professional Education for Business*, pp. 98–100.

others fall in between and manage to view the degree as being *both* a professional and graduate degree, with perhaps several routes open to the degree depending on the student's undergraduate background and the nature of his specialized interests.

4) All of these issues are related to the question as to what is the best kind of undergraduate preparation for postbaccalaureate training in business. The exclusively graduate schools take the view that any kind of undergraduate background (but preferably not in business administration) is acceptable. Among the schools also offering undergraduate work, there are a small but growing number that plan their master's programs on the assumption that students will not have majored in business administration as undergraduates. But most of the "mixed" schools with both undergraduate and graduate programs find themselves on the horns of a dilemma. Tradition and the large stake they have in their undergraduate curricula oblige most of them to take the view that some undergraduate training in business is necessary before the student starts a master's program At the same time, they are pulled in the opposite direction by a growing volume of applications from students without business training, by the spreading acceptance of the idea that the master's degree is a professional degree, by the current emphasis on the desirability of an undergraduate background in liberal arts or engineering, and by the view that business education, to be effective, calls for a degree of maturity and singleness of purpose which is lacking in undergraduates.

TYPES OF MASTER'S PROGRAMS

Taking these and other differences into account, we can distinguish the following types of master's programs now being offered:

1   Integrated two-year programs which assume no previous preparation in business subjects and require a substantial core of graduate level courses oriented toward managerial problem-solving. These programs are found chiefly in the exclusively graduate schools and tend to fall into one of two subgroups: a) Those that emphasize the development of administrative skills, particularly through the use of cases, but do not place much emphasis on subject matter. b) Those that put more emphasis on subject matter and the underlying disciplines and, unlike the first group, require a field of specialization.

2   "Hybrid" programs which require from one to two years of work, depending on the student's background. These fall into two groups: a) Two-year programs with a substantial core which, in effect, is

divided into two parts, from the first of which a student may be excused if he has had the corresponding undergraduate courses. These programs tend to emphasize preparation for general management careers and generally do not put much emphasis on specialized subject matter. b) Modifications of the conventional one-year program, in which students without the necessary prerequisites spend a year making them up in special graduate sections. These programs typically have little or no core in the second year, which is largely devoted to a field of specialization and electives. In this respect they resemble the next group.

3   Strictly one-year programs built on a set of undergraduate prerequisites. Students without these prerequisites make them up in undergraduate courses. Most such programs tend to have little or no required core, emphasize specialized subject matter, and are geared more to the needs of the staff specialist, public accountant, research worker, or teacher than to those of the future administrator. This is still the most common type of master's program. A few do have a substantial core of required courses emphasizing preparation for general management careers, but they are in a small minority.

GRADUATE PROGRAMS IN INDUSTRIAL ADMINISTRATION

The preceding classification refers to the master's programs in schools and departments of business in the universities and colleges. Master's degrees in business are also offered in a number of engineering schools, where the field is likely to bear such titles as industrial administration, industrial management, and engineering administration. In Chapter 10, we described the undergraduate version of a program in industrial administration and distinguished it both from the field of industrial engineering and from the typical undergraduate curriculum in business administration.

Graduate programs in industrial administration, unlike their undergraduate counterparts, contain practically no formal work in engineering. They largely attempt to meet the same needs as other graduate business programs. The content of graduate work in industrial administration, however, tends to be on a higher analytical plane than in conventional graduate business programs and tends also to involve a greater degree of sophistication.

The difference is due to the backgrounds of the students, all of whom have had a significant amount of undergraduate work in mathematics, the sciences, and usually engineering. In addition, some of these programs prefer that applicants have some operating experience of an engineering or manufacturing nature before beginning their graduate work. This kind of student body should be contrasted with the usual M.B.A. candidate: undergraduate degree in business or liberal arts with little or no science or mathematics, no engineering training, and little or no experience except for military service. Even when the conventional graduate business program attracts a significant number of students with an engineering background, the latter are in the minority; and the courses offered assume little or no training in mathematics, science, and engineering.

Some of the graduate departments in industrial administration are gripped by the same uncertainty that afflicts many of the M.B.A. programs. They have not yet decided whether the degree they offer is a conventional master's degree building on a similar undergraduate degree, or whether it is a professional degree standing essentially independent of the undergraduate training, except for the necessity of specifying a minimum preparation in science and mathematics. Thus in a number of schools the master's degree requires from one to two years depending on the student's undergraduate training. What we would call the better programs, however, generally assume no previous training in business administration.

The two-year program in industrial administration tends to be quite similar to those in the better graduate schools of business. There is a substantial core of required work in the fundamental business subjects; the development of management skills is emphasized; and the narrower aspects of engineering are largely ignored. At the same time, the students' background in science and mathematics makes possible a more sophisticated treatment in some fields and permits the program to develop advanced work on the application of the newer analytical techniques to management problems. Carnegie Tech and M.I.T. probably represent the two best known examples of two-year master's programs in industrial administration built along these lines, but there are others.

Other types of master's programs in industrial administration vary over a wide range. Some require no core but tailor-make programs for individual students; others have a required core which may in varying degrees reflect an engineering orientation; in some the core depends on the student's undergraduate background. In addition, some have specialized programs, such as Case Institute's program in Operations Research.

FLEXIBILITY AND CHANGE

In the rest of this chapter, we shall examine these different types of programs in considerable detail and, as in the several preceding chapters, suggest the directions in which we think improvement is needed. As before, our proposals are to be interpreted merely as offering general guidelines. Flexibility, experimentation, and the tailoring of curricula to the particular needs, resources, and interests of individual schools are no less desirable here than in the case of the undergraduate programs. But in the graduate as well as the undergraduate case, there is increasing agreement as to the general direction in which the business schools should move. The need for flexibility is never an adequate excuse for what is generally agreed to be a poor program.

The situation described in the following pages is as we found it during the time our material was collected (1956–58), although we take some note of changes in particular schools that have occurred since then. We said in Chapter 1 that business education is in ferment. Various schools have recently revised their master's programs or are now in the course of doing so. On the whole, however, the picture drawn of the state of business training at the master's level can be taken as describing the situation in the fall of 1959 virtually as well as it does that during the period in which our material was being compiled.

One-Year and Two-Year Programs and the Problem of Prerequisites

In Chapter 7 we recommended that the master's degree in business require two years of full-time work, approximately half of which would consist of a core of required courses covering the same broad areas recommended for the undergraduate curriculum. This was on the assumption that candidates for the master's degree had not majored in business administration as undergraduates. We argued against the arrangement followed by most schools, which is to rely on undergraduate work for the core of required business subjects so that the master's degree represents primarily a year of electives and specialization building on the undergraduate core.

The exclusively graduate schools, with one exception, require two years of work for the master's degree and specify no undergraduate business prerequisites. In only one, apparently, is it clearly possible to secure the master's degree in one year by offering undergraduate business courses previously taken.

Most of the "mixed" schools which have both undergraduate and graduate work typically require about thirty units of work for the master's degree, over and above the undergraduate prerequisites that are specified. The range, among the schools we examined, was from twenty-two to thirty-six units, with something over half requiring exactly thirty units.[4] Apparently nonmember schools are more inclined to require in excess of thirty units than are the member schools; on the other hand, a larger fraction of the total may be satisfied by undergraduate courses.

It is only by an act of charity that a number of these master's programs can be considered graduate programs at all. It is common to permit a student to meet as much as 50 per cent of the credit requirements by taking undergraduate courses, even after he has met the usual undergraduate prerequisites. The proportion may run higher, particularly in schools with small faculties and limited resources.[5]

It is a fairly common practice among American universities to list certain courses as being for both graduate and undergraduate students. Where this is true, a large part of the work for the master's degree is likely to be in such courses, and the "graduate" student may have little opportunity to study in classes composed entirely of graduate students. Some attempt is made to meet this problem by requiring extra work from those who wish graduate credit for a course of this sort, but this obviously is no substitute for courses intended exclusively for graduate students.

What is required in the way of undergraduate prerequisites varies somewhat but in general consists of the core of business courses which the school requires of its own undergraduates.[6] The total required varies from less than twenty to more than thirty semester units. Sometimes a fair amount of flexibility is permitted; in other cases, the required undergraduate courses are spelled out in detail, and the student is forced to make up any such courses that he has missed. There seems to be some trend toward greater flexibility in administering rules regarding undergraduate prerequisites as the number of applicants without previous training in business increases.

---

[4] A few schools state their requirements as being from forty-eight to sixty semester units but then allow credit up to thirty units for undergraduate work previously taken. Students coming from an undergraduate business school may not get a full year's credit for their undergraduate work, with the result that more than one year may be necessary for the master's degree.

[5] At one member school we visited, a thesis seminar in each of the special fields constituted virtually the only exclusively graduate courses available. For the rest, the master's candidate apparently took undergraduate courses. Kozelka comments on the tendency "for telescoping undergraduate and graduate sections, but using the fiction of separate course numbers." *Professional Education for Business*, p. 106.

[6] Sometimes the requirement is stated as the equivalent of an undergraduate major at any school which is a member of the Association. This, of course, may permit a wide variation in standards. Cf. Kozelka, *Professional Education for Business*, pp. 103–104.

In the great majority of schools, master's candidates lacking some of the undergraduate prerequisites are simply put into undergraduate courses. This is virtually universal among schools which are not members of the Association. Some of the member schools have tried to meet this problem by creating special graduate sections in which the master's candidates can secure the necessary elementary background but cover more ground and at a higher analytical level than in purely undergraduate classes.

The use of special graduate sections for this purpose seems to be spreading. While few schools yet provide such graduate sections for all specified prerequisites, probably a fourth or more of the member schools with conventional one-year master's programs that we visited had graduate sections available for some courses. The quality of the work in these special courses varies. Sometimes it is little better than what is required of undergraduates, but some of these courses provide a real challenge to good graduate students.

Setting up special graduate sections for the undergraduate prerequisites represents an attempt to meet a new set of needs by modifying an old program instead of developing a new one suited to the purpose. The one-year type of master's program to which has been attached a "graduate" version of the school's undergraduate core is not, in our opinion, a satisfactory substitute for a freshly planned program which treats the two years as an integrated whole.

It seems to us that there is a better way of providing a program for students with different undergraduate backgrounds. This would be to have a large required core of courses extending into the second year, from part but only part of which a student might be excused because of undergraduate courses previously taken. The program would be planned primarily to meet the needs of students without an undergraduate background in business administration. The student who had majored in business would thus become the special case, rather than the other way around.[7] This is as it should be if the standard for a good business education is to be graduate training preceded by a broad undergraduate preparation in nonbusiness subjects. Equally important, an antiquated one-year master's program cannot be satisfactorily overhauled by permitting students to make up undergraduate prerequisites that were established long ago. The situation is, of course, much worse if the student spends his first "graduate" year making up his prerequisites in the regular

---

[7] A suggested program of this sort, which a few schools now have, is described in this chapter and is summarized in Table 19.

undergraduate courses. It is made still worse if part of his second year is also spent in undergraduate classes.

THE PROBLEM OF NONBUSINESS PREREQUISITES

In considering the undergraduate curriculum in Chapter 8, we stressed the importance of an adequate background in English, economics, the other social sciences, the physical sciences, and mathematics. It is clearly desirable that graduate students in business also have some minimum preparation in these preprofessional fields, for their "professional" training cannot but suffer if their background in these areas is deficient. This problem is certain to be of growing seriousness as the scientific basis for managerial decision-making continues to expand.

At present, the position of the exclusively graduate schools seems to be that any sort of undergraduate preparation (except possibly in business administration) is equally acceptable. All avoid specifying prerequisites in the form of particular courses. The catalogues of some offer no guidance at all as to what might be desirable. One suggests that work in certain fields is useful but not required. One of the most detailed statements of a desirable undergraduate background is to be found in the 1958–59 Bulletin of the Stanford Business School, which reads as follows:

The professional training offered by the Graduate School of Business is especially suited to students who have had their academic backgrounds in the various fields within liberal arts such as economics or political science, and in engineering or science. Undergraduate business majors should not apply without consultation with the Admissions Committee. No specific courses are required for admission, but it will be helpful to have had basic courses in economics and science. One year of college mathematics or its equivalent will be very helpful to candidates. Thorough training in written and oral English is important. Undergraduate students with interest in definite phases of business can advantageously plan their programs accordingly. For example, a student interested in production may select an undergraduate engineering major; a student directing himself toward foreign trade may major in history, language, or geography; one interested in marketing or personnel may select a social science major. However, the program of study in the Graduate School of Business is organized to allow students who enter without this preparation the opportunity to supplement their training in courses at the School or in other departments of the University.

The business schools offering graduate programs need to give more thought to the question as to what is a desirable undergraduate background for graduate training in business. We suggest that they seek in their public announcements to encourage either of two kinds of undergraduate work for students who are planning to attend a graduate business school. They might recommend, first, a liberal arts program which, whatever the student's major, would call for a minimum amount of work in economics and the other social sciences, English and speech, mathematics, and the natural sciences. (See the program recommended in Chapter 8.) The second alternative would be a special type of engineering program calling for much less of the conventional engineering subjects and much more in the social sciences and humanities than the engineering schools now permit. Obviously the second alternative would not be feasible without special cooperation from the engineering schools.

This brings us to another troublesome question. If certain types of preprofessional subjects are a desirable background for a good program in business administration, what should the graduate schools do about the students who come to them with deficiences in these subjects? Several alternatives are available.

One is to introduce the needed introductory material into some of the required graduate courses. This is common procedure now in graduate offerings in economics and in administration and human relations. Another alternative is explicitly to introduce the needed preprofessional course into the graduate curriculum. The University of Chicago, for example, has just introduced a survey-type course in the behavioral sciences into its graduate business program; some other examples could also be cited. Another possibility is to add some elementary nonbusiness courses to the graduate core and waive them for the student who has had the corresponding undergraduate courses.[8]

Still another alternative is to let the students pick up the necessary background "on their own" as they go along. In this case, the graduate business courses would assume that the students had the necessary background, however acquired. While this may make life difficult for some students, it is better than "watering down" courses or spending an undue amount of time on elementary material.

The preprofessional subjects that are chiefly at issue here are elementary economics, psychology and sociology, and mathematics. No simple solution suggests itself, but we do recommend that 1) graduate business courses assume such background knowledge in the underlying disciplines as the latest developments in each business field may suggest are necessary, and 2) each school develop its own program for remedying deficiencies in students' backgrounds. Eventually, it is to be hoped, students will enter graduate school with adequate undergraduate preparation in the necessary background fields.

[8] This suggestion is further developed later in this chapter.

The Graduate Core[9]

Most of the exclusively graduate schools require of all students a core of required courses constituting a year's work or more. Six of the eight graduate schools referred to in Table 17 had such a required core in 1957–58, and a seventh was planning to introduce one. There is some variation in the extent to which core requirements may be waived because of undergraduate work previously taken. The least amount of waiver seems to occur at Harvard and perhaps Stanford. Chicago in the past has been somewhat more liberal in this respect.[10] But in most cases waiver of a required course because of previous preparation does not reduce the time necessary for the degree. Electives are substituted for required courses. Increasingly, the attitude in the graduate business schools is that the student must spend two years in graduate level courses to earn the M.B.A.

A different situation prevails among the schools offering both the bachelor's and master's degree. In these cases, there is apt to be little in the way of a graduate core beyond the undergraduate prerequisites. Among our sample schools, nearly two-thirds had specific requirements of no more than six semester units beyond specified undergraduate prerequisites; about 30 per cent had no core at all beyond the possible requirement of a master's thesis. On the other hand, slightly less than a quarter of the schools in our sample specified five or more semester courses.[11]

[9] In the remainder of this chapter we shall make use of the same sample of member and nonmember schools offering undergraduate programs that we studied in Chapter 9, supplemented by the complete list of exclusively graduate schools. We have also selected five graduate programs in industrial management or administration. Of the thirty-seven member schools in the earlier sample, thirty-three had master's programs in 1955–56. This excludes New York University, which is here treated as an exclusively graduate school. Of the thirty-seven nonmember schools, twenty-one had master's programs in 1955–56. Several member and nonmember schools have added master's degrees since then. The data derived from this sample largely describe the situation as it was in 1955–56 or 1956–57. In the text, however, we shall occasionally refer to changes that have occurred since then. The sample of schools is further described in Appendix E.

[10] In its new program, Cornell permits the waiver (by examination) of up to five specified courses out of the fifteen required by the core (see p. 259, below). In its newly revised program, Chicago will continue to permit substitution of undergraduate courses previously taken for some of the required core, but this will no longer reduce the time required for the degree below two years. Formerly, it was possible to secure the degree in anywhere from three to six quarters, depending on the student's background.

[11] The Carnegie Corporation Survey of Business Education provides some more evidence on this point. Of the more than 100 responding schools with master's programs, about half reported that they had no required core at all. About a fifth required twenty semester units or more. As few as ten required as much as a full year's work in the core. The majority of these were presumably the exclusively graduate schools. See the Survey's *Summary of Preliminary Findings* (revised August 1, 1958).

A few of the schools with both undergraduate and graduate offerings have master's programs which resemble those in the exclusively graduate schools. Northwestern and Washington University, for example, each have in effect a two-year master's program with a large core planned as an integrated unit. In one case, eight out of fifteen core courses may be waived for students who have had undergraduate equivalents; in the other, up to thirty out of forty-eight semester units in the core may be waived. In both cases, the time required for the degree is thereby reduced. A somewhat similar situation has existed at the University of Pennsylvania. No undergraduate prerequisites are specified, but some part or all of the graduate core of sixteen semester units may be waived for students with the appropriate undergraduate background. How large one considers the core at these institutions depends on the way one treats these elementary core courses that can be waived.[12]

A few schools start from a one-year master's program which has little or no graduate core for the student with a bachelor's degree in business administration, but require the student without a previous background in business administration to spend his first graduate year making up prerequisites in special graduate sections. For the latter this becomes the graduate core. Both types of students then go on to a year of specialization and electives.[13]

There is undoubtedly room for several different ways of handling the core requirements. The important thing is to plan an integrated two-year program in which the school lays out the work it feels the student must cover. Some schools may wish to pay no attention to the special situation of students who have had some undergraduate business courses and, indeed, to discourage such students. Refusal to waive any part of the graduate core is justifiable, particularly if the basic graduate courses attempt to do much more than can be expected in the corresponding undergraduate classes. However, a problem is likely to arise in a few courses, for example, accounting, in which the student may feel that in good part he is being made to cover already familiar ground.

A school wishing to waive some of its first-year core courses for students who have had corresponding undergraduate work should do so with several qualifications. First, the student should still spend more than one year getting the degree, although a full two years may not be necessary. Second, there should in most cases be a second required course in the field in which the first course was waived, from which the student cannot

[12] A number of other schools have one-year programs with a significant core of required courses but also specify the usual undergraduate prerequisites.

[13] Recent examples have been Indiana and the University of California at Berkeley, but the same system exists, at least in part, at a number of other schools.

be excused. Thus the school insures that the student is exposed to more advanced material and to the kind of development of his problem-solving and other skills which cannot be expected in an undergraduate course. And, finally, it would be highly desirable if the student used the time saved through being excused from certain elementary business courses to remedy deficiencies in his general education that may exist because he concentrated on business subjects as an undergraduate.

This last proposal suggests a general way in which the graduate schools might insure that their students have had the preprofessional background which is important for business students. If it is considered important, for example, that graduate business students have a minimum background in economics, the other social sciences, or mathematics, introductory courses in these areas might be added to the graduate core and then waived for students who have had satisfactory undergraduate work in these fields.

The Cornell Graduate School of Business and Public Administration seems to have made a start in this direction. In its heavy core of fifteen semester courses, five may be waived by examination: economics, government, business law, accounting, and statistics. The assumption seems to be that in the typical case some of these will be waived. The presence of economics and government in this list is particularly to be noted. This procedure could easily be widened to include in the core elementary or survey courses in psychology or the behavioral sciences, science and technology, and mathematics, from some or all of which the student might be excused either by examination or on presentation of evidence of a satisfactory undergraduate course previously taken. In the quite unlikely case that a student could not satisfy any of these preprofessional requirements, the master's program would entail more than two years of work.[14]

Components of the Graduate Core

We have argued that the curriculum leading to the M.B.A. should contain a substantial core of required subjects covering essentially the same professional areas described in Chapter 9. Graduate courses in these fields would naturally carry the student further than the corresponding

---

[14] Some schools might wish to consider the interesting possibility of a two-year master's program with a core of business and nonbusiness courses (including prerequisites) that would attempt to put students with both a business administration and liberal arts background on roughly equal footing. The total requirement would add up to more than two year's work. The former business undergraduate would be excused from some first-year business courses but would presumably have to take some of the nonbusiness courses. The reverse would be true of the student who had majored in liberal arts. Special provision would probably have to be made for the engineering student.

TABLE 17

NUMBER OF MASTER'S PROGRAMS REQUIRING GRADUATE COURSES
IN THE VARIOUS CORE FIELDS IN SAMPLES OF FOUR TYPES OF
BUSINESS SCHOOLS

Field	Eight Exclusively Graduate Schools	33 Mixed Member Schools	21 Mixed Nonmember Schools	Five Engineering Schools
Accounting	6	7	3	2
Statistics	5	5	2	2
Integrated "controls"	1	3	3	1
Managerial economics	2	8	1	2
Applied macroeconomics[a]	1[b]	5	1	3
Other economics	3[c]	8	5	2
Organization—administration	4	4	0	3
Human relations—personnel	4	8	1	2
Management principles	1	3	1	0
Finance	6	10	0	3
Marketing	6	9	1	3
Production	6	5	2	3
Industrial relations	0	1	3	3
Legal, political, social framework	4[d]	6	3	2
Business policy	4	9	4[e]	1

[a] Including business cycles, national income, and forecasting, but excluding aggregative economic theory as taught in economics departments.
[b] Four schools apparently cover some study of national income concepts and analysis in other courses.
[c] Two of these are fairly elementary survey courses.
[d] Two schools not included here require a course in business law which might qualify as a "framework" course if broadly enough taught.
[e] Four additional schools have a "business problems" course.
Source: The samples are described in Appendix E. Data are from catalogues and replies to the questionnaire prepared by the Carnegie Survey of Business Education, supplemented in the majority of cases by material gathered in personal visits. Tabulations describe the situation prevailing in 1955–56 or 1956–57. In cases in which a school had both an M.B.A. and M.A. or M.S. degree, only the M.B.A. was included.

undergraduate courses. The analysis should be more rigorous, with more emphasis on managerial problem-solving and greater use of complex cases, and with more of a systematic attempt to develop the other basic skills that are important.

INFORMATION AND CONTROL

All schools require their master's candidates to have an elementary background in accounting, and nearly all take the same attitude regarding statistics. However, leaving aside the exclusively graduate schools and the better graduate programs in industrial administration, only a minority insist on further work in these subjects beyond what the student could be expected to have acquired in undergraduate courses.

The situation is portrayed in Table 17. Of the exclusively graduate schools, six required work in accounting, and a seventh required a course in "control" which dealt with both accounting and statistics. Two of the five graduate programs in industrial administration required graduate work in accounting, and a third required an integrated course in "quantitative control."[15]

The situation is different in the "mixed" schools that offer both graduate and undergraduate work. In the great majority of these schools, the student who has already had the undergraduate prerequisites in accounting and in statistics is excused from further work in these areas. This is true of both member and nonmember schools.

It seems to us a mistake to permit students to satisfy a graduate requirement in accounting and statistics with the usual sort of elementary courses offered to undergraduates. At the master's level particularly, it is essential that the student be thoroughly trained to *use* accounting and statistics. The emphasis needs to be on the managerial uses of these tools, i.e., on analysis and interpretation, which are just the respects in which the undergraduate elementary courses in both accounting and statistics tend to be weak.

A two-year master's program, we suggest, should require at least a year (or even three semesters) of accounting and statistics, with the emphasis on the use of these tools for managerial problem-solving and control. Schools which gear their master's program in part to the needs of students with an undergraduate background in business administration should insist on a minimum of one and preferably two semesters of interpretive accounting and statistics combined, which would build on the elementary undergraduate courses already taken. In addition, students should be made to use their background in statistics as well as accounting in other courses.

The reader is referred to the more extended discussion in Chapter 9 on what needs to be emphasized in the basic courses in accounting and statistics for business students. The kinds of courses we recommend there are also what we have in mind for a master's program, except that in the latter case advantage should be taken of the greater maturity and serious-

---

[15] Table 17 refers to eight exclusively graduate schools, whereas we listed nine in Chapter 2. The difference arises because in this chapter we have included Carnegie Tech in our small sample of engineering schools having graduate programs in industrial administration.

ness of the student, and the managerial uses of these quantitative tools should be emphasized even more than in the corresponding undergraduate courses. There also should be greater emphasis on the newer kinds of quantitative techniques for solving business problems, although what is possible here is limited by the mathematical sophistication of the school's students.[16] The graduate programs in industrial administration have an obvious advantage in this respect.

MANAGERIAL AND AGGREGATIVE ECONOMICS

In our discussion of the undergraduate curriculum, we suggested that as a minimum business students should take, in addition to elementary economics, more advanced courses in managerial economics and in what might be called applied aggregative economics. The same considerations apply to the master's program. Courses in managerial and applied aggregative economics need to be included in the required core; in addition, economic analysis will inevitably enter into other courses, particularly those in the functional fields.

Current practice varies widely from the desiderata we suggest. It is a rare school that requires of its master's candidates solid work in both managerial and aggregative economics at a reasonably sophisticated level. This was true of fewer than ten of the sixty-seven schools whose core requirements are summarized in Table 17.[17]

This is an area in which the exclusively graduate schools make an unsatisfactory showing. Only two of the eight graduate schools required a course in managerial economics. What is more surprising, only one required a full course in aggregative economics, although several more cover some material on national income and related topics in other courses. Two of the five graduate programs in industrial management required managerial economics; three required aggregative economics. In these two groups taken together, only three schools seem clearly to have required both. There are indications that this number will increase somewhat in the next several years.

Of the thirty-three member schools in our sample that have both bachelor's and master's programs, eight had a graduate requirement in

---

[16] Chicago plans to introduce into its required core a quarter's course in Econometrics, which combines economics and statistics. Carnegie Tech requires a two-semester course in the second year in Advanced Business and Engineering Economics. An increasing number of schools are introducing elective courses with such titles as Statistical Control, Operations Research, Decision Theory, etc.

[17] The number would be somewhat larger if we added undergraduate prerequisites to graduate requirements. As we saw in Chapter 9, however, only a small minority of schools have undergraduate requirements in these two areas. This is particularly true of managerial economics.

managerial economics, and five required a course in applied macroeconomics. Eight of these schools had other requirements in economics, including a few that required a course in economic theory not oriented toward managerial economics. As for the nonmember schools, there seems to be almost no interest in requiring of their students advanced work in economics of the sort that we recommend. (See Table 17.)

These schools, which have for the most part one-year master's programs built on undergraduate prerequisites, can assume that their students have had some elementary background in economics. But not many students enter a master's program with much if any training in using the tools of economic analysis in managerial problem-solving. And not many more can interpret intelligently current economic conditions or assess the significance of new developments in government economic policy.

We recommend that the schools whose programs assume no undergraduate training in business require the equivalent of a year's course in moderately advanced economic analysis, including managerial economics, national income and business fluctuations, and some consideration of the economic aspects of government policy. This need not all be done in the same course; there are opportunities for integrating various parts of this sequence with other courses.[18] We also suggest that these schools emphasize in their catalogues the desirability of the student's taking an elementary course in economics as part of his undergraduate program, whatever may be the field in which he chooses to concentrate.

Master's programs that cater to students having had undergraduate work in business administration should also include a year of economics as part of the required core. Some students might be excused from part of this requirement because of undergraduate work previously taken, although at present relatively few students would qualify for such a waiver. We recommend caution in excusing students from a graduate course in managerial economics because the student previously took an undergraduate course with the same title. Waiver of the graduate course in aggregative economics may be easier to justify. To the extent that the graduate school has its own system of combining subject matter which does not correspond to the conventional boundaries separating undergraduate courses, the argument for permitting substitution of under-

---

[18] The University of California (Berkeley) is conducting an interesting experiment in the special graduate sections it provides for master's candidates who need to make up the undergraduate prerequisites that the school specifies. It has been attempting to integrate in special courses some or all of the usual material in the economics of the firm, aggregative economics, statistics, and accounting. A study committee at Columbia has proposed that some managerial economics be combined with other tools of rational decision-making, human relations, other aspects of administration, and some limited contact with the functional fields into one large integrated course.

graduate courses previously taken for part of the graduate core is considerably weakened.

ADMINISTRATION-ORGANIZATION-HUMAN RELATIONS

The M.B.A. program, even more than the undergraduate curriculum, needs to include some required work in the related fields of organization theory, "management principles," and human relations.[19] We believe that at least a year's work is needed in these interrelated areas, however the necessary material may be organized into particular courses.

All six of the exclusively graduate schools having substantial core programs required some work on organizational behavior, particularly in human relations. Course titles vary, and so does course content. Four of the schools required courses which we have classified under the heading of "Organization—Administration," and four required work in what is clearly human relations, but we probably should go no further than to say that all six required work in this general area. (See Table 17.) In addition, one school required a course in management principles. Three of the five graduate programs in industrial administration required work in organization-administration, and two required courses in human relations.

Of the thirty-three Association schools in our sample offering both bachelor's and master's degrees, eight required a graduate course in the human relations area; four, in organization-administration; and three, in "management principles." Among our twenty-one nonmember schools, however, we found only one graduate course required in human relations and one in management.

This situation is clearly in need of correction. The "mixed" schools, nearly as much as the exclusively graduate ones, look on the M.B.A. program as representing professional preparation for the practice of business. As likely as not, "management" or "administration" will be a word that occurs in a school's statement of its objectives. In view of all this, it seems obvious that the school offering a master's program in business should accept responsibility for doing what it can to develop its students' organizational skills.[20]

In Chapter 9 we offered some tentative suggestions as to how undergraduate work in this field might be offered. We suggest something along the same lines for the master's program, the required work amounting to

[19] The sections on management and organization in Chapter 9 are essential background for this discussion and provide a reasonably precise definition of the areas in administration-organization which are here being discussed.

[20] This is being increasingly recognized, and several schools have introduced or revised requirements in this area since our survey was made.

about two semester courses. The student should be exposed to the important literature and to whatever significant generalizations are available. Beyond this, particularly at the graduate level, he should have a generous amount of practice in coping with various types of organizational and interpersonal situations. Some schools have used a variety of techniques for "clinical" teaching in this area. In addition to cases, use can be made of visual aids, role-playing, team assignments, oral reports, and other techniques. A skill-development course along these lines also presents a good opportunity for giving students the practice in oral communication that most of them badly need.

There are undoubtedly many ways of developing the needed organizational knowledge and skills. Certainly no rule can be laid down as to how much should be taught, and in what ways. The greatest agreement exists as to the need for work in human relations. In addition, some schools are struggling to develop a body of teachable material in "organization theory." "Management principles," apparently, is not very often a required course, although some material that belongs under this heading may enter into other courses. Offerings in this particular area tend to be on an elective basis and, of course, are usually a part of whatever management major the school offers.[21]

THE FUNCTIONAL FIELDS

Of the six exclusively graduate schools with core curricula, all required some work in the functional fields of finance, marketing, and production. (Table 17.) Somewhat surprisingly, not one required a course in labor and industrial relations.[22] As we have seen, all require some work in human relations, which may also include something in personnel management.

The virtual unanimity among the exclusively graduate schools regarding the importance of work in the functional areas is to be expected. In general, these schools give a strong managerial emphasis to these courses, although some do so more than others. Cases are extensively used, but the student also has the opportunity to acquire some of the essential background he needs through supplementary reading. The approach is generally much less descriptive than it is in the usual undergraduate course, although some schools do less to develop a significant body of generalizations than we might wish.

[21] For an extensive survey of courses now being offered (but not necessarily required) in administration and related areas, see C. E. Summer, Jr., *Factors in Effective Administration* (1956), especially Appendix 3; also his more complete report reproduced as *The Development of Administrative Effectiveness, Appendix III* (n.d.).

[22] One plans such a requirement beginning in the year 1959–60.

Let us look now at the business schools which offer both graduate and undergraduate work. Of the thirty-three member schools, ten required a course in finance, nine in marketing, and five in production. (See Table 17.) Only one required a course in industrial relations, although eight specified some sort of work in human relations and personnel. As we have seen, the majority of nonmember schools have little or nothing in the way of a core requirement. Hence, it is not surprising to find from Table 17 that few required any work in the functional fields. In keeping with their general approach to the master's degree, these nonmember schools put almost exclusive reliance on the student's undergraduate work to provide a background in the different functional areas of business.

Our recommendations here parallel at a higher level those that we made in Chapter 9. The equivalent of perhaps a semester's work should be required in each of the fields of finance and marketing and probably also in production and in the combined area of industrial relations and personnel.[23] While there should be considerable emphasis on managerial problem-solving and a liberal use of cases, the student also needs to be given the analytical tools with which to work and, where appropriate, an understanding of the functioning of the particular markets which impinge upon managerial decision-making in the different functional fields. The course in production should be an analytical course in the management of physical resources generally and should not be confined to manufacturing processes. It should include some treatment—how much depends on the background of the student—of the newer developments in providing a quantitative basis for rational decisions in the area of operating management.[24]

The need for an overall view of the interrelationships among the different functional aspects of management is coming increasingly to be emphasized among the leaders of business education. To some extent, this need is met in a good course in business policy. In some quarters, however, there seems to be a feeling that this is not enough—that more effective ways need to be developed of viewing the enterprise as a system of interconnected functions. In two cases that we encountered of planned revisions of the master's program of a school, this feeling has led to the proposal that no separate courses in the functional fields be required. Instead, the various functional areas would be dealt with in integrated courses concerned with the structure and functioning of the enterprise.

The less radical procedure is to offer separate functional courses, but to attempt some integration through the use of common cases or through

[23] See our more detailed formulation in Chapter 9.
[24] See the section in Chapter 9 on teaching the basic production course.

a case-analysis or report-writing course which serves a dual function: to improve the student's skill in written communication and to impress him with the fact that most business problems have more than one facet.

We have no strong views on how or how much of such integration should be attempted. Certainly there is nothing sacred about a "basic" course in each of the functional fields. We suggest that the equivalent of three or four semester courses be reserved for the functional fields and that schools experiment with whatever kind of integration seems best to them. Particularly in the case of students without any previous background in business administration, there are fairly strong grounds for continuing to offer a fairly substantial body of theoretical and case materials in marketing, finance, etc., even though some integration (beyond the course in business policy) is also attempted. The student should gain some experience in dealing with substantive problems in these areas at the same time that he is being impressed with the fact that the anatomy and physiology of the business enterprise must be viewed as a whole.

THE NONMARKET ENVIRONMENT

Few would deny that the master's program should require considerable work on the broad nonmarket environment of business. The aim should be two-fold: first, to impress on the student the multifarious and changing ways in which business interacts with its institutional environment, and second, to develop in him a sharpened interest in and a sense of responsibility for the kind of society in which he will live and work.

The exclusively graduate schools, on the whole, seem to agree with this view. Four of the six schools with substantial core requirements had courses which point in this direction. A fifth is planning to introduce such a requirement. Columbia, in the planned revision of its M.B.A. program, proposes to require the equivalent of three to four semester courses on the nonmarket environment of business, and its dean has strongly emphasized the need for stressing the philosophical and historical aspects of the role which business plays in American society.

Of the thirty-three member schools in our sample offering both graduate and undergraduate work, only six required as much as a course on the legal, social, political, or intellectual environment of business. Only three of twenty-one nonmember schools had such a requirement.

The kinds of courses required in this general area vary widely. Harvard requires a course on Business Responsibilities in the American Society which, according to the 1957–58 catalogue, seeks "to begin to familiarize the student with the economic-legal-political-social environment within which business decisions are made and the business process takes place, the impact of such environmental factors on the shaping of business decisions, and a recognition of the impact of such business decisions on the economy itself." This comes close to describing what we have in mind, with the qualification that in our view such a course should strongly emphasize the element of *change* in the environment of business. Actually, the Harvard course seems to be confined largely to the economic environment of business, with particular emphasis on national policy relating to competition and to economic stability.

Carnegie Tech requires a semester of Government and Business in the first year and, what is more interesting, a course on Ideas and Social Change in the second. Tulane requires a course in Business and Society, in the teaching of which a sociologist and a philosopher have participated. Northwestern requires a course in Social Problems in Administration, which the 1956–57 Bulletin describes as follows:

This course is concerned with the forces—economic, governmental, and social—which affect the climate in which business operates. The responsibility of the executive to the community, the interaction of business decisions within society, and the way external forces limit business influence are explored through the discussion of cases.

A number of other schools require some sort of course in Public Policy, Government and Business, or the like.[25] It is fair to say, however, that few schools require courses with the breadth and the kind of intellectual challenge that are needed by students who have a good chance to become leaders of the community.

We think all graduate schools would be well advised to require the equivalent of a year's course on the evolving legal, political, social, economic, and intellectual environment of business. A wide selection of both readings and cases should be used. Some schools might wish to experiment with a year's course so arranged that students might be excused from some part of it, depending on the strength of their undergraduate background in history, political science, and economics. But all students should be exposed to some of the kind of readings and discussion that a well-taught course along these lines can provide.

There is little need in the M.B.A. program for the narrow and conventional kind of course in business law that we criticized in Chapter 9. What is needed is a broad treatment of the kinds of legal institutions that help to shape the environment of business. Naturally, this would be an essential part of the more general course just proposed. So far as we can determine, three of the exclusively graduate schools now require a course in business law, although we cannot say how broadly or narrowly they

[25] Cornell, in addition to a semester's course in Private Enterprise and Public Policy, has also required two semester courses in business and economic history.

are all taught. In large part, we suspect, they are a carryover from an earlier day, although in one instance the course is being continued in the new program the school is developing.

BUSINESS POLICY

The need for an integrating, case course in business policy in the master's program is too obvious to call for much comment. Four of the six exclusively graduate schools with core programs have required such a course in the recent past, and the two which have not are planning to do so in their revised programs. In addition, Columbia plans to require such a course in the new core which it is developing. Only one of the five graduate programs in industrial administration requires a policy course.

Of the thirty-three "mixed" schools in our sample which are members of the Association, only nine required a course in business policy. Only four of the twenty-one nonmember schools required such a course, although four others required a course in "business problems" which, in some cases, may have qualified as a policy course. Thus, despite the virtually unanimous testimony as to the value of an integrating case course in business policy for students planning a business career, apparently less than a third of the mixed schools require such a course of their master's candidates. Here is an excellent illustration of the failure of most business schools to adapt their master's programs to the new emphasis on managerial problem-solving and on training for administrative careers in business.

Every master's program should require at least a semester's (or quarter's) course in business policy. The objectives of such a course would be several: to integrate the students' work in the various special areas so as to show the ramifying implications of most business decisions, to give students practice in identifying problems by confronting them with complex business situations, to develop further their problem-solving skill in approximations to real life situations, and through oral and written reports to improve their communication skills.[26]

RESEARCH, REPORT-WRITING, AND THESIS REQUIREMENTS

Only one of the exclusively graduate schools requires the writing of a master's thesis. The situation is different with the other business schools. About half of all the schools with graduate programs reported a thesis requirement.[27] More than a third of the member schools in our own sample required a thesis; this was also the case in more than three-

[26] See also the more detailed discussion in Chapter 9.
[27] Carnegie Survey of Business Education, *Summary of Preliminary Findings.*

quarters of the nonmember schools. Several additional schools had an optional thesis requirement for which something else could be substituted, for example, additional course work.

A considerable number of the member schools require a research course of some type, frequently but not always as a part of the thesis requirement. In some cases this course is the vehicle through which a long report is required of the student.

A formal thesis requirement can be dispensed with if the master's degree in business is viewed as a professional degree for students planning on careers in business management. Significantly, it is among the nonmember schools that the thesis requirement is most popular. We do not, however, argue that a thesis should never be a part of the master's program. It would be quite appropriate to retain it as an option for those students looking forward to a career in teaching or research.

A course on research and report writing can play a useful role in the graduate curriculum, although the requirement of a separate course is not absolutely essential. Certainly there should be plenty of opportunity for report writing, and several long reports should be required. A separate course or seminar on the writing and presentation of reports can offer the student systematic help in organizing, analyzing, and writing up his material and in presenting a summary of his findings orally to his peers. Some schools explicitly plan report-writing courses along these lines. At some schools a course on business research and report writing is the only course specifically required (beyond the undergraduate prerequisites).

Quite clearly, the greatest possible emphasis should be placed on report writing and presentation. Two things both need to be stressed. One is the research side: planning a project, collecting and analyzing the material, and drawing inferences from less than complete information. The other is written and oral communication: the presentation of results both in a well-organized, well-written document and by effective oral summarization before an audience.[28]

Specialization at the Graduate Level

Our findings in Part II strongly suggest that, even at the graduate level, students planning on management careers do not need a particularly

[28] The graduate program at the University of Virginia attacks this problem in several ways. Full-year courses are required in both written and oral communication, and in addition there is a semester of Supervised Business Study involving a substantial research project. The two communication courses require that the students carry on a moderate amount of research on a variety of business and nonbusiness problems, including a certain amount of field work.

specialized business training. There is a place for a moderate degree of specialization in the master's program, however, particularly for those planning on staff careers that call for a command of technical skills of a high order.

As we saw in Chapter 3, preparation for careers in the various staff specialties of business is a legitimate objective for the business schools, although our findings in Chapter 5 and 6 suggested that, with only a few exceptions (notably accounting), business itself, with the help of evening and extension courses, can supply most of the specialized training needed. While the student wishing a specialized career need not be discouraged from obtaining some special competence in the master's program, certain rules need to be followed by a school which chooses to set up fields of concentration for its students.

First, the fields should be broadly defined and, as a corollary, should be few in number. Second, each field should probe deeply, should make use of the best available analytical tools, and should investigate as thoroughly as possible what the various underlying disciplines can contribute to an understanding of that particular aspect of business. This, in turn, implies that the future specialist in a business field should use his undergraduate years in part to obtain the necessary mastery of the tool subjects which he will later need—in mathematics and statistics and the physical and social sciences.

If a field of concentration is taken, it should never require more than a moderate fraction of a student's time. We shall define "moderate" as not more, and preferably less, than one semester of full-time work (i.e., fifteen semester units). While this maximum is obviously arbitrary, it comes close to being all that the student can afford in a two-year program if something more than a year is invested in the required core and if there is also to be some opportunity for electives. Most students will not need fifteen semester units of specialized work in one field, and usually the amount of specialization should probably be restricted to less than this amount.

PRESENT PRACTICE

In their attitude toward specialization, the exclusively graduate schools tend to divide into two groups. Those in one group require a field of concentration; the others do not and tend to limit the number of course offerings in one field so that excessive specialization is impossible. A few of the latter schools formally forbid any considerable degree of specialization.

Most of the "mixed" schools require a field of concentration. Indeed, as we have seen, many master's programs represent primarily a year of specialization built on the undergraduate major in business. In those schools which have developed a substantial core of required graduate courses, the amount of specialization naturally tends to be small. A few of the nonmember schools also do not emphasize a field of concentration, but often this is because the school has so few graduate courses that much specialization is impossible.[29] Some schools limit their fields of concentration to two or three areas so that, except for accounting, no great degree of specialization is required. A few schools, for example, list only accounting and "management" as fields of concentration.

Some schools permit considerable flexibility in the choice of courses to constitute a field of concentration. In some cases this flexibility is so great that it can hardly be said that a formal concentration requirement exists. But in a good many schools the requirement is both relatively inflexible and heavy. These cases are, for the most part, examples of the traditional master's degree, with little in the way of a graduate core, oriented toward subject matter, and permitting relatively heavy specialization.

Just as we found in the case of the undergraduate curriculum, the great majority of students major in a very few fields. The most popular, in order of preference, are management (including general business), accounting, marketing, and finance. The most marked change in the last six or seven years has been the increase in the popularity of management as a field of specialization, in itself a significant index of the trend away from much specialization at the graduate level.

As a general rule, the graduate offerings of the business schools do not contain as many narrowly vocational courses as do their undergraduate offerings. While many specialized graduate courses are available, they are more the sort one would expect in any graduate department—concerned, at a more or less advanced level, with some branch of specialized subject matter. A number of schools, because of principle or limited resources, offer only a few courses in each special field, some of which are of the seminar or "problems" type. However, the narrow, "how-to-do-it" kind of course is not completely absent by any manner of means.[30]

---

[29] However, this does not deter some member and nonmember schools. For example, the graduate program in one member school requires sixteen semester hours of concentration, but it offers no exclusively graduate courses except for a research or thesis seminar in each major field.

[30] Thus the graduate bulletin of one school listed courses in "The Preparation of Annual Reports," "Advertising Typography and Printing," "Visual Presentation of Financial Data," "Credit Procedures and Practices," "Techniques of Job Rating and Administration," "Current Federal Estate- and Gift-Tax Practice," and others of a similar nature.

In addition, virtually all "mixed" schools permit graduate students to meet part of the degree requirement with undergraduate courses, some of which are of the extremely specialized, vocational type. Moreover, a number of master's programs permit fields of specialization which are as bad as some of those (described in Chapter 9) which are available for the bachelor's degree. Indeed, in many schools the fields of concentration for the master's degree are precisely those listed in the undergraduate curriculum.

Toward a Two-Year Professional Master's Program

Some recapitulation is in order at this point. We have taken the view that the M.B.A. should be treated as a postbaccalaureate professional degree for students planning on careers in business or in some aspect of economic management in nonbusiness organizations. This interpretation of the M.B.A., it seems to us, requires that the business schools move from the one-year type of master's program that presumes an undergraduate major in business to the broader type of two-year program that does not require an undergraduate concentration in business subjects.[31]

Already, in a substantial number of business schools, graduate students whose bachelor's degree was not in business administration outnumber those who had an undergraduate major in business. In well over half of the schools, however, students who did have an undergraduate business major form a majority of the graduate student body.

In the exclusively graduate schools the proportion of students who had undergraduate majors in business is usually less than 25 per cent.[32] It is less than half, and sometimes only a fifth, at other schools that have developed graduate programs to appeal to the liberal arts or engineering graduate. The proportion also tends to be less than 50 per cent at several

[31] One of our consultants argues persuasively that a good master's program does not require two years and points out that most of the second year in our recommended program is available for specialization and electives, much of which can be dispensed with if the students are carefully selected, are well trained in the basic (non-business) tool subjects, and are not afraid to work hard. We grant that this argument has considerable merit. We have been influenced by current practice in the leading graduate schools and by the fear that much compression of the curriculum will lead to some degree of intellectual indigestion. Given the amount of background material students must pick up on their own and the fact that teaching that emphasizes problem-solving and the development of communication skills is inevitably time consuming, we are inclined to retain our standard of two years for most graduate programs. But some schools, particularly those with very select student bodies, may prefer to offer a program confined to three semesters or four or five quarters, even for students without previous training in business administration. Such a program would, of course, have to consist almost entirely of required courses and would not provide time for a field of specialization.

[32] In a few it is under 10 per cent.

schools that enroll large numbers of part-time students who are already in business and who feel the need to supplement their earlier education in engineering or liberal arts. The graduate programs in industrial management, of course, attract students with backgrounds in science or engineering.[33]

The tendency for master's programs to be dominated by students who have already had undergraduate business training is strongest in the state universities that have large undergraduate programs. These schools have, for the most part, continued with the kind of master's degree that penalizes rather than attracts students whose undergraduate backgrounds are not in business administration.

Whatever recommendations we make, therefore, must cope with a number of interrelated and partly conflicting considerations. While the need is for a broad two-year type of master's program, preferably for students who did not major in business as undergraduates, yet for the indefinite future large numbers of students with bachelor's degrees in business will insist on continuing on through the master's degree. There is also one additional fact that is relevant, to which we have so far alluded only in passing. In addition to the specialized needs of the accountants, some students seek graduate training in business as preparation for specialized research careers or careers in teaching.

All this suggests that a flexible approach must be taken to the master's program. To meet these varying needs, we propose that schools plan on either of two types of M.B.A. program, which we shall call "Type A" and "Type B." In addition, we also propose a special degree in accounting to provide a fifth year for students who plan on careers in public accounting.

THE "TYPE A" MASTER'S PROGRAM

Our "Type A" variant aims entirely at the needs of students who did not major in business as undergraduates and is similar to the kind of curriculum which most of the exclusively graduate schools now offer or are planning to have. It is also similar to the best of the graduate programs in industrial administration. It would call for two years of study which could not be reduced because of undergraduate business courses previously taken. It would have a required core comprising a bit more than half of the two years' work. It might or might not require some specialization in the second year.

[33] These generalizations are based on a study of the educational backgrounds of students in the samples of exclusively graduate, member, and nonmember schools used in the earlier sections of this chapter, supplemented by the Carnegie Corporation Survey of Business Education, *Summary of Preliminary Findings.*

This program is summarized in Table 18. Although it calls for a minimum core of thirty-six semester units, the total might be considerably larger. We list the areas which should be covered, but it is not essential that a separate course be given in each field. Experiments in integration are to be encouraged, and different schools may wish to experiment in different ways. We do assume, however, that little if any of the core

TABLE 18

PROPOSED "TYPE A" M.B.A. PROGRAM FOR STUDENTS WITHOUT AN UNDERGRADUATE MAJOR IN BUSINESS ADMINISTRATION[a]

Subject	Approximate Semester Hours
Administration-organization-human relations	6
Economics	6–9
Managerial economics	
Aggregative economics	
Government economic policy affecting business	
Information and control	6–9
Managerial accounting	
Statistics and related topics	
Functional areas	9–12
Report writing and research	0–6
Legal, social, and political environment	6
Business policy	3–6
Total core	36–54
Specialization	0–15
Electives, including nonbusiness courses[b]	——

[a] See discussion in text. Assumes total degree requirement of sixty semester units.
[b] The number of semester hours available for electives will depend on size of core and concentration requirement.

would be waived because of a student's undergraduate preparation.[34] A school under this program would be free to plan each course, combining elementary and more advanced material as it wished, without reference to the student who had had some undergraduate business courses. If any of the core were waived, electives would be substituted so that the program would require two years' work of all students. This is the main dif-

[34] We repeat again our suggestion that the requirement for the degree might be made larger than sixty semester units to the extent of several preprofessional courses considered essential, with the idea that these would be waived for students with adequate undergraduate preparation.

ference between this and the "Type B" program to be discussed in a moment.

Schools with this kind of program might or might not permit a field of concentration. If they do, it should not exceed fifteen semester units and might well be less. If it takes the form of a major and minor, the combined total should not exceed eighteen units.[35] The larger the required core, the less emphasis, presumably, there would be on a field of concentration.

We should expect that virtually all of the first year's work would be prescribed and that a small part of the core (at least the course in business policy) would be left for the second year. There is also considerable advantage in leaving for the second year at least some of the material on the interaction of business with its nonmarket environment.

We need not repeat at length what we have said regarding the kinds of material that should be covered and how courses in this sort of program should be taught. The emphasis would be on managerial problem-solving and the development of the necessary organizational and communication skills. But the emphasis would be analytical as well as clinical; the case method of teaching would be used extensively but not exclusively; the student would be made to look for significant generalizations, and the contributions of the underlying disciplines to the solution of business problems should be thoroughly investigated; and written and oral communication would be stressed at every opportunity. We suggest also that in both the "Type A" and "Type B" programs, a comprehensive examination be required, probably during the student's last semester.

THE "TYPE B" PROGRAM

The program just discussed pays little or no attention to the special needs of students with substantial undergraduate work in business who wish to go on for the M.B.A. While we might argue that what these students need more than additional business courses is to correct their deficiencies in general education, particularly in the underlying disciplines most important to business, it would be unrealistic to assume that all business schools will ignore the demand for graduate business training from this source. Bowing to the inevitable, we suggest a "Type B" program for students who have had substantial work in business as undergraduates. A minimal variant of this program is summarized in Table 19.

This table divides the proposed core into two parts, one of which can be waived because of work previously done and the second of which cannot. Starting from the standard of a two-year program of sixty semester

[35] In this case it would be highly desirable for the minor to be in a related *nonbusiness* field.

TABLE 19

PROPOSED "TYPE B" M.B.A. PROGRAM FOR STUDENTS WITH AND
WITHOUT AN UNDERGRADUATE MAJOR IN
BUSINESS ADMINISTRATION[a]

| | Approximate Semester Hours | |
Subject	Can be Waived	Cannot be Waived
Administration-organization-human relations	3	3–6
Economics Managerial economics Aggregative economics Government economic policy affecting business	3	3–6
Information and control Accounting Statistics and related topics	6	3–6
Functional areas	6–9	6–9
Report writing and research	0	0–6
Legal, social, and political environment	0	6
Business policy	0	3–6
Total core	18–21	24–45
Specialization	0	0–15
Electives, including nonbusiness courses[b]	0	—

[a] See text. Assumes total degree requirement of sixty semester units, part of which may be waived because of previous undergraduate work.
[b] The number of hours of electives which cannot be waived will depend on size of core and concentration requirement. Some electives should be made available.

units, we would permit undergraduate courses to be substituted for eighteen to twenty-one units, leaving thirty-nine to forty-two units to be met by graduate courses. Waiver should ordinarily be possible, however, only by passing an appropriate examination; credit should not be automatically given merely because the student has had an undergraduate course in a particular field. Under this minimal program, a student who had a bachelor's degree in business could not secure the master's degree in one academic year. He could, presumably, meet the requirement in a year and two summers, or in three semesters, or, for schools on the quarter system, in four or five quarters. The student whose background was in liberal arts or engineering would need the full two years, as in the "Type A" case.

In the "Type B" program, a student might, if he were able to secure necessary waivers, be excused from the first course in administration-organization, from a semester of economics, from the first semester in accounting and statistics, and from the first courses in two or three functional fields. He would then go on to take the rest of the core shown in the second column of Table 19. He would have to take at least one advanced course in administration, in economics (probably managerial economics), in two or three functional fields, in the legal, political, and social framework of business, and in business policy. More than a semester might be required in each case, and the school might wish to experiment with integrating the work in two or more of these fields. For obvious reasons, the student should not be excused from the course in business policy. We think it wise also to require him to take the work on the legal, social, and political framework of business. In general, the required courses from which he could not be excused would build on the earlier courses which might be waived. They would deal with more advanced material; they would utilize cases and report writing to an extent that is not practical in an undergraduate class; and in general they would be conducted at a considerably higher analytical level than would be the case in undergraduate courses, even of the kind we recommended in Chapter 9.

In exceptional cases, one of the second group of courses might be waived for an able student who, as an undergraduate, had done advanced work in the field in question. But such a student should be required to substitute an elective for the course from which he had been excused.

We do not think that many schools would be likely to adopt the maximum core under the alternatives described in Table 19. The minimum core of forty-two units (eighteen plus twenty-four) is much more likely to be acceptable, particularly since most of the schools to which this proposal is addressed are likely to wish to require a field of concentration. Here, as with the "Type A" program, we suggest that specialization be held to a maximum of fifteen units (and preferably less). We also recommend that students who took more than six units of undergraduate concentration in a special field not be permitted to specialize in the same field in the master's program. (An exception might be made for the accountants.) Some schools may prefer not to encourage (or even permit) specialization at all, limiting the work beyond the core which a student might take in a single field to, say, two semester courses. A more flexible arrangement would permit the student to specialize (within the limits indicated) or not, as he preferred.

The program summarized in Table 19 is minimal and in some ways unsatisfactory. It is unsatisfactory because students who majored in business administration as undergraduates presumably have too weak a foundation in general education. Our Type A program presumed four years of general education followed by a two-year graduate program in business. A student who completes our Type B program may have had the equivalent of only two years of general education, combined with something more than three years in business administration.

A more satisfactory variant of our Type B program immediately suggests itself. A full two years of work might be required of everyone, including those who were undergraduate business majors, and a student excused from some of the business courses listed in Table 19 would be required to take a corresponding number of nonbusiness courses, graduate or undergraduate, the particular courses to depend on an evaluation of his undergraduate preparation.[36] Given the general position taken in this report, the logic of this proposal can hardly be gainsaid.

THE M.B.A. AS A TEACHING AND RESEARCH DEGREE

It might be argued against our recommendations that they do not provide adequately for the student who wishes to embark on a teaching or research career. It might be claimed that the conventional type of one-year master's program, complete with thesis and a heavy field of concentration and superimposed on an undergraduate major in business, better meets the needs of such students than does the broader type of program we propose, with its emphasis on the development of managerial skills.

We have already stated our objections to the kind of one-year program offered by the majority of business schools and believe that the needs of future teachers and research workers (assuming that they do not go on to the doctorate) can better be met in other ways. Specifically, we suggest that two alternatives be open to these students.

The first alternative would be to take the "Type B" program with a field of specialization, with electives (or a report-writing and research course if one is required) being used for additional research training. Such additional training would include not only further work in research methods but also a research project and report beyond what would otherwise be required.

The other alternative would be for the student to take an M.A. or M.S. in the most appropriate underlying discipline (psychology, economics, etc.), including in his program such graduate business courses as he

---

[36] We raised earlier the possibility that less than a full two years might be required for the degree, even in the Type A program. The proposal made here could apply whether the basic degree requirements were 45 or 50 or 60 semester units. For any business courses waived, the student would substitute nonbusiness courses.

needed, assuming that the department concerned would accept them in partial satisfaction of the course requirements for the degree. Obvious opportunities exist here for joint arrangements between the business school and other departments. Master's candidates in psychology, economics, or public administration should be able to take individual courses or "minor" in the business school. It should also be possible for the M.B.A. candidate to take electives or part or all of his concentration in a nonbusiness field.

We do not think that the need for a research and teaching degree warrants the retention of the conventional one-year master's degree in business. Too many sins have been committed in its name; it seldom involves more than a limited amount of work at the graduate level; and most of the students who become candidates for such a degree are looking forward to careers in business. The only way to make these programs serve their primary purpose is to convert them into something like the "Type B" program that we propose. The needs of the minority of students who want to prepare for teaching or research can be met in the other ways we suggest. Those who count on teaching business courses need the training provided by our recommended core even more than they need advanced training in some specialty; this is nearly as true of many of those who aspire to being staff specialists in business and other organizations.

THE SPECIAL CASE OF ACCOUNTING

We are prepared to make an exception in the case of public accounting, for which it might be desirable in some cases to have a one-year master's degree, with its own designation, which builds on an undergraduate business major of the sort described in Chapter 9.[37] This would provide the fifth year that the public accountant presumably needs if he is not to overspecialize in his undergraduate years and thereby sacrifice some of the essential elements of a reasonably broad education. We do not, however, recommend such a five-year program for those planning on a career in *private* accounting. These students, who will be concerned with the informational and control activities of some business concern, should take the regular two-year master's program, with accounting as their field of specialization.[38]

The year of graduate work for the future public accountant would presumably consist in substantial part of advanced and specialized accounting courses and such courses in related fields (law, finance, etc.) as

[37] A five-year program leading to a special bachelor's degree in accounting would be equally acceptable.

[38] We are prepared to argue that this is also the best preparation for those who look forward

were considered necessary. Some work should also be required in other business areas that will help the practicing accountant to meet the increasingly broad range of demands for his services. He should have a basic familiarity with the various functional activities of the firm; he needs a command of economics and statistics; and he, no less than the business manager, should be informed about the changing nonmarket environment of business (beyond the knowledge of the tax laws that he is in any event expected to have).[39]

While public accounting may have special needs that call for a special master's program, we are inclined to believe that these needs can also be met, and in some respects perhaps met better, through the broader type of M.B.A program which permits a field of specialization. Under the "Type B" program, for example, a student with the kind of undergraduate major described in Chapter 9 (with a minimal concentration in accounting) could have waived all of the more elementary courses in Table 19 and could concentrate to the extent of fifteen semester units in accounting (possibly even more by substituting a course in accounting or a related field for the course in managerial control required of other students). Something along these lines is standard practice in schools which have an M.B.A. program with both a substantial core and a field of specialization.

The "Three-Two" Program

We raised in Chapters 6 and 7 the possibility of a "three-two" program in which three years of general education would be followed by two years of concentration on business subjects. Such a program could lead to either the bachelor's or master's degree.

EXISTING PROGRAMS

While this sort of five-year program has been widely discussed in the last few years, there is only one well established example in business administration that we can turn to for guidance. This is at the Amos Tuck

to moving into responsible positions in the large public accounting firms.

[39] Cf., for example, the following: "The CPA comes in contact with many types of people in his activities. To work successfully with such people requires a broad background, not only in his own field, but in many fields which touch upon accountancy. He needs a knowledge of public affairs and of recorded history, of the manner in which business events and transactions are consummated, of production, marketing, finance, and economics, and some knowledge of engineering, statistics, and business policy. Technical training is of course important, but CPAs (and businessmen) are beginning to realize that a broadly trained person is, in the long run, likely to be a better prospect for employment than the individual with only technical training." Commission on Standards of Education and Experience for Certified Public Accountants, *Standards of Education and Experience for Certified Public Accountants* (1956), pp. 18-19.

School at Dartmouth. Several graduate schools have, in effect, a three-two program for able students, who are permitted, on a selective basis, to enter the graduate program at the beginning of their senior year.

The "three-two" plan has had considerable use in engineering. Here the plan involves the cooperation between a liberal arts college, at which the student spends his first three years, and an engineering school at which the final two years are spent. Well over 100 liberal arts colleges have cooperated with more than thirty engineering schools in these arrangements.[40] There seem to be several advantages to these arrangements so far as they apply to engineering. The student avoids some of the narrowness in the typical four-year engineering program because of the extra year. He secures the benefit of a liberal arts atmosphere during the first three years, and he can also defer the final commitment to engineering as a vocation until the end of the junior year. The liberal arts college finds it unnecessary to establish an engineering curriculum of its own.

While the students who have transferred to engineering schools under such a cooperative arrangement seem to have performed satisfactorily and the plan has continued to spread, reactions to the plan have been somewhat mixed. One of the more important obstacles to a wider use of the arrangement has apparently been the reluctance of students to give up the anticipated pleasures of spending their senior year on their "home" campus. Another objection has been the extra year, compared to the four years required in a conventional engineering program. In addition, it has been said, the three-two plan does not fit in well with the usual arrangements for fulfilling military service obligations.[41]

MOVING TO A THREE-TWO PROGRAM

A three-two arrangement is a compromise between exclusively graduate training and a purely undergraduate program. It is clearly better than a program that confines business training to the undergraduate years.[42] It is not as good as a four-two arrangement that leaves the undergraduate years free for general and preprofessional education and defers professional training until after the student has received his bachelor's degree. In the latter case, professional training benefits both from the

[40] Cf. T. H. Carroll, *Business Education for Competence and Responsibility* (AACSB, 1956), p. 7.

[41] On the use of the three-two plan in engineering, see H. H. Armsby, "The 'Three-Two' Plan—An Educational Experiment," *Higher Education*, x (December, 1953), 61–64; J. B. Sanders, *General and Liberal Educational Content of Professional Curricula: Engineering* (U. S. Office of Education, Pamphlet No. 114, 1954), p. 16.

[42] Cf. Miller Upton, "The Rising Tide—and A' That," in *Future Supply of Teaching Personnel*, (School of Commerce, University of Wisconsin, 1956).

larger undergraduate base and from the additional maturity and stronger motivation of the student.

For schools planning a gradual move from undergraduate to graduate business education, a three-two plan might be a useful transitional device. Some may wish to try it with the idea of keeping it as a permanent arrangement. Particularly the publicly supported institutions would find it easier to "sell" than a complete elimination of the undergraduate business program. And there is a significant saving for the student in both time and money compared to the four-two arrangement.

If a three-two program is adopted, the professional training in the fourth and fifth years should follow the general lines of the "Type A" master's program described earlier in this chapter. Since it might be possible to treat all five years as an integrated unit, particularly if the fourth and fifth years were taken chiefly by students who had spent the three preceding years on the same campus, it might be possible to insist on certain prerequisites—for example, elementary economics, statistics, some minimum of mathematics, and accounting.[43]

Additional flexibility can be introduced into the three-two plan by arranging the fourth year (in which most of the basic courses in the core would be taken) as an independent unit. Students unable or not motivated to take the fifth year could secure the bachelor's degree at the end of the fourth year with an abbreviated core of business subjects making up about 25 per cent of his total four years' work.[44] While this is a possible arrangement, it also has its difficulties. A fourth-year core program cannot serve equally well as a base for the fifth year's work and also as a terminal program for those who will graduate at the end of the fourth year. A single year's professional training does not permit of sufficient "carry-through" in the development of the student's problem-solving and organizational skills, and he is likely to graduate with an inadequate understanding of the functioning of the business enterprise and of the environment within which business operates.[45]

[43] The larger the number of preprofessional requirements specified in the first three years, the greater becomes a problem of some importance. If there is much specification, the student must make an early commitment to the program, a commitment he may later regret. The counterpart of this problem concerns the student who decides only at the beginning of his junior year to major in business. He may then have substantial requirements to make up. The latter difficulty would exist for transfer students also.

[44] Cf. Carroll, *Business Education for Competence and Responsibility*, p. 12.

[45] In such a fourth-year core, a student would have available at the maximum thirty semester units, assuming he had no other graduation requirements to make up (apart from R.O.T.C.). Our minimum undergraduate core was thirty-six units; the "Type A" graduate core is also thirty-six. In addition, the task of absorbing nearly the whole core in one year, while the student is still subject to undergraduate distractions, suggests that some mental indigestion is likely to result and that the quality of instruction is likely to be impaired.

On the whole, we suspect that the three-two plan will not prove to be popular with the business schools for the following reasons.

1   The plan is easiest to administer when the only students involved are those who have spent the first three years in the same university. If they have enjoyed their campus life, students from other colleges will be reluctant to transfer at the beginning of their senior year. Hence, students from other institutions (liberal arts colleges, for example) will enter the program chiefly after they have their bachelor's degree. Thus the first "graduate" year must mix college seniors from the host university with college graduates from other schools. The situation is made worse if some of the seniors are using the fourth year as a terminal year.

2   There is some evidence that most undergraduates in their senior year are not quite ready for a rigorous program of the sort that we recommend. They find it somewhat difficult to break away suddenly from the social and extracurricular activities that characterize undergraduate life. They lack, to some degree, the necessary maturity and motivation. There is no question that the actual process of graduation from an undergraduate college, with all its formal and informal symbolism, helps psychologically to prepare a student for the more exacting educational experience of graduate professional training, whether it be in business, law, or medicine.

3   A three-two program does not fit well with the growing junior college movement, with its attendant transfer of students to four-year colleges at the beginning of the junior year. While junior college transfers can prepare themselves in their junior year to shift to the business program for their fourth and fifth years, this increases the number of academic adjustments to which the student is subjected. It is easier for him to transfer directly into an undergraduate business school or to wait until after graduation for his business education.

4   A three-two plan is not well suited for the urban business school which enrolls large numbers of part-time students in its master's program, the courses in which are offered chiefly in the afternoon or evening. These part-time students are employed people of some maturity, and they are not likely to mix well with college seniors. In addition, the latter face a difficult adjustment if they have to

move from a normal undergraduate daytime program to late after-noon and evening classes.[46]

Of course, it would be possible for a school to offer both a day-time three-two program for its full-time students and a special master's program in the evening for college graduates who are already employed.

5   If a school adopts a three-two program, it is likely to find that a considerable number of students will take their bachelor's degree and drop out at the end of the fourth year. We have pointed out some of the weaknesses of such a three-one arrangement, which are certain to lower the quality of the program as a whole.

It may be that we are overimpressed by the difficulties of administer-ing an effective three-two program. Further experiments in the use of the plan should be welcomed so that the business schools might have addi-tional evidence to assess. In the absence of such evidence, schools not wishing to experiment can concentrate on improving their master's and undergraduate programs. In this connection, they need to face up to the issue as to how far they are prepared to go in emphasizing their graduate program at the expense of the undergraduate.

Evening Programs and the Part-Time Graduate Student

In many business schools, the majority of master's candidates are part-time students, taking courses in the late afternoon and evening after being fully employed during the day. Some of these students majored in business as undergraduates. To a growing extent, however, college grad-uates *without* previous training in business administration are flocking to these evening programs. Their undergraduate background is in liberal arts, engineering, education, etc., and they now feel a need for formal training in business. In some localities, there has been a marked influx of engineers into these evening M.B.A. programs. These students need chiefly a broad training in business fundamentals—essentially in what we have included in our proposals for the core in the master's program.

[46] If, as in some urban schools, the undergraduates are also part-time students, this is not much of a problem. However, the part-time undergraduate, who needs more than four years to earn his bachelor's degree, is likely to resist the additional requirement of a fifth year of full-time work, which for him may mean two years or more of part-time study. He is likely to seek out the school that will offer him a strictly undergraduate program. Needless to say, graduate work of any kind is difficult for any student who is forced to drag out his under-graduate education through more than four years of part-time study.

An evening M.B.A. program populated by part-time students with full-time jobs presents both a serious problem and a great opportunity for a business school. The nature of the students themselves creates the opportunity. They tend to be mature men with some business experience and strong motivation. To the extent that they did not major in business as undergraduates, they create an approximation to the ideal case we have described in this report, in which the student gets his business training after a broad, nonbusiness undergraduate education, but only after several years of work experience.

But there are also offsetting disadvantages. These students have limited time for study; they come to their classes after a full day on the job; there is limited opportunity to use library facilities; and a full master's program may drag out over a number of years. Maintaining an instructional staff also poses problems. Unless such evening teaching is made a part of the instructor's regular teaching schedule (with a corresponding reduction in his daytime load), the alternatives are either an extra load for the regular faculty (for additional compensation) or the use of part-time instructors who themselves hold other jobs. Both alternatives are unsatisfactory.

THE PRESENT SITUATION

Evening master's programs, as would be expected, are to be found primarily in the major urban areas, chiefly in the large private universities. They are a minor factor in the state universities and on the smaller and rural campuses.

Three of the exclusively graduate schools have large part-time enrollments. The entire program at one of these, New York University, is largely geared to the needs of the student already employed. Some of the "mixed" schools have master's programs which are almost entirely evening affairs for part-time students. Exclusively part-time M.B.A. programs are somewhat more prevalent among nonmember than among member schools. Most of these programs are subject to all the criticisms previously raised against the conventional one-year master's degree with little or no core and extensive undergraduate prerequisites. In addition, in the poorer of these schools, students continue to take a good many undergraduate courses even after they have met the prerequisites; too much specialization is frequently encouraged; too many part-time instructors are used; and there are the additional difficulties previously mentioned arising from the fact that the students have limited time for study and inadequate access to a library.

It seems to us that the argument for the kind of master's program recommended earlier in this chapter is even stronger for the part-time student who is already employed than it is for the full-time student who goes on to a master's degree immediately after graduating from college.[47] The argument is strongest of all for the evening student who did not major in business.

This is recognized by some schools, which offer good to excellent evening M.B.A. programs for employed college graduates. These programs consist largely of a broad core of required courses along the lines we previously suggested and are aimed chiefly at those who did not major in business as undergraduates. Unfortunately, these still constitute a minority of the evening M.B.A. programs available. In the more typical case, the graduate core is small, the business prerequisites are large, and no special provision is made for students with a liberal arts or engineering background.

The urban schools quite clearly need to give more attention to this problem. The demands of part-time, employed students, particularly those without an undergraduate degree in business, deserve to be met with programs of maximum effectiveness. We suggest that some adaptation of our "Type A" or "Type B" program be utilized, depending on the extent to which the school wishes to provide for students who majored in business administration as undergraduates. Ideally, all evening master's programs should meet the following conditions:

1 The curriculum and standards of instruction should be the same as the school would expect to have in a day program for full-time students (subject to inevitable qualifications regarding the quantity of written work and library assignments that can be expected of employed students).

2 Evening courses should ordinarily be taught by full-time faculty as part of their regular teaching load. If some outside instructors are used on a part-time basis, they should be fully qualified by day-faculty standards. They should also be required to attend such faculty meetings as are needed to insure that their courses are fully integrated into the program as a whole, and they should be expected to make a reasonable amount of time available to students beyond regularly scheduled classes.

3 Standards of admission should be high—as high as for a full-time day program.

4 Reasonable library facilities should be easily available to evening students, as well as quarters for study and discussion before and after classes.

---

[47] We should add one qualification. An evening M.B.A. program might well require something less than the equivalent of two years of full-time course work.

5   It should not be a major purpose of the evening master's program
to offer specialized, vocational training aimed at helping students
with their present jobs. This should be the function of extension-
type, nondegree courses which the school, within the limit of its
facilities, may wish to make available to the community.[48] The
master's degree should represent much more than a certificate that
the student has taken a minimum number of technical courses in
some narrow specialty.

A Note on Admission Standards

It is tempting to offer the sweeping suggestion that the business schools
should use more selective screening procedures and thereby seek to improve the average quality of their graduate students. Certainly this is a
desideratum that needs to be taken to heart by a good many schools that
admit to accepting students of inferior ability. As we shall point out in
Chapter 13, graduate students in business make the same unfavorable
comparison with those in other fields as do undergraduates.

On the whole, the exclusively graduate schools have reasonably high
standards of admission; in some, the quality of students is very high. The
majority of these schools use the Admission Test for Graduate Study in
Business (ATGSB) as well as the evidence presented by undergraduate
scholastic records, work experience and military service, student activities, and, in some cases, personal interviews and recommendations. A
few schools, particularly Harvard, have devoted a good deal of research
to the development of appropriate selection standards.

The situation is much more spotty in the "mixed" schools that offer
both the bachelor's and master's degree. Some attempt to be highly selective. While in general schools try to insist on a C plus to B minus undergraduate grade record, a good many in effect accept any student with a
bachelor's degree, subject to the minimum entrance requirements of
their university's graduate division. Most schools are not yet using the
ATGSB, although the available evidence suggests that use of this test adds
significantly to the information provided by the undergraduate record.[49] It is also our impression that most schools are paying too little at-

---

[48] These courses are discussed in Chapter 12.

[49] Cf. Marjorie Olsen, *The Admission Test for Graduate Study in Business as a Predictor of First-
Year Grades in Business School, 1954–1955* (Educational Testing Service Statistical Report
57–3, January, 1957). This was also confirmed in personal interviews. It should be added
that, like all such tests, the ATGSB has many limitations, and we by no means recommend
exclusive reliance on it. For a detailed study of its predictive value at one school, see E. S.
Nourse, *A Study on the Validity of the Admission Test for Graduate Study in Business* (unpublished
master's report, University of Chicago School of Business, May, 1957).

tention to the kinds of evidence that bear on the nonmental qualities that are most significant.

There is not much doubt that admissions standards generally need to be raised and more selective screening procedures used. We recommend the general use of the ATGSB, insistence on better than average undergraduate scholastic records, and judicious consideration of other relevant evidence—work and military experience, student activities, letters of recommendation, etc. It would also be helpful if the AACSB would show more leadership in making generally available information regarding the experience of various schools and in encouraging the more general acceptance of higher entrance standards.

The current climate of opinion points toward an increasing emphasis on an expansion of master's programs. But expansion should be accompanied by an improvement in quality—of students as well as curriculum. The anticipated rapid growth in the number of college graduates, the increasing recognition of the value to the businessman of the kind of business education we propose, and some de-emphasis of undergraduate programs should provide ample opportunity to improve quality and increase graduate enrollments at the same time.

Graduate Standards and the Role of the AACSB

Until 1958 the AACSB refrained from setting any standards for postbaccalaureate work in business. At its annual meeting in that year, it adopted a set of minimal standards, the most relevant parts of which are reproduced below.

1 *Admissions.* As a general practice, admission to the graduate program in business shall be limited to holders of a baccalaureate degree from a recognized institution. Special consideration may be given to integrated programs in which the student is admitted to a two-year graduate program following three years at the undergraduate level.

2 *Graduate offerings.* As a minimum, the school shall regularly offer one full year of course work or equivalent (open only to graduate students in their final year) in at least three of the following areas: accounting, finance, marketing, statistics, economics, and management. For purposes of comparison, "a full year of course work" shall correspond to six semester hours in a conventional university program. A thesis course shall not be considered as meeting the area requirement.

3 *Curriculum requirements.* It is assumed that the minimum requirement for a Master's degree shall be the equivalent of one academic year of full-time work for the holder of a baccalaureate in business. Up to one additional year may be required for holders of other baccalaureate degrees. At least

half of the student's work in his final year shall be in courses open only to graduate students.

4 *Faculty*. From the full-time faculty, there shall be, as a minimum, the equivalent of three senior men devoting full time to the graduate program in business. At least two-thirds of the exclusively graduate classes shall be taught by members of the instructional staff with the appropriate doctorate.

5 *Evening and branch graduate work in business*. The same standards shall apply for the evening and branch program as are established for the day program.

. . . .

7 *Facilities*. For approval of a graduate program in business, member schools shall have adequate library, laboratory and classroom facilities, and suitable accommodations and services for the faculty.

8 *Maintenance of program*. A school of business which meets the necessary Standards for the Master's degree shall be registered by the Association. A school which fails to maintain or meet the minimum Standards shall not be registered. Absence of registration of the graduate program shall not prejudice the school's membership in the Association. . . .

The minimal character of these recommendations will be all too obvious to the reader of this chapter. No admissions standards are proposed beyond possession of the bachelor's degree; no curriculum suggestions are offered. Its minimum of graduate offerings (although more than some schools offering the M.B.A. now have) are no more than a small start toward the bare essentials of a satisfactory master's program. The question of a minimum core is not touched, nor is the problem of prerequisites. And in general these standards would require little change even in the more unsatisfactory master's programs that we have described. Probably the section on faculty would involve the most significant change, particularly in some of the smaller schools. It is significant also that failure to live up to these standards would not jeopardize a school's membership in the Association.

This cautious and not very meaningful step illustrates the greatest weakness of the Association. While it has been a strong force making for a *minimum* level of acceptability in collegiate business education, it has not been able as an organization to generate the active and imaginative leadership needed to raise standards above this level. It is largely the vehicle of what we earlier called the great middle class of collegiate business education—which includes most of the conventional, "mixed" schools with many more undergraduate than graduate students. The Association's first step toward a set of standards for the master's degree has been slow and halting because, presumably, a significant part of its membership is not yet ready to commit itself to a type of program substantially better than that which many schools are now offering.

chapter 12

NONDEGREE PROGRAMS

FOR BUSINESSMEN

THROUGHOUT this report, we have stressed the fact that education for business competence is a continuing process that should extend throughout the businessman's career. The demand for formal business education is not confined merely to those who look forward to future business careers; those already in business also need additional education and training.

The demand by practicing businessmen for further educational help has expanded greatly since the Second World War.[1] Of the several million businessmen in the United States, there are few who cannot benefit from additional education and training; and the number who currently seek such educational help, in one form or another, exceeds the number of students enrolled in the full-time degree programs in the business schools. As Clark and Sloan have put it, education has "come into its own, not only as a prerequisite to an industrial career, but as a continuous adjunct to it."[2] The need for further education and training is felt at all levels of business.

This demand for continuing business education is met from several sources: individual employers, trade associations and other business supported groups, the public school systems through their adult education activities, and the colleges and universities. The educational activities of business itself—as represented both by in-company programs and those conducted by other business groups—constitute an educational phenomenon of the first magnitude. Despite their unquestioned importance, however, we shall not consider in this chapter the programs conducted by business itself, nor shall we be concerned with the adult education provided by public school systems, including the community colleges. We shall confine ourselves to the nondegree educational activities of the

---

[1] For a discussion of a comparable development in England, see D. K. Clarke, "A Survey of Management Education in the United Kingdom," *Journal of Industrial Economics*, IV (February, 1956), 95–106.

[2] H. F. Clark and H. S. Sloan, *Classrooms in the Factories* (1958), pp. 11–12.

four-year colleges and universities so far as they are directed at the needs of businessmen and other administrators.[3]

The Nature of the Need

The adult business education provided by the universities serves two purposes. It may provide part or all of a college education that an individual was unable to obtain earlier and on a full-time basis, and it meets some part of the need for additional training that arises after a person embarks on a business career. The first objective is met through evening courses and degree programs, in which are enrolled part-time students who obtain their college education while they carry full-time jobs. While we shall have more to say about these students, our chief interest is in the second category of needs just mentioned, which involves a good deal more than merely offering standard college courses in the evening.

This latter type of need arises in several ways. The requirements of particular jobs and occupations, for example, may call for specialized skills and knowledge, sometimes in quite narrow areas, which the universities cannot appropriately provide as part of their regular degree programs. Then there is the need for a less particularistic but still specialized body of skills or knowledge in recognized fields or subfields, the need for which develops only as the person's career unfolds. Thus an accountant may find it desirable to take further work in some branch of the law or of accounting. The production manager may want further training in some special phase of engineering or in industrial psychology. The sales manager may feel the need for more training in sampling survey methods, consumer motivation, or some aspect of advertising.

In addition to this call for specialized knowledge, there has been a rapidly growing demand for educational help in developing managerial competence as a whole. This is a part of the trend toward more rational decision-making and the professionalization of management to which we have referred at various places in this report, and reflects a growing recognition of the relative shortage of topflight managerial talent.[4] Most

[3] There are a number of studies dealing with different aspects of the educational activities performed by business itself, and others were in progress as this study was being written. See, for example, Clark and Sloan, *Classrooms in the Factories;* D. S. Bridgman, "Company Management Development Programs," in Frank C. Pierson *et al., The Education of American Businessmen* (1959); the series of studies published by the American Management Association on *Management Education for Itself and Its Employees* (4 parts, 1954); and the forthcoming study by O. N. Serbein, *Educational Activities in Business.* Our own survey of companies developed a good deal of material on company training programs of which we have not been able to make full use in this report.

[4] See in particular the latter part of Chapter 1 and the discussion of the ingredients of business competence in Chapters 4 and 5.

concerns (particularly the larger ones) give much time and thought to how to select and train those with the highest potential for executive leadership, and "management development" has become a phrase heard at every turn.[5]

This demand may take two forms. First, educational help may be sought to remedy deficiencies in some particular dimension of business competence. Thus there may be a demand for courses in human relations or conference leadership or for any of the standard subjects taught in the core of a university program in business administration. This is the piecemeal approach, which best fits the needs of those who know what their most serious deficiencies are.

Alternatively, companies and individuals may express a demand for an integrated educational package. In this case, educators are expected to determine the elements of business competence to be stressed and to devise an educational program that will develop all of these elements taken together. From these efforts have stemmed the executive development programs now offered by many universities, by individual companies, and by such organizations as the American Management Association. In a sense, the rising enrollment in evening M.B.A. programs represents the same sort of phenomenon. A similar demand, but somewhat more specialized in character, has led to various kinds of certificate programs.

Businessmen, like their fellow citizens in a free and literate society, also express a demand for nonbusiness education—not only for its own sake but sometimes also for its supposed contribution to business competence. On occasion, as in the case of the Bell Telephone System, a planned curriculum in general education becomes a particular type of executive development program. Some material in the humanities and in the physical and social sciences enters into other executive development programs that devote their chief attention to business subjects.

Finally, because business and the world around it are changing so rapidly, there has been a growing demand for educational offerings that will help businessmen keep abreast of new developments—not only in particular business fields but also in the social, political, economic, and technological environment of business. Thus there has grown up a variegated demand—from individuals, companies, trade associations, and local business groups—for courses, institutes, and conferences in everything from current world affairs and "new challenges to management"

---

[5] The literature on management selection and development has by now reached imposing proportions. A small sample of this literature was cited in Chapter 5 and some additional references are given in Appendix A. See also Bridgman, "Company Management Development Programs," in Pierson *et al.*, *The Education of American Businessmen*.

to changes in the tax laws or new developments of special interest to bankers, traffic managers, insurance underwriters, real estate brokers, furniture manufacturers, retailers, and others.

Most of these demands reflect a real need, although as often as not the nature of the need has not been clearly evaluated by the business groups or educators concerned. The total demand imposes a considerable burden on the limited resources of the business schools. To a considerable extent, what the universities do to satisfy the demand results from local pressures, considerations of institutional prestige, the possibilities of additional income, and the promotional zeal of a few individuals. As likely as not, the programs that are undertaken do not reflect a careful appraisal of what needs are most important and how they can most effectively be met without seriously interfering with the university's primary responsibilities to teach its regular students and to advance knowledge through research.[6]

The universities attempt to meet the demands for adult business education in three chief ways: through evening and extension courses, through special conferences, institutes, and short courses, and through executive or management development programs. While it is the last of these methods that has attracted the greatest attention among business educators in recent years, it is the first two that affect the largest number of people. We shall organize our discussion in the rest of this chapter around these three forms of adult education for businessmen.

Management Development Programs

The newest and most rapidly growing of the educational services which American universities offer to business is the management development program. In 1950, only four such programs were in existence: M.I.T.'s Executive Development (Sloan) Program, which was started in 1931; Harvard's Advanced Management Program and Chicago's Executive Program, both begun during the war; and Pittsburgh's course in Management Problems for Executives, the first of the postwar programs.[7] By the end of 1953, there were seventeen underway; by 1955, more than two dozen; and by 1958, there were over forty, with more being planned.

---

[6] Cf. R. L. Kozelka, *Professional Education for Business* (1954), pp. 117–18.

[7] Unlike the others mentioned, the Chicago program is a nonresidential evening program, extending over two years and leading to the master's degree for college graduates, and perhaps for this reason is not included in some lists of executive development programs. A list of forty-two programs with their birth years is provided in Kenneth R. Andrews, "University Programs for Practicing Executives," in Pierson *et al.*, *The Education of American Businessmen*. Andrews' chapter provides an excellent introduction to the subject.

The movement has extended to other countries, not only to Europe but also to South America and to the Middle and Far East.

Management development programs differ in several significant respects from the other two main types of adult business education offered by the universities. First of all, there is the marked difference in clientele. Management development programs are limited to responsible and experienced businessmen; that is, to "executives."[8] Second, participants are, in virtually every case, sent by business firms, which take the initiative in selecting those who are to attend. Third, the programs are on such a scale that they require a substantial investment of time and money and presuppose, therefore, results of some significance. Time is measured not in hours or days, but rather in weeks and months. A corollary of this third characteristic is that the students are usually absent from their normal responsibilities for a considerable length of time, which may range from two weeks to a year.[9]

Why do the business schools offer these programs, and why do companies send their officials to them with such alacrity? We have already offered one answer in the opening pages of this chapter. There has been a growing demand since the war for educational help in developing managerial competence as a whole. One form this demand takes is that for an integrated educational package, devised by the educators themselves, which aims to improve the managerial skills of those already in the middle and top levels of management. The enthusiasm with which such programs have been offered by the universities and received by the business world suggests that substantial success in attaining this objective has been achieved. But this conclusion holds only with some significant qualifications, the nature of which will become apparent in the course of the detailed appraisal that follows.

While these programs can be classified in various ways, we shall use a simple three-fold differentiation: 1) programs aimed at developing general managerial competence, with considerable emphasis on improved understanding in the more important subject-matter fields of business but with no attempt to concentrate on the special problems of any particular

[8] Actually, university programs may be geared to various levels of management. Thus Harvard has had both an Advanced Management and a Middle Management program. M.I.T.'s long standing Sloan program for younger executives has recently been supplemented by a shorter course for senior executives.

[9] There are some exceptions. Thus, U.C.L.A. and Chicago, to cite two examples, have part-time evening programs meeting once or twice a week over an extended period. Santa Clara's program meets one full day a week for twelve weeks. North Carolina requires a week in residence at the beginning and end, with a series of week-end sessions in between. All of these are briefly described in Ward Stewart, "Executive Development Programs in Collegiate Schools of Business," *Higher Education*, May, 1958, pp. 1–5.

industry or function, 2) programs that do so specialize, and 3) programs that seek to improve managerial competence by concentrating on non-business rather than business subjects.

PROGRAMS TO DEVELOP GENERAL MANAGERIAL COMPETENCE

It is this first type of program that is usually meant when the term "management development" or "executive development" is used, and most of the university programs for executives fall into this category. These programs all have the same ostensible objective: to improve managerial competence—or, as is sometimes put, "executive effectiveness." What this means in somewhat greater detail has been summarized by the National Industrial Conference Board as follows:[10]

... through these courses, the educational institution is trying to teach the executive to improve his thought processes and his analytical abilities. Most university people would be happy if they could be sure that their executive students were going home with the habit of sound thinking thoroughly fixed. They know the practical value that would inevitably result—improvement in the batting average of right decisions.

Beyond this single broad objective are several others that seem to reflect the stated aims of most or all of these university programs. These objectives may be expressed as follows:

To broaden the outlook of the individual; to give him an appreciation of his responsibilities in community affairs and of the other areas of management outside his own specialty.

To teach the executive to think through the problems that confront him in his job, whatever that may be.

To make the individual a more effective executive in his present job.

To increase the potential abilities of the executive to handle higher-level jobs later on.

These objectives seem to indicate that the universities have analyzed the executive job in terms of three major elements: the executive as a problem analyzer, as a leader of men, and as an influencer of community affairs.

Program brochures repeatedly stress the points enumerated in this quotation. Particular emphasis is put on achieving these objectives through broadening the executive's mental horizon. A common assumption is that the most important single problem in management development has to do with how to convert capable specialists into even more capable generalists. To some schools, this seems to mean chiefly acquiring "an organization-wide" view, or "a top-management perspective," or a "general management approach." Here breadth is taken to mean a

---

[10] National Industrial Conference Board, *Executive Development Courses in Universities* (Studies in Personnel Policy No. 160, 1957), p. 5.

broad or company-wide view of, primarily, the internal problems of the firm. To other schools, the job of creating a generalist attitude means in good part orienting the executive away from the internal problems of management toward "changes in markets, government controls, levels of business activity, technologies, and society," or toward "corporate association with community and national issues, and awareness of the problems and opportunities of leadership in a free business society."

Most programs, of course, concern themselves with both types of orientation, but there is considerable variation in the extent to which emphasis is placed on the internal-managerial and on the external-environmental aspects of the executive's problems.

Mere statement of educational objectives is not enough, of course, to explain why so many business schools have rushed in to offer executive development programs. Actually a number of incentives have been at work, of which the most important have probably been the opportunity (or feeling of obligation) to provide a service requested by some part of the business community, the desire to fill a need in business even though the service had not been requested, the possibility of additional income for the school and the faculty, the opportunity to improve the school's relations with and support from the business community, and the general prestige value of such programs, in the academic as well as the business world.[11] The faculty also stands to benefit in other ways, particularly through more extensive business contacts and the opportunity to engage in a particularly challenging kind of teaching, but these have been by-products rather than important reasons for initiating the programs.

THE CONTENT OF THE PROGRAMS

Most management development programs bear some resemblance to the broader type of M.B.A. curriculum described in Chapter 11, and the topics usually dealt with include many of those listed in the kind of M.B.A. curriculum we recommended in that chapter. Virtually all schools having executive development programs also offer the M.B.A., and a good deal of the teaching materials used in the former are borrowed from the M.B.A. courses. Typically, some of the same faculty is used, and there is also some transfer to the executive development sessions of the faculty's general approach to business administration and of the teaching methods used in the master's program.

While a considerable range of topics is usually covered, three areas in

---

[11] Cf. *Executive Development Courses in Universities*, pp. 5–6.

particular tend to be emphasized.[12] The first centers around financial management and control. Both financial analysis and managerial accounting may be treated under this heading. Finance is ordinarily dealt with both as an aspect of internal administration and as a major point of contact with the firm's market environment (i.e., the money and capital markets).

The second area is the management of human resources within an organizational context. The kinds of problems dealt with vary widely among schools, but most programs, in one way or another, pay considerable attention to the problem of human relations. A number also concern themselves with industrial relations or the more conventional aspects of personnel management. Most also bring in other material on administration and the administrative process, frequently in the form which we described in Chapter 9 under the heading of "management principles." But whatever the emphasis and the details of the approach used, the trend is toward helping the executive increase his organizational effectiveness and his skill in interpersonal relations, which, as we saw in Chapter 6, are two of the basic elements of managerial competence.

The third area always covered is the firm's nonmarket environment.[13] This usually includes some material on national income and related topics, the place of business in society (including the relations between government and business), and the responsibilities of business to the community. The technological environment of business is dealt with less often than the economic and political, but it is not uncommon to offer some material on this subject.

The three "core" areas mentioned seldom make up all of an executive development program. Among other topics frequently included are marketing management, production management, further material on general management and administration, some elementary statistics, personal development (usually reading and speech skills), some managerial economics, and, more often than not, business policy. Since these programs are intended to be broadening, one seldom finds much if any time being devoted to problems of particular industries, the specialized subdivisions of the various functional fields (purchasing, advertising, etc.), or to the technical aspects of production engineering.

In addition to the work in business administration and related areas,

---

[12] The same three areas are mentioned by Kenneth R. Andrews in the first of two articles on "Is Management Training Effective?", *Harvard Business Review*, xxxv (January-February, 1957), 86.

[13] There are a few programs, such as the Business Executive Program of the University of Southern California and the M.I.T. Program for Senior Executives, which are largely devoted to this range of problems.

a number of programs present material derived from a variety of non-business fields. This is done through lectures, discussion, and some assigned reading. Some schools offer a few unrelated lectures; others present an integrated series of sessions, usually conducted by faculty members from other departments. The topics are frequently drawn from the humanities, but the speakers may also deal with some aspect of science, education, political affairs, or any other topic of general significance.[14] Here again the aim is to broaden the perspective of the business manager and, in this case, to inspire him to view the world in other than business terms.

For the most part, this type of management development program draws its students from a wide variety of industries. Indeed, the opportunity to exchange views with men having other types of experience is supposedly one of the most important benefits the individual derives from this form of adult business education. There are, however, a few programs which, while emphasizing general managerial competence, are limited to executives from a particular industry—for example, banking, transportation, or public utilities. Examples are Michigan's program for public utility executives and Stanford's transportation management program. In neither of these programs is more than a small fraction of the total time spent on problems of the particular industry. For the most part, attention is concentrated on the same topics emphasized in a general program for executives without regard to industry. These programs are to be contrasted with those which are not only confined to the executives of one industry but also deal primarily with specialized subject matter.[15]

TEACHING METHODS AND MATERIALS

As we should expect, the case method is utilized more in management development programs than in the regular degree offerings of the business schools. There is also much less use of the simple lecture method. With these qualifications, the pedagogical techniques and teaching materials utilized in the M.B.A. courses are in good part carried over into these programs for practicing businessmen. Some schools, as in their regular graduate courses, rely almost exclusively on cases; others, while

[14] Thus guest lecturers at the 1956 University of Kansas program included, among others, professors of history, education, home economics and sociology, physical education, music education, zoology, journalism, English, and chemical engineering. The University of Indiana program, according to its 1957 brochure, includes a course in "Current Trends in Literature." The Case Institute program is another that systematically provides for some exposure to the humanities, science, and other nonbusiness fields. Other examples could also be cited.

[15] Thus Columbia's program in transportation management, unlike Stanford's, deals almost entirely with the problems of the transportation industry.

making use of cases, combine them with other readings. A combination of discussion and informal lectures is widely used. In most programs, with varying degrees of success, the effort is made to involve the students deeply in the learning process. They participate actively in discussion; there are reading and problem assignments and reports on cases; and "bull sessions" outside the classroom are an important part of the total educational process.

In planning the curriculum, the business schools use some combination of two different approaches to the material to be covered. Under one arrangement, separate courses are set up in each of the subject-matter fields to be covered, and each course is given at a certain time each day in much the same fashion as in the regular degree programs. This has been referred to as the "compartmentalized" approach, in which business and management are dealt with as a set of separate although related fields.[16]

In the second, "non-compartmentalized" approach, the material is organized in terms of broad problem areas. Thus Top Management Policy and Administration and Managerial Responsibilities and Their Limits were the two areas or "courses" around which Northwestern's 1957 Institute for Management was organized. This second approach puts less emphasis on subject-matter and more on problem-solving and the development of a broad perspective. On the whole, this approach tends to lead to deeper involvement by the student and to more active discussion and less lecturing. It also implies extensive use of the case method.[17]

Most programs make some use of both methods, but usually a school leans toward one or the other approach; and a few represent nearly pure examples of one of the two extremes.

In addition to lectures, reading assignments, discussion, and cases, other teaching methods are also used, including role playing, conference sessions, and panels and committees. And the use of business games is spreading rapidly.[18]

SOME BENEFITS OF THE PROGRAMS

The general objective of these programs is to help the participants develop into better executives capable of assuming larger responsibilities.

[16] Cf. National Industrial Conference Board, *Executive Development Courses in Universities*, pp. 9–10.

[17] It also is relatively costly in terms of time and, for maximum effectiveness, requires a resident student body.

[18] For a brief discussion of business games and their value as a teaching device, see p. 367, below.

While little clear-cut evidence is available as to how well this objective is being achieved, there is widespread agreement that businessmen do benefit in certain respects from the better of these programs; and it is assumed as a corollary that a higher level of managerial competence does result. The more important of the advantages usually cited are the following.

First, the participants gain most from being exposed to the viewpoints and experiences of other participants. As Melvin Anshen has written, "Perhaps the greatest contribution of the better programs . . . is the opportunity they give a man to rub his mind against the minds of executives from other industries, companies, functions, and places. . . . His imagination is stirred by discovering that other organizations, facing problems similar to those confronted by his own firm, have used different solutions successfully. Formally and informally, in daytime classes and nighttime bull sessions, his thinking is challenged, prodded, stimulated, exercised, and broadened."[19]

Second, there is the opportunity for reading, reflection, and self-evaluation in a new and relaxed atmosphere. As a result, the participant "gains a sense of perspective, a chance to look back at his job and the way he has been handling it without the distractions of company affairs and family, and free from the pressures of decisions, deadlines, and commitments."[20]

These are the two advantages most often cited, and it is noteworthy that neither depends very much on what is formally taught in these programs. There are, of course, other advantages, depending on the program and the man, which do reflect the material taught and the stimulus of the faculty—for example, new knowledge and insights, the acquisition of new tools of analysis, and, more generally, the development of a broadened perspective and a greater capacity for systematic and sustained thought.

None of this, however, provides any guarantee that the graduate of one of these programs "is now an x% better executive than he was before he took the course."[21] There is an untested presumption that he is, but our present knowledge does not permit us to say more.

SPECIALIZED PROGRAMS

As we noted earlier, one category of management development pro-

[19] Melvin Anshen, "Executive Development: In-Company vs. University Programs," *Harvard Business Review*, xxxii (September-October, 1954), 85. See also Andrews, *Harvard Business Review*, xxxv (January-February, 1957), 86–87.

[20] Anshen, *Harvard Business Review*, xxxii (September-October, 1954), 86.

[21] National Industrial Conference Board, *Executive Development Courses in Universities*, p. 17.

grams deals with the special problems of a particular industry or business function. The aim is usually twofold: to improve general management skills *and* to develop the special kind of competence presumably needed in a particular field of business. This second objective means that considerable stress is placed on an appropriate body of specialized subject matter.

Programs of this type are offered by a number of business schools, sometimes in conjunction with a trade or professional group, for example, one of the bankers' associations. They tend to be shorter than the general type of executive development program; some are brief enough to qualify as the kind of short conference or institute described later in this chapter.

Examples of this type of program are the banking schools at a number of universities, the Transportation Management Program at Columbia, the Institute of Investment Banking at Pennsylvania, the Graduate School of Savings and Loan at Indiana, the Management Development Conference for mutual savings bank officials at Dartmouth, and the Executive Controls Program at Syracuse.[22]

LIBERAL ARTS PROGRAMS

One of the most striking recent developments in the field of education for practicing executives has been the initiation of a number of programs that concentrate exclusively on the liberal arts and eschew all business subjects. Interestingly, business itself rather than the universities has taken the lead in promoting this type of program. Of the ten or so programs of this sort that have been started, one (the Executives Program of the Aspen Institute for Humanistic Studies) is not associated with a university, and five others, although located on a campus, are part of the Bell System's experiment in liberal education for executives.

These programs are so new and so few in number, and their form and content vary so widely, that it is difficult to offer a brief summary description. The Bell System programs at Dartmouth, Northwestern, Pennsylvania, Swarthmore, and Williams have varied both in length (eight weeks to ten months) and in content. The other programs also differ widely in format—from the community wide plan jointly sponsored by the Memphis (Tennessee) Adult Education Council and Southwestern University, which offers Memphis executives "the liberating effects of the higher arts" in a series of weekly half-day sessions extending over

[22] For other examples see Andrews, "University Programs for Practicing Executives," in Pierson *et al.*, *The Education of American Businessmen*.

two years, to Wabash College's program in which students attend for about ten weeks spread over five years.

The emphasis in these programs is on the liberal arts primarily in the sense of the humanities, although the social and physical sciences are not ignored. The first of the Bell System programs, that begun by the Bell Telephone Company of Pennsylvania at the University of Pennsylvania in 1953, included during a recent year material in the fields of logic, economic history and thought, music, art, literature, ethics, social science, history and meaning of science, industrial relations, and American civilization.[23]

Liberal education for executives can serve two interrelated purposes. It may seek simply to develop the "whole man" so that he can live a fuller and more fruitful life and be a more useful citizen. But a liberal education can also help, directly or indirectly, to improve managerial competence. It is this latter view that lies behind the Bell System's liberal arts program, just as it provides the basis for the many statements by prominent executives regarding the value of a liberal education for businessmen. Liberal education can contribute to executive effectiveness in a number of ways: through a wider knowledge of the nonmarket environment of business, through the development of breadth of perspective and flexibility of mind, and through the inculcation of new attitudes of mind toward oneself, one's job and company, and one's place in society.[24] In general, the idea is that by helping them to be better men, liberal education helps executives also to be better businessmen.

Limitations of time have not permitted us to study the relatively few liberal arts programs now being offered as carefully as they deserve, and, in any event, the evidence needed for a careful evaluation is lacking. Not only are these programs very new, but what they contribute to executive effectiveness is even more difficult to evaluate than is the case with the more conventional type of executive development program that addresses itself directly to the improvement of management skills.

By the nature of the case, the business schools will not be the ones to carry on this experiment in liberal education for executives. This is an

[23] See, for example, E. D. Baltzell, "Bell Telephone's Experiment in Education," *Harper's Magazine*, March, 1955, pp. 73–77; Abbott Kaplan, "Liberal Education in a Business Civilization," in *Research in Management*, Report of the First Annual Conference Sponsored by the Institute of Industrial Relations, University of California at Los Angeles (September, 1957), pp. 22–23. Kaplan's paper also contains a brief description of the Southwestern program in Memphis, as does the chapter by Dyer in Pierson *et al.*, *The Education of American Businessmen*. The Wabash College program is described in National Industrial Conference Board, *Executive Development Courses in Universities*, pp. 81–82.

[24] See the earlier discussion on the role of liberal education in Chapters 3 and 7, especially pp. 46–47 and 142–43.

area of management development that lies largely outside their field of competence. But, assuming these programs are judged to be reasonably effective, we can envision a fruitful relationship between business and the liberal arts colleges (including the liberal arts departments of the universities) from which both sides can draw substantial benefit.

A BRIEF EVALUATION OF UNIVERSITY PROGRAMS

"The problem of how to evaluate executive development programs, university-sponsored and company-sponsored, in terms of what they do for the men who attend them remains to be solved."[25] While most participants feel that they get something of value from the management development programs offered by the universities, a thorough evaluation remains to be made. The participating companies lack the evidence to judge whether they are getting their money's worth, and the business schools do not have an adequate basis for judging whether they are making the most effective possible use of their resources in offering these programs. The presumption is that they are worthwhile—from the point of view of the participating executives, their companies, and the business schools—but the case remains to be proved.

The fact that business itself has thus far been unable to make a systematic evaluation is illustrated by the following statement from a very large company which has made extensive use of both university and its own in-company programs. Similar comments were made by a number of other firms during the course of our company survey.[26]

We do not have any systematic evidence as to the impact of such experiences on the personal skills and performance of the men who have attended these programs. The intuitive judgments of their superiors are still the primary basis on which we evaluate these experiences. We also receive some help from the reports which the men themselves give us regarding the programs. We hope that more systematic ways of evaluating the benefits will be developed from our experiences and the experiences of other businesses.

The evidence available comes chiefly from the reactions of the individual participants as reflected in reports to their employers and in replies to questionnaires from the schools. As Andrews points out, this evidence is probably more valuable to the schools in planning how to revise their programs than it is to the companies trying to decide what, if any, programs to use and whom to send.[27] Other useful evidence can come

---

[25] Anshen, *Harvard Business Review*, xxxii (September-October, 1954), 89. The same point has been made by a number of other writers.

[26] The company survey is described in Appendix B. The quoted statement is contained in a letter to the authors from one of the companies interviewed.

[27] *Harvard Business Review*, xxxv (January-February, 1957), 87.

from the observations and judgments of the superiors, associates, and subordinates of the participants after they return to their jobs and from the reactions of the faculty members in the programs. Nearly all of this evidence is subjective, in part because we do not yet know how to measure executive effectiveness. But some systematic studies resting on more or less objective evidence are beginning to be made.[28]

Such evidence as exists seems to support the following tentative conclusions.

1) There is universal agreement that executive development programs, whether given by the universities or the companies themselves, "should constitute only a part of a long-range plan for the development of an executive."[29] Only if firms do have carefully thought out, long-range plans for the development of managerial talent can they select the right men for the right university programs and supply the conditions necessary so that these men can build on this experience after they return to their jobs. Both business and the business schools need to remember that "the university program can only play a relatively small part in the development of executive leadership in a company."[30] Too many business schools "sell their programs to prospects without stopping to explore with each organization its long-range management staffing plan. They neglect to relate program content and method to the special educational requirements of each potential customer."[31]

2) Given the emphasis on breadth and on new ways of thinking about business problems, these programs should be evaluated in terms of their effect on the long-term growth of the individual, not in terms of the immediate effect on the way a manager performs his job.[32]

3) Not all managers benefit from these university programs. Further, for those that do, it is important that the man be fitted to the program. In general, senior executives and men from middle management do not fit well into the same program. Even for officials at the same level, some

[28] On all this, see the two-part article by Andrews in the *Harvard Business Review*, xxxv (January-February and March-April, 1957); also his chapter in Pierson *et al.*, *The Education of American Businessmen*. Professor Andrews now has in progress a large scale research project the results of which should give us a much more substantial basis for evaluating the effectiveness of these programs.

[29] A. V. MacCullough, "University Courses for Executives," *Management Record*, xix (May, 1957), 170.

[30] H. W. Johnson, "A Framework for Evaluating University Executive Development Programs," paper read at Industrial Relations Conference, Princeton University, September 19, 1956 (mimeographed).

[31] Melvin Anshen, "Better Use of Executive Development Programs," *Harvard Business Review*, xxxiii (November-December, 1955), 68.

[32] Cf. Andrews, *Harvard Business Review*, xxxv (March-April, 1957), 68.

will benefit more from a particular school's program than will others.[33]

There is room for programs that cater to top executives and for those that seek to meet the needs of men in the lower levels of management. While in both cases the courses should stress breadth and not narrow technical skills, it is generally agreed that those intended for senior executives should place a heavier emphasis on the external environment of business than do the programs for lower ranking officials.

4) Since the students learn chiefly from each other and from actively participating in the educational process, provision must be made for discussion both in and out of the classroom and for a good deal of problem and case work. This can be done better by programs that are on a full-time residential basis than by those which are not, but the latter type, if carefully planned and of sufficient length, can also serve a useful purpose.[34]

5) These programs can offer an extremely valuable teaching experience to the business school faculty and, incidentally, can lead to useful business contacts. But not all faculty members are qualified to teach in the programs, and those that do participate should be carefully selected in terms of their ability to command the respect and stimulate the thinking of the businessmen who attend.

6) Particularly if offered in the summer, these programs need not represent an unreasonable drain on the business school's resources. If the program is well planned, if the students and faculty are wisely selected, if the program is not only self-sustaining but yields some additional revenue that can be used for other essential activities, and if the school has the resources to meet its primary responsibilities to its regular students and to research, it seems reasonable to conclude that the benefits, both to business and the university, warrant the investment both by the companies and the business school. It is probably true, however, that some schools have rushed into these programs without adequate faculty resources, with the result that they have had to offer a poor program for businessmen, or their other and more essential activities have suffered, or both.

7) There is clear need for continuous study, evaluation, and improvement of these programs. Thus far, despite important differences in detail, most university programs are cut from much the same pattern, have the same ostensible objectives, and make much the same educa-

---

[33] Cf. Johnson, "A Framework for Evaluating University Executive Development Programs"; also Anshen, *Harvard Business Review*, xxxiii (November-December, 1955), 69.

[34] Cf. Andrews, *Harvard Business Review*, xxxv (January-February, 1957), 87, and xxxv (March-April, 1957), 69.

tional assumptions. It seems to us that there needs to be more significant differentiation based on a careful reformulation of objectives and re-evaluation of the best means of achieving them. But for this differenti-ation to be meaningful, the schools must have a clearer conception of the range of possible needs for management education, some notion of which are most urgent, and some basis for judging what needs can be most effectively met with the resources available to each particular school.

We suspect that, among other possible bases of re-evaluation, there will be with the passing years increasing opportunity for programs tailored to the needs of those in the upper levels of management who have already attended the conventional type of university or in-company program or have obtained an equivalent educational experience in other ways. The process of self-development should never end, and the uni-versities should be able to help in this process at various stages in the executive's career. This can provide one basis for more differentiation among university programs than now exists.[35]

In Part II we concluded that managerial competence rests upon four sets of basic skills—problem-solving, handling organizational relation-ships, interpersonal relations, communication—and that these skills are applied in dealing with the firm's market and nonmarket environment and to internal problems of organization and of economic management. With varying degrees of success, university executive development pro-grams seek to improve all of these fundamental skills and to provide the businessman with new perspectives and some additional knowledge re-garding the broad problem areas mentioned. But not all managers at all levels need the same kind of improvement in the same skills; this is a matter of the man, his background, and the particular point at which he is in his career. Nor do all executives need precisely the same kind of further education with respect to these different problem areas—nor do all react in the same way to the same kind of educational stimulus.

In short, while many businessmen can undoubtedly benefit from the kind of educational experience which the university management de-velopment programs attempt to provide, there is a range of changing needs—not a single, uniform, and unchanging one. It should be the business school's responsibility, with possibly some help from business, to identify the particular set of needs it is best qualified to meet and to de-vise the best educational program it can to satisfy this set of needs—pro-vided it is satisfied that it has the resources required without sacrificing

---

[35] It is our impression that most university programs are based on the assumption that the participants have not had the equivalent of much formal training in business administration. This assumption will become less justified as the years go by.

other essential activities and (what may demand a superhuman degree of objectivity) that no other agency can do the job better.

Evening and Extension Programs

We turn now to a second type of adult business education—the evening and extension courses taken by part-time, working students. These students comprise a far more heterogeneous throng than the select clientele served by the executive development programs. The demands of this larger group for further education and training are met by the evening colleges and extension divisions of the larger universities and, to some extent, directly by the business schools themselves.

Students in the evening courses offered by the business schools constitute a somewhat more homogeneous group than do those in the separately administered evening colleges and extension centers.[36] The age range is somewhat wider than among day students, but educational backgrounds are not greatly different. The evening students are for the most part enrolled in degree programs similar to or identical with the day program, although a larger number of specialized courses are likely to be available in the evening and there are fairly certain to be more "special" students who are not candidates for a degree but enroll in one or two courses.

So far as we know, there are no data available on the relative numbers of students taking evening courses offered directly by the business schools and of those taking business courses administered by separate evening colleges and extension divisions. The students in the separate evening colleges and extension divisions cover a wide range—in age, in educational background, in occupational interests, and in ability and motivation.[37] If they are candidates for a degree, and nominally most of them are, presumably they are high school graduates. But an increasing number have some college education. While the majority of students apparently register as degree candidates, only a small fraction actually complete all of the work required for the bachelor's degree.

[36] Something less than half of the separately organized business schools offer evening classes. (Cf. Carnegie Corporation Survey of Business Education, *Summary of Preliminary Findings* [revised August 1, 1958], Table XXI.) In the remaining cases, if evening business classes are offered at all, they are administered by a separate evening college or extension division, which may also exist in a university or college that does not have a business school. For a brief survey of the types of evening colleges, see J. P. Dyer, *Ivory Towers in the Market Place* (1956), pp. 27–30.

[37] Dyer, *Ivory Towers in the Market Place*, chap. 1; and J. R. Morton, *University Extension in the United States* (1953), chap. 7.

In 1957, the 175 members of the two national associations of evening and extension schools—the Association of University Evening Colleges and the National University Extension Association—reported an enrollment of almost 650,000 part-time students, excluding enrollments in noncredit courses. It is impossible to judge how many of these are seeking to develop competence in business, but one authority estimates that some 35 per cent were enrolled in "credit courses related to business."[38]

THE NATURE OF THE CURRICULUM

Business schools that have evening programs offer in the evening essentially the same curriculum that is available to day students. The evening program may go further, however, and offer additional specialized and vocational courses that are not given in the day. Practice with respect to offering degree credit for specialized courses with a strong vocational orientation varies. Broadly speaking, three different policies may be followed.

Some schools give degree credit in the evening only for courses equivalent to those in the regular day program and exclude from the latter all courses with a strong vocational orientation. If any of the latter are offered in the evening—for example, a C.P.A. review course—no degree credit is granted. At the other extreme, some schools not only offer a range of narrow vocational courses to both day and evening students, but also give degree credit for them. Some schools seek unsuccessfully to straddle the issue, refusing to offer certain types of courses during the day but giving them with degree credit in the evening. Where this occurs, one can expect that many vocationally minded day students will seek out these evening courses, thereby foregoing more essential work they might have taken.

Similar problems arise when the business courses are offered by an evening college or extension division. Most such courses are similar to daytime courses and count toward a degree.[39] But the number of noncredit courses is growing as businessmen turn to the universities for specialized educational help of a sort that does not fit into the framework of the regular academic program. Often such specialized courses reflect

[38] Dyer, "Business Education in Evening Colleges and Extension Divisions," in Pierson *et al., The Education of American Businessmen.*

[39] Only a small fraction of the evening colleges offer their own degrees. (Cf. Dyer, *Ivory Towers in the Market Place,* p. 42.) The rest, together with the extension divisions, offer credit courses which count toward a degree administered by a day college. Approval of the day college is usually required for such credit courses. This approval typically covers not only the general content of the course but also the qualifications of the instructor, although it is our impression that this requirement is frequently very loosely enforced. Cf. Kozelka, *Professional Education for Business,* p. 111.

the interests of and pressures from particular trade or professional groups.[40]

We are not concerned here with the variety of cultural courses offered in the evening but only with those courses which presumably contribute in a fairly direct way to the student's business competence. These can be of three broad types.

The first group consists of basic courses, more or less identical with those given during the day, in the fundamental business subjects and related nonbusiness fields. The second type consists of both elementary and advanced courses in the various specialized business fields such as insurance, real estate, retailing, advertising, and transportation. Included in this group are those special courses aimed at preparing the student for professional-type examinations such as those given for the C.P.A. or C.L.U. certificate. These courses may or may not carry degree credit. The third category of offerings includes courses dealing with "new developments" in various fields. Such courses are becoming increasingly popular in such areas as, for example, insurance, collective bargaining, tax accounting, data processing, and operations analysis.

Whenever an institution offers evening instruction in business subjects, all three of these types of courses are likely to be found, but the relative emphasis on the three types varies considerably. The more limited programs concentrate on the first group of courses and on the less specialized courses in the second group. The more active and service-minded programs do much more with the second and third categories, with a liberal sprinkling of tailor-made courses to meet the needs of particular business and professional groups.

Evening courses may be integrated into various kinds of degree and certificate programs. Certificate programs are usually designed to meet the needs of particular occupational groups, as in insurance, advertising, industrial relations, retailing, or industrial management. Some students seek to earn a degree to make up for a college education that was missed earlier and which cannot be sought during the day. Some are candidates for an advanced degree, usually the M.B.A.[41] Some seek to develop or improve some form of specialized business competence by taking the courses specified in a particular certificate program. And many, without the aim of earning a certificate or degree, take the particular courses which they

[40] For a distribution of business courses in resident centers, extension classes, and through correspondence, classified by level and whether or not they carried credit, see Morton, *University Extension in the United States*, chap. 9.

[41] Problems associated with the evening M.B.A. program were discussed at some length in Chapter 11.

think will remedy specific deficiencies that they may have or add to their skill or knowledge along particular lines.

THE EVENING FACULTY

The teaching staff for evening courses comes primarily from two sources: the regular daytime faculty and part-time instructors brought in from the outside.[42] Thus it is largely true, as Dyer states, that "the evening college is charged with doing a first-rate academic job with a faculty whose basic interests lie elsewhere."[43] To only a slightly less extent, this is true when the business school itself offers the evening courses. It is least true when a business school offers most of its courses in the evening and has little or no daytime student body.

Daytime faculty members may teach in the evening under either of two arrangements. The most common practice is to teach in the evening for extra compensation, with the evening courses representing a net addition to a full daytime teaching load. The less common practice—which, however, seems to be growing—is to include evening teaching as part of the faculty member's full-time load, with a corresponding reduction in the number of hours taught during the day and with no additional compensation.

The first of these two arrangements is open to serious objections, and there is no doubt that it has been abused. In some cases, the overload of evening teaching may amount to 50 per cent of the day load, and 25 per cent is quite common.[44] As we shall see in Chapter 14, full-time teaching loads are by no means light; they are typically twelve hours in member schools and higher in nonmember schools and departments of business. It is fair to say that, in these circumstances, the quality of both day and evening teaching suffers. The effect on the faculty member's scholarly activity is likely to be even more serious.

The more desirable arrangement, clearly, is to have evening courses included as part of the faculty's full-time teaching load. But there are almost insuperable obstacles to imposing this as a general rule. Many instructors object to evening teaching, and until salaries are raised substantially above their present levels, those who are willing to teach these courses are likely to insist on additional compensation.

As we shall see in Chapter 14, there are serious objections to the use in the regular degree offerings of the business school of part-time teachers

---

[42] In addition, there are some full-time instructors who teach only in the evening, but they represent only a very small fraction of the total evening faculty.

[43] *Ivory Towers in the Market Place*, p. 117.

[44] Cf. Kozelka, *Professional Education for Business*, p. 19.

drawn from the business community. These objections also exist to their use in evening courses, especially if the courses carry degree credit and cover the usual academic subjects. These difficulties are much less serious, and indeed may virtually disappear, in the case of highly specialized offerings, particularly those stressing actual procedures or new developments in business practice. It is only logical to have such courses taught by well qualified practitioners. There are other types of technical courses, especially those stressing new developments in a particular discipline, which scholarly inclined staff experts from business can teach with considerable success.

It is clear that evening teaching in business subjects will continue to be done largely on a part-time basis, with the staff drawn either from the day faculty or the business community. The quality of teaching might be improved, however, to the extent that some or all of the following steps could be taken.

1) Wider use of the arrangement under which faculty members teach both evening and day courses as part of their normal teaching load.

2) Tighter control over the amount of teaching for extra income which the individual faculty member would be permitted to accept.

3) More careful screening of part-time teachers drawn from the business community.

4) More systematic use of procedures, such as faculty meetings, that will lead to greater uniformity in the quality of teaching and provide for better communication among the instructors in the evening program. More adequate provision also needs to be made for faculty-student contacts outside the classroom.[45]

We are reluctant to suggest that the evening colleges try to build up larger full-time teaching staffs. In fact, we doubt that this is either wise or possible in the case of two types of instructors: those who teach subjects largely concerned with business practice and those who teach academic subjects that carry degree credit in the day program. The former need to be drawn for the most part from business, and the latter should have, if possible, some daytime teaching experience.

We do see one additional source of full-time faculty members for the evening school which is suggested by our recommendations in earlier chapters. If the business schools were substantially to reduce the degree of course proliferation and eliminate some of the overspecialized fields and courses which they now make available in their regular degree pro-

---

[45] Speaking of evening courses generally and not merely in business administration, Dyer remarks that student-teacher contacts outside the classroom are "conspicuously absent." *Ivory Towers in the Market Place*, p. 131.

grams, some faculty members who found it impossible to adjust to the new order of things might be shifted to the evening program, where they could continue to teach in their respective specialties. In short, one way of reducing excess specialization in the day curriculum is to transfer both courses and instructors to the evening program. There is more justification for many of these specialized courses in the evening, where they need not carry credit toward a degree and where they can serve the legitimate needs of those already in business for particular kinds of specialized training. The obstacles to this kind of transfer are too obvious to require comment. But there is a good deal of logic in the suggestion, and it permits a university to protect the tenure of a highly specialized faculty member who can not adjust himself to a new and broader day program.[46]

SOME FINAL COMMENTS ON EVENING COURSES

In some ways, the demand for part-time evening education presents the universities with even more of a dilemma than do the other kinds of nondegree programs discussed in this chapter. Evening programs must satisfy the demand for a college education by those unable to get it on a full-time basis and at the same time cope with the requests for the various kinds of supplementary education that were described at the beginning of this chapter. Both types of demand reflect important needs, some part of which can be appropriately satisfied by the universities.

Specialized and vocational types of training belong in these evening programs and not in the undergraduate degree curricula of the business schools, but, even in the evening, the universities should try to be more selective than some of them now are. They should not try to provide educational services which they are not particularly well qualified to offer or which can be equally well or better managed by other agencies. Nor should they try to do so much that the effort weakens their regular degree programs or diverts the faculty from essential research activities.

Here, as in the case of the other types of nondegree educational activities, a partial answer lies in more careful evaluation of the community's needs. This implies an ability to resist local pressures if, in the judgment of the university, the demand is not one that it can appropriately meet. Even more, it implies cooperation with other agencies—for example, the public schools, the local community college, and various trade and professional groups—to arrange an effective division of labor.

Beyond this, we would offer only one other suggestion. We suspect that the evening schools could develop a more effective counseling service for the local business community than they now provide. This service could

---

[46] The possibility of such a transfer was being considered at one urban university we visited which was on the verge of a radical revision of its day program.

be made available both to companies and individuals. Frequently businessmen, particularly the officials of smaller concerns, feel a need for supplementary education and training but lack the information to decide which of the evening courses currently available at the local university will be of greatest help to them. The availability of such a counseling service could be widely publicized.

Institutes and Conferences

Every year, thousands of businessmen attend a wide range of conferences and institutes under university auspices.[47] These affairs are tailor-made to fit the interests and needs of particular groups. They are typically of short duration, seldom lasting longer than a week and usually only a day or two, and they are frequently cosponsored by a trade or professional group and the university.

TYPES OF PROGRAMS

There has been a substantial increase in the demand for these short programs since the war. The range of subjects that can be dealt with is virtually limitless, including problems of small business, estate planning, labor arbitration, recent tax developments, transportation and traffic management, automation and data processing, supervisory training, and some aspect of banking or real estate or insurance. Increasingly, conferences are being held for firms in particular industries: life insurance underwriters, mortgage bankers, building materials distributors, retail hardware dealers, petroleum jobbers, furniture manufacturers, motor vehicle fleet operators, and many others. Some of these programs are aimed at employees below the managerial level, for example, a Prescription Shoe-Fitting Workshop, a Secretaries Institute, and many programs on some aspect of selling. Programs are arranged not only for industry or professional groups but also for individual companies, particularly in the form of so-called "short courses."[48]

[47] "Conference activities were among the earliest means for extending the use of university resources. Perhaps more than any other medium of university extension service, they have been continuously and specifically requested by many different groups." Morton, *University Extension in the United States*, p. 54. This source contains useful information on the place of conferences and institutes in the work of university extension divisions.

[48] A "short course" typically consists of a series of meetings, usually weekly, extending over a period of up to two or three months. It may be on or off the campus. These courses may be offered for individual companies or for a wider audience. Several hundred such courses have been given in various parts of the country for small businessmen under the joint sponsorship of various universities and the Small Business Administration. When given at the request of a single company, the short course may be a "prepackaged" course which has been given before or it may be tailor-made to the company's specifications.

The short conference-type programs are usually directed toward those in a particular occupation or functional specialty (accountants, personnel managers, etc.) or toward owners or managers in a particular industry. While a few draw from more or less of a national audience, participants come predominantly from the local area. For the most part, these programs attempt to do one of several things: review recent developments of interest to practitioners in a particular field (for example, taxation), help improve general business competence and technical skills among members of a particular group who have a range of problems in common (small businessmen, bankers, sales or traffic managers, etc.), review new developments in a body of specialized subject matter (such as data processing or operations research) that may be of wide interest, and, finally, provide a general mental stimulus and broadening influence.

These programs are often jointly sponsored by both the university and one or more industry or professional groups. Sponsorship by the latter is frequently considered necessary to insure satisfactory attendance. More often than not, these groups take the initiative in proposing a conference or institute.[49] Arrangements are likely to be handled by an extension division, if one exists, but some institutions have special agencies to administer these programs. Some schools actively seek all of this kind of business they can get; others take little initiative and even reject many of the requests for special programs they receive from business groups.

Some universities have residential centers for continuing adult education, and their business conferences are held chiefly at these centers. Two substantial examples are the Continuing Education Centers at the University of Georgia and at Michigan State University, which have modern hotel, conference, and classroom facilities. Continuation centers exist also at several other state universities and land grant colleges, not to mention the special conference facilities available at such places as Columbia University's Arden House or New York University's Gould House. The more elaborate of these conference centers are costly to maintain, and the substantial overhead expense creates some pressure to keep them continuously occupied with paying guests who are attending conferences.

EVALUATION

It is not unfair to say that these conference programs have spread and grown with little planning and even less evaluation of the results that can be expected of them. In many cases, they clearly represent an uneconomic use of the university's resources, and they not infrequently are of

---

[49] "More than any other type of extension activity, conferences are the outgrowth of requests made by the users of this type of service." Morton, *University Extension in the United States*, p. 124.

doubtful value to the businessmen who participate. While some are carefully planned, deal with significant topics, have effective speakers, and draw interested and attentive audiences, others are hastily put together with a minimum of concern for either subject matter, the quality of the participating faculty, or the needs of the audience. It is a tribute to the desire of businessmen for further education, as well as perhaps to their naïveté, that these conferences are so frequently well attended.

The majority of these programs have a number of weaknesses that impair their educational effectiveness. Most of them are too short for there to be much of a cumulative impact, although in most cases greater length undoubtedly would significantly reduce attendance.[50] Frequently the programs are not well planned. The choice of topics is often haphazard, with too little consideration of the needs supposedly being served. The effectiveness of the speakers and discussion leaders often leaves much to be desired. All too often, there is a reluctance to make those attending participate actively in the educational process. Superficiality is an inevitable result. This is particularly true of very short conferences, in which there is likely to be no assigned reading, emphasis is put on lectures, and such discussion as takes place is undisciplined and on a superficial level.[51] The situation is in marked contrast to the better of the management development programs, which turn out to be an arduous intellectual experience for many executives. There are, however, a number of workshops, seminars, and short courses to which the preceding criticisms to not apply and which do provide a valuable educational experience for the participants.

Universities undertake these programs for a number of reasons, some of which also lead them into evening courses for part-time students or into full-fledged management development programs. The motive of service should not be minimized, although it frequently may suffer from an excess of organizational zeal by the staff of the division responsible for this type of activity. There is a long and respectable tradition of service to the community in both the urban and state universities. But there are also other important reasons. The type of service represented by conference programs possesses a good deal of public relations value, from which may come a more favorable climate of public opinion, financial

[50] Of about 3,700 conferences in both business and nonbusiness subjects held by thirty-four universities in 1951–52, approximately 2,000 lasted only one or two days, and another thousand had a duration of three to five days. (Morton, *University Extension in the United States*, p. 57.) Our own survey of a large number of brochures of conferences and institutes held in 1956–57 suggests that these proportions are still about the same.

[51] See the similar views expressed by Andrews in Pierson *et al.*, *The Education of American Businessmen*, chap. 21.

support for various of the university's activities, and greater ease in placing the business school's graduates. Finally, there are the immediate
benefits in the form of revenue from fees for the university (which may
be substantial) and extra income and additional business contacts for the
participating faculty members. An occasional additional benefit—although it is seldom an important reason for planning a conference, institute, or workshop—may result from the contribution which participation
in these programs may make to the professional competence of the
faculty member.

While these are important reasons for undertaking this type of activity,
they must be weighed in the light of the answers to two fundamental
questions. Is an important educational need being met in a reasonably
effective fashion? And does the satisfaction of this need, taken in conjunction with the other benefits mentioned, outweigh the costs involved—
above all, the cost entailed in diverting the university's resources from its
primary responsibilities?

In this as in many other cases, it is easier to offer a general statement
of the issues than a set of specific and workable recommendations that
will improve existing practice. While more general than we should like,
the following propositions are worth stating.

1) Taken as a whole, conference-type programs can serve an important need. If well done, they may help to develop management skills,
or at least to awake participating businessmen to the need for improvement. They can help the businessman keep up with new developments
that are important to him. More generally, they can provide a meeting
place in which viewpoints and experiences can be exchanged and businessmen can be exposed to new ideas.

2) The university's resources should obviously be conserved for those
types of programs in which it can make its most effective contribution.
In general, these will be programs which stress recent developments in
fields in which the faculty has particular competence, help to develop
professional and business skills with respect to which particular business
groups need assistance that cannot be provided in other ways, or offer in
condensed form and in a manner interesting to adults material drawn
from the regular degree offerings on the campus.

3) More attention should be paid to the quality of the educational
services being offered. In particular, there should be less adherence to
the idea that a significant contribution to professional knowledge and
skill can be made in the course of one or two days of listening to lectures
or of casual participation in undisciplined discussion.

4) Business schools and their associated service bureaus and extension

divisions should work closely with local firms and trade and professional associations with a twofold purpose in mind: first, to obtain a systematic and continuing evaluation of the educational needs of the business community and, second, to arrange for a fruitful division of labor whereby the university will be asked to provide only those programs in which it can make an effective contribution without impinging on its other responsibilities. With possibly a slight amount of help, business firms and trade groups can provide for themselves some of the educational services which they now request of the universities, and they can probably provide them equally well.

Adult Business Education: A Concluding Note

Little doubt can remain that the business schools have a considerable opportunity for useful service in the field of adult business education. Directly or through their sister evening colleges and extension divisions, they can make a significant contribution to each of the kinds of need described at the beginning of this chapter. If, however, the universities are to make their maximum contribution, they must develop a carefully formulated educational philosophy that will help them decide how much emphasis they should place on this type of educational service in view of the other demands on their limited resources. It will also help them decide what particular educational needs of the business community they should try to satisfy, and how this can best be done.

In addition to their desire to provide a service of clear value to the business community, the universities have other reasons for wishing to satisfy some considerable part of the demand for adult business education. In particular, the universities stand to benefit in three ways: improved relations between the university and the business community, increased revenue for the university (some of which may accrue to the business school), and gains to the faculty both in income and in the extent of their contacts with the business world.

These benefits, of course, entail a cost. The most obvious cost is the faculty time that can be absorbed in these programs. Moreover, there is the danger that these additional activities may drain off the faculty member's energies and divert his interests from essential scholarly activity. There is no doubt that on some occasions these and other costs substantially outweigh the benefits received, either by the business community or by the business school and the university. But many of the educational service activities are so clearly worth performing that they justify a considerable effort on the part of the university. The problem is to strike an appropriate balance and, in the programs that are offered, to provide as high a quality of educational service as is possible under the circumstances.

Both the university and the business community are likely to gain most from those educational programs that make the most effective use of the day faculty's talents (without seriously interfering with their regular teaching and research activities) and at the same time make a contribution to the faculty's intellectual and professional development. Therefore, in the field of adult business education, the universities should put their greatest emphasis on those areas which are taught in the daytime degree programs and on the development of interesting and challenging programs aimed at improving the higher managerial and staff skills. This can best be done in some versions of a management development program, through evening M.B.A. programs of the sort recommended in Chapter 11, by making available in the evening variants of day business (and preprofessional) courses for which there is the greatest demand, and by the better type of carefully planned short conference, institute, or seminar. While there may be some doubt as to how deeply the universities should become involved in the more specialized and vocational kinds of adult business education, there are opportunities here which at least some institutions may appropriately exploit—less through use of their regular faculty than in providing physical facilities, assisting in planning programs, and acting as intermediaries in finding competent teachers from the business and professional world.

The most important need at the moment is for the universities to take stock of what they are doing in the field of adult business education—to develop a clear-cut philosophy and set of objectives and to appraise the needs to be served and the resources available for meeting them. It is to be hoped that in the future there will be less tolerance of superficiality, less emphasis on the prestige and public relations aspects of the programs, and a greater willingness to resist local pressures for programs that the university cannot conveniently or appropriately provide. We hope there will be greater emphasis on what these programs can contribute to the professional development of the faculty as well as of the business community. We also hope there will be greater insistence that, for a particular program of adult business education to be offered, reasonable evidence be given that the university can provide the kind of training desired better than any other available agency and without serious conflict with the other (and prior) claims on the staff and resources available.

PART IV

Students, Faculty, Teaching, and Research

chapter 13

IMPROVING THE

QUALITY OF STUDENTS

PREVIOUS chapters have considered at length the problems of objectives and curriculum but have only touched on the other necessary ingredients of a successful educational operation: competent faculty and students. Important as curricula are, the best curriculum in the world can not compensate for an inadequate faculty, a poor student body, and the resulting lack of a stimulating atmosphere. In this chapter we shall look at the kinds of students who now seek a business education in college. Chapter 14 will deal with the business school faculty.

The Quality of Undergraduate Students

Two questions in particular need to be considered. First, do business students have the mental aptitude to handle and benefit from the more rigorous kind of program recommended in earlier chapters? It has frequently been argued that significant reform in undergraduate business education would be difficult because of the inferior mental quality of many business students. It has also been argued that only a small minority of college students are qualified for the kind of graduate business program proposed in Chapter 11.

The second question has to do with the nonmental traits of business students. As we saw in Chapters 5 and 6, business success and the social usefulness of a business career depend on more than the kind of mental aptitude which is measured by intelligence tests.

Unfortunately, there is very little evidence bearing on this second question. We can say a few positive things about the motivation of business students and a little about some of their attitudes toward themselves and their environment. We can also draw a few inferences that bear on their ability to handle social relationships. Beyond this, the available evidence has to do with mental ability. We shall, therefore, concern ourselves primarily with the first of the two questions we have posed: How good are business students in terms of mental ability, and how does the answer bear on the feasibility of the kind of educational program that we are proposing? As we proceed, we shall also consider what little information we have regarding nonmental traits.

TABLE 20

INDICATIONS OF STUDENT ABILITY BY FIELD OF STUDY

| | Selective Service College Qualification Test, 1951-1953 | | | | College Graduates (ACE Psychological Examination) Median Score (AGCT Scale) |
| | Freshmen | | Seniors | | |
Field of Study	Mean Score	Per Cent Exceeding Critical Score (70)	Mean Score	Per Cent Exceeding Critical Score (75)	
All fields	70	53%	74	50%	121
Agriculture	68	40	71	29	119
Biology	71	60	73	46	121
Business	*68*	*38*	*73*	*43*	*119*
Education	66	28	69	20	117
Engineering	72	68	76	67	124
Humanities	70	52	74	47	122
Physical sciences	72	66	76	68	127
Social sciences	70	56	74	51	120

Note: A Selective Service College Qualification Test score of 70 corresponds to 120–121 on the AGCT scale.

Sources: Freshmen and senior scores on the Selective Service College Qualification Test are from Educational Testing Service, *Statistical Studies of Selective Service Testing, 1951-1953* (Report SR-55-30, 1955). Median scores of college graduates (bachelor's level) on the American Council on Education Psychological Examination (converted to the AGCT scale) are from the Commission on Human Resources and Advanced Training, *America's Resources of Specialized Talent* (prepared by D. Wolfle, director, 1954), and are based on test scores of a sample of 10,000 men and women students who graduated in 1950 from 41 colleges and universities.

ARE BUSINESS STUDENTS INTELLECTUALLY INFERIOR?

An article in *Fortune* a few years ago posed the question: "Is poor scholarship particularly characteristic of men going to business schools?"[1] The answer, based on data gathered by the Commission on Human Resources and Advanced Training, was in the affirmative.[2] It was found that students in some fields were more highly selected in terms of intelligence scores than were students in other fields and that business students

[1] Duncan Norton-Taylor, "Business Schools: Pass or Flunk?" *Fortune*, June, 1954, p. 240.

[2] The Commission's report was prepared by its director, Dael Wolfle, and published as *America's Resources of Specialized Talent* (1954).

as a group were clearly below average. Analyses by the Educational Testing Service of the scores made by nearly 500,000 male college students on the Selective Service College Qualification Test (SSCQT) confirm the poor showing of students in business.[3]

Let us examine both sets of data as they are summarized in Table 20. It is clear that business schools and departments enroll a disproportionate share of very weak freshmen.[4] Only 38 per cent of the freshmen in business equalled or exceeded the qualifying or "passing" score. For no other identifiable group of freshmen except those in education did such a large proportion fail to qualify. In fact, business, education, and agriculture were the only fields in which a majority of the freshmen did not qualify.

The showing in the senior year was slightly better, business students having improved more since the freshman year than those in any other field. Yet business students were still below the average of all college seniors, and, at this level, 57 per cent of the business students failed to register qualifying scores. Again, only students in agriculture and education did as poorly as those in business. Among students receiving the baccalaureate degree, business students ranked well below those in engineering and the sciences and below the average for all college graduates. It is also clear that business attracts a smaller proportion of really good students—only 12 per cent of its graduating seniors stand in the top 20 per cent of all college graduates.[5]

[3] *Statistical Studies of Selective Service Testing, 1951–1953* (E.T.S. Statistical Report 55–30, 1955). For further information, see Henry Chauncy, "The Use of the Selective Service Qualification Test in the Deferment of College Students," *Science*, CXVI (1952), 73–79, and M. H. Trytten, *Student Deferment in Selective Service: A Vital Factor in National Security* (1952).

[4] Four-year schools of business tend to have the same minimum standards for admission to their freshman classes as do other undergraduate colleges on the same campus. Yet the data show that business freshmen are, on the average, significantly inferior to freshmen generally. The inescapable conclusion is that at that level, at least, business is peculiarly attractive to the weak student. The Commission on Human Resources noted this tendency in a more general context: "In general, . . . fields which have the reputation of being 'hard' get somewhat brighter groups of students than do fields which have the reputation of being easy. This is true whether one thinks of broad areas . . . or of individual fields. . . . Thus the physical sciences, languages, engineering, and law are all fairly close to the top of the lists, while education, business, some of the social sciences, home economics, and physical education are close to the lower end." *America's Resources of Specialized Talent*, p. 202.

[5] The Commission on Human Resources (*America's Resources of Specialized Talent*, p. 196) reported the proportion of graduates in engineering and business by quintiles; the first quintile includes the poorest students; the second, the next best, etc.

	Quintiles				
	First	Second	Third	Fourth	Fifth
Business graduates	27%	25%	20%	16%	12%
Engineering graduates	15	17	21	22	25
All college graduates	20	20	20	20	20

SOME QUALIFICATIONS

The evidence raises serious questions regarding the past and present standards in American business schools. Yet perhaps the picture is not quite as bad as it seems. First of all, while it is clear that freshmen in business are much weaker than those in most other fields, some of the gap is closed by the senior year. This suggests that business schools—particularly the four-year ones—tend to have high attrition rates.

A second qualifying circumstance concerns the size of the differences involved. Aside from the question of statistical significance, we doubt that much practical meaning can be read into the small differences between some of the average scores in Table 20. The Commission's data show that business school graduates had median aptitude scores of 119 as against 121 for all graduates; the sscqt comparison for college seniors is 73 as against 74.[6] All in all, it would not be inaccurate to say that, in terms of mental ability, those graduating from the business schools differ only slightly from the average of all college graduates. They are about on a par with seniors or graduates in the social sciences, biology, agriculture, and the humanities, and are perhaps a little better on the average than those in education. Certainly they are below the average level in engineering and the physical sciences, but in this respect business students have a great deal of company.

This difference between business, on the one hand, and the physical sciences and engineering, on the other, is very real. Particularly is this true if we look at the students in the top quintile, although other fields also attract a less than proportionate number of the very best students.[7]

[6] The Commission noted that "small differences are somewhat unreliable; a repetition of the study would probably show reversals of some of the ranks. But . . . it is unlikely that most fields would move up or down the list by more than one or two places." (*America's Resources of Specialized Talent*, p. 202.) In the case of the Selective Service tests, even though the large numbers of students involved mean that the difference of one or two points between the average scores of business school and all college graduates is "statistically significant," we doubt that much importance can be attached to such a small difference.

[7] "Every field draws some of the top quality students. The fields differ considerably, however, in the proportion of their membership which is drawn from the top levels of ability. . . . For each graduate who majored in the natural sciences or in the humanities and arts and whose intelligence test score was among the top fifth of all graduates there were three of lesser ability. In the social sciences and in education the top level people were each working with four of lesser ability, and this was the average ratio for all fields. In business and commerce the dilution was greater than average; for every student from this highly selected range there were about six from lower levels of ability." See *America's Resources of Specialized Talent*, p. 204.

Of the 1,350 exceptional students who participated in an "early admission to college" program, for example, only twenty-seven indicated that business administration was to be their major field.[8] A study conducted in 1955 of a group of high school boys of superior ability revealed that only 7 per cent preferred business as a major in college, whereas 24 per cent preferred engineering; 8 per cent, physical science; and 10 per cent, education.[9]

In light of these findings, is business receiving an adequate supply of really competent people? To answer this question, we should have to know more than we now do regarding the needs by business for persons of superior intellectual ability. It may well be that the need for such people is not quantitatively great. In this case average ability is less relevant than the number at the top of the scale. We have seen that business schools do attract people in the top quintile, although there are not many of them. But perhaps business is getting all such students that it needs. Further, business may also recruit some superior people from the noncollege population and from among nonbusiness graduates. And, finally, it should always be remembered that business students as a group, while possibly less able in some sense than students in certain other fields, are definitely above the population as a whole in intelligence.[10]

It should also be borne in mind that there is a great disparity in academic standards among institutions. In all probability, the variation in ability among fields on the same campus is less than the variation among campuses. The difference between even the poorer students at a good college and the average at a very weak school may be considerable. It is also apparently true that colleges with low academic standards are particularly likely to have business programs.

To summarize the evidence thus far, it is clear that the business schools, at least at the undergraduate level, are attracting considerably more than their proportionate share of poor students and a less than proportionate share of the good ones. Despite this, the average quality of the students

---

[8] The Fund for the Advancement of Education, *They Went to College Early* (1957), p. 95. Similarly, few of the recipients of National Merit Scholarships, all of whom are exceptional students, intend to major in business.

[9] But 20 per cent indicated that their probable field of study would be business. About 10 per cent of the group *wanted* to have careers in business. The sample included only boys who were high school seniors, stood in the top third of their class, and contemplated college. C. C. Cole, Jr., *Encouraging Scientific Talent* (College Entrance Examination Board, 1956), pp. 142, 144, 150.

[10] If the average intelligence of the entire population is taken as 100, the average of all those entering college is 115 and the average of those graduating from business schools is 119. See *America's Resources of Specialized Talent.*

graduating from business schools is not as low as we might otherwise expect. Several factors contribute to this result. A large number of students of average ability study business; attrition rates among the poorer business students seem to be very high; and some other fields which also attract poor students—for example, education—help to hold down the average for all fields. We also need to differentiate among business schools. But, although there are a few schools with high standards, the conclusion is inescapable that the undergraduate business schools are today admitting too many poor students. We think it is also true that they are still permitting too many of their present students to graduate.

This last conclusion results from comparing the findings in the preceding pages with the conclusions reached in Part II, where it was argued that truly professional training implies standards which are higher than those which need to be applied to the college community as a whole. Yet, as we have seen, the average ability of students graduating from business schools is slightly below the average for all fields.

The Effect of Higher Standards

There are a few undergraduate business schools which seem to have standards that are higher than those of most of the liberal arts departments on the same campus. We visited a number of other schools where we were told, but usually with no corroborating evidence, that the business students were as good as those in liberal arts. On no campus did we find evidence or hear the claim that business undergraduates were on a par with those in engineering or the physical sciences.[11] This is consistent with the statistical evidence presented earlier in this chapter.

Of the schools that do maintain reasonably high standards at the undergraduate level, most are two-year schools that do not have the burden of accepting and then screening a large group of freshmen, as do the four-year schools. It is possible to have a four-year school of business which, by choice or necessity, admits to the freshman class any high school graduate and then applies scholastic standards which force the incompetent and weak to drop by the wayside. Few schools, however, are likely to apply such a policy as rigorously as our suggested standards require, although it is clear that a good many business and liberal arts

---

[11] With one exception. At one land-grant college we were told that business and engineering students were on a par, although both groups ranked below students in the physical sciences. The "near-business" programs of the engineering schools, i.e., the industrial administration curricula, typically have students who are, on the average, inferior to engineering students generally.

faculties are discouraging large numbers of weak freshmen and sophomores from continuing.

Although it is encouraging to find that some four-year faculties are attempting to hold to reasonable scholastic standards, the high attrition
rates that usually result are somewhat disturbing for a number of
reasons. First, they are costly in terms of scarce faculty resources (and
faculty morale). Second, the screening device sometimes used—for example, the elementary accounting course—is not necessarily efficient as
a criterion of eligibility for further study in business. Third, the cost in
terms of student anxiety and anguish is invariably high. This is particularly true in some "soft hearted" schools where weaker students are
not dismissed but simply are not permitted to graduate. Most important
of all, the large numbers of poor students, before they are weeded out,
drag down the quality of instruction and prevent the better students from
getting out of their courses all that they might. All this suggests that the
four-year schools should either adopt more realistic admissions standards
that would exclude more of those students who do not have a reasonable
chance of graduating, or else should shift to an administrative arrangement (e.g., a one-three or two-two plan) under which standards are
easier to maintain.

This is not to advocate that any university deny the youth of its con-
stituency an education. But we do believe that professional schools should
conserve their resources for the preparation of those who are most able
to profit from such training and have the personal qualifications necessary for personally fruitful and socially useful professional careers.[12] Few
would argue that engineering and medical schools should accept all who
apply. While the argument may be somewhat less strong for the business
schools, the same reasoning is applicable and is becoming more so as
business problems become more complex.

Raising admissions and performance standards to the minimum levels
suggested here would result in the exclusion of a significant number of
poor students—students lacking the requisite mental ability or motiva-

---

[12] The position taken here can be defended at much greater length than we have chosen to
do in this section. It is one which is held by most leading business educators as well as by many
of those who are concerned with education in a broader context. Cf. particularly Byron S.
Hollinshead, *Who Should Go to College* (prepared for the Commission on Financing Higher
Education, 1952); V. C. Gildersleeve, "The Abuse of Democracy," *The Saturday Review*
(November 24, 1956), pp. 15ff.; Rockefeller Brothers Fund, *The Pursuit of Excellence—Education
and the Future of America* (Special Studies Report v, 1958); The President's Committee on
Education Beyond the High School, *Second Report to the President* (July, 1957); and The Presi-
dent's Commission on Higher Education, *Higher Education for American Democracy* (December,
1947), vol. i.

tion or both.[13] To the extent that most of these are not of college caliber to begin with, there can be little basis for opposing the move. Inevitably, however, adoption of our recommendation would mean exclusion from the business school of some weak students who not only will eventually move into a business career but are also just good enough to qualify for degrees in a liberal arts or community college. This, it seems to us, is as it should be if the business schools are to offer the kind of program that this study suggests is needed and if they are to acquire the standing as professional schools to which they aspire. While the excluded students may well go into business anyway, they are likely to gravitate toward the kinds of positions that require neither a high degree of mental ability nor a great deal of formal business training—for example, in selling, in the lower levels of management, or as owners of very small businesses. These students would have available to them the service offerings in business described in Chapter 10 (if they remain on the campus of a four-year college) or the business courses available in the terminal programs of the junior and community colleges. In this way, the poorer students can get some background that will be useful to them in business, and they are free to go as far in the business world as their talents and opportunity will take them.

Very little is known about how to select those young men and women who are most likely to be successful in business. Given our ignorance of the most effective selection criteria, it is possible and indeed probable that the standards we suggest would exclude from collegiate business schools some students who might become successful businessmen anyway. There are two compelling reasons for taking this risk. First of all, the risk cannot be very great. The standard we propose is, after all, not such a very high one. While the available evidence indicates that, above some minimum level, mental ability may not be highly correlated with the various measures of business success, it is also apparently true that a moderate degree of mental ability is indeed an essential (but by no

[13] How many, of course, we do not know. It has been suggested (Hollinshead, *Who Should Go to College*) that college opportunities should be made available to the top one-fourth of the population in terms of mental capacity. Translated into I.Q. units, this would exclude students with aptitudes lower than 110. Using the data of the Commission on Human Resources, we derived the rough estimate that from 18 to 23 per cent of those who receive bachelor's degrees in business have aptitudes below 110. We agree with Hollinshead (p. 14) and others that chances for success in a respectably rigorous collegiate program are reasonable only for individuals in the top quarter of the population. Hollinshead notes that the National Research Council estimates that college seniors average about 116, that the Armed Services find 110 to be a reasonable cut-off for its officer training programs, and that most college admissions officers think an I.Q. of less than 110 does not augur well for success in college. Cf. also *Higher Education for American Democracy*, vols. I (pp. 39–44) and VI (p. 11).

means a sufficient) condition. More important still, unless the inferior students are excluded, it is not possible to give the other students the kind of preparation that will contribute most to their effectiveness as businessmen and as leaders in a democratic society.

The additional screening we recommend would be of two sorts. More students would be refused admission on the basis either of tests or scholastic record or both. And, by higher grading standards applied in courses that would be made more difficult, a higher level of performance would be necessary to secure passing grades. We are not recommending that business schools adopt an arbitrary cutoff point on the basis of some intelligence test. What we do urge is that standards of student performance be raised, and that students be refused admission or dropped who, it is judged, cannot meet this performance level. Motivation, the particular configuration of a student's aptitudes, or other factors, as well as what is measured by intelligence tests, may explain a student's failure to meet the desired performance standards.

It would be unrealistic to expect all schools to follow this prescription. It is unfortunate but true that some schools must continue to accept students of such a caliber that a reasonably high-level professional program in business is impossible. Inevitably, then, there will be some second-rate schools catering to second-rate students. But we do not believe that they need be members in good standing of the AACSB. The Association needs to give more attention than it has so far done to the admission and performance standards of present member schools as well as of those newly applying for membership.

The Quality of Graduate Students

Thus far we have been speaking chiefly of undergraduates. We must now look at the graduate students, all but a tiny fraction of whom are candidates for the master's degree. The chief evidence available comes from the Commission on Human Resources.

The Commission's most significant finding in this connection is that "the differences among the fields are about the same regardless of the educational level at which the students are studied."[14] Thus graduate students in business tend to have about the same relative ranking as do undergraduates. (See Table 21.) Graduate students in business had a median AGCT score of 121 and thus ranked below fourteen of the twenty

---

[14] *America's Resources of Specialized Talent*, p. 197. As before, the discussion uses group medians on tests, the results of which are converted into the scale of the Army General Classification Test (AGCT).

TABLE 21

DISTRIBUTION OF SCORES ON AGCT SCALE OF
COLLEGE GRADUATES AND GRADUATE STUDENTS
SPECIALIZING IN DIFFERENT FIELDS OF STUDY

| | *Percentile Scores (on AGCT Scale) of Each Group* | | | | | |
| | *College Graduates* | | | *Graduate Students* | | |
Field of Specialization	*25th Percentile*	*Median*	*75th Percentile*	*25th Percentile*	*Median*	*75th Percentile*
All fields combined	114	121	128	116	124	132
Agriculture	114	119	125	122	127	133
Business and commerce	*112*	*119*	*126*	*114*	*121*	*128*
Economics	115	122	129	116	125	133
Education	109	117	124	114	121	128
Engineering	117	124	132	118	126	134
Health fields	—	—	—	118	125	132
History	113	120	127	116	124	131
Home economics	105	113	119	111	116	122
Humanities and arts	115	122	129	117	125	134
Law	—	—	—	115	124	128
Natural sciences	116	123	130	120	128	135
Psychology	114	123	130	125	132	138
Social sciences	112	120	127	116	124	133
Social work	—	—	—	114	121	127

Source: *America's Resources of Specialized Talent*, Appendix I. See also Table 20.

fields (not all of which are shown in Table 21). They scored below the average (124) of all graduate and professional students. The difference between business and the most highly selective fields was greater for graduate than for undergraduate students. Perhaps 15 per cent of the graduate students in business had AGCT scores below 110; only two fields —home economics and physical education—attracted more weak students.

Deans and faculty members in the business schools generally believe that their graduate students are superior to their undergraduates. This certainly seems plausible; and the tables of this section tend to substantiate this claim. What is more significant, however, is that the relative position of the business student deteriorates between graduation from college and graduate school. Taking all fields together, the median AGCT score rises from 121 for all college graduates to 124 for all graduate students. For business students the increase is only from 119 to 121. Over 40 per cent of the graduate students in business were apparently of lower ability than the average graduating senior in business.[15] More than 60 per cent of the graduate students in business had AGCT scores of below 125—the level which has been identified as the minimum for "satisfactory graduate work."[16] And only one-fifth of the business graduate students scored as high as AGCT 130—roughly equivalent to the cutoff point on the Selective Service College Qualification Test for seniors desiring to enter graduate or professional school. (Nearly half of the seniors in business who took the SSCQT managed to score that high or higher.[17])

At a few schools we were informed that the better undergraduate students in business seldom continue their studies beyond the baccalaureate degree. We suspect that a large number of the graduates from undergraduate curricula who do go on to take master's work in the multipurpose schools are not especially outstanding students, particularly if their goal is business practice rather than teaching or research. There are several reasons for believing that this is the case.

The able business undergraduates, intent on an active business career and confident of their own abilities, are likely to take a position immediately upon graduation or after military service. The less able and the more insecure, provided their undergraduate records are a bit better than average, may seek to improve their competitive position by spending another year getting the master's degree. The average level of ability at the multipurpose or "mixed" schools is raised by some of the more able students preparing to be technical staff specialists, research workers, or teachers—and by graduates from nonbusiness curricula who desire an M.B.A. before embarking on a business career. The cream of the candidates for the master's degree tends to be skimmed off by a few of the exclusively graduate schools with high admission standards. Further, the bulk of the students admitted to the exclusively graduate schools did not

---

[15] Cf. *America's Resources of Specialized Talent*, Appendix I.

[16] C. G. Wrenn, "High Level Research Talent," in National Research Council, *Human Resources and the Fields of Higher Learning*, p. 25, as cited in Cole, *Encouraging Scientific Talent*, p. 22.

[17] Business students taking the SSCQT were apparently substantially superior to those represented in the data of the Commission on Human Resources. Based on the scores of 6,310 males seeking to qualify for draft exemptions, the SSCQT average for business seniors was AGCT 126. The Commission on Human Resources average of AGCT 121 for *graduate students in business* is based on a much smaller sample, including both men and women and drawn from forty to fifty universities. The difference between 126 and 121 is, no doubt, partly due to implicit selectivity factors in the case of the SSCQT (i.e., males seeking draft exemption presumably so they could go on to graduate or professional schools of one kind or another). Despite this bias in the data, we believe that the text suggestion that relatively few of the bright seniors in business go on to take advanced business degrees is justified.

major in business as undergraduates. In short, the poorer graduate students are largely concentrated in the one-year master's programs for which undergraduate business training is, in effect, a prerequisite, and they are more likely than not to have majored in business as undergraduates.

Although it would help to know more about the undergraduate origins of the weaker graduate students in business, it is nevertheless clear that too many schools now have unsatisfactory standards at the graduate level. Probably not much more than 5 per cent of those who receive bachelor's degrees in business each year go on to do graduate work in business.[18] If these students were to come from only the top half of the preceding year's graduating class, the average quality of business graduate students would improve substantially—except perhaps for those few graduate schools that already have very high entrance standards.[19]

The chief way of improving the quality of M.B.A. candidates, however, lies in another direction. If graduate standards were generally raised and graduate programs made more attractive and challenging, at the same time that undergraduate specialization in business was discouraged, there would be an ample supply of good candidates for the master's degree. The best of the graduate schools illustrate the appeal which a well planned and challenging graduate program in business can have for above average students who have taken their first degree in nonbusiness fields. In this connection, a study made at the Educational Testing Service of the effectiveness of the Admission Test for Graduate Study in Business offers some suggestive findings. While those who were business majors as undergraduates had better undergraduate grade records than either the engineering or liberal arts students, both of the latter groups scored higher on the Admission Test than did the business majors. In addition, both engineers and other nonbusiness students tended to have better grades during the first year in graduate school than did the undergraduate business majors.[20]

---

[18] This estimate is based on 1) the ratio of graduate to undergraduate business degrees and 2) the proportion of graduate students in business who majored in business as undergraduates. Cf. The Carnegie Corporation Survey of Business Education, *Summary of Preliminary Findings* (revised August 1, 1958), Table XLII, and this report, Table 1.

[19] The median score for graduate students in business would be raised from 121 to 126 on the assumption that the same percentage of graduating seniors in each percentile above the median went on to graduate work. See Table 21.

[20] Marjorie Olsen, *The Admission Test for Graduate Study in Business as a Predictor of First-Year Grades in Business School, 1954–1955* (Educational Testing Service Statistical Report 57–3, 1957). The 1,205 students covered by the study represented ten graduate programs. About 30 per cent had been undergraduate business majors, 20 per cent had engineering degrees, and the remaining 50 per cent had liberal arts and other kinds of undergraduate degrees.

Nonmental Characteristics of Business Students

There are other respects, besides mental ability, in which it is frequently assumed (usually with little supporting evidence) that business students differ from those in other fields. For example, it has been alleged that many business students are not strongly motivated toward business as a field of study or as a career—that they have vague aspirations focussed on business only because nothing else attracts them more. It is also claimed that a relatively large number of business students come from the lower socioeconomic strata and have parents who did not go to college. Another widely held belief is that the business student has a personality which differs somewhat from that of the typical nonbusiness college student. These are the kinds of questions about which little information has been collected.[21] And that which is available tends to be quite subjective.

MOTIVATION

We discussed the question of motivation with groups of students and individual faculty members on several dozen campuses. The impression was widely held that relatively few undergraduates concentrate in business administration because they are intellectually attracted to the subject. (Not infrequently an exception was made for accounting.) Often they major in business because they feel that they will wind up in business and that it is therefore only reasonable to take a business degree.

On the other hand, some students quite positively want and are seeking what they consider to be a career in business. Some of these go to the university *only* because they can major in business—they want to be businessmen, and they want the business degree because they believe it will help them achieve their primary goal. They usually are highly motivated. This group often contains a large proportion of young people who look upon a career in business as a way of moving upwards socially and economically. They look on the college degree partly as a status symbol, but chiefly as a way of breaking into and moving up in the business world. Students with this attitude often express a desire for a "practical" education which will, in some way or another, give them higher starting salaries and higher lifetime earnings than any alternative. They often are impatient with instruction which apparently does not have this orientation. Taking a narrowly "practical" view, many of them may

[21] See, however, Norman Frederiksen and W. B. Schrader, *Adjustment to College* (Educational Testing Service, 1951) for a study of a large sample of veteran and nonveteran students.

show little interest in the broader implications of how a private enterprise system functions. And they may not be greatly concerned, at least at this stage of their careers, about the social responsibilities of the businessman.

While this prototype of the strongly motivated business student with narrow interests certainly has some validity, probably more so in the "downtown" urban universities than anywhere else, the picture can easily be overdrawn. The strong motivation toward material success is not necessarily incompatible with some breadth of outlook. Moreover, self-centeredness and a lack of concern for what is going on in the world are also characteristic of many nonbusiness students. We doubt, for example, that the interests of the typical engineering student are any broader than those of the business student, and the same might be said of many liberal arts students who drift through four years of college life and then graduate with no broader cultural or social outlook than when they entered.[22] As a matter of fact, we collected some impressionistic evidence on a few campuses that business students tend to be better informed about current political and economic affairs than do other students.[23]

A third category of business student includes those who are in the business school by default. This is the residual element. They either could not find anything else that appealed to them, or they expected business administration to require less work than any other field. Students in this group tend to be weak academically or to have very little in the way of ambition, or both. They have no career aspirations, are not strongly motivated to improve their social or economic standing, and of course have no strong intellectual interest in the subject matter of the school. They are the ones, in particular, who have given the undergraduate business schools a reputation for having weak students. So far as we can determine, they are found in significant numbers in nearly every undergraduate business school. A substantial move in the direction of a high-level professional degree with high academic standards would eliminate many of the students in this last group. This, we believe, is as it should be. The social return from the investment of educational resources in these students is very low, and they pull down the level of performance of those who can gain most from a good undergraduate education.

[22] For some supporting evidence, cf. Frederiksen and Schrader, *Adjustment to College*, p. 390.

[23] We gathered little evidence worth citing regarding some of the student characteristics which William H. Whyte, Jr., cites with such concern in *The Organization Man* (1956)—the tendency toward conformity, the desire for stability and security, the bias toward staff work, a passive kind of conservatism, etc. Whyte presents little evidence to differentiate business from other students in these respects. As for his criticism of the emphasis on a "practical" education and narrow specialization, these are matters that we have already discussed.

We have little to offer on the other personal qualities of business students. We were sometimes told that students in business are more "people-oriented" and are more likely to be extroverts than are, say, engineers. This is a plausible assertion—so much so that it was not always clear whether such statements were based on observation or assumption. We did accumulate some evidence that business students, more than either engineering students or students in general, engage in a significant amount of extracurricular activity.[24] This is an important point in view of the findings in Part II regarding the significance of organizational and human relations skills for a successful career in business—particularly at the higher levels. We have already suggested that these qualities can be partially developed by at least some types of extracurricular activities.

Very few schools attempt to select undergraduate students on the basis of other than intellectual qualities.[25] Admittedly this is a difficult thing to do. The logic of this report, however, suggests that the undergraduate schools should give some consideration to nonintellectual attributes.[26] We are not competent to say how this should be done. Clearly, this is an area greatly in need of exploration, one in which possibly the business school and the psychology department might find a common research interest.

SOCIOECONOMIC STATUS

A related area about which little is known concerns the sociological dimensions of students in various fields. At one urban school we were told that most of the business students were from "blue collar families" and that the faculty felt obliged to shape the curriculum accordingly. Similar views were encountered at some other schools. While this generalization can be made too strongly, it may be true that, at least in the urban schools, relatively more undergraduate business students come from families at a low socioeconomic level than is the case of the college population as a whole.[27] This is consistent with the finding of the Commission on Human Resources and Advanced Training that the "higher

[24] This was also true of the sample of students studied by Fredericksen and Schrader. See *Adjustment to College*, Appendix A.

[25] The better graduate schools do attempt to do so and give weight to such factors as the applicant's work and military experience, undergraduate extracurricular activities, etc. In addition, the Harvard Business School has for some years been engaged in an elaborate "Selection Study," hoping to identify personal characteristics that are related to business success.

[26] This point is also made by Richard Kozelka in his report, *Professional Education for Business* (1954), pp. 47–49.

[27] See, for example, Chris A. Theodore, "Boston University Graduates in Business and Industry," *Boston University Business Review*, III (Spring, 1956), 23–24.

the socioeconomic level of the home, the greater the likelihood that the child will earn a degree in a liberal arts or science field" rather than in vocational subjects.[28] It is interesting, in this connection, to note the finding by Warner and Abegglen that, among their sample of business leaders who had graduated from college, a much larger fraction of the sons of unskilled and skilled workers took some business training in college than was true of any other socioeconomic group.[29]

There is a substantial body of evidence to confirm the general impression that there is a strong positive correlation between family social standing and going to college.[30] But the democratization of higher education is proceeding apace; and a steadily increasing percentage of children from poorer families, in which the parents did not have a college education, are going to college. The most able of these students with this kind of background are likely to be motivated towards and to be able to qualify for study in one of the more difficult professional or academic fields. A significant fraction of the remainder wind up in a business school or some other type of vocationally oriented program. They are likely to have narrow interests oriented toward what they believe is practical, although there are, of course, numerous exceptions.

Business Students in the Future

The kind of educational program recommended in these pages requires a more carefully selected student body than can be found in most business schools today. Clearly, the average quality needs to be raised, more by eliminating students at the lower end of the scale than by increasing the number in the top few percentiles. It has already been suggested that it is better, so far as possible, to achieve these higher standards by a more selective admissions policy than through higher attrition rates alone.

The program proposed here also implies a student group with a reasonably high level of positive motivation toward careers in business or other forms of "economic management." Many students now in the schools meet this stipulation. But many, as we have seen, do not. They take business courses by default and have little notion as to what they want out of college. Such students are better off, we submit, in a general arts program. Certainly their presence in a high level professional curriculum is bound to be wasteful of scarce educational resources. In addition, the student himself has lost an opportunity to explore a wider range

[28] *America's Resources of Specialized Talent*, p. 209.

[29] *Occupational Mobility in American Business and Industry, 1928–1952* (1955), pp. 109, 112

[30] Cf., for example, Hollinshead, *Who Should Go to College*, pp. 35–37, 171–81.

of human knowledge and perhaps thereby to find a field in which he might better develop his talents. From an administrative viewpoint, the problem is made simpler by the fact that the students with low levels of motivation and no positive interests are often the same students who lack the intellectual equipment to complete a professional degree program of high quality.

Improvement in the quality of the student body requires not only more careful selection on the basis of mental ability and motivation, but also greater insistence on an adequate academic preparation both in secondary school and in the first years of college. A commercial, technical-vocational, or nondescript high school diploma does not prepare a student for a collegiate business program of respectable caliber. Some business schools have tended to neglect such matters in the past, but they cannot afford to do so in the future.

Given a good foundation laid in high school, insistence on a sound pre-professional preparation along the lines described in Chapter 8 will be a strong force for changing the character of the business school student body. Students will have more of a common background; they will have been screened by the preprofessional courses; and fewer of them will be campus floaters. Engineering students are more homogeneous and more carefully selected than are students in business, not because of their engineering courses but because the preprofessional work in mathematics and the sciences tends to screen students in terms of ability, interests, and level of motivation, as well as to give them a common intellectual background. The general education core of Chapter 8 could have much the same result in business administration.[31]

A final word needs to be said about nonmental qualities. We have tried to translate the stress on skill development in this report into curriculum recommendations. But the development of most of the skills considered in Chapters 5 and 6 presupposes certain innate qualities—qualities that apparently can only be shaped and perhaps sharpened but not created *de novo* by classroom experience. This suggests that schools should either guide their admissions policies in part by a consideration of what innate qualities are considered to be desirable, or else they should develop a program under which students with the intellectual but not the other necessary qualities are eventually identified and given the opportunity

[31] When we speak of the need for a more homogeneous student body, we have in mind only such characteristics as mental aptitude, possession of the necessary analytical and communication tools, seriousness of purpose, and interest in what is being studied. We make no plea for conformity in any other respect. Indeed, it is our hope that the broader and more rigorous type of program that we recommend will attract to the business schools types of students they do not now attract, and that in some respects the diversity in interests and backgrounds will be greater, not less, than it now is.

to change their educational goals. Given our present state of ignorance, and the limited resources of most schools, the former policy is extremely difficult to implement, particularly with undergraduates. (This is another argument for deferring business training to the graduate years.) A few schools make some attempt to follow the latter policy. But most schools pay no attention to the problem at all (except in accounting).[32] This is understandable, in view of the paucity of knowledge about these matters. We hope that research in this area will be accelerated; there seem to be signs that it will be. The need for more knowledge about these matters is urgent.

One last comment seems necessary on the "quality gap." The quality of students at the better schools is far above that at the average school of business, not to speak of the weaker schools. It seems certain that the better schools will have even higher standards in the future than they have now. Thus there is a good chance that the quality gap between the better and poorer schools will widen rather than narrow, a possibility which points up the need for concentrated effort to improve the position of the poorer schools. The problem is likely to become particularly acute at the graduate level. The gap is already very wide between the best of the graduate programs and those which are only of average quality or less. As the demand for graduate training expands, much of the growth will have to come in these poorer programs.

All of this presents a problem to the American Association of Collegiate Schools of Business which thus far it has apparently been reluctant to face. While the Association has been very much concerned with the quality of collegiate business education, this concern has manifested itself chiefly regarding such matters as curriculum, terminal degrees of faculty members, and teaching loads. We think that the time has come for the Association to concern itself also with the quality of students and standards of student performance. We admit this is no easy task.[33] But given the role it plays in establishing standards of minimum acceptability and in setting the climate of opinion among the rank and file of business schools, the Association has an obligation to work actively for higher standards in both admissions policy and student performance, including the initiation of studies that will help to achieve agreement as to the form such higher academic standards should take, how they can best be implemented, and the steps the Association itself should take to establish and maintain these standards.

[32] The extent of student counseling within the business school varies widely, but in general there is less of it than there should be. Cf. Kozelka, *Professional Education for Business*, p. 53.

[33] Among other difficulties is the fact that admissions and performance standards are often determined by central university authorities (or by trustees or by legislatures).

chapter 14

THE BUSINESS FACULTY

THE EXPANSION in the student population has already outrun the ability of the business schools to find qualified teachers. In the absence of strong and positive action, the worst of the faculty shortage is yet to come. In recognition of this fact, the AACSB sponsored a conference in 1955, the proceedings of which have been widely read and discussed.[1] As a result there has come to be a greatly increased awareness of the seriousness of the problem, and some steps have been taken to cope with it.

But as serious as this quantitative problem is, the issue of quality is even more important. Indeed, the two are inseparably connected. One answer to the faculty shortage—the inevitable answer in the absence of positive measures—is increasing reliance on inadequately qualified teachers. One of the most important issues facing the business schools is how, in the face of the pressures created by mounting enrollments, they can not only maintain but improve the quality of their faculties. Without such improvement, the higher standards of business education proposed in this report are not likely to be attained.

Characteristics of Business Faculties

More than 10,000 persons were engaged in 1956 in teaching one or more business courses in a college or university.[2] About 60 per cent of these were regular, full-time faculty members of schools or departments of business. The remainder were employed part-time in either day, evening, or extension programs.

Part-time instruction may create relatively few problems when it is used for specialized, nondegree courses offered as a service to the community. It is only natural that such courses, which can provide valuable supplementary training for those already in business, be offered by practicing specialists. The serious problems arise when part-time instructors are used extensively in the regular degree offerings of a school. Such in-

---

[1] The proceedings were published as *Faculty Requirements and Standards in Collegiate Schools of Business* (AACSB, 1955).

[2] The Carnegie Corporation Survey of Business Education, *Summary of Preliminary Findings* (revised August 1, 1958), is, unless otherwise specified, the source for most of the figures cited in the remainder of this chapter on the size and characteristics of business faculties.

structors may appear on the campus only for the hour needed to give a class. They take little or no part in faculty discussions and the school's planning; they are not readily available to students; their teaching is not easily coordinated with that of the rest of the faculty. And, while they may enrich their teaching with the results of their own business experience, they do not enrich it with the results of wide reading and their own research.

A somewhat different but also serious problem arises out of the widespread tendency for regular faculty members to take on extra teaching for additional compensation in evening and extension programs. This is, of course, a reflection of the low level of salaries that generally prevails. Daytime teaching loads of twelve or fifteen hours are frequently increased by four to six hours of evening teaching in the search for extra income.[3] The results of this extra teaching on the faculty member's research and on the extent to which he keeps up with his field are too obvious to call for further comment.

WORK LOADS

It is fair to say that college teachers of business subjects carry heavy work loads and, like college teachers generally, are not particularly well paid.[4] Teaching loads in the business schools are typically twelve hours per week; in departments of business, the load is typically fifteen hours. The student-faculty ratio tends to be high, usually more than 20:1. With heavy teaching loads, moderately large classes, the usual committee and other administrative chores, and a minimum of grading and clerical assistance, it is not surprising that many business school teachers do little research. (Given these facts and the additional one that business courses seldom require expensive equipment or other large overhead costs, we can also understand why many universities look on their business schools as an important source of revenue.) To this picture we need to add the almost irresistible temptation confronting many faculty members, particularly in urban areas, to supplement modest salaries by taking ad-

[3] R. L. Kozelka speaks of the practice of permitting 25 to 50 per cent additional teaching loads through evening and extension classes. *Professional Education for Business* (AACSB, 1954), p. 19.

[4] As a general rule, it is not true that business school faculties are paid significantly more, rank for rank, than their colleagues in the liberal arts departments. In about two-thirds of the cases that we studied, business school salaries were no higher than in the liberal arts college, and in a few cases they were actually lower. However, there is more "rank inflation" in the business schools, and promotion is likely to be more rapid. (This means that it is the younger men who benefit most.) The major financial difference between business school and liberal arts faculties is not in salaries but in the opportunities for earning additional income—chiefly through consulting activities or evening teaching.

vantage of the relatively plentiful opportunities for additional teaching or outside consulting jobs.

EDUCATIONAL BACKGROUNDS

About 40 per cent of the full-time faculty members in business schools hold an earned doctor's degree. The percentage is about the same for college teachers in all other fields taken together, although this latter figure is expected to fall to perhaps 20 per cent by 1970.[5] The 40 per cent figure for business school faculties drops significantly if we include part-time teachers in the day, evening, and extension programs, since most of these do not have the doctorate.[6]

Most of the doctorates held by business school faculties—85 to 90 per cent—are in economics or business.[7] The degrees in economics outnumbered those in business in the ratio of about seven to five.[8] Here is further evidence of the close relationship which has traditionally existed between economics and business administration and of the important role which economics departments have played in training business school teachers. It also helps to explain some of the resistance to the introduction of material from the behavioral sciences into the business curriculum. The remaining doctorates are distributed among education, psychology, other social sciences, and a scattering of other fields.

Doctorates in economics are somewhat more heavily concentrated in

[5] *Teachers for Tomorrow* (Fund for the Advancement of Education, Bulletin No. 2, 1955), pp. 25 and 62. This decline has already begun and has been more rapid in business administration than in most other fields. See, for example, *Teacher Supply and Demand in Colleges and Universities, 1955–56 and 1956–57* (National Education Association, 1957), p. 19.

[6] The proportion of doctorates reported by a business school is subject to some administrative juggling, into which some deans feel they have been forced by the way in which the terminal degree requirements of the Association have been stated. Thus, inclusion of the economics department in the school increases the proportion of doctorates, since most economists above the rank of assistant professor are likely to have the PH.D. (Similarly for political science or sociology.) Transfer of the evening program to another administrative unit also raises the percentage of doctorates since it removes the part-time instructors who do not have advanced degrees.

[7] According to the Carnegie Survey of Business Education the figure is about 85 per cent. It was about 90 per cent in the samples of schools that we examined intensively.

[8] The sample of 74 schools, used in Chapters 8 and 9, yielded the following distribution of doctorates held by full-time, regular business faculty (948 degrees in the sample).

Field of Doctorate	Association Schools	Nonmember Schools
Business administration	35%	35%
Economics	56	48
Psychology	1	3
Education	2	4
Other	6	10
	100%	100%

member than in nonmember schools, and more at the full professor level than in the lower ranks. A disproportionate share of the persons holding doctorates in education and the social sciences are in the junior ranks—presumably an indication of their relatively recent arrival on the scene.

The membership standards of the AACSB specify that at least half the instructional hours "on either the Junior-Senior level or on an overall basis will be taught by full-time faculty members having terminal degrees. . ."[9] About 65 per cent of business school faculty members have terminal degrees satisfactory to the AACSB.[10] In the case of the member schools, about two-thirds of the terminal degrees are doctorates, but only a little over half of the terminal qualifications represent doctorates in the case of the nonmember schools.[11] Of those having terminal degrees other than doctorates, a substantial majority are accountants with a master's degree and the C.P.A. Most of the rest have law degrees.

About 65 per cent of the student credit hours offered in a recent year were taught by faculty members meeting the minimum terminal qualifications specified by the Association.[12] The range among schools was quite wide—from 90 per cent or more to as low as 27 per cent among the schools we examined. The member schools, of course, make a much better showing than nonmember schools. There is also a considerable disparity among fields. Among the core fields, accounting, business law, and economics ranked high; the functional fields and statistics ranked much lower; marketing fared particularly badly with considerably less than 50 per cent of student credit hours being taught by instructors with the appropriate terminal qualifications.[13]

In view of the growing faculty shortage, it is too much to expect the Association to insist that more than 50 per cent of the teaching be done by instructors with the appropriate terminal degrees. The Association would probably be wise, however, to redefine some of its present terminal degree requirements. Clearly, a law degree by itself is inadequate; it

[9] *1958 Standards for Membership.*

[10] A 1955–56 self-survey of member undergraduate schools prepared by the AACSB also indicated that about two-thirds of faculty members had acceptable terminal qualifications. In our sample of nonmember schools, the figure was about 62 per cent.

[11] For member schools, the source is the AACSB self-survey cited in the preceding footnote. The estimate for nonmember schools is based on a tabulation from our sample of such schools.

[12] The self-survey previously mentioned is the source for some of the information presented in this paragraph.

[13] Accounting ranks high because the combination of a master's degree and the C.P.A. certificate is quite common. Business law is taught by lawyers with the necessary law degree. In economics, the doctorate is typical in the upper two ranks. The functional fields rate poorly because quite often both the basic and some of the more specialized courses are taught by instructors with only the M.B.A. Statistics, usually a sophomore course, is frequently taught by young instructors without the doctorate.

should be combined with either the M.B.A. or an advanced degree in one of the social sciences. We suspect that advanced teaching in accounting should be reserved for those who have the doctorate rather than the M.B.A.-plus-C.P.A. Terminal qualifications probably also need to be raised in other fields. Advanced engineering degrees, for example, probably should not be considered terminal for teachers of industrial management unless supplemented by evidence of advanced work in business administration or economics.

On the whole, however, significant improvement in the quality of business school faculties is not likely to come from a preoccupation with terminal degree requirements.[14] Like most of the Association's standards, specification of terminal degrees is at best a minimum and somewhat inflexible safeguard against an amount and kind of incompetence that borders on the intolerable. In the long run, the raising of standards and the improvement in the quality of business school faculties must rest with the schools themselves. Universal possession of the doctorate by itself will not bring about a sound curriculum and imaginative teaching, nor will it alone generate the fundamental research or high standards of accomplishment that are needed. The rut from which collegiate business education is now trying to emerge is dotted with doctoral hoods, which sometimes have the quality of keeping their wearers' eyes fixed on the past instead of on the opportunities that lie ahead.

Nonetheless, there are many reasons for insisting that some minimum fraction of a business school faculty have the doctorate, particularly if the school wishes to foster research or offer graduate instruction. We are inclined to suggest that more flexibility be introduced into the Association's standards, perhaps by its giving up the specification of terminal degree requirements by fields. Instead, the Association might require that some minimum fraction of the faculty have the doctorate (the fraction perhaps varying depending upon the relative importance of graduate and undergraduate instruction), and that the remainder have at least a master's degree in business administration or a related underlying discipline.

About half the schools that we visited insisted in principle that their faculty members have the doctorate—because it was university policy, because of the belief that the degree was necessary as a screening device, or for similar reasons. About a quarter of the deans we interviewed wanted more of their faculty members to have the doctorate not because of any conviction as to the value of the degree, but merely because of its

[14] For further discussion of terminal degree requirements, see Kozelka, *Professional Education for Business*, pp. 11–14.

prestige value and the need to adhere to the standards set by the Association. About a dozen schools took what we felt to be a sensibly flexible attitude. They wanted a considerable number of doctorates in their faculties, particularly in the case of the men who were interested in carrying on research, but they did not consider the degree essential in every case if there was other adequate evidence of competence. A corollary of this flexible attitude in a few schools was insistence on the degree in the case of younger men (for whom other evidence was not likely yet to be convincing) but a willingness to waive the requirement of the doctorate in the case of more experienced persons of proved scholarly or professional competence, particularly if there were also some evidence as to teaching ability.

Inbreeding has been a serious problem in some of the large schools that have their own doctoral programs, although this particular academic disease is by no means confined to business faculties. It is far easier and usually cheaper to obtain new faculty recruits from an institution's own new PH.D.S than to bid in the open market for young instructors who have been trained elsewhere. At one campus we visited, 80 per cent of the business school faculty members having doctorates received their graduate training at that institution. While this is an extreme case, a high degree of inbreeding exists at several other schools.

The evils of faculty inbreeding can be quickly stated. A particular set of attitudes within the faculty tend to perpetuate themselves; new and fresh viewpoints developed elsewhere are kept out or are introduced into the school very slowly. Curriculum, teaching methods, and attitudes toward research tend to become frozen if considerable new blood is not introduced from the outside. Advances in all these respects are spread widely among the better business schools; no institution has a monopoly on the best ideas. Hence, it is important that the faculty of a school be drawn from a number of different kinds of training and that it have been exposed to more than one kind of academic environment.

In addition, it is difficult to avoid personal favoritism if a school recruits regularly from its own graduate students. Senior professors push their own protégés for faculty appointments; the "logrolling" that results impairs faculty morale and, more often than not, fails to lead to the appointment of the best available candidate. Sometimes the effect on the successful candidate is also bad. Although now a member of the faculty, he is likely to remain tied to the apron strings of his sponsor and inhibited from setting off on new paths of which his former teacher may disapprove.

TYPES OF FACULTY MEMBERS

The search for prototypes is usually dangerous, but it may be worth the risk of overgeneralization to suggest some of the broad categories into which faculty members in the business schools fall.[15]

Applied social scientists. Here we include the applied mathematicians and statisticians, as well as the economists, psychologists, and other social scientists who, while primarily concerned with some basic discipline, are also interested in applying the analytical tools of their field to business problems.

There is growing recognition that business administration is a respectable field of study for social scientists *qua* social scientists and that it is possible to have in the business schools challenging programs of both teaching and research. During the last few years, there has been a sharp upsurge of interest among the business schools in acquiring behavioral scientists, statisticians, and applied mathematicians—not necessarily with the idea that these men will settle down to teaching conventional business courses, but with the hope that they will contribute research findings important to business and indicate ways of enriching the teaching in the business fields with more material gleaned from the underlying disciplines. A few psychologists and sociologists have already been doing this in some schools—for example, working in the areas of human relations, personnel, organization theory, and consumer behavior. Quite a few economists have been doing essentially the same thing, teaching and doing research in managerial economics, banking and finance, the economics of marketing, and some of the industry fields. In addition, some economists in the business schools have done research and taught in the broader areas of interest to businessmen, for example, taxation and problems of economic instability. In the last few years, a number of business schools have acquired statisticians and applied mathematicians to help develop work in operations research, linear programming, advanced statistics, and the like.

In all probability, this group of what we have called the applied social scientists—now a small minority in the business school—will grow sig-

[15] We exclude here, as elsewhere in this report, faculty members in nonbusiness fields who are in the business school by administrative accident. These include members of the economics department located in the business school if they have no interest in the applications of economics to business problems. Sometimes a department of sociology, journalism, etc. will be in the business school, and the members of these departments we also exclude—as we do also the teachers of English, mathematics, science, etc. when the business school offers its own service courses in these fields.

nificantly in the years ahead, as will their influence on curriculum and research. The reasons for this lie in the advances now being made in various of the social sciences and in the applications of statistics and mathematics to business problems. The recent appointments of men in these various nonbusiness fields by a number of the better schools are being closely watched. In addition, there have been unmistakable stirrings of interest among the teachers of conventional business subjects, who are increasingly looking to see what new light the underlying disciplines can throw on problems in their particular business fields.[16]

The various types of business specialists. Much the largest part of the business school faculty is made up of the men who, whether trained originally in economics, business administration, or some other field, teach in the various business specialties. Of this group, probably more were trained in economics than in business administration, although a few started out as engineers, psychologists, lawyers, etc. They specialize in some particular business field—for example, accounting, marketing, production, insurance. Some do a respectable amount of research, but the majority do little or none.

These business specialists as a group carry the largest influence in nearly every school and are chiefly responsible for shaping educational policy. They do not, however, constitute a homogeneous group, and it is therefore worthwhile to distinguish several subgroups. There are, first, the scholarly inclined specialists (usually trained in economics or occasionally in another social science) who do considerable research and textbook writing, emphasize subject matter rather than skill development in their teaching, and maintain some connection with one or more of the underlying disciplines.[17] Second, there is the managerially oriented group, which emphasizes subject matter less and managerial problem-solving more than the first group. These faculty members make extensive use of the case method of teaching, do little research, but have extensive contacts in the business world and do a great deal of consulting. Next, we have a group of what we may call the textbook teachers. These were

---

[16] The seminars dealing with new developments in business administration supported by the Ford Foundation have played a very useful role in this connection.

[17] Particularly in the case of those trained in economics, it may be difficult sometimes to distinguish between those whom we have called "applied social scientists" and this group of "scholarly inclined business specialists." The chief bases of differentiation lie in the way the faculty member views his interests, the nature of his scholarly activity, and what he chooses to teach. The applied social scientist will view himself as, for example, a psychologist or economist, not as a specialist in personnel or marketing; he is more concerned with keeping up with developments in psychology or economics than with detailed developments in the business fields; and his teaching will not be confined to the standard courses in any one special business field.

either poorly trained in the first instance or else have failed to keep up with their fields. They do no research; their teaching is descriptive and largely follows the latest textbook; they do only a little consulting (chiefly of a very routine kind) but seek out opportunities for extra teaching to supplement their incomes.

Finally, at the end of the spectrum, are the vocational teachers. These are the specialists concerned with a low level of skill training and detailed description of current practice, whether it be in typing and shorthand, bookkeeping, office procedures, advertising copywriting, personal selling, insurance claims, restaurant management, or what not. The "vocationalists" tend to attract the poorer students wanting a "practical" training. By the nature of the case, they are not interested in research. They do little thinking about the field of business administration as a whole, and, perhaps even more than the other business specialists, they defend the inviolability of their own specialties.

Significant reform in collegiate business education depends on the broad middle range of this spectrum. Of particular importance are the "scholarly inclined subject matter specialists" and the "managerially oriented" group. These need to move closer together in their approach both to teaching and research, and both need to look more actively for help from the underlying disciplines, as their more progressive members are beginning to do. In partnership with a growing number of applied social scientists (and statisticians and mathematicians) interested in business problems, these politically powerful groups in the faculties of the better of the Association schools can provide the impetus and necessary support for the kinds of reform recommended in this report. Some of the most difficult problems will be to reduce the existing emphasis on specialization (of which the better managerially oriented teachers are probably less guilty than most of the other teachers of business subjects), to increase faculty interest in and competence to do fundamental research (about which little can be done in the case of the vocationalists and probably the textbook teachers), and to create a willingness on all sides (including the central administration of the university) to run the risk of reduced enrollments in the interest of higher standards.

The Shortage of Faculty

Taking its cue from the anticipated doubling in collegiate business enrollments between 1953 and 1970, the AACSB conference at Arden House in 1955 anticipated the need for a corresponding doubling of business school faculties. Calculations based on this assumption indicated an annual need for new faculty (for replacement and expansion) rising from nearly 500 in 1958 to about 1,000 in 1967 and declining to 700 in 1970. If the present standards regarding possession of the doctorate are to be maintained, this suggests the need for 275 holders of the doctorate in 1958, rising to more than 500 by the mid-1960s.[18] All indications suggest that these requirements cannot be met from the anticipated supply of new holders of the doctor's degree who are likely to be available for business teaching.

Ways of coping with this anticipated shortage have been treated at some length in the recent volume published by the Association on *Faculty Requirements and Standards* and therefore need not be considered in detail here. It may be worthwhile, however, to deal briefly with a few of the more important issues. One problem that we shall avoid, despite its critical importance, is the need to raise salaries—an issue that faces not only the business schools but all of higher education. We have little to add to the large body of literature that already exists on this troublesome subject.[19]

INCREASING THE NUMBER OF AVAILABLE DOCTORATES

In 1958 about 100 doctorates in business administration were conferred.[20] A concerted effort is now under way to increase this number substantially. Existing doctoral programs are being expanded, new ones have been started, and more of an effort is being made to induce able M.B.A. candidates to continue toward the doctorate.[21] These efforts are discussed further in Chapter 17. The business schools probably cannot expect to get a significantly larger share of the PH.D.s in economics, although greater opportunities for research and high-level teaching might attract some young economists who now seek employment outside the business schools. The number of doctorates in business, however, can be expected to increase fairly rapidly during the coming decade.

[18] *Faculty Requirements and Standards*, p. 55.

[19] On the subject of business school salaries, see in particular C. C. Brown and O. N Serbein, "The Competitive Position of Collegiate Teaching Careers in Business Administration," in *Faculty Requirements and Standards*, pp. 184–200. On college salaries generally, see Beardsley Ruml and D. H. Morrison, *Memo to a College Trustee* (1959), and Beardsley Ruml and S. G. Tickton, *Teaching Salaries Then and Now* (1955), both published by the Fund for the Advancement of Education.

[20] See Table 1. The number of PH.D.s in economics awarded annually has typically been about twice the number of doctorates in business administration. John Lewis has estimated that about 40 per cent of the doctoral output in business and economics combined goes into business teaching. *Faculty Requirements and Standards*, pp. 56–57.

[21] It should be remembered, however, that not all those receiving the doctorate in business administration (or economics) go into college teaching. Cf. *Teacher Supply and Demand in Colleges and Universities*, pp. 74–75.

Increasing attention is being given to the possibility of attracting to the business schools holders of doctorates in fields other than business and economics.[22] As we have seen, 10 to 15 per cent of the doctorates held by business school faculties are in nonbusiness fields, and about a third of these are in the other social sciences. Two possibilities exist here: to attract to the business schools already established scholars from other fields, and to induce young social scientists, before or at the time they receive their doctorates, to work on problems of interest to business and to throw in their lot with a business school faculty.

The first of these possibilities can hardly be important in terms of numbers, although the addition of even a few more able social scientists and other scholars might have an important catalytic effect on a number of business school faculties.[23] Given the appropriate inducements, a modest increment to the supply of new faculty recruits might come from new PH.D.S in the social sciences, mathematics and statistics, and possibly other fields. Two conditions in particular are necessary to increase the supply available to the business schools from these sources: improvement in the intellectual atmosphere in the business schools (including a broadening and deepening of the teaching, as well as a greater emphasis on research), and stronger incentives to graduate students in these other fields to interest themselves in business problems.[24]

Although the business schools should continue to look beyond business administration and economics for faculty recruits, the total addition to the supply likely to come from these other fields will probably remain small. While not large in terms of numbers, this increment to the supply is nonetheless important because of its probable effect on quality—particularly on the quality of the research carried on by business school faculties but also on the quality of teaching.

THE USE OF BUSINESSMEN AS TEACHERS

This much debated issue resolves itself into two subsidiary issues: the use of businessmen on a part-time basis and the appointment of former businessmen to full-time positions either before or after they retire from business. (We include here also those in military or civilian government service.)

There is general agreement that the use of businessmen as part-time teachers is an expedient to be avoided as much as possible, particularly

[22] This has been urged by Dean G. L. Bach. See his paper, "Business School Faculties: Potential New Sources," *Faculty Requirements and Standards*, pp. 111–25.

[23] Such an effect has already made itself felt at several schools in the last few years.

[24] The Program in Economic Development and Administration of the Ford Foundation has sought to stimulate progress in both of these directions.

in the regular day program of the business school.[25] The use of such part-time instructors should be confined, if at all possible, to evening courses not carrying degree credit.

An exception should be made, however, for the highly qualified business expert who keeps up with the latest developments in his field and maintains university contacts as a normal part of his work. Such a person may make a valuable contribution to a business school even on a part-time basis. This may be the only way a school with limited resources can man some advanced technical courses, particularly in relatively new fields.

The use of former businessmen on a full-time basis is more debatable. A majority of the deans we interviewed doubted the wisdom of an extensive reliance on this source of supply, and we are inclined to agree with them. But certainly a flexible attitude is necessary. A businessman or government official who has had advanced training, has scholarly interests, has kept abreast of his field, and is still a considerable distance from normal retirement age may make an excellent faculty prospect, particularly if he has also had teaching experience. While the salary differential makes it difficult to obtain such people, high surtax rates reduce this obstacle somewhat, and improving faculty salaries may reduce it still further.[26]

The argument is fairly strong against much use of businessmen who have nothing to offer but the fact that they have been in business and now prefer the quieter life of a university campus. As one group of businessmen has put it, "a businessman cannot qualify as a teacher simply because he was successful in business; in order to qualify, he must have the traits we expect in any faculty member."[27] Least desirable of all is the retired businessman in his late sixties or seventies, who is likely to have little to offer students except anecdotes and reminiscences. There may occasionally be, however, the opportunity for a short-term visiting appointment of a truly distinguished person who, through lectures, seminars, and informal discussion, can offer a stimulating experience to both students and faculty.

While the business schools should probably not rely to any significant degree on former or present businessmen to man the business school's

[25] This was the general view among the deans we consulted and seems, on the whole, to be the official view of the Association. The latter's statement on this point is rather loosely worded, except for the requirement that at least five faculty members exclusive of those in general economics must give full time to instruction in business administration. Cf. also Kozelka, *Professional Education for Business*, pp. 14–15.

[26] Cf. *Faculty Requirements and Standards*, esp. pp. 119–20.

[27] *Business Looks at Business Education* (School of Business Administration, University of North Carolina, 1958), p. 19.

regular courses, most faculty members should have a significant amount of responsible business experience, whether obtained through an interlude of full-time business practice or through consulting activity. First-hand familiarity with business practice is *one* of the ingredients that make a good business school teacher (at least in the more applied fields), but it must be combined with large doses of scholarship and teaching ability.

INCREASING FACULTY EFFECTIVENESS

Frequent reference has been made in the last few years to the possibility of improving faculty productivity. We believe that the size of classes can be judiciously and selectively increased without any deleterious effect on the quality of teaching. We share the view expressed by others that the virtues of the small class have been exaggerated.[28] There are also clear opportunities for increasing faculty effectiveness through the use of teaching assistants, more clerical and grading help, more use of nonteaching personnel for administrative and counseling chores, closed circuit television, and so on.[29] All this has been said before. While there has perhaps been some improvement and a few schools have been willing to experiment, accomplishments to date have not been impressive. Higher education is not noted for its efficiency, not even in its schools of business administration.[30]

But these means of increasing faculty effectiveness only touch the edges of the problem. The business schools have hardly begun to explore the two most important ways of improving the teaching effectiveness of their faculties and at the same time providing more time for research. One lies in the area of curriculum planning. The other, very simply, lies in teaching fewer and better students.[31]

The faculty resources of most schools could be substantially increased by a carefully planned and significant reduction in the number of fields

[28] Cf. *Better Utilization of College Teaching Resources* by the Committee on Utilization of College Teaching Resources (Fund for the Advancement of Education, 1959), pp. 35–42; and Ruml and Morrison, *Memo to a College Trustee.*

[29] The Fund for the Advancement of Education has been supporting a series of experiments by selected colleges on ways of meeting the shortage of college teachers that would improve rather than reduce the quality of college education. The University of New Mexico, including its College of Business Administration, has been one of the participating institutions. For the experiments conducted and results achieved the first year, see University of New Mexico, *General Report on the Program for the More Effective Utilization of Teaching Resources* (September, 1957, mimeographed). See also *Better Utilization of College Teaching Resources*, which reports on a variety of experiments by a number of colleges.

[30] Cf. Daniel Seligman, "The Low Productivity of the 'Education Industry,' " *Fortune*, October, 1958, p. 135. This is, of course, entirely consistent with the fact that college teachers (and administrators) typically carry very heavy work loads.

[31] Cf. Miller Upton, "The Rising Tide — and A' That," in *Future Supply of Teaching Personnel* (School of Commerce, University of Wisconsin, 1956).

of specialization and number of courses offered, and perhaps also in the frequency of course offerings. It was pointed out in Chapter 9 that forty to fifty courses should be adequate for any undergraduate program. Major reforms in this direction still remain to be made. Until they are made, a significant part of the faculty shortage cannot be considered a shortage at all.

Much more of the present and anticipated faculty shortage would disappear if the business schools stopped trying to provide for virtually a fifth of all the men seeking a college education (and a seventh or eighth of all men and women students combined). If the best undergraduate schools were to shift to a graduate (or three-two) basis and if the remaining schools were substantially to raise their standards, the numerical aspects of the faculty problem would take on much more reasonable proportions. Even the intermediate step of raising standards and revamping the undergraduate curriculum along the lines proposed in Chapters 8 and 9 would afford considerable relief to most schools—and significantly improve the quality of the education being provided. It should also lead to a marked improvement in the quality of business school faculties.

Improving the Quality of Faculty

The elements that make a good faculty are essentially the same for any professional school.[32] In the case of the business school, these factors can be stated as follows. Each faculty member should have a thorough and up-to-date command of his field, which should be viewed as an intellectual discipline as well as a set of basic skills. Not only should he be a reasonably good teacher, but he should help the school to be progressive in its educational planning. The faculty as a whole should generate a substantial amount of significant research that continuously pushes outward the frontiers of what is known, and it should make important contributions to the improvement of business practice.

Most business school faculties must be judged seriously wanting in some or all of these respects, and significant improvement in the quality of faculty is perhaps the most critical need now facing business education. The nature of the most serious deficiencies will be considered in more detail in the next two chapters, which will deal with teaching and research in the business schools. But some of the broader issues need to be raised at this point.

[32] See, for example, Columbia University, *The Educational Future of the University* (1957), pp. 122–24. See also the qualities of a good faculty member described in the Report of the President's Commission on Higher Education, *Higher Education for American Democracy*, vol. IV (1957), p. 2.

It can be said of only a modest minority of business school teachers that they have a thorough and up-to-date command of their fields, as is revealed both in the relevant literature and in the best of current business practice. Too many faculty members view their own areas of interest both too narrowly and too superficially and are too little concerned with what has been called "the intellectual foundations of professional work."[33] This is not merely our own impression. It is confirmed by other informed observers and was further documented by many of the deans and better faculty members to whom we talked during the course of this study.

The situation differs among schools and among faculty members. In this connection, it is useful to refer back to the faculty prototypes described earlier in this chapter. The better of the applied social scientists and what we called the scholarly inclined business specialists are apt to keep up with the scientific literature in their field, although the latter may be weak on important developments in other areas that bear on the field in which they specialize. Both, however, may be poorly informed about current business practice. The managerially oriented teachers are likely to know much more about business practice than they do about the important scientific literature. The textbook teachers by definition fail to keep up with their fields; they convey to their students second-hand information which is frequently out of date by the time their students receive it. The vocationalists are familiar with current business practice in their specialties—and that is all.

It is fair to say that many business school faculties have been suffering from a creeping intellectual obsolescence, although many individuals and some schools can be cited as notable exceptions. This obsolescence shows up in many ways—poor teaching that emphasizes descriptive detail, the absence of a stimulating intellectual atmosphere, the small volume of significant research, lack of familiarity with the latest analytical tools, a too narrowly specialized approach to subject matter, and so on. In some cases, the difficulty is a lack of native ability. More often the trouble lies in other directions, such as poor graduate training, the enervating influence of poor students, failure to keep abreast of new developments for a number of reasons (including heavy teaching loads and low salaries), a preoccupation with teaching students what is immediately useful, and the geographical isolation of some schools.

A further word needs to be said about the failure of so many business school teachers to keep fully abreast of the most recent developments in their fields. First of all, something akin to an "explosion of knowledge" has been taking place. It is not surprising that faculty members find it

---

[33] Columbia University, *The Educational Future of the University*, p. 124.

difficult to keep up, particularly when a considerable amount of the new relevant knowledge is in areas in which they have had little training (as in mathematics, statistics, the behavioral sciences, or the more esoteric parts of economics). Second, communication of new ideas in business administration tends to be impeded by a number of difficulties, of which only two need be mentioned here. Business firms are under no obligation to publicize their own particular contributions to improved business practice. Also, a variety of scientific vocabularies and kinds of analytical tools are needed to understand the scientific literature in the many diverse fields on which business administration increasingly has to depend.

Intellectual obsolescence is not confined to the poorer undergraduate schools. It exists in varying degrees in nearly all schools. (Of course, business administration is not unique in this respect.) Some business schools can show an excellent record in curriculum planning, in the development of case and other teaching materials, and in consulting and other service activities. But, in good part because of the time and energy devoted to these aspects of the school's program, research is neglected, and faculty members do not have the time and energy (and sometimes the training) to keep up with the latest developments in the underlying disciplines that are relevant to their respective business fields.

As we shall point out in Chapter 16, the record of the business schools is particularly poor on the side of research. We do not argue, however, that every business school teacher should seek to grind out a steady stream of articles and books. The important need is for an increased interest (and competence) in *scholarship*. What is needed is the desire and ability to probe deeply and to ask searching questions about what is known and not known in the area of one's interests. Such scholarship can be applied in the field as well as in the library. It illuminates teaching, and it *may* also result in publication. It greatly enhances the ability of the business school to serve the business community and other segments of society. Scholarship in this sense is what makes a university; without it a business school is not really a part of the university community.[34]

The intellectual atmosphere in the business school frequently compares unfavorably with that in other schools and colleges on the same campus, although the situation is likely to be no worse than in some of the other undergraduate professional schools. In some cases, the situation

---

[34] Cf. V. W. Bladen, "The Role of the University," *University of Toronto Quarterly*, XXVI (July, 1957), 493; J. H. S. Bossard and J. F. Dewhurst, *University Education for Business* (1931), p. 550. See also A. N. Whitehead, "Universities and Their Function," in *The Aims of Education* (Mentor edition, 1949), especially pp. 103–104.

in the business school merely reflects the general lack of scholarly interests and activity on the campus generally. Sometimes, it is our impression, the university administration offers little support to significant improvement in the business school, whether because it expects nothing better, or because the revenue yielding properties of the school might be impaired, or because more scholarly activity might interfere with the service functions which the school is expected to perform for influential business groups.

While there is need for improvement in all the dimensions of quality, the primary needs are quite clear. They are to create in the business schools a more stimulating intellectual atmosphere, to bring the less progressive faculty members up to date with the latest scientific literature and business practice in their own and related fields, and to generate the capacity and desire to ask more probing questions and to engage in more significant research. In this sort of environment, academic standards will necessarily be high, the achievement of more effective teaching should not be difficult, and the ability of the business schools to serve the business community and society at large will be enormously increased.

These are broad generalizations and, if carried no further, represent no more than wishful thinking. In the next two chapters we shall spell out some of these matters in greater detail, particularly as they bear on the present situation with respect to teaching, research, and professional activities in the business schools.

chapter 15

THE NEED FOR

BETTER TEACHING

PROPOSALS for curriculum reform and higher standards clearly imply the need for better teaching. While this is in good part a question of academic goals and the quality of faculty, something more is also involved. Good teaching requires an adequate educational philosophy and an appropriate selection of teaching methods and teaching materials.

Improving Teaching in the Business Schools

Chapters 6 and 7 set forth some general criteria which, in our opinion, should govern the way in which students are instructed in the business schools. The student needs to acquire a command of systematic knowledge at as high an analytical level as he can handle, and then be made to put this knowledge to use in problem-solving situations that will help him develop the basic skills he will need as a businessman. In short, the business schools need to emphasize both "principles" and clinical teaching. The aim should be to make the student participate actively in the learning process and to help him develop for himself the problem-solving, organizational, and communication skills that he will need all his life.

Taken as a whole, the business schools do not live up to these standards. While a number of schools and a good many individual faculty members give much time and thought to improving the quality of their teaching, and while the situation generally is tending to improve, the over-all quality of teaching is not high. In good part, this is a reflection of the poor intellectual climate in most business schools. More specifically, the factors responsible for poor teaching include 1) the failure of most undergraduate schools to hold to sufficiently high standards, with the resulting poor quality of students and student performance, 2) the poor training and background of many faculty members, 3) the tendency toward overspecialization and, in some schools, toward vocationalism, 4) the small body of significant and verified generalizations on which teaching can be based and, partly for this reason, 5) the poor quality of the teaching materials that are generally used, 6) the fact that many teachers are overworked, 7) failure to make the most effective use of the teaching methods that are available, and, helping to explain several of the preceding weaknesses, 8) failure to develop a satisfactory educational philosophy related to the proper objectives of business education. The first four of these factors have already been treated at various points in this study (as has the last one in the list). We shall return to the fourth in connection with our consideration of research in the next chapter. In what follows we shall be concerned chiefly with the problem of teaching materials, teaching methods, and, more generally, the educational philosophy or general approach which should govern the teaching of business subjects.

While the general quality of teaching in the business schools leaves much to be desired, let it be said that the situation is probably no worse—and indeed it may be somewhat better—than in many other departments on the campus. Most business schools do emphasize the need for good teaching, although their standards as to what constitutes good teaching frequently leave something to be desired. There are some excellent teachers in the business schools, and a few schools have done an excellent job in developing new teaching materials and improving teaching methods. Nowhere is teaching neglected in the way that research often is. Nonetheless, there is wide room for improvement.[1]

THE KINDS OF EMPHASIS NEEDED

In Chapter 7 we pointed out that business courses could be taught with any one of three kinds of emphasis, which we called the *descriptive*, the *analytical*, and the *managerial-clinical*. The emphasis in business school teaching is now weighted too heavily toward the description of existing institutions, procedures, and practices. What is needed is a greater emphasis on the analytical and on the managerial-clinical aspects of the various business fields.

Greater emphasis on an analytical approach means giving students a command of useful analytical tools, seeking out significant generalizations, and in general developing in students the kind of sophisticated understanding of the relevant underlying relationships that will enable them to cope with concrete problem-solving situations.

The kinds of problem-solving situations which are important to the businessman are those which he encounters in an administrative capacity.

---

[1] In the majority of schools we visited in which the question arose, deans and faculty members seemed reasonably content with the quality of teaching. The kind of improvement desired which was most often mentioned was wider use of the case method. Other desired changes sometimes mentioned were smaller classes, more grading assistance, less use of inexperienced junior instructors, and experimental use of television.

Hence, there is need also for a managerial and clinical emphasis in which problems are considered not only from the viewpoint of the detached observer, but also from that of the manager who must cope with them and reach a workable solution within the limitations imposed by his immediate environment. A managerial-clinical emphasis implies considerable use of cases, but other types of problem materials and teaching techniques can also be used in courses which have this kind of orientation.

The present situation obviously varies widely, not only among schools but among instructors and courses in the same school. The emphasis on description, routine drill, and memory work is greatest in the more elementary courses, in many of the more specialized vocational courses, and wherever the instructor does little more than have the class recite from a textbook. A significant amount of analysis—involving a search for significant generalizations and the development and application of analytical tools—does enter into some advanced courses, particularly in the better schools. The amount of clinical teaching that emphasizes problem-solving situations as the business manager sees them also varies widely. A few schools emphasize this approach almost to excess. Others make moderate use of it, particularly in the more advanced undergraduate and graduate courses. Some schools and some instructors shun this approach entirely, whatever the subject or the level of instruction. On the whole, however, the last decade has witnessed a significantly increased emphasis on the point of view of the managerial decision-maker and on the use of business cases as teaching materials.

While it is clear that business schools need to increase the analytical content of their courses and place more emphasis on managerial problem-solving, the appropriate blend of the analytical and clinical approaches will vary with the course, the background and maturity of the student, and the tastes and abilities of the instructor. In general, it seems reasonable that the early courses should stress principles more than a clinical approach to managerial problem-solving; later courses can stress the managerial-clinical side much more.[2] "Tool" courses such as those in accounting and statistics, while emphasizing managerial use and interpretation, would make less use of case materials than a course in marketing management or financial administration. In some courses—such as accounting, statistics, marketing research, or operations analysis—"problems" rather than "cases" may be most appropriate. Of the courses in the undergraduate core, probably only the course in business policy should rely almost exclusively on long cases of the Harvard type.

As is only to be expected, the situation is much better at the graduate

[2] It will be remembered that in Chapter 9 we warned against too much reliance on cases in the first or "basic" courses in the various functional fields.

than the undergraduate level. In general, there is much less description, there is more analytical content, and there is greater stress on a managerial point of view and more extensive use of cases. At the better graduate schools students are exposed to a fairly rigorous program. Some graduate schools emphasize a clinical approach to managerial problem-solving almost to excess, with some consequent neglect of essential analytical tools and insufficient attention to significant generalizations. Others pay more attention to systematic analysis and the search for principles and put too little emphasis on problem-solving in the kinds of situations businessmen actually face. The contrast between these two types of schools, however, has been tending to lessen.

Teaching Materials and Methods

TEACHING MATERIALS

One safe generalization can be made immediately about the teaching materials currently being used in undergraduate business schools. There is too much reliance on textbooks, many of which are of indifferent quality or worse.[3] In nearly half the schools we visited, it was the general practice for an instructor to make his assignments almost exclusively out of a single text, particularly in the less advanced courses. We have seen any number of course outlines in which the reading assignments consisted almost entirely of the chapters in a single book, and in which the topics considered were (as often as not) taken up in the precise order in which they appeared in the text. In such cases the library is hardly used at all; there are few if any written assignments except for tests; and the student's intellectual horizon is confined to the covers of the one textbook. Many college students—and not only those in business administration—graduate with little more knowledge of the resources of their college library than they had as entering freshmen.

In a fair number of schools, stress on a single text is supplemented either by some library readings or the modest use of cases or both. An increasing number of texts are including a selection of cases, and there is a growing supply of casebooks which instructors can use in conjunction with the standard textbooks. Extensive library assignments, however, do

---

[3] L. C. Marshall's caustic comment of a generation ago still has a great deal of validity. "If, however, any doubt concerning the poor quality of instructional material lingers in the mind, that doubt will be quickly expelled by an examination of the formal texts and other 'business literature' which is pouring in floods from our printing presses. Its quantity is exceeded only by its mediocrity." See "The School of Commerce," in Raymond A. Kent, ed., *Higher Education in America* (1930), p. 101.

not seem to be common in most undergraduate courses. A few under-graduate schools—a very few—do make extensive use of a wide variety of reading and problem materials: selections from a variety of books, periodical articles, government documents, court cases, as well as long and short business cases and problems drawn from a variety of sources.

A few schools concentrate upon the use of cases in undergraduate courses, to which textbook and other reading is subordinated. For the most part, the cases used are drawn from published casebooks or the Harvard collection of cases, but a few schools devote considerable faculty time to the preparation of their own case materials—usually, however, for graduate rather than for undergraduate courses.

The situation is much better at the graduate than the undergraduate level.[4] Reading is seldom confined to one text; there is considerable reliance on case and other problem materials, even in the schools which do not have a strong managerial orientation; and the graduate student learns to use the resources of the university library. Naturally, the volume and quality of the reading and other teaching materials vary considerably among schools and even among instructors in the same school.

A larger volume of more challenging reading material, more written work, and more good problems and cases for class discussion are among the major needs of undergraduate teaching. For maximum effectiveness, they need to be accompanied by the kind of teaching and instructor-student contacts that inspire the student with an interest in the subject and a willingness to stretch his mental powers to their utmost.[5]

As in other fields, a growing volume of audio-visual aids is becoming available to help the business instructor. Practice varies widely in the extent to which such materials are used. Detailed evaluation of the kinds of aids available lies beyond the boundaries set for this study, but we do venture to make two suggestions. Instructors need to keep an open mind about the usefulness of such aids and to be willing to adopt those which seem to be genuinely useful. But they also need to beware of the kind of "gimmicks" which do not really add to the students' understanding or contribute to the skills that need to be developed. Above all, techniques and materials should be avoided that leave the student merely a passive

[4] It is better if the school actually makes available graduate courses to its graduate students. In this connection, see what was said in Chapter 11 about the use of undergraduate courses by M.B.A. students.

[5] These same suggestions have been made in one form or another by various observers. Cf., for example, R. D. Calkins, "Objectives of Business Education," *Harvard Business Review*, xxv (Autumn, 1946), 54–56; J. H. S. Bossard and J. F. Dewhurst, *University Education for Business* (1931), chap. 15; and L. C. Marshall, "The School of Commerce," in Kent, ed., *Higher Education in America*, pp. 97–104.

observer. The very first condition of good pedagogy is that the student must become an active participant in the learning process.

Some schools have already begun to make limited use of television, particularly of the closed-circuit variety. The experiments we encountered were chiefly in the elementary accounting course, lectures by television being followed by the usual laboratory-discussion sections. Reports, on the whole, were favorable. Students whose contact with the lecturer is through the television screen apparently do as well or better on examinations (provided they have the usual laboratory-discussion experience) than do those who listen to lectures in the traditional way. The great limitation of television is that it does not provide for active participation by the student. Its chief advantages lie in the opportunity it provides for all students to hear particularly able lecturers and in the fact that a variety of teaching aids and illustrative material can be used more effectively than in the conventional classroom lecture.[6]

One other possible type of teaching material (if it can be called that) should be mentioned: the student's activities outside the classroom. While there are obvious dangers in the suggestion, the possibilities here deserve further investigation. All students have organizational experiences of one kind or another—in their extracurricular activities, in their part-time work, in formal and informal social groups, and in their family life. They become personally involved in these organizational relationships in a way that cannot be duplicated when they are asked to consider problems and cases dealing with situations which they have not personally experienced. They might be asked to prepare reports on some aspect of their own organizational experiences, making full use of the analytical concepts that have been developed in class. To serve their purpose, such reports would have to contain some significant amount of analysis which related the student's experiences to important generalizations being developed in the course.

TEACHING METHODS

Excluding laboratory work, college classes are generally conducted in one of three ways: the straight lecture, the discussion method, and a combination of lecture and class discussion.[7] All three, of course, are found in the business schools.

[6] See *Teaching by Television*, A Report from The Ford Foundation and The Fund for the Advancement of Education (May, 1959). See also *Better Utilization of College Teaching Resources* by the Committee on Utilization of College Teaching Resources (Fund for the Advancement of Education, 1959). This report deals with a variety of experiments in the use of new teaching methods.

[7] Lecture and discussion may be combined in two ways. If the class is not too large, the instructor may alternate lecture and class discussion. (This usually happens to some extent

We are impressed by the extent to which, on the whole, the business schools (even the poorer ones) seek to maintain reasonably small classes and to provide the opportunity (at least nominally) for class discussion. Virtually every school has a few courses conducted by the lecture method, sometimes in very large classes, but most schools seek to keep their upper division classes reasonably small and to provide opportunity for student participation in class discussion.[8] The results, however, frequently leave much to be desired, and for this there are a number of reasons.

In the first place, teaching by the Socratic method is an art which some teachers never acquire. In addition, many business schools are able to maintain small classes only by extensive use of young and inexperienced teachers, many of them graduate students working for an advanced degree. The result is that many instructors in classes small enough for extensive student participation do little but lecture, and discussion is largely confined to an occasional question from the class.

The two chief difficulties probably center around the quality of the students and the quality of the teaching materials used. There is little point in seeking to stimulate discussion in small classes if the students' reading is confined to a textbook that raises few challenging questions, if a good many of the students have an inadequate background, no intellectual curiosity, and little capacity for logical thinking or oral expression, and if the teacher cannot present significant and challenging questions and then help his students to reason their way to as much of an intellectually satisfying answer as is possible in the circumstances.

We doubt that undergraduate classes, particularly in the elementary business courses, need to be kept as small as many schools try to keep them. A more effective allocation of resources probably calls for a somewhat larger typical class size. What is saved in this way can be invested in the preparation of better teaching materials and the provision of reading assistance for a greatly expanded amount of written work, not to mention higher salaries or more time for research.[9] (As we noted in earlier chapters, a substantial amount of resources can also be saved by scheduling fewer courses.) In the advanced courses, the argument for

in classes supposedly conducted entirely through class discussion.) In very large courses, the instructor may lecture, say, twice a week, and the course may be broken into "quiz" sections for the third weekly meeting.

[8] Cf. R. L. Kozelka, *Professional Education for Business* (1954), p. 23.

[9] See, for example, University of New Mexico, *General Report on the Program for the More Effective Utilization of Teaching Resources* (September, 1957, mimeographed), and Beardsley Ruml and D. H. Morrison, *Memo to a College Trustee* (1959). See also the conclusion that "In these times the burden of proof is still on the advocate of the small class." *Better Utilization of College Teaching Resources*, p. 41.

small classes is stronger, although even here it is not always overwhelming. At the graduate level, with more mature and serious students, class discussion in classes of forty or fifty should be possible, at least in the first year courses, and the experience of the Harvard Business School suggests that the case method of teaching can be used successfully in classes of seventy-five or more. Harvard's success with the case method in relatively large classes illustrates a point that we have emphasized in this and earlier chapters. If the students are able, mature, and strongly motivated, if a great deal of written work is required, if there is adequate provision for preparing teaching materials and grading papers, and if cases and problems are used that stimulate group discussion outside the classroom, then teaching can be effective even in relatively large classes. However, in the more advanced graduate courses, particularly of the seminar type, small classes (ranging, say, from ten to twenty-five) are usually necessary.

The system of lecturing to large groups (of 100 or more), which are then divided into discussion sections conducted by junior instructors, may frequently be an alternative that works as well or better than the proliferation of small classes, many of which are handled entirely by junior faculty members.

At this stage we are on highly controversial ground, and there is much respectable evidence in support of the advantages of the small class. The main point to be made, however, does not require that we seek to resolve this issue. That point is that *small classes do not make up for inadequate teaching materials, insufficient written work, poor students, and generally low standards.* If these deficiencies can be substantially remedied, the business schools will do a much more effective teaching job even if the average size of classes is significantly increased. This proposition, it seems to us, is hardly debatable.

Nor can there be much debate about the kinds of tests and examinations to which students should be exposed. There is entirely too much use of objective-type examinations in the business schools. The great argument for such examinations is that they can be easily graded. But too high a price is paid for this advantage if all the student is asked to do is to place check marks by true-false or multiple-choice questions. Examinations should constitute an exercise in written communication and challenge the student to use his logical faculties in applying what he has learned to significant problem situations. Thus, tests should consist chiefly of essay questions, problems, and short cases. The business schools should bend every effort to provide enough reading assistance to permit major reliance on this type of test wherever classes are too large and the teaching load too heavy for the instructor to do his own grading.[10]

Under the heading of class discussion we need to include not only talking *about* a problem but also what is generally called "role-playing," in which students act out in class various types of situations that illustrate principles that are being learned in the course. Role-playing is frequently used to illustrate various types of organizational problems, including that of face-to-face communication. It has been used successfully, for example, in courses in business policy, administration, human relations, personnel management, and salesmanship.[11]

Role-playing can serve a useful purpose in some courses, but we think that this technique also can easily be abused. Extensive reliance on this pedagogical device may mean that essential reading and the development of analytical tools are being neglected.

One kind of role-playing probably needs to be used more widely than is now the case. That is the oral report presented under conditions that simulate those which the student is likely to encounter in the business world. Emphasis should be placed on the organization and substantive content of the report, as well as on the manner in which it is presented.

We can only mention another kind of "role-playing" which may have considerable use in the future, more so in graduate and executive development programs than in undergraduate teaching. This is the "business game," some variant of which has already been used or tried experimentally by a number of institutions. The business game seeks to simulate some of the demand, cost, and other conditions facing a group of hypothetical firms. Teams of students "manage" these firms, and, after such analysis as is possible, make the decisions that are called for; an electronic computer may be used to determine the market results of these interdependent decisions. Given the results of their previous actions, the players proceed to make further decisions (within the rules laid down for the game).

Such games probably can serve several useful purposes. They give students experience in making decisions under pressure and in the face of limited information. They develop the habit of looking for the significant variables and relationships that determine the results that ensue from

---

[10] We have urged throughout this report the need for more emphasis on written and oral communication. In the case of written reports and tests, it would also be advisable to require students to rewrite them as often as necessary to make them satisfactory. This assumes that the necessary reading assistance is available.

[11] The last named course may consist of virtually nothing but role-playing and, as usually conceived and taught, does not, in our opinion, belong in the business school curriculum.

alternative lines of action, and they point up the multifaceted character of most business problems. Perhaps even more important, the student gets a dramatic demonstration of the *dynamic* and *interdependent* character of the forces which typically operate on business firms. The chief limitations of these games arise from their artificially simple character and the possible need for expensive computer equipment.[12]

The Case Method

In all probability, wide differences will continue to exist among business schools in the extent to which, and in the ways in which, they make use of the case method of teaching. But, on the whole, the debate on this issue seems to be subsiding. The values of the business case for class discussion, for written reports, and even for examinations is by now generally recognized; the use of cases is spreading rapidly; and many business faculties now undertake to prepare for themselves some part of the cases they use. At the same time, the case method has come to carry more flexible connotations than it once did. There is a useful place for both long and short, complicated and simple cases. And teaching by the "case method" may range from the "nondirective" kind of discussion characteristic of classes at the Harvard Business School to closely supervised discussion centering around specific questions which the class is asked to consider.[13]

In short, the argument about the virtues of the case system is coming to be in good part a matter of emphasis. The strongest advocates of the case system do not deny the need for other types of teaching materials or

[12] For brief description of business games, see John McDonald and Franc Ricciardi, "The Business Decision Game," *Fortune*, March, 1958, and James R. Jackson, "Learning from Experience in Business Decision Games," *California Management Review*, I (Winter, 1959), 92–107. For a more technical and analytical discussion, including consideration of the uses of business games as more than merely a teaching device, see Richard Bellman et al., "On the Construction of a Multi-Stage, Multi-Person Business Game," *Operations Research*, v (August, 1957), 469–503.

[13] A business case has been defined as "a carefully written description of an actual situation in business which provokes in the reader the need to decide what is going on, what the situation really is, or what the problems are—and what can and should be done." K. R. Andrews, "Executive Training by the Case Method," *Harvard Business Review*, xxix (September, 1951), 73. Under the heading of "cases" we include also those descriptions of situations that do not necessarily require each member of the class to reach an action decision. The case method can also be considered to comprehend the "incident process" of teaching. In addition, several schools have utilized successfully "living cases," in which officials of an actual company present to a class something of the history and problems of their company, and after discussion and some research, students prepare a report evaluating the issues raised and offering their own solutions. Cf. J. W. Towle and Carl A. Dauten, " 'Living Cases' for Management Education," *Advanced Management*, xxii (May, 1957), 24–26.

the need to develop the student's command of analytical tools.[14] On the other side, advocates of more traditional teaching methods are coming to grant the usefulness of business cases in developing the student's ability to apply the analytical tools that he has learned. In addition, there is little disagreement as to the great value of cases in stimulating student interest.

While emphasizing the elements of a consensus that has begun to appear, we do not want to minimize the differences that still exist among schools and among individual faculty members. The important issues that are still being argued center, in effect, around the place of systematic knowledge in the learning process and in the development of the important business skills. The most uncompromising advocates of the case method are those who are most skeptical regarding the existence of a *teachable* body of systematic knowledge on which the practice of business can be said to be based.

Since, in our opinion, something like a working consensus is developing regarding the use of the case method, we shall confine ourselves to mentioning briefly some of the important issues which, it seems to us, business faculties should keep in mind in preparing and using cases in their undergraduate and graduate programs.[15]

1 There are few places in the curriculum where cases should be the *only* kind of teaching material used, and few where the possibility of cases should be ignored completely. But, at the same time, emphasis on the case method is more suitable in some circumstances than others.

Use of elaborate cases is less appropriate in the basic undergraduate courses than in graduate and advanced undergraduate courses, although even in the former there is room for some use of cases to illustrate generalizations, to apply what has been learned, and to help in developing problem-solving and communication skills. Shorter and simpler cases are most appropriate in the early courses. The "tool" subjects such as accounting and statistics lend themselves less well to the case method than do the functional fields

---

[14] See, for example, Pearson Hunt, "The Case Method of Instruction," *Harvard Educational Review*, XXI (Summer, 1951), 175–92.

[15] For more detailed discussion of the case method, both pro and con, see M. P. McNair, ed., *The Case Method at the Harvard Business School* (1954); J. W. Culliton, " 'The Question That Has Not Been Asked Cannot Be Answered,' " in *Education for Professional Responsibility* (1948), pp. 85–93; Bossard and Dewhurst, *University Education for Business*, pp. 506–11; J. A. Bowie, *Education for Business Management* (1930), pp. 156–65; Alvin Brown, "The Case (or Bootstrap) Method," *Advanced Management*, XXI (July, 1956), 11–13; and the references cited in the other footnotes in this section.

(especially in their managerial aspects) and, above all, the integrating course in business policy.[16]

2   More cases are needed that deal with problems in the lower levels of management. Since virtually all students begin their careers on the lower rungs of the business ladder, they need more training than they now get in dealing with the kinds of substantive and organizational problems that arise at these lower levels. Too much of the case material they now get is concerned with the problems of top management. This is *not*, of course, to urge that the schools emphasize the specialized subject matter with which the student will have to deal in his early years in business. Rather, what we are suggesting is that he be given some experience in applying the results of a broad training to some of the kinds of problems he will encounter in the lower as well as in the higher levels of management.

3   Instructors need to develop skill in preparing and using cases.[17] There is much accumulated experience that the teacher just beginning to use case materials will find useful. The Harvard summer seminars in the use of the case method for business school teachers have been quite valuable, and it is to be hoped that they will be continued in some form and made widely available. A small amount of case preparation might well be made a part of the program for the doctorate, particularly for those going into teaching.

4   While each faculty member, at least in the more applied and managerially oriented fields, should have the experience of preparing a few cases based on real-life situations, it is a waste of resources for many schools to build up their own elaborate case collections when good case materials already exist elsewhere for the asking. Clearly, some division of labor and an efficient system of pooling cases on a national basis are desirable.[18] For some years, the Harvard Business School maintained, in effect, such a national pool by making its large collection of cases available to other schools. More recently the AACSB has established an Intercollegiate Case Clearing House, which is administered for the Association by the Harvard Business

[16] Cf., for example, C. S. Richards, *Graduate Training for Business Management and Administration in Great Britain, Europe and North America* (1954), p. 45. See also our discussion of these courses in Chapter 9.

[17] On some of the skills needed by the teacher in a course utilizing Harvard-type cases, see Pearson Hunt, "The Case Method of Instruction," and several of the papers in McNair, ed., *The Case Method at the Harvard Business School.*

[18] Institutional prestige is a complicating factor here. A few schools feel that prestige requires that they compile most of the cases they use. The deans and some faculty members feel embarrassed if their students are asked to use cases prepared at another institution.

School. Cases may be submitted by individual authors and are reproduced and sold to the schools wishing to use them. Periodic bibliographies are prepared and made generally available.[19] It is to be hoped that this sort of arrangement will be continued and that schools will make extensive use of it. In addition, an increasing number of commercially published case books are becoming available.

5   There is room for wide variation in the kinds of cases used and in the ways that they can be employed in the classroom. While cases should preferably be based on the true experiences of actual companies, even well-designed hypothetical cases can be useful. The use of cases as a basis for class discussion and oral and written reports can serve a variety of purposes.[20] But whatever purposes are emphasized, the essence of the case method is that it is student (as well as problem) oriented. The student, not the teacher or the author of the text, is forced to play the leading role in the classroom. This kind of personal involvement should be an important part of the student's total learning experience if he is to develop the ability "to think in the presence of new situations."[21]

6   Heavy reliance on the case method involves two serious dangers. Systematic knowledge may be neglected, and the student may be left to use relatively crude and weak analytical tools when he might have been trained to use more refined and powerful ones.[22] Equally or more important, preoccupation with the preparation and teaching of cases may lead a faculty to neglect research on significant problems. Teachers who heavily emphasize case teaching tend to distrust generalizations; they become preoccupied with

[19] See, for example, *Intercollegiate Bibliography: Cases in Business Administration*, vol. II (1958).

[20] Among these are: to provide illustrations from real life of generalizations the students have previously learned; to give students practice in recognizing problems and in applying to their solution techniques of analysis which they have been studying; to drive home the fact that business decisions typically affect more than one aspect of a firm's operations; to provide practice in marshalling evidence and weighing the alternatives on the basis of which a decision must be made; to teach inductively by letting the student develop his own generalizations through contact with specific instances; to show how often business problems do not lead to clear-cut answers but nonetheless require that a decision be made; to help develop in the student the courage to make decisions on the basis of inadequate information; to offer a certain amount of "experience by proxy" which may give the student a "feel" for handling various types of problems and confidence in dealing with new situations; and to provide extensive practice in oral and written communication and in the give and take of group debate.

[21] A. S. Dewing, in McNair, ed., *The Case Method at the Harvard Business School*, p. 3.

[22] There is some evidence that inductive learning that is not preceded or accompanied by the use of general concepts is inefficient compared to that which does make use of such concepts. Cf. L. E. Cole, *Human Behavior* (1953), chap. 16; also S. S. Stevens, ed., *Handbook of Experimental Psychology* (1951), pp. 661-62 and 1277-78.

the individual instance and rely on *ad hoc* analysis; they become so wedded to a clinical approach that they may lose interest in the kind of research that goes on in the university library or the faculty member's study; or they do not have time (which often means that they also do not have the inclination) for painstaking research on significant problems.[23] It is no secret that this has been a problem with many faculty members in those schools most dedicated to the case method.

7   The case method also involves two significant costs. It takes a great deal of class time to cover a given body of material or range of problems. And it is an expensive method of teaching if the school prepares a large part of the case material it uses.

Some Other Matters Regarding Teaching

COOPERATIVE AND INTERNSHIP PLANS

Ideally, the business student's formal education should be combined with business experience of a sort that will help to give greater meaning to his formal professional training. The opportunities for doing this, however, are limited. In practice, business educators have confined their attention to a few ways: internship programs (chiefly in accounting and retailing), reports on summer work experience, and occasional use of the cooperative plan.[24]

This is a subject on which we have little to add to what has been said by others.[25] Ideally, students *should* have supervised practical experience to go with their formal training on the campus. In practice, this is difficult to achieve for a number of reasons. The jobs likely to be available to students are at too low a level to add significantly to what is learned

[23] A. R. Towl discusses some of the uses of cases for research in McNair, ed., *The Case Method at the Harvard Business School*, pp. 223–29, but his limited discussion in no way invalidates the statements we make in the text. The search for generalizations through the use of case studies is an entirely appropriate form of research, but not a great deal of significant research of this sort has so far been done by those faculty members who most strongly emphasize case teaching.

[24] A few schools stress part-time work concurrently with formal education. At the College of the City of New York, for example, selected seniors in various of the business majors are placed with business firms for training under joint college and employer supervision. Such supervised work experience carries a limited amount of course credit. Without integrating work experience into the curriculum, several schools encourage their students to hold part-time jobs and take this into account in scheduling classes.

[25] See, for example, Bossard and Dewhurst, *University Education for Business*, pp. 511–17; Kozelka, *Professional Education for Business*, pp. 81–86.

in the classroom. Much emphasis on working while going to school is likely to interfere with the process of formal education. It is difficult to induce business firms to take on students chiefly for the educational benefit to the student, particularly if the period of employment is short and involves much supervision.

It seems reasonable to suggest that business schools might require their students to have some moderate amount of work experience before graduation, particularly during summers, and it might be wise to require a report on some aspect of this work experience. Such a report should be not a set of random notes or reminiscences, but should be pointed toward some limited problem that permits of detailed reporting and some analysis.

The cooperative plan holds out certain attractions, but we think it can be taken for granted that not many schools are prepared to face the administrative problems that are involved.[26] On our part, we have some doubts that the gains are worth the cost for most schools. While we are prepared to grant some of the advantages usually attributed to the cooperative program, it is not clear that these advantages are so great that schools not on the plan should be urged to go over to it. It might be added that the *prima facie* case for a cooperative plan in engineering is stronger than it is in business administration.[27]

HONORS PROGRAMS

We believe that the undergraduate business schools might make greater use of special honors programs than they now do. Such honors work would be limited to upper division students and perhaps only to the senior year.

[26] The cooperative plan has been most widely used by engineering schools. Two undergraduate business schools on the cooperative plan are those at the University of Cincinnati and Northeastern University. For discussion of the advantages of the cooperative plan and a brief bibliography, see Thomas Alva Edison Foundation, *Cooperative Education and the Impending Educational Crisis* (1957); also Bossard and Dewhurst, pp. 513–17.

[27] In all fairness, the usual advantages of the cooperative plan should be cited at this point. They include: 1) Their job experience helps to teach students how to work with people. 2) Through their work experience students see the application of what they learn in the classroom, and their formal business education becomes more meaningful to them. 3) The period of work gives the student a chance to digest what he has learned during the previous period on the campus. 4) The students are able to find out early the kinds of jobs they are suited for. 5) They are able to get a head start on a business career through their on-the-job training and through establishing an employment relationship while still in college which becomes permanent as soon as they graduate. 6) The cooperative arrangement permits students to earn their college expenses. We should also add one disadvantage which seems to us of some importance. The cooperative arrangement, when a student stays with one employer through most of the program, may lead to making a permanent job commitment earlier than is in the student's long-range interests.

Honors programs can take a variety of forms.[28] They may consist merely of a special senior seminar limited to the most able students. They may involve also such elements as a senior thesis and special tutorial arrangements involving the substitution of reading and library research for some formal course requirements. In a professional school it would be appropriate if the best students could be exposed to particularly fruitful kinds of clinical teaching or experience—for example, a specially designed case course or special internship arrangements with selected employers who would be interested in investing time in helping to supervise and train particularly bright students.

It can be fairly said that few undergraduate schools are offering enough of an intellectual challenge to their brightest students. If the business schools are to continue to operate on the principle of mass education, it becomes imperative that the most promising candidates for future positions of leadership be identified and that their training be patterned to bring about the maximum possible development of their talents.[29]

Similarly, a fairly strong argument can be made for some rough segregation of students by ability in some or all courses that are large enough to have several sections. At least the brightest students can be put in special sections and thus offered a more challenging intellectual experience than their less well-endowed classmates. Such honors sections can cover more ground, deal with more difficult problems, and make greater use of challenging case materials than can classes that are geared to the pace and abilities of the average student.

Honors undergraduates should also be encouraged to do extra work in the nonbusiness areas, including physical science, mathematics and statistics, and advanced economics and psychology. Unlike his counterpart in a liberal arts college, the honors student in a business school should not utilize the honors program as a means of specializing much beyond what is called for in the standard curriculum available to all students. Business administration itself is already enough specialization at the undergraduate level. The exceptional student should be encouraged to secure a more thorough grasp of analytical tools and to dig more deeply into the underlying disciplines on which the study of busi-

[28] A new journal, *The Superior Student*, has recently been established to disseminate information regarding honors programs and to encourage their wider use in American higher education. Some discussion of honors programs specifically for business schools will be found in Bossard and Dewhurst, *University Education for Business*, pp. 501–503. See also the discussion by F. H. Harrington of the need for honors programs in professional schools in *The Superior Student*, II (February, 1959), 2–4.

[29] For a description of the new honors program in business administration at the University of Washington, see *The Superior Student*, II (February, 1959), 15.

ness is based. What he learns in this way can be applied to business problems in an honors seminar or thesis or in other ways.

Honors programs are expensive, particularly in faculty time, and add to the heavy administrative burden that business schools already carry. For this reason, they are probably beyond the resources of many schools. The better endowed schools, however, should give more thought to the possibility of a well-planned honors program than most of them have thus far done.

chapter 16

RESEARCH IN THE
BUSINESS SCHOOLS

WE CONCLUDED in Chapter 14 that there is a critical need to develop in the business schools a more stimulating intellectual atmosphere and to generate within their faculties the capacity to ask more probing questions and to engage in more significant research.

As part of a university, the business school must create as well as transmit knowledge. As a professional school, it must be concerned with research as well as teaching. Research by a university faculty serves two purposes, and this is as true in a professional field as in the arts and sciences. First of all, it is through research that man advances his understanding of the world in which he lives. Much of this research must take place in the university, since the "wit of man has thus far contrived no other comparable agency."[1] Secondly, research—or at least scholarship—contributes to stimulating and imaginative teaching. Because this is so, professional education "can only be satisfactorily accomplished where research and teaching are effectively combined."[2]

If the business school belongs in the university, then research belongs in the business school. Must, therefore, all business schools emphasize research, and must all faculty members engage in research? The answer we give must take account of the limited resources of most schools, the many drains on the time and energy of the faculty, the poor research training of many faculty members, the excessive orientation in many schools toward what is practical, and the infrequent presence of a lively intellectual atmosphere. Nor should we minimize the inherent difficulty of carrying on significant research in the field of business, which is still new and but indistinctly defined as a subject of scientific inquiry and

[1] Abraham Flexner, *Universities: American, English, German* (1930), p. 14.
[2] J. B. Conant, *The Citadel of Learning* (1956), p. 65. See also A. N. Whitehead, "Universities and Their Functions," in *The Aims of Education* (Mentor ed., 1949). Appropriately, Whitehead's essay was originally presented (in 1927) at a meeting of the American Association of Collegiate Schools of Business.

which must rely on evidence which business firms may be reluctant to release.[3]

We believe that the correct answer to our question runs about as follows. We may begin with Whitehead's dictum that "one good test for the general efficiency of a faculty is that as a whole it shall be producing in published form its quota of contributions of thought. Such a quota is to be estimated in weight of thought, and not in number of words."[4] Schools with limited resources should have a modest program of research publication, but they should insist that there first be something worth publishing. Schools with more generous resources, and particularly those with graduate programs, should put greater stress on research and on the publication of *significant* research results.

In addition, *all* schools should insist that their faculty members be scholars as well as teachers—that is, that they have the desire and ability to probe deeply and to ask searching questions about what is known and not known in the areas in which they teach. This means a thorough and up-to-date knowledge of one's field. In the more applied fields, such knowledge encompasses both business practice and the relevant analytical literature. This does not mean, however, that all professors should be expected to publish the results of their scholarship. Such pressure has already led to many publications that represent a needless burden on limited library shelf space. The kind of scholarship to which we refer can illuminate teaching, stimulate students and colleagues, and feed the store of ideas that makes a university, even if there is no publication at all.

Hence there is room in the business school both for scholar-teachers who may publish little and for those who concentrate upon formal research and are widely known for their publications. The particular blending of teaching and research will vary with the individual faculty member and will vary also among schools. The demand for professional training for business is so great, and the human talents and physical resources required for basic research are so limited, that there cannot possibly be a significant research center at every business school that may otherwise be serving an important educational function. It is inevitable that a relatively few leading institutions will be the centers for research and advanced graduate training. The rest should concentrate on professional training at a higher level than is now the case and on the creation of a scholarly atmosphere that stimulates inquiry, with a limited amount of formal research and publication as a secondary objective.

[3] Not only are business firms not available as subjects for controlled experiments (a problem with which all the social sciences are familiar) but, worse, it is frequently not even possible to observe and record for general use many of the kinds of internal operations which the student of business administration would like to study.

[4] *The Aims of Education*, pp. 103–104.

The Kinds of Research That Are Needed

Most thoughtful observers are agreed that the research performance of the business schools has so far been unsatisfactory. Our understanding of business behavior is clearly of the most rudimentary kind, and in most business fields there is a paucity of significant generalizations that can be taught in the classroom or used by businessmen and other administrators. This situation exists despite the substantial amount of research activity going on in some business schools and the flood of articles, pamphlets, monographs, and books that continue to be published.

Much if not most research in the business schools attempts merely to describe current practice or, going a short step further, to develop normative rules which summarize what is considered to be the best of prevailing practice. The business literature is not, in general, characterized by challenging hypotheses, well developed conceptual frameworks, the use of sophisticated research techniques, penetrating analysis, the use of evidence drawn from the relevant underlying disciplines—or very significant conclusions. A substantial amount of the publications now emanating from the business schools represents activities that scarcely qualify as research—textbooks of varying degrees of quality, contributions to handbooks, semi-popular articles in trade journals, journalistic reports on current developments, and the like.

In describing the quality of academic research in business administration, O. W. Phelps comments:[5]

The showing to date is impressive primarily on the grounds of volume. In quality of analysis, depth of penetration, and significance of subject matter, much of it is deficient.... By far the greater proportion of it is purely descriptive, being accumulations of data describing business activities or procedures in individual cases or as aggregates. Where more than description is attempted, the analysis often betrays lack of association with principles, the evidence—where offered—is insecure, and the problem is frequently extremely narrow in scope and the conclusions equally restricted in their application.

In many schools, no more than lip service is paid to the need for research. In those schools that emphasize undergraduate teaching, little time, energy, or resources are left for research activity. It is also true that many deans have little conception of what might be significant lines of research. To some, it is important only that enough of something be published to make a respectable list in the reports prepared for the central university administration, the school's alumni, or the state legislature.

[5] "Academic Research in Business Administration," *The Journal of Higher Education*, XVIII (February, 1947), 82–83.

BUSINESS AND THE BUSINESS SCHOOLS

In some professional fields, the professional school is, in effect, the research arm of the profession. Through its research activities the professional school creates the new knowledge on which future professional practice will be based. Thus, the university blazes the way for the practitioner, providing him with ever more powerful tools with which to deal with once intractable problems. Medicine, of course, is the classical case of this.[6]

The relation between business and the business schools is much different. In the matter of significant research, business firms (particularly the larger ones) are more likely to blaze the way than are the business schools. This is not to deny that specialists on business school faculties frequently provide important consulting and "research" services to business. But they do so as staff specialists, applying to specific problems the store of existing knowledge which is in their custody.

Company officials to whom we talked in the course of this study showed, on the whole, very little awareness of any significant research going on in the business schools. When research activities were mentioned (excluding those having to do with science and technology), the reference was most often to work outside the schools. Moderately frequent reference was made, for example, to behavioral science research (such as that at the Michigan Survey Research Center), to work in industrial and human relations at the various research centers concerned with this range of problems, to a wide range of psychological research being conducted outside the business schools, and to recent developments in operations research (again chiefly outside the business schools). Some of the conventional lines of academic business research were occasionally mentioned, for instance, in marketing, finance, personnel management, and urban land economics. But, in general, the lack of familiarity with the research activities of the business schools was quite striking.[7] So also was the frequency with which reference was made to current research activities in other parts of the campus, in what we have called the underlying disciplines.

[6] See, for example, J. E. Deitrick and R. C. Berson, *Medical Schools in the United States at Mid-Century* (1953), chap. 3. Cf. also A. J. Harno, *Legal Education in the United States* (1953), pp. 188ff.

[7] It must be mentioned that our results were somewhat biased in two different respects. Top-level executives are likely to know much less about what kinds of research are being conducted in the universities than the staff specialists who work under them. Secondly, by the nature of the case, we spent more time with officials concerned with personnel, management development, and organization planning than with those in other areas—although our respondents also included company presidents, operating vice presidents, financial officers, etc.

It is fair to say that, at least so far, more significant knowledge of ultimate value to business has come out of the nonbusiness departments of the university than out of the business schools. This is true, we think, even if we exclude the physical sciences and engineering. Major contributions to our understanding of business behavior and to the ability of business to deal with some types of problems have come from psychology, mathematics and statistics, economics, and sociology.[8] This has been particularly and increasingly true since the war. Sometimes research results in these underlying disciplines or tool fields have been such as to be directly applicable to business problems. To some extent, faculty members in particular business fields have acted as middlemen in order to develop these applications. This, of course, is in line with what we should expect and in line with what tends to happen in other professional disciplines—except that, in business research, less sophisticated use is made of the findings of the underlying disciplines than tends to be the case in the traditional professional fields.

TYPES OF BUSINESS RESEARCH

Business research may be of several kinds. There is, first of all, the distinction between pure (or fundamental) and applied research. *Pure* research in business administration implies more than abstract concepts and the broad generalizations of theory. It implies going back to the foundation disciplines on which the study of business must rest and seeking to develop theories and concepts which may ultimately be useful in the study of business behavior and business problems. Pure research can, of course, be "problem-solving." Its problem-solving character depends on the kinds of questions that are asked and on the operational nature of the statements that are made, and not on the degree of abstraction that may be involved.

Applied business research may be at several levels. It may be analytical, descriptive, or merely observational. It is analytical if an attempt is made to draw significant generalizations from a body of data through systematic use of the best analytical tools that are available or can be constructed. The scientific and imaginative quality of the analysis can vary,

---

[8] Perhaps cultural anthropology and political science should also be included. However, as Robert Dahl points out, political scientists have shown little interest in applying their concepts to the structure and behavior of business. ("Business and Politics: A Critical Appraisal of Political Science," *American Political Science Review*, LIII [March, 1959], 1–34.) Also, political science has not, on the whole, developed analytical tools as obviously useful in the study of business problems and business behavior as have the other social sciences. This is beginning to change as political science takes on a more empirical, positivist, and behavioristic coloration. We should add that we exclude public administration here because we look on it, like business administration, as a "derived" field which draws on the various underlying disciplines.

of course, from very bad to excellent. Descriptive research records and classifies; it offers descriptive generalizations but does not use analytical tools to draw general inferences. Observational studies are what the term implies—the collection and reporting of facts.

The weaknesses in the larger part of the research going on in the business schools can now be stated in terms of the preceding categories. There has been too little pure research and not enough of the right kind of applied research. The construction of useful theories and analytical concepts has been left in good part to those in the underlying disciplines, who have only a limited interest in business problems. There has been a flood of applied research, but most of it has been observational, descriptive, or at a low analytical level.

This is not to suggest that no research of high quality is going on in the business schools. Some pure research and a considerable amount of applied research at a high analytical level are being carried on, particularly at the leading institutions. The results of this work can be seen in the recent journal and monographic literature. But the amount of such work is still only a small fraction of the total research and writing in the business schools.

Thus the business schools need to develop both more pure or fundamental research and, using the best tools now available, more applied research at a high analytical level. The former requires bringing the underlying disciplines directly into the business schools. The latter implies the formulation of challenging hypotheses, the development and use of more sophisticated analytical tools, including more utilization of concepts and findings from the various social sciences and greater reliance on the tools of mathematics and statistics, and the systematic collection of detailed and reliable data on the internal working of different kinds and sizes of business firms.

We may also indicate some of the kinds of research that are needed by referring to the four broad types of problems or "basic elements" described in Chapter 4: organization-administration, the nonmarket and market environment of business, and economic management.

Research on organizational problems is still in its infancy.[9] Here clearly the behavioral sciences have much to contribute. We still have little tested knowledge on such problems as how alternative organizational arrangements affect various kinds of decision-making, the conditions of organizational viability, and the factors that influence the interactions between the individual and his organizational environment.

---

[9] See, for example, Chapter 9, above, and J. G. March and H. A. Simon, *Organizations* (1958), chap. 1.

There is need for more of a "behavioral" approach to the study of organizations, particularly to the study of large groups. Considerably more study has been made of small group behavior than of large groups. As March and Simon remark, the study of formal organizations is an area in which there is "a great disparity between hypothesis and evidence. Much of what we know or believe about organizations is distilled from common sense and from the practical experience of executives. The great bulk of this wisdom and lore has never been subjected to the rigorous scrutiny of scientific method."[10]

The business schools have contributed relatively little to our understanding of the interactions between business and its nonmarket environment. This has been largely left to economists, historians, political scientists, and students of the law. A few business schools have encouraged the study of business history; there has been a little work on the interrelations between business and scientific and technological change; and there is a growing interest in the business schools in the factors that make for steady economic growth as well as for instability. But, in general, it is fair to say that the important contributions to our knowledge about the nonmarket environment of business have come from outside the business schools and have then been woven by the latter into their teaching. This is a range of topics on which business school faculties should do more research than they are now doing. Here again they will need the help of scholars in the various social science disciplines.

Naturally, business school research has paid much more attention to the market environment of business, although probably the most important contributions have come from other parts of the university.[11] Of course, a great deal of various types of market research goes on in the business schools, and there are numerous studies of particular markets and particular industries. While some of this research has been at a high analytical level, much has been largely descriptive in character. There has been some useful work in the study of financial markets, but here again, with some important exceptions, most financial research in the business schools has not been at a high analytical level.

As would be expected, a good deal of the research in the business

[10] *Organizations,* p. 5.

[11] As we should expect, our knowledge of labor markets owes much to the various industrial relations centers, many of which are not connected (or are only indirectly connected) with business schools. Research on financial markets goes on in both economics departments and business schools. Some of the major contributions to the study of commodity markets have arisen out of the economists' theory of price determination and their studies of industrial markets. Our understanding of consumers' behavior owes much to the social psychologists, sociologists, and statisticians. And so on.

schools has been concerned with problems of economic management. While an increasing amount of very good work is going on, most business school research in this area has not been of a very high order. In particular, the schools have been slow to develop more powerful analytical tools which would contribute to more rational decision-making in business—whether in production, finance, marketing, or personnel management and industrial relations. We do not wish to minimize the useful work that some business school faculties have done in various of these management areas. But the business schools have so far played only a minor role (although there are some important exceptions) in the development of the new "management sciences" and in the applications of linear programming, game theory, decision theory, etc. to business problems. As might be expected, the business schools that have done some of the most important work here have been those at technical institutions. More recently a few other business schools have begun to develop research programs in this area.

In all the areas of management, there is need for more fundamental theoretical work, for a better understanding of the interrelationships among the variables with which the business manager must deal, and for better ways of identifying and evaluating the alternatives from which choices must be made.[12] Much of the research in functional management now carried on in business schools attempts merely to describe current practice or seeks to formulate normative rules on the basis of insufficient evidence and without the help of the best available analytical techniques.

While this is an accurate generalization as things now stand, the situation is clearly changing for the better—more in some business schools than in others. The improvement is also showing itself in the monographic and journal literature—not only in some of the new journals like *Management Science* but also in the contents of various of the older journals concerned with particular aspects of management.

Whether the aim is to improve our understanding of business behavior (i.e., to search for significant generalizations) or to develop better techniques and rules for decision-making, it is clear that business research needs to become more analytical, to develop a more solid theoretical underpinning, and to utilize a more sophisticated methodology. This means not only more applied research of the sort that makes the best possible use of the methods of analysis that we now have, but also the development of new and more useful theories and concepts. This in turn

---

[12] If management is to become scientific in nature, "research is mainly required on the fundamental subjects upon which the technology of management must grow—especially on psychological, social and economic aspects." Alexander King, "Management as a Technology," *Impact of Science on Society*, VIII (June, 1957), 83.

requires that the business schools turn for help to the underlying disciplines such as the behavioral sciences and mathematics and statistics, as well as to economics. Hence it is essential that there be close co-operation between conventionally trained members of business school faculties and those who are working in these other areas.

None of the preceding discussion is intended to minimize the importance of field investigations, detailed case studies, and, in general, the systematic collection of more and better information about business behavior. This is the essential raw material for the study of business—but it is only the raw material. Similarly, case collection is an important activity for the business school, both because of its contribution to teaching and because of its value as training for the faculty member. But case collection by itself is not research in the usual sense of that term. It can, however, become the raw material for research, since, through careful and discriminating analysis, significant generalizations can sometimes be drawn from the study of a large number of cases.

This leads us to suggest that, as the quantity of business cases of various sorts steadily accumulates, it should become increasingly feasible, by careful analysis, to throw some light on a variety of hypotheses regarding business behavior. The modern emphasis on quantitative measurement and statistical tests has to some extent caused many scholars to ignore the possibilities of what may be called the case study method of research. Defenders of the Harvard Business School's emphasis on case collection have not been altogether wrong in emphasizing the potential contribution of business cases to systematic research.[13] Unfortunately, however, neither at Harvard nor elsewhere has there been much of an attempt systematically to analyze and draw generalizations from this storehouse of raw material. While the search for uniformities in case materials prepared for other purposes is never altogether satisfactory and has to be supplemented by other evidence, this kind of material can frequently be very valuable for research purposes.

Methods of Supporting Research

The poorer business schools, particularly those that concentrate on undergraduate teaching, typically have little or no resources for faculty research. Teaching loads are heavy; it is difficult or impossible to arrange time off for research; and virtually no money is available for research assistance, travel, computing help, and so on. At the other extreme, a

[13] See, for example, A. R. Towl, "The Use of Cases for Research," in M. P. McNair, ed., *The Case Method at the Harvard Business School* (1954), pp. 223–29.

few institutions can offer very generous support for research, and the chief limitation on research output becomes the willingness and competence of the faculty. The majority of schools fall in between these two extremes.

A number of different administrative arrangements exist for supporting research. The most common is the Bureau of Business Research, which typically is more concerned with service activities for the local business community than with support of fundamental research. We shall discuss these bureaus in more detail in a moment. Some schools—for example, those at Harvard and U.C.L.A.—have a Division of Research. The director typically administers the school's research funds, receives applications for research help from the faculty, allocates financial aid and recommends relief from teaching when needed, and negotiates with potential donors for research grants for projects initiated by faculty members that require outside financial help.[14] In some cases the school's research funds are administered by a committee rather than a director. In some schools, such matters are handled directly by the dean, often with the help of an advisory committee.

Some schools have specialized research agencies that administer programs in particular fields. An institute or center for research in industrial relations is sometimes closely affiliated with the business school. Specialized bureaus or institutes, or less formal faculty groups, sometimes exist to foster research in such areas as real estate, some aspect of marketing, transportation, management science, accounting, or insurance.

Funds for research come from a variety of sources. The more fortunate schools have an allocation for research in their regular budgets. Foundation grants may be available, either on an unrestricted basis or to support particular projects. Industry or government may finance particular pieces of contract research, and industry groups may provide funds for continuing research in specialized areas. A number of schools have followed Harvard in setting up a group of Associates, made up of business firms and individuals, who contribute funds that may be used for re-

[14] The situation at U.C.L.A. is unusual in that there are two research facilitating agencies. The Bureau of Business and Economic Research makes research assistance available to both the economics department and the business school. In addition, there is a Division of Research within the business school with its own budget and program of activities. The Division allocates funds for faculty research, is involved in negotiations on contract research, includes a Management Sciences Research Project, assumes main responsibility for publication of the *California Management Review*, administers a case research program, and engages in some other activities concerned with research. See, for example, *Annual Report of the Division of Research, 1957–58* (U.C.L.A. Graduate School of Business Administration, mimeographed). Harvard also has long had a Bureau of Business Research, which is now a part of the School's Division of Research. The Bureau is well known for its annual studies of department store and variety chain operating costs and also performs a number of other, chiefly statistical, services.

search, case collection, faculty salaries, or perhaps other purposes. If a bureau of business research exists, it will have its own budget, most of which may be committed to its continuing service activities, although some funds may be available for assisting individual faculty members.

In the vast majority of business schools, there is no centralized planning of research, and no conscious attempt is made to develop a central "theme" around which faculty members plan their research.[15] Of course, where specialized research institutes exist, there is some planning and direction of group research activities along predetermined lines. But, in general, research in the business schools rests on the initiative of individuals or of small groups, and little in the way of centralized planning and coordination is attempted. On the whole, also, it is our impression that business school faculty members have engaged in less group or team research than has characterized most of the social sciences in recent years.

BUREAUS OF BUSINESS RESEARCH

There are more than fifty bureaus of business and economic research on university campuses, virtually all of them affiliated with or a part of the school of business administration.[16] In many cases, the economics department is also involved. Some of these are fairly large operations with substantial budgets. Many are very small affairs.[17]

Several things can be said immediately about these bureaus. First of all, for most of them, their primary function is service to the business community rather than significant research of any sort. (The value of this service function is weighed in part in terms of its public relations value for the business school and the university.) Second, the fact gathering and small amount of research performed by these bureaus is largely concerned with local and regional conditions. Third, and in part responsible for the first two characteristics, the bureau of business research is overwhelmingly a phenomenon of the state university. About four-fifths of all the university bureaus of business research in the country are on state university campuses.

This helps to explain why research in these bureaus typically means

[15] The Graduate School of Industrial Administration at Carnegie Tech is the best known example of planned research around a central theme. Even when there is no central planning, however, a general theme or approach may be apparent in the publications of the faculty.

[16] See Associated University Bureaus of Business and Economic Research, *Membership ana Personnel Directory* (1958); R. W. Coleman, *A Survey of Functions of Bureaus of Business and Economic Research* (West Virginia University, 1957).

[17] In Coleman's survey of bureaus of business research, the range in number of employees reported was from three to thirty-one. See also D. S. Vaughn and E. S. Hobbs, *Bureaus of Research in the South and in the United States, 1957–58* (University of Mississippi Bureau of Public Administration).

not much more than collecting and publishing data on local business conditions and similar service activities for the local and regional business community. These services are not without value, and some bureaus go a step further to make studies of a local or regional nature that have some analytical content. But the amount of significant research is, in the typical case, very small indeed.[18]

There are obviously exceptions to these generalizations. There are a few bureaus or divisions of research that have no other purpose than to facilitate faculty research. There are some others that, in addition to their service activities, carry on research programs of their own and make substantial research assistance available to individual faculty members. But for the bulk of the bureaus of business research, our earlier generalizations stand. If one were interested in locating the most significant research to come out of the business schools in the last decade, very little time would need to be spent with the publications of bureaus of business research.[19]

The failure of these bureaus to engage in a larger volume of significant research is not to be ascribed solely to a preoccupation with local service activities or to limited budgets. In the majority of the schools that we visited which had bureaus, the faculty did not make full use of the research facilities which the bureau was prepared to put at their disposal. It is true that extension-type service work does absorb a large part of the budgets of most bureaus. But in most cases there are still resources left to support a moderate amount of additional faculty research, if the faculty could be induced to make greater use of these resources. The lack of significant research in the bureaus is in good part a reflection of the inability or disinclination of most business school faculty members to undertake significant research projects.

There are no simple panaceas that will lead immediately to a significant improvement in the quality of work done by bureaus of business research. Probably the greatest hope lies in a general improvement in the intellectual atmosphere in the business schools. A better trained and more scholarly inclined faculty will certainly be reflected in a higher quality of research and service activities. Beyond this, we venture to

[18] In a recent survey, bureaus of business research reported their main types of activities in the following order of importance: publishing periodic surveys of business conditions, publishing special studies of the local or regional economy, publishing regular articles on business and economic conditions. Facilitating faculty research was listed as an important objective much more often than it was cited as an important activity in which the bureau was actually engaging. See the survey by Coleman cited in footnote 16.

[19] See, as an example, Associated University Bureaus of Business and Economic Research, *Index of Publications of Bureaus of Business and Economic Research, 1957* (Bureau of Business Research, University of Oregon, 1958).

offer the following suggestions, which are more relevant to the situation in some bureaus than in others.

Almost everywhere there is need for a careful stocktaking of existing activities. Current data collecting programs need to be reappraised in terms of their value to the region and the school. Undoubtedly a good deal of information is now being collected that is of little value to anyone. A similar reappraisal needs to be applied to present publishing activities. The monthly reviews published by most bureaus contain very little meat beyond the usual statistical data on local economic conditions and an occasional analytical article of some local interest. Certainly there is no point to publishing surveys of national business conditions, much better versions of which are readily available to the local community in government and private publications at little or no cost.

Local and regional studies need to be given a more analytical content. Some bureaus might wish to concentrate on a long-range regional research program that builds around a central theme, using interested faculty members from the school as well as its own professional staff (if it has any). Contract research for public and private agencies should be avoided unless it involves issues of general significance and research personnel are available to do a competent and analytical piece of work which will be available for publication. Many bureaus now follow the wise rule that research will not be undertaken for private firms unless the problem has general interest, the investigator is to have the normal freedom of the scholar, and the bureau is free to publish the results in its own way. If these conditions cannot be met but local conditions require that the assignment be undertaken, the job should be turned over to a member of the bureau or business school staff to be handled under a private consulting arrangement.

Bureaus of business research should assume more responsibility for stimulating and guiding the research of the business school faculty. This means more than making some research facilities available. It implies having available on the bureau's staff persons capable of providing technical help in the design of projects and in research methods. It implies also that the bureau might well take the leadership in such activities as organizing faculty seminars and bringing in outside experts for talks to students and faculty. The bureau can also play an important role in providing research training for graduate students who act as research assistants. Many bureaus now accept this as one of their functions; but, since so little challenging work is done, the training is frequently of only limited value.

On the side of service to the community and the school, it might be desirable for some bureaus to seek, among other things, to become the coordinating agency for the faculty's consulting activities.[20] This might lead to some improvement in the quality of the faculty's consulting work (much of which is now of a very routine nature). It could contribute to a better distribution of such work among members of the faculty. And, depending on the initiative shown by the bureau and the availability of faculty personnel with the right kinds of technical competence, it might stimulate local firms and government agencies to seek the business school's help on more interesting and challenging problems than is now usually the case.

The preceding paragraph assumes that local service activities are accepted as an important part of the bureau's functions. If this is in fact the case, it should be openly recognized and perhaps reflected in the title of the bureau.[21] If the primary emphasis is to be on research, this also should be recognized and the bureau's activities reorganized to bring about more effective implementation of the research objective. At present, too many bureaus profess to engage in or sponsor research when, in fact, they act as a not very effective service agency for the business school. To the extent that local pressures and the availability of technically qualified personnel permit, most schools would probably be well advised to put less emphasis in their bureaus on service work disguised as research and more on improving the scholarly quality of the faculty and on encouraging a moderate amount of applied research at a truly analytical level.

Some Needed Steps

A number of things can be done to improve the quantity and quality of research in the business schools. Some of the kinds of action that might be taken are spelled out in the recommendations presented in our final chapter. At this stage, we shall confine ourselves to a few main points.

IMPROVING THE INTELLECTUAL CLIMATE

A general improvement in the scholarly climate in the business schools is the first need—for its effect on teaching as well as its possible long-run effects on the quality of research. This is not to suggest that every business school is to be built up into a research center. This, of course, would

[20] Cf. J. A. Bowie, *Education for Business Management* (1930), pp. 170–71.
[21] Only two or three bureaus include any reference to service in their titles. Most call themselves simply bureaus of business (and possibly economic) research.

be a flagrant waste of resources. But, although the main advances in knowledge will continue to come from the relatively few research-oriented schools that are centers of both graduate training and research, it is important to increase the level of technical competence and scholarly activity at all schools.

A number of steps would contribute to this end. We should like to mention several in particular.

First, there is urgent need for arrangements that will help existing faculty members to bring themselves up to date with recent developments in their fields and in the related underlying disciplines. The need for "retreading" programs of this sort is far greater than that for additional funds for formal research projects. One of the most promising developments along these lines has been the summer seminars on new developments in business administration, now being conducted by the Graduate School of Industrial Administration of Carnegie Tech and the School of Business of the University of Chicago with the help of grants from the Ford Foundation. Summer programs of this sort, spotted in various parts of the country, are needed to accommodate hundreds rather than the few dozen who have thus far attended these seminars.[22]

Other arrangements to serve the same purpose would also be desirable: leaves with pay and fellowships so that faculty members can study for periods from a summer to a year at one of the leading graduate and research centers; faculty seminars at individual schools to deal with important new developments in business administration and the related disciplines; joint seminars with representatives of other departments; visits by leading authorities from other institutions for periods long enough to provide a real stimulus to the faculty.[23]

It is also important to find ways of releasing more faculty time for scholarly activity and formal research. At present, teaching, administrative chores, and outside activities (mainly for extra income) leave the typical faculty member with little time for anything else. If salaries were high enough, business schools might more effectively restrict the efforts of their faculty members to earn additional income through routine out-

[22] Seminars of this type provide an opportunity "for bringing new technical developments to the attention of an academic generation that was not exposed to them in its own professional training but is still intellectually young and flexible enough to want to add to its analytical equipment." From an unpublished report on the value of the first summer seminar conducted by Carnegie Tech.

[23] Several of the programs of the Ford Foundation have been pointed toward the needs described here. These include, in addition to the summer seminars on new developments, visiting professorships for social scientists, mathematicians, and statisticians at selected business schools, a mathematics institute for teachers of business administration, and summer and full-year faculty fellowships.

side activities and extra teaching. The possibilities here are, of course, quite limited. But something can be done to free faculty time by reducing the number and frequency of course offerings, increasing the size of some classes, and providing more grading and clerical assistance. Financial help is also needed to provide for research leaves or reduction in teaching load for those faculty members who can make the most effective use of time released from teaching.

Free time, greater technical competence, and an aroused scientific curiosity are the chief needs if there is to be a significant improvement in the scholarly quality of business school faculties—and with it a larger volume of significant research results. Further evidence is supplied by the answers of the deans we visited to the question: What kinds of aid are needed to encourage research? A virtually universal reply was: funds to permit more time off for the faculty. Other frequent suggestions included: fellowships to enable faculty members to bring themselves up-to-date with new developments, more summer institutes for business school teachers, rotating research professorships, summer research grants in lieu of teaching, and grants to facilitate completion of doctoral theses by younger faculty members.

CLOSER RELATIONS WITH THE UNDERLYING DISCIPLINES

One of the most striking developments of the last few years in business administration has been the rapidly growing application of material from the behavioral sciences, mathematics, and statistics to the study of business problems. This trend is certain to continue. Improving the quality of business research therefore calls for closer cooperation between research workers trained in the business fields and economics and those whose backgrounds are in the other fields mentioned. This implies seeking to interest more behavioral scientists, mathematicians, and statisticians in business problems (whether they move into a business school or not), more interdisciplinary research, and more training in these related areas for doctoral candidates in business and for present faculty members seeking to keep up with the latest developments.[24]

[24] The Ford Foundation has already provided important support in this general area. A recent interesting step was to commission papers by, respectively, a political scientist, a psychologist, and a sociologist, in which each author was to survey the relevant literature in his field and suggest ways in which his discipline could contribute further to an understanding of the structure and functioning of business. See the paper by Robert Dahl, "Business and Politics: A Critical Appraisal of Political Science," previously cited; Mason Haire, "Psychological Problems Relevant to Business," to be published in the *Psychological Bulletin;* and the paper by Paul Lazarsfeld scheduled for publication in an early issue of the *American Journal of Sociology.*

OTHER MEASURES TO AID RESEARCH

The need for an adequate amount of unrestricted research funds is too obvious for comment. The chief sources available include the regular university budget, the foundations, and the business community. Most of the research funds will continue to flow to the larger research centers, and this is as it should be. But some modest amount of research money should be available to all business schools as part of a systematic program to encourage scholarly activity, good teaching, and professional competence. Each school, with such help as it can get from the university authorities, its alumni, and the business community, should have some amount for research in its budget. In addition, the more research-minded members of these faculties should receive a sympathetic hearing from the foundations.

The business community can provide not only financial aid but also assistance in other ways—particularly through making information available for research purposes. More communication between the business school faculty and the more research-oriented executives and staff specialists in business firms should not only contribute to the professional competence of the faculty member but also contribute problems, information, and hypotheses that will make for more meaningful research.

We do not think that we should suggest how research should be organized or pursued by the more able scholars and in the larger research centers. Here again free time for research is a necessary condition for the rapid advancement of knowledge. There is also need for better communication among research workers on new problems and methods in their respective fields, something which might be provided through more frequent conferences. In addition, more extensive interchange is needed between research workers in the universities and those in government and business.

Some schools, with a core of able people interested in a particular area of research, may find it useful to set up specialized research centers which will bring together scholars with related interests, encourage group research, and provide for time off from teaching. This pattern is already in use in some schools.

In general, at the leading schools and for the best men wherever they are located, there is no serious shortage of research funds. The funds needed for promising research projects by good men are either already available or else can be obtained without undue difficulty. The main needs are time, ideas, and, in some areas, factual information.

Consulting and Other Professional Activities

In addition to their teaching and scholarly activities, every business school faculty should have continuing contacts with the business community. Such contacts serve a number of purposes. They help to keep the faculty member informed regarding current business practice. They yield direct observations on the kinds of business behavior and problems about which the faculty member attempts to teach and write. Hence, such contacts can enrich teaching and provide some of the raw material for research. Such contacts also help to enlist the support of the business community for the business school and, in the form of consulting activity, may provide useful services to business and government.

Contacts with business may take a variety of forms: consulting activities (which usually mean extra income for the faculty member), participation in meetings of trade groups and professional societies, preparation of business cases, visits to business firms, speeches to trade groups, service clubs, and the like, and other activities of a similar sort. Of these activities, it is that which goes under the heading of consulting that creates the most important problems for the business school.[25] While consulting activity can and should contribute to a faculty member's teaching and research, all too often it has the opposite effect.

In the majority of the schools we visited, we were told that most of the faculty had had some consulting experience, although many of these were not now engaged in consulting work. A smaller but still considerable number of faculty members had had some previous full-time business experience. While the situation varies from school to school, three kinds of problems typically arise to prevent faculty members from securing the kind of responsible and continuing experience that contributes to their teaching and scholarly activity. 1) Some faculty members exploit the consulting privilege and spend too much time off the campus. 2) Much of the "consulting" work is at a low level and contributes little to the professional competence of the faculty member. More often than not, outside "consulting" activities amount to no more than a succession of routine part-time jobs taken on primarily for the extra income.[26] 3) It is

[25] Cf. L. C. Marshall in Raymond A. Kent, ed., *Higher Education in America* (1930), p. 99. An excessive amount of additional teaching for extra income is also a problem, but one with which we are not concerned here.

[26] Outside work activities "tend powerfully to be or soon do become 'pot-boiling' activities —work essentially routine in nature, making no challenging demands upon the doer, and contributing nothing to professional competence. Such kinds of routine activities are overwhelmingly frowned upon by administrators—at least they say they frown on them." From a report on *Policy of American Institutions of Higher Education on Outside Work for Pay*, prepared for the AACSB (1953, mimeographed).

difficult to get some faculty members to do any outside professional work at all, either because opportunities are limited (particularly in the more isolated schools and more so in some fields than others) or because of lack of inclination. These problems are encountered in different combinations in different schools, but one or another of them exists in every school. Solution of the latter two problems requires the cooperation of business itself, a point on which we shall have something more to say in the last chapter.

Almost without exception, business schools permit outside activities for extra income, and the majority actively encourage outside work.[27] Three limitations are usually put on such activities. They should not involve more than a specified amount of time (usually one day a week). There should be clearance in advance with the dean or his representative. And the work should be of a kind that contributes to the professional, teaching or scholarly competence of the individual or otherwise brings advantage to the school. Sometimes these rules are formally stated; sometimes they exist only as an informal understanding. In either form, they are frequently and widely violated. It is the third rule that probably causes the most trouble. Much of the "consulting" in which many faculty members engage is simply hackwork, the only purpose of which is extra income.[28] Yet, as long as faculty salaries remain so low, deans naturally find it difficult to curb such routine activities. In the usual case, they make no attempt to do so, despite their ostensible objections to such work.

We have no suggestions to offer regarding these problems except the obvious ones. Higher salaries would permit business schools to enforce a policy which, in many schools, is now probably unenforceable. If more faculty members had a high degree of technical competence, business firms could perhaps be induced to offer them more responsible assignments. And most important, again, a livelier intellectual atmosphere and a greater emphasis on scholarship within the school itself would make faculty members less willing to take routine jobs that contribute nothing to their professional advancement.

Beyond this, we think the time has come for business schools to eliminate the more flagrant cases of neglect of university duties for the sake of outside business activities and extra income—even if the outside work is of an acceptable nature. There should be no place in the regular faculty for men so involved in their business affairs that they are on the

[27] This is the evidence both from our own survey and from the report cited in the preceding footnote.
[28] More centralized solicitation, screening, and coordination of consulting assignments within the school might help to eliminate some of the more routine jobs that some faculty members are tempted to accept.

campus only long enough to hold their classes. Yet something approaching this not infrequently happens. Some faculty members derive an income from their outside work which is larger than their regular salaries. While it may be difficult to stop underpaid professors from earning a modest supplement to their salaries from consulting work or additional teaching, certainly the man who doubles or trebles his salary through his outside activities can hardly plead financial hardship if the dean insists that he devote an appropriate amount of time to his teaching, to scholarly activity, and to his other university duties.[29]

---

[29] We recognize that sometimes an unusual person can do a good deal of consulting but still find time for his students and be a productive scholar. Conversely, many faculty members of limited abilities and aspirations do little or no consulting but also do no research and fail to keep up with their fields.

chapter 17

DOCTORAL PROGRAMS

IN BUSINESS

THERE ARE about two dozen active doctoral programs in business in the United States.[1] These programs have a critical role to play in the future of collegiate business education because, as we saw in Chapter 14, they constitute the most important source of supply of future college teachers of business administration. Thus far, however, the flow of doctorates in business has been quite small—an average of less than a hundred degrees per year during the last decade.

Table 22 indicates that there is a substantial amount of concentration of doctoral work and that a handful of universities account for the bulk of the doctor's degrees awarded in business. Recently a number of schools have instituted work for the doctorate or have revised and expanded programs that they already had, and several other schools are likely to inaugurate doctoral programs in the near future. Clearly, the number of programs will continue to grow, but it is equally clear that the bulk of each year's graduates will come from relatively few schools.

Objectives of the Doctoral Program

Doctoral programs are ordinarily viewed as preparing students for careers in either teaching or research. As others have noted, however, this is an overly sharp distinction. We stressed the point in earlier chapters that every college teacher should be also a scholar, even if he does not publish. In addition, it usually happens that those who formally carry on research, at least in the universities, also teach, although it is true that holders of the doctorate may have research careers in government or business or, as sometimes happens, move into administrative positions that make some use of their technical training.

Quantitatively, the greatest need is for well trained and scholarly col-

[1] There are perhaps a dozen more that either are relatively inactive (with virtually no graduates in recent years), are so new that they have yet to award their first degrees, or are programs which, while permitting the study of business fields, are officially offered in the economics department.

TABLE 22

DOCTOR'S DEGREES AWARDED IN BUSINESS, 1948–1958

University	Doctorates Awarded in Business and Commerce (by academic year)				
	1947–48 through 1957–58	1954–55	1955–56	1956–57	1957–58
1. New York University	145	28	16	0	17
2. State University of Iowa	99	16	9	5	5
3. Ohio State	93	12	10	10	6
4. Indiana	85	15	12	7	6
5. Harvard	78	7	17	9	14
6. Texas	71	6	9	14	0
7. Chicago	59	14	6	2	7
8. Illinois	59	6	3	6	14
9. Columbia	54	6	6	5	5
10. Michigan	33	6	5	5	3
11. Wisconsin	30	4	2	6	3
12. Northwestern	25	5	4	0	4
13. Cornell	24	7	2	0	1
14. Stanford	18	3	2	2	2
15. Alabama	17	1	2	8	4
16. University of Washington	17	1	5	5	3
17. Minnesota	16	1	6	2	2
18. Louisiana State	13	2	1	2	2
19. St. Louis	9	1	2	2	4
20. Pittsburgh	7	0	0	0	0
21. Missouri	5	0	0	0	1
22. Carnegie Institute of Technology	4	0	0	2	2
23. Buffalo	4	0	1	1	1
24. Florida	3	2	0	0	0
25. Nebraska	3	1	0	0	0
26. George Washington	3	0	1	0	2
Total	979ᵃ	144	121	93	109ᵃ

ᵃ The total for 1947–48 through 1957–58 includes one degree from each of five institutions not included in the above list, four of which awarded no degrees in business during the academic years 1954–55 through 1956–57; the fifth awarded its only degree of the period in 1957–58.

Source: For 1947–48 through 1954–55, American Council on Education, *American Universities and Colleges, 1956* (1956), Table 9. For 1955–56 through 1957–58, see Appendix D.

lege teachers.[2] But the need is also great for well trained and imaginative research workers, on whose efforts we must rely for expansion in our knowledge of business behavior and for significant generalizations that

[2] While some holders of the doctorate in business will go on to successful careers as practicing businessmen, it is not the function of the doctoral program to prepare students for such careers. This is the primary objective of the M.B.A. program

can be taught. Most but not all of these research workers will also teach. Doctoral programs in business, therefore, should prepare students both for teaching *and* research, and certainly not for the former alone. There is room, however, to blend these two kinds of preparation in different ways. Some business schools may choose to put their primary emphasis on research training; others may concentrate on the kind of training that emphasizes teaching. But *all* doctoral programs in business administration should place considerable stress on the development of scholarly attitudes and on training in the methods of scholarship.[3]

This raises a somewhat related issue, the counterpart of which exists also in some of the other professional fields, such as engineering or education. Should the doctoral program in business have a "traditional" or a "professional" orientation?[4] Schools that lean in the former direction have requirements similar to those of the traditional PH.D. in the humanities and social sciences. These programs emphasize scholarship and an advanced command of specialized subject matter. Two foreign languages are usually required, as is an elaborate dissertation which allegedly makes an "original contribution to knowledge." As applied to business administration, the traditional program is likely to emphasize theoretical analysis, some command of research tools, and in general the detached view of the scholar-observer.

In contrast, the professionally oriented doctoral program tends to stress the point of view of the business manager. The emphasis is on how managers go about solving business problems. The doctoral candidate is being trained chiefly to teach future businessmen, to prepare teaching materials, and to keep informed regarding the best of current business practice. This kind of doctorate, sometimes designated D.B.A. rather than PH.D., builds on the foundation of the M.B.A.; there is little emphasis on either theoretical abstractions or refined research methods; there are no language examinations; and there is only a minimal thesis requirement. On occasion a doctoral program will have a nominal professional orientation, although it resembles the traditional doctorate in virtually all respects except the foreign language requirement.

Many thoughtful observers believe that the time has come for im-

[3] Along with many others, we believe that good teaching is scholarly teaching. (Cf. The Committee of Fifteen, *The Graduate School Today and Tomorrow* [Fund for the Advancement of Education, 1955], pp. 28f., and *The Education of College Teachers* [reprinted from the 1957–58 Annual Report of the Carnegie Foundation for the Advancement of Teaching], pp. 10f.) By scholarly teaching we mean teaching which is accompanied by and which draws stimulus from some type of continuing research investigation which may or may not lead to formal publication.

[4] The distinction being made here is essentially that described by George P. Baker and David B. Tyack, "Doctoral Programs in Business and Business Administration," in *Faculty Requirements and Standards in Collegiate Schools of Business* (AACSB, 1955), pp. 91ff.

portant reforms in the traditional PH.D. program, even in the humanities and social and physical sciences for which it was originally intended. The desire of the newly emerging professional and applied disciplines, including business administration, for a teaching and research degree that more obviously fits their special needs is entirely understandable. The protest has been particularly strong against the foreign language requirement and the need to prepare an elaborate and time-consuming dissertation. This has been accompanied by a desire for the kind of training that would emphasize systematic observation of and participation in the real world of the professional or business practitioner.[5]

It seems to us, as it has seemed to others, that we do have to recognize that the professional fields are different from the older arts and sciences. Literal and inflexible application of traditional doctoral requirements in a professional field is likely to mean either that the legitimate needs of the field are not met, and thus its development is retarded, or else that the professional faculty rebels and seeks to offer its own "professional degree." Unfortunately, when the latter course is taken, the reaction against the traditional form may be so strong that standards of quality and scholarship are sacrificed.

The proper solution would seem to lie in some modification of the traditional form of the doctorate to meet the needs of the new disciplines (business in this case), while at the same time maintaining the standards, scholarly values, and hard-won respectability associated with the "traditional" doctorate. In the pages that follow we shall examine the different ways in which the business schools offering doctoral work have sought to achieve this objective.

Types of Doctoral Programs

Any meaningful classification of doctoral programs must consider more than catalogue requirements.[6] The same set of requirements can mean quite different things on different campuses. Wisconsin, for example, requires a candidate for the PH.D. to offer four fields for the degree—economics and three fields of the student's choice. Indiana, in much the same way, requires economics and four elective fields of its D.B.A. candi-

[5] See, on this range of problems, E. V. Hollis, *Toward Improving Ph.D. Programs* (1945), esp. chaps. I and VII; The Committee of Fifteen, *The Graduate School Today and Tomorrow; The Education of College Teachers;* and R. L. Kozelka, *Professional Education for Business* (1954), pp. 105–106.

[6] The description of types of programs in this section is based on a study of twenty-six doctoral programs, all in schools that we personally visited. Twenty-two are included in Table 22. The others are either new, did not award at least two degrees during 1955–57, or else were listed by the U.S. Office of Education as awarding degrees in economics rather than business.

dates. Aside from the relatively extraneous issue of languages, the two programs are essentially alike in form. Yet the two faculties differ considerably in their views of doctoral work in business administration and in the implementation of their respective programs.

If we look not only at the formal requirements but also at a school's general approach to doctoral training and the field of business administration, we can distinguish four broad types of doctoral programs. We shall consider these under the following headings: 1) programs which view business administration as primarily applied economics, 2) those that emphasize a broad background in business, but chiefly in terms of subject matter, 3) those that concentrate on a special field within business, again with a subject matter emphasis, and 4) those that emphasize organization and administration in their approach to business problems. Naturally, not all doctoral programs fit neatly into one of these categories, but we think that the classification has some descriptive as well as analytical value.

APPLIED ECONOMICS

The first type of program, which approaches business as applied economics, is probably still the most common. As offered by some business schools, it evolved out of the traditional PH.D. in economics, passing through an intermediate stage in which the economics department permitted candidates to offer one or more business fields in addition to the required work in economic theory and economic history.[7] Eventually, the business faculty began to offer its own doctorate but retained the form and flavor of the traditional PH.D. in economics—with the same emphasis on research, essentially the same requirements in economic theory (and possibly other areas in economics), and the same language and thesis requirements. This kind of doctoral program in business may differ only in detail from that offered by the economics department.[8]

As might be expected, the functional fields of marketing and finance and the industry fields of insurance and transportation fit easily into this pattern, as do industrial relations and statistics. Schools with this sort of emphasis on applied economics generally do not view with favor the

[7] Some programs, such as those at the University of Pennsylvania and at M.I.T., are still in this intermediate stage. The degree is taken in economics, although the student's work in the applied fields (as well as the writing of the thesis) is supervised by the business faculty. Until very recently, this was also the situation at the University of California (both at Berkeley and Los Angeles).

[8] See, for example, the reference by D. W. O'Connell to the "decided orientation toward formal economics" of the Columbia doctoral program in business. *American Economic Review*, XLVI (May, 1956), 572.

fields of personnel administration, human relations, or organization theory; they do relatively little case teaching and tend not to have extensive business contacts; and they seldom permit the substitution of business tools (e.g., accounting) for one or both of the foreign languages. The schools with this kind of program are likely to have a tradition of scholarship and tend to maintain reasonably high academic standards. They are inclined, however, to be unsympathetic to the view that treats business administration as an independent discipline, with its own methodology, philosophy, and body of knowledge. There is also likely to be relatively little emphasis on managerial problem-solving in their treatment of the various business fields.[9]

Of the doctoral programs that seem to approach business administration primarily from the point of view of applied economics, the program at one large midwestern state university we visited may be taken as an example. In addition to meeting requirements in statistics and two foreign languages, the student must offer economic theory, two additional fields from a list of nine (some of which are administered jointly with the economics department), and a minor field in some area other than economics. Students may enter the doctoral program immediately after receiving the baccalaureate degree—which is usually in economics or business. They do not have to take the M.B.A. degree before proceeding to the PH.D., although most of them do. Several other business schools offer doctorates which closely resemble this one in their requirements and general orientation.

GENERAL BUSINESS PROGRAMS

Our second type of doctoral program calls for a broad command of business subjects but does not emphasize a required core in economic theory.[10] The student must offer work in a number of business fields, but no field is designated as a major field, although one is usually the disser-

[9] Although some schools in this category have been doing a good job of selecting and training scholarly teachers, their contributions have been smaller than they might have been because of their overly narrow view that business administration is still a branch of economics. The Harvard Business School led the way in the struggle for emancipation more than a generation ago, but at the time it went too far in denying the existence of a systematic body of knowledge (including but going much beyond economics) on which the study of business could be based. It has since retreated somewhat from that position, as can be seen from the latest revision of its doctoral program, its increased emphasis on research, and the nature of some of its recent faculty appointments.

[10] Some schools have continued with a diluted requirement in economics which they, rather than the economics department, administer. If the remaining requirements consist of work in an array of business fields no one of which is emphasized over the others, we should include such programs in this "general business" group despite the presence of a nominal economics requirement.

tation field, and no particular area of business (or economics) is considered so fundamental that it is required of all candidates. Typically the doctorate is based on the M.B.A. degree. To cite one example, the doctorate at one well known graduate business school requires the M.B.A. degree or at least the M.B.A. core, qualifying examinations in four business fields chosen from a list of ten or more, and a minor field in a non-business area. The candidate is not required to gain a mastery in depth of any field, but he is expected to have a reasonably good acquaintance with several; he acquires no theory or tool skills beyond what are provided by the introductory M.B.A. courses; and his training proceeds as if business administration were essentially a collection of separate business specialties rather than an integrated discipline. The requirement of an outside minor field contributes to the emphasis on breadth.

EMPHASIS ON A SPECIAL FIELD

In the third type of program, one of the business fields chosen by the student is designated as a major field and receives a greater stress than do the others. The faculty and the student think of the doctorate as being in marketing, accounting, etc., even though the degree normally bears a more general designation. The level of competence required in the areas of business other than the major field is typically not much if any higher than what would be expected of an advanced undergraduate or M.B.A. student.[11] Where a special field is so heavily stressed in the doctoral program, graduate teaching tends to concentrate upon a command of specialized subject matter. Not much attempt is made to view business administration from the point of view of managerial problem-solving, and management is likely to be considered just another field, coordinate with, for example, finance or statistics. Two foreign languages are typically required; not many members of the faculty are likely to be sympathetic toward teaching by the case method; and considerable emphasis is put on the dissertation. As schools in our first group consider economics to be the best undergraduate preparation for a doctoral candidate, so schools with this third type of program favor work in business administration as the best kind of undergraduate preparation.

One of the southern state universities offers an example of this third kind of program. The doctoral candidate must choose a major or primary field and also offer two minor fields. The preparation expected in the major field is about twice that required in the minor fields. The equiva-

---

[11] Some of the doctoral programs with this special field approach, like some of those in our second category, still cling to a vestigial requirement in economics, but the requirement is so elementary that they must be considered as belonging to this rather than the "applied economics" group.

lent of an undergraduate major in business administration is in effect a prerequisite, so that a general background in business at the undergraduate level is assumed. Other requirements include a foreign language, "business statistics," and, of course, the conventional kind of dissertation. Several other business schools have similar programs.

PROGRAMS STRESSING ADMINISTRATION

Our fourth type of program features in one way or another the central theme of administration and managerial problem-solving. Business administration is viewed as more than either applied economics or a collection of special business fields. In effect, the attempt is made to develop a doctoral program on the assumption that business administration can be viewed as a more or less independent and integrated discipline. At least two variants of this approach need to be distinguished.

The first is represented by the Harvard Business School. Harvard's doctoral program was "designed for advanced study of the kinds of thinking and methods of analysis useful in administration and to acquire knowledge of the background and facts of business life as they bear importantly on the administrative process."[12] But an understanding of the "administrative process" was not to be obtained by mastering some body of systematic knowledge. In this respect Harvard's approach to the M.B.A. carried over to its D.B.A. program. Administration is an "art," involving "wisdom" and "judgment;" it does not rest on any central body of theory or principles that must first be mastered. Since a corollary of this view is that business administration should be taught largely by the case method, Harvard has put considerable stress on training in the preparation and use of cases.

Harvard's D.B.A. program of a few years ago illustrated this general approach quite clearly. The candidate's qualifying examination tested him substantially on the work he had done for the M.B.A.[13] Beyond this, the candidate wrote a thesis and presented himself for an examination in a special field. The thesis requirement could be characterized as a large case study emphasizing the managerial aspects of the problem being studied. Thus:

The thesis should demonstrate an administrative point of view and professional competence in using primary data in a scholarly manner to develop a contribution to the understanding and knowledge of management problems.[14]

[12] Catalogue of the Harvard Graduate School of Business Administration, 1957–58, p. 89.
[13] The official description of the doctoral program for 1955–56 stated that the "Doctoral Program is built upon the M.B.A. program." This statement was not included in the bulletin for 1957–58.
[14] From the School's *Program for the Degree of Doctor of Business Administration*, 1955–1956, p. 8.

In addition, while writing his thesis, the student participated in a year's seminar in "Research and Its Presentation," strongly oriented toward the preparation and use of cases.

Thus the program provided little or no training in research methods other than case preparation. No central body of theory was recognized, nor were there any core fields required of all candidates beyond what was necessary for the M.B.A. And, as in the M.B.A. program, managerial problem-solving was emphasized.

Harvard has now begun to move away from this extreme "administration-as-an-art" emphasis in its doctoral program. The school is attaching more importance to systematic knowledge and to training in research methods, and the program is now conceived as building on more than what is required for the M.B.A. degree.

To implement this shift in emphasis, a number of innovations have been introduced. An effort is being made to identify possible candidates for the doctorate early in their second M.B.A. year so that they may be directed to those courses "specifically keyed to the Doctoral Program." Thus it is explicitly recognized that the regular M.B.A. courses cannot provide all of the foundation necessary for the erection of a rigorous doctoral program.[15]

While the same form of qualifying and special field examinations has been retained, the 1957–58 description of the D.B.A. program suggests that more attention is being put on a command of the relevant literature. In the special field examination the candidate is "expected to show a considerable command of the substantive content and literature of his chosen field." A principal purpose of the thesis has become "to demonstrate a candidate's capacity to make fruitful use of research methods appropriate to his problem. . . ." Since 1957 the School has, we understand, taken further steps to build analytical content and training in research methods into its doctoral program.

The second variant of the administrative approach seeks to base the study of managerial decision-making on a central core of systematic knowledge and analytical tools. "Administration" is looked on as a currently evolving synthetic discipline which rests ultimately on an array of underlying fields, including but not confined to psychology, sociology, and economics. Stress is also placed on the development of technical aids

[15] In 1957–58, the "keyed" courses included: Advanced Economic Analysis I and II, Business History, Concepts and Research Methods of the Behavioral Sciences, Statistical Methodology, Field Reading Seminars, Research and Its Presentation, and Teaching by the Case Method. Except for Advanced Economic Analysis I, one of the reading seminars, the research seminar, and the case teaching seminar, courses of study are worked out on an individual basis. Only the research seminar is unequivocally required. But there seems to be an inference that all or most candidates will take the other three courses just mentioned.

to rational decision-making and on research methodology, with a consequent emphasis on mathematical and statistical analysis and, again, on the analytical tools of economics and the behavioral sciences. It might be said that a doctoral program of this type seeks to prepare students for the scientific study of decision-making in an administrative context, chiefly but not exclusively in business.

As the Harvard Business School is the chief example of the first type of administrative approach, so the Graduate School of Industrial Administration at Carnegie Tech is the outstanding example of the second. Building on a foundation comprising half to two-thirds of the regular M.S. curriculum, the doctoral program calls for advanced work in preparation for examinations in four areas: quantitative analysis, organization and administration, business institutions, and one of the related social sciences.[16] The student selects one of these areas for even more intensive work, and this then becomes the dissertation field. The program is flexible, and it can be shaped to individual interests. After course work and examinations (four to five semesters after the baccalaureate), the student "devotes substantially full time to research, usually working closely on a tutorial basis with members of the faculty on on-going research projects."[17]

The Carnegie Tech program prepares its students particularly for active careers in research, and especially in the new frontier areas in which many of its faculty have been working. Teaching, however, is not neglected, and graduates of the program have begun to move out into teaching positions in the more research-minded business schools. Doctoral training at Carnegie Tech is obviously much more oriented toward a sophisticated kind of research training than it is at Harvard, which emphasizes research training much less and preparation for teaching considerably more.

Some other schools are beginning to emphasize administration in their doctoral programs, and a number are beginning to require more training in mathematics and statistics. The University of California (Berkeley), for example, requires that students take qualifying examinations in both economic theory and administration, and requires certification in

[16] Certification is also required in mathematics and one foreign language.

[17] From the School's 1958–1960 *Announcement*, p. 15. In another place it is stated: "The School believes that such participation [in faculty research] helps the student gain deeper insight into the nature of practical business and economic problems and into the process of extending the frontiers of knowledge and putting new research findings to work in industry." It should also be added that the psychology department at Carnegie Tech offers a doctoral program that involves some of the members of the faculty of the Graduate School of Industrial Administration. The doctoral programs in industrial administration and in psychology are described as alternative ways of carrying on advanced study in the behavioral sciences.

two out of the three "tool" areas of mathematics, statistics, and accounting. U.C.L.A. has a similar set of requirements. Work in administration is also required in several other of the newer doctoral programs.

There are some schools which, while recognizing the importance of the behavioral sciences and quantitative methods for the student of business administration, refuse to consider administration or organization as a separate and self-contained field. Instead, they bring the behavioral sciences directly into their teaching in the various business fields, and the student must obtain some command of the various behavioral science areas and of the research tools used in these fields. Recent changes at the University of Chicago business school reflect this point of view. It is probable that an increasing number of doctoral programs will require some background in the behavioral sciences, whether or not the area of administration-organization comes to be more generally required as a field for the doctorate in business administration. It is noteworthy that one of the new courses Harvard has introduced for its doctoral program is entitled Concepts and Research Methods of the Behavioral Sciences.

EMERGING TRENDS

We have purposely drawn fairly sharp lines between the four broad types of programs described in the preceding paragraphs. Actually, the doctorates offered by most schools have features drawn from two or more of our categories and in that sense are hybrids. Most still reflect the fact that they grew originally out of the PH.D. in economics, even if the emphasis now is on training over a wide range of business fields or primarily in some special field of business.

The general direction which the doctoral programs in the best schools will take in the years ahead is beginning to be clear. The applications of the behavioral sciences will be stressed more than in the past; so will training in quantitative methods; and work for the doctorate will be increasingly built around an analytical core that encompasses more than conventional economic theory. In one or another variant, the theme of the doctoral program is likely to become "the scientific study of managerial decision-making," whether or not a separate field of administration-organization is recognized. The business schools will continue their efforts to shed the traditional language requirements, and it can be expected that some attempt will be made to find a satisfactory substitute for the conventional thesis requirement. Such experimentation is to be encouraged as long as it is accompanied by sound and rigorous training in the areas most relevant to the study of business behavior, an appropriate emphasis on research methods, and recognition that most doctoral candidates need some training in teaching as well as research.

Formal Requirements for the Degree

Requirements for the doctorate ordinarily include: 1) selection of a set of fields to study, some of which may be required of all students; 2) qualifying examinations testing the student's competence in the several fields; 3) certification of competence in certain areas considered to be necessary tools of the scholar (such as foreign languages and statistics); and 4) preparation of a dissertation. In the pages that follow we shall examine in some detail these and other possible requirements for the degree.

A REQUIRED CORE IN THEORY

The preceding pages suggest quite strongly that all doctoral candidates should be examined on a central core of analytical material. We believe that a dual requirement would be desirable, covering not only economics but also a range of material from the behavioral sciences—the latter possibly organized into a field of organization or administration.

The requirement in economic theory would cover both macro- and microeconomics, with more emphasis on the latter. This would not be precisely the same requirement for which doctoral candidates in economics are held, since the needs of business students are somewhat different. Perhaps the term "economic analysis" might be used (as it is at Indiana) in order to suggest that applications are covered as well as theory *per se*. Thus, although standards should be the same as for the economics degree, the subject matter should differ somewhat. There seems to be no need to require other fields in economics of everyone, although several schools now do require economic history or history of economic thought of their doctoral candidates. Elective work in economics certainly should be available to all candidates, particularly to those whose applied interests require a greater than average familiarity with some particular branch of economics.

The other part of the "theory" core should be in the area of administration-organization—or, alternatively, in those parts of the behavioral sciences which are most relevant for the analysis of business problems. It is probably too soon to expect agreement as to what should be included and taught in this general area, although wide agreement could probably be reached on the need for the inclusion of some topics. Our own view is that this body of knowledge should be organized around the theme of decision-making in an organizational context and should include treatment of possibly all four aspects of "administration-organization" as they were distinguished in Chapter 9 (aids to rational decision-making, "organization theory," "management principles," and human relations).[18]

The doctoral candidate should, in our view, be held for qualifying examinations in each of the two parts of the core—economic analysis and organization-administration or behavioral science theory. Each examination should presume the equivalent of at least a year's formal course work *at the graduate level* and should carry the student beyond what is required for the M.B.A. Probably this work should come chiefly in the second graduate year, in part to accomodate students who, after working for a year in the M.B.A. program, are encouraged to aim for the doctorate.

TOOLS OF RESEARCH

In the traditional PH.D. in the social sciences and humanities, the tools of the scholar have been considered to be some central body of theory, possibly the history of the field, foreign languages, and some kind of research methodology. In the social sciences—and therefore in business administration—statistics and, to a less extent, mathematical analysis have come to be essential parts of the scholar's analytical equipment. For the student of business, a moderate acquaintance with accounting is also indispensable. While a knowledge of one or more foreign languages is desirable, it is seldom essential to the teacher or research worker in business administration. Even so, about three-quarters of existing doctoral programs in business continue to require one or more foreign languages, although, as in most other fields, the requirement seldom results in the student's acquiring a usable knowledge of any foreign language.

Strangely, only a few schools formally require statistics of their doctoral students, although it is reasonable to assume that most students do get exposed to the subject. Of equal concern is the level of the statistics requirement. Rarely does it go beyond one year's elementary work, essentially what an undergraduate business major would get in his second course, and this clearly does not meet the need of the doctoral candidate for sophisticated, research-oriented training in statistics. We would suggest a requirement which would presuppose the equivalent of one semester's graduate work in statistics beyond what we recommended at the undergraduate level, that is, a year's graduate course for those without prior work in the field.[19]

[18] See pp. 179–82, above. The need for required work in either administration or behavioral science theory would apparently now be accepted by a number, perhaps most, of the leading business schools.

[19] See Chapters 9 and 11 for discussions of the role and content of statistics in the business curriculum.

Intimately related to statistics is mathematical analysis. All doctoral candidates in business would benefit from being introduced to the power of modern mathematics in business research, and indeed in business operations. This is all the more true if they are to do work in organization-administration, economic analysis, and modern statistics, if they hope to understand the recent literature in some business fields, if they are to be at least as sophisticated as many of their future students probably will be, and, finally, if they hope to make a significant contribution in their own scholarly investigations. This is not to imply that business students should be trained as applied mathematicians. But the business schools do need to become more sensitive to current and prospective trends in both the business literature and business practice and to the kind of teaching, research, and consulting tomorrow's scholars will be required to do.[20]

A third important tool area is accounting. Although few doctoral programs state a formal requirement in accounting, it is generally assumed that the candidate has acquired a working knowledge of the field in his previous work for either the bachelor's or master's degree.

Thus we recommend that all doctoral programs in business have requirements in statistics, mathematics, and accounting. The requirements could be met by qualifying or certifying examinations, by graduate course work, or by the presentation of satisfactorily completed undergraduate work.

These three tool requirements might be substituted for one language and possibly for both. The more research is to be emphasized, the greater is the justification for dropping both languages and requiring more in each of these tool areas. The more the school wishes to emphasize general cultural advantages and the literature and business practice in other countries, the more reasonable it would be to retain one language. Little can be said, however, for retaining the traditional requirement of *two* foreign languages. Insistence on a knowledge of two foreign languages in a school that finds it necessary to stiffen its requirements in the theory core and in the other tool fields can only result in a steady debasing of the language requirement until it becomes virtually meaningless. This, unfortunately, is already happening—not only in business administration but also in other fields.[21]

The total required core recommended here is no more than is currently common. The economic analysis requirement could represent formal

[20] See Chapter 8 for a discussion of the kind of mathematics we have in mind.

[21] For an argument for the study of foreign languages as "a useful skill and a liberating experience," see William R. Parker, "Foreign Languages and Graduate Study," *Journal of Proceedings and Addresses of the Fifty-fourth Annual Conference of the Association of American Universities and Fifth Annual Conference of the Association of Graduate Schools* (1953), p. 31.

(graduate) course work of about one year or a bit more, as would the requirement in administration or behavioral sciences. The accounting, statistics, and mathematics requirements could be met by a total of four semesters' work, assuming some undergraduate background in one or more of these fields. The actual amount of work required in graduate school would vary from school to school and from one student to the next. There might or might not be a specification of competence in one foreign language.

ROLE OF THE OPTIONAL AND MAJOR FIELDS

Schools differ in whether there should be a major field for the degree or whether business itself is the major. The Office of Education recognizes this distinction by reporting doctorates according to whether they are in "business and commerce—specialized field" or in "business and commerce—general." About a fourth of the doctoral programs we examined required, essentially, that one of the fields of business offered for the degree be designated as a major, implying among other things that this would be the dissertation field. Typically two other business fields were also required, sometimes with additional nonbusiness, tool, or theory requirements. The remaining schools took a more general view. The degree is considered to be in business administration *per se*—although all of them require two or more particular business fields.

Our general recommendation is that the degree require two optional fields beyond what has already been proposed for a core. One of these fields might be designated the major, provided, however, that doing so does not result in regarding the degree as being in marketing, accounting, etc., with the implied neglect of all areas other than the special field. The degree should be in business (or business administration), although the student would normally study one subfield of business somewhat more intensively than the others. In any event, the thesis requirement implies a fair amount of specialization in a particular business field, even if no field is emphasized above the others in the qualifying examinations.

The fewer the number of conventional fields required for the qualifying examinations, the more desirable is it that the school require that the doctoral candidate have an elementary background in the standard "core" fields of the undergraduate program. Evidence of such background might be provided by simple certifying examinations or by courses previously taken. This is not often a problem since most doctoral candidates have had the equivalent of the undergraduate core courses or else find it easy to secure the necessary background.

Some schools require a large number of fields, apparently on the assumption that the doctoral candidate should be informed generally about as many fields of business as possible. Intimately bound up with the question of number of fields is the problem of the degree of competence to be required. It is obvious that the schools specifying five, six, or seven fields expect less than those requiring two or three. Explicit recognition of this is made at a few schools that differentiate among fields in terms of the level of competence required.

A further problem arises out of the custom of a minor field. The minor field is sometimes a business field or one closely allied to business, but it is often permitted to be in any department of the university, regardless of its relevance to the student's overall program. We lean to the view that the requirement of a minor is an anachronistic appendage which the business schools would be well advised to abandon. We do not object to the student's being permitted to choose one of his optional fields from a nonbusiness area. On the contrary, we favor this practice as long as it contributes to a rationally planned program and the outside field is explored in reasonable depth. The current use of the outside minor field seldom meets either of these conditions.

LEVELS OF COMPETENCE AND THE QUALIFYING EXAMINATIONS

The particular form of the doctoral examinations is in good part a matter of local custom and in any event is frequently determined by the university's graduate division. But the business school is free to specify the level of competence required in each of the areas in which the doctoral candidate presents himself, and on this subject it may be worthwhile to offer a few comments.

In some of the areas required for the doctorate, the level of competence required might be equivalent to that obtained in a good undergraduate program or in the required core of an M.B.A. program that assumed no undergraduate prerequisites. Thus the doctoral candidate might be expected to demonstrate a competence in mathematical analysis such as would be obtained in a year's undergraduate course of the sort described in Chapter 8. Similarly, undergraduate competence in accounting should be sufficient. In statistics, the level should be somewhat higher, representing the result of at least a semester's graduate work beyond the typical introductory course. This graduate course should have a different orientation and be at a more advanced level than that which we recommended in Chapter 11 for the core of the M.B.A. program. Competence at the required level should be tested either by a special examination or by a satisfactory grade earned in the appropriate course.

A minimum of a year's graduate work should be required in each of the two core areas of economic analysis and administration-organization (or behavioral science). In each case, the work required should carry the student beyond what is typically expected of M.B.A. candidates, with the result that a student without some undergraduate background will probably need to take more than a year of course work in each of the two areas. His competence in these fields should be tested by qualifying examinations.

The candidate's competence in his optional fields should also be tested by qualifying examinations. Course work alone should not be enough. The level of performance to be expected depends on the number of fields that must be offered. If two are required, the examinations can assume about a year's graduate work in each field beyond the typical introductory (M.B.A. or undergraduate) course. In addition, the student should be expected to obtain an even greater command of the field in which he writes his thesis, and on this he might be tested in a special examination or in the final examination which follows completion of the dissertation.[22]

To recapitulate, the student would take qualifying examinations which assume a year or more of graduate work in each of the areas of economic analysis, administration-organization (or behavioral science), and two optional fields. In addition, he would have to demonstrate his competence in mathematics, statistics, and accounting—and possibly a foreign language—at the levels suggested. Beyond this, he would have to write a dissertation and demonstrate an unusually thorough command of his thesis field.[23]

THE DISSERTATION

In the traditional view of the PH.D., the formal training of the first two or three years of the doctoral program merely qualifies the student for the last great step—the writing of a dissertation that will make an "original contribution to knowledge." The examinations that precede the dissertation are merely "preliminary" or "qualifying" tests, the passing of which permits the student to "advance to candidacy" for the degree. It is by writing a dissertation that makes an original contribution that the candidate demonstrates his right to be admitted to the community of scholars.

[22] The thesis field can be one of the optional fields or one of the core fields or a field which is not presented for the qualifying examinations at all (including one which overlaps two or more conventional fields and which is tailor-made to fit the candidate's interests).

[23] How much time these requirements would actually take depends on the student's undergraduate preparation and on whether he has been through some part or all of the M.B.A. program. This matter is discussed later in this chapter.

The results of this fiction are well known and have been summarized by F. W. Strothmann as follows:[24]

Such a dissertation not only fails to be, in the honorific sense of the term, a contribution to knowledge, but it also lacks value both for the future researcher and for the future teacher. Its futility is not the result of specialization as such, but rather the result of specialization without end and purpose. It is probable, however, that by defining the dissertation as 'an original contribution to knowledge,' pointless research is more often encouraged than discouraged. For it is under the tyranny of this definition that the candidate is sent into 'virgin territory' even if he cannot possibly come back with more than a handful of pebbles.

The dissertation requirement should be a constructive educational experience rather than a test of the candidate's endurance. For many graduate students who have the potentiality to become good college teachers, completion of the massive tome of minutiae that is ordinarily expected becomes a traumatic experience which does nothing to spur their interest in continued scholarly activity. We share the opinion of the "Committee of Fifteen" that:[25]

the dissertation can, and should, be one of the most exciting intellectual experiences of the future college teacher. It should be primarily a contribution to the knowledge of its author, an instrument of his intellectual growth, and the result of an adventure, not necessarily into virgin territory, but into the world of ideas that are worth wrestling with.

We should like to echo the Committee's suggestion that the conventional thesis requirement be replaced by one which would have the candidate produce, after a period of carefully supervised research and writing, a readable and well reasoned report on his investigations, whether or not the result was an "original contribution" to the store of human knowledge.

To this extent, we are in agreement with those business schools that have sought to substitute a "professional" D.B.A. for the traditional PH.D. But while we agree that the traditional thesis requirement is in need of revision, we are also prepared to argue that the doctoral program must provide the future scholar-teacher or research worker with a working command of modern research techniques, an understanding and appreciation of the scientific method, and the ability to bring systematic knowledge to bear on the solution of practical problems. The thesis requirement should, therefore, provide a positive and intellectually exciting learning experience for the candidate and at the same time test his command of

[24] Committee of Fifteen, *The Graduate School Today and Tomorrow*, p. 27.
[25] *The Graduate School Today and Tomorrow*, p. 27.

the subject matter of some special field, his ability to use the research methods appropriate to the problem he investigates, and his ability to prepare a readable and reasonably sophisticated research report.[26] The report need not be overly long—much closer to a long article or short monograph than to the several hundred pages that the doctoral candidate usually writes.

The kinds of problems suitable for the dissertation can vary over a wide range, and they may or may not involve the student intimately in the research being carried on by some faculty member. But whatever the topic, the candidate should be required to examine critically some body of literature, to show a command of the relevant analytical tools, and to organize his findings into a well reasoned and well presented report. The thesis might represent the attempt to apply what is known to the solution of a specific business problem; it might or might not involve a field investigation; it might be concerned with the theoretical implications of some issue. But it should be more than the preparation of a business case —and both more and less than the ponderous and badly written descriptive studies that are now so frequently submitted.

The time to be spent on the dissertation is a question of some importance. At present, this period is typically much too long. A reasonable goal would be to hold the effort represented by the dissertation to the equivalent of one year of full-time work, although part-time employment may stretch the total time elapsing between beginning and ending the thesis to something more than this. Every effort should be made to provide whatever financial support is necessary so that the thesis can be completed within a reasonable period, preferably not more than two years. Prolonged delay negates the primary purpose of the dissertation, which is to provide an educational experience for the candidate and a final check on his training and ability to do scholarly work.[27]

OTHER REQUIREMENTS

Several other requirements might be included in the doctoral program, and some of these are now found at some schools. Thus, the M.B.A. course

---

[26] Hollis queried employers of PH.D. recipients and reported as follows on the subject of the dissertation: "They [the employers] would prefer to see the candidate's thesis research demonstrate initiative, intellectual maturity, and grasp of the investigational procedures used rather than to have it exemplify what the academicians call an 'independent and genuine contribution to knowledge.' " *Toward Improving Ph.D. Programs*, pp. 34–35.

[27] Needless to say, the level of analysis and sophistication which the candidate is expected to demonstrate will vary considerably among schools. Standards vary in doctoral programs as they do at the level of the master's or bachelor's degree. What standards are imposed for the dissertation will depend largely on the training of the faculty and the standards of scholarship they impose on themselves.

in business policy might be an additional requirement for those who have not already had it. Such a course is good training in a number of respects and would help to prepare candidates to teach such a course if they eventually join a business school faculty. It might also be wise to include some sort of requirement in business history or the changing environment of business. This might be met by passing certain specified courses and could be waived for those who had had comparable work as undergraduates or in an M.B.A. program.

Beyond the required work in statistics, a seminar on research methods might be required of all candidates at the thesis writing stage. Such a seminar might not only help to integrate the student's previous work in the tool areas and introduce him to more advanced research techniques. It could also provide a forum in which students could share and report on their experiences in planning and carrying through their research projects.

Since most doctoral candidates will become college teachers, some training in pedagogy should be required or at least made available. This is now done by most schools through a system of apprenticeship, in which doctoral candidates act as teaching assistants or junior instructors in the elementary courses. For most schools, this is the most important way of offering financial support to doctoral candidates.[28] In addition, a seminar on teaching methods in general, or on the collection and use of cases, might be required or made available. It is our impression that there has been a new interest in offering additional training in teaching as the leading business schools have taken stock of and considered possible revisions in their doctoral programs.[29]

Sources of Students and the Problem of Timing

The program described in the preceding pages implies from three to four years of full-time work (exclusive of summers) following receipt of the bachelor's degree. There is general agreement that it should not take longer than this to meet all of the requirements for the doctorate. Whether in fact this desideratum is achieved depends on a number of circumstances, including the student's undergraduate preparation, whether he completes a full M.B.A. program before becoming a doctoral candidate, the need to meet language and other supplementary requirements, the

[28] In exclusively graduate schools, of course, this alternative is not open, but advanced doctoral candidates might be used as assistants in the larger M.B.A. courses, as graders, and (what is common practice at several schools) in the preparation of cases.

[29] For further discussion of the need for better training of college teachers and of some of the experiments now being tried in providing teaching experience and training, see Committee of Fifteen, *The Graduate School Today and Tomorrow*, and *The Education of College Teachers*.

way in which the thesis requirement is viewed, the availability of financial support, and the extent to which the school is prepared to insist that the student adhere to a schedule, particularly with respect to completion of the thesis. Several of these points call for further comment.

SOURCES OF STUDENTS FOR THE DOCTORAL PROGRAM

One of the complicating factors in designing an effective doctoral program is the fact that students may come from a number of different sources, thus having different backgrounds. The chief source has been the M.B.A. program, the objectives of which differ significantly from those which are appropriate to the doctorate.

The essential purpose of the M.B.A. program is the preparation of practitioners for the middle and upper levels of management. The doctoral program, on the other hand, has the objective of developing that set of attitudes, knowledge, and skills which characterize the scholar-teacher. A well designed M.B.A. program with a strong managerial orientation can provide some but not all of the predissertation training that the doctoral candidate requires. The latter needs additional work in theoretical analysis and in research methods, and his command of subject matter needs to be carried further than is possible in most M.B.A. courses. While most of the courses in a high-level M.B.A. program can be taken by doctoral candidates, depending on their background, there also need to be courses which are designed chiefly for doctoral students.

Here we encounter a problem that has bothered a number of business schools. If, for example, a student has spent two years in the kind of M.B.A. program recommended in Chapter 11, he will still need to do a considerable amount of work to prepare for the qualifying examinations we described earlier. Unless the courses taken in his second year as an M.B.A. student were chosen in order to meet the doctoral requirements, he may need as much as a year's additional work before he can begin on the dissertation. As the leading schools have sought to expand their doctoral programs in recent years, they have given increasing attention to this problem and have sought to attract able M.B.A. candidates into the doctoral program during their second year of work for the master's degree.[30]

Doctoral candidates may come from sources other than the M.B.A.

---

[30] The 1957–58 announcement describing the recently revised D.B.A. program at Harvard notes (p. 22): "Men at the Harvard Business School in the M.B.A. Program can make their decision to become Doctoral candidates at any time up to midyear of their second year and fit smoothly into the Doctoral Program. On the other hand, if they wait until after midyear to seek admission it will be difficult for them to get the full value of the Program without spending additional time to pick up courses offered in the second half of the year, some of which they might well have missed." Other schools have also sought to identify potential doctoral candidates early in the second year of the master's program.

program. They may come straight from an undergraduate college, where their major may have been in business administration or in some other field. The typical undergraduate business curriculum, at least as it now exists in most schools, is not a promising source of supply for a high level doctoral program. The student's training is likely to have been too narrow, with important deficiencies in the underlying disciplines. Further, as we saw in Chapter 13, undergraduate students inclined toward a scholarly life do not typically major in business administration, and the best of those who complete an undergraduate business program do not typically go on to do graduate work in business. This situation might improve if undergraduate business schools were more generally to adopt the kind of curriculum and standards that we recommended in Chapters 8 and 9. In the meantime, more attention should be paid to attracting into the doctoral program students who did their undergraduate work in engineering, science and mathematics, and the social sciences. These students, of course, will also have deficiencies, particularly in the elementary business subjects, that will have to be remedied. For the most part this can be done in the first-year M.B.A. courses and by extra reading. If desired, provision could be made for such students to take a master's degree en route to the doctorate.

RESIDENCE AND TIMING

It may help to give concreteness to our suggestions if we indicate in more detail the kind of program which might be taken by students with the different kinds of backgrounds described in the preceding paragraphs.

For the student with no previous training in business administration, our suggestions imply four or five graduate semester courses in economic analysis and organization-administration (or behavioral science), possibly four semester courses in mathematics and statistics, a semester of accounting, two or three semester courses in each of two optional fields (more in the field in which the thesis is to be written), the equivalent of an elementary background in those parts of the first year M.B.A. core not otherwise covered, and possibly additional requirements in research methods, case preparation and teaching, a foreign language, etc. This program adds up to a total of from sixteen to twenty semester courses, depending on the student's previous background. For a student with little undergraduate background in economics, statistics, or mathematics, and with no previous work in any of the business fields, a minimum of five semesters of full-time work would be required. A school with the necessary resources might offer special graduate courses for such students so that they could quickly catch up with those who had been through the M.B.A. program. It would be more economical, however, to let such students spend the first year taking chiefly the courses that we proposed in Chapter 11 for the "Type A" M.B.A. program. In his second year, the student could go on to more advanced courses in economics, statistics, organization-administration or behavioral science, and his optional fields. This would carry over into the first semester of the third year.

Students who entered the doctoral program only after receiving the M.B.A. would probably need an additional year for advanced work in economics, organization-administration, statistics, and the optional fields and to make up deficiencies in mathematics. In most fields probably an additional semester's course or seminar would be necessary. This would add up to about a year's work, particularly if a year's course in mathematics were necessary and a foreign language requirement had to be met.

In brief, a student who starts in the doctoral program directly after receiving the bachelor's degree will need about five semesters before he can begin work on the dissertation, which should then (assuming full-time work) be comfortably completed by the end of the fourth year. The graduate of a broad M.B.A. program will need about one year of additional full-time work, plus another year or so for the thesis. The M.B.A. candidate who moves into doctoral courses by the middle of his second year can be ready for his dissertation by the second semester of the third year. Thus it would seem that a well designed M.B.A. program can provide for perhaps three semesters of the total work required (other than the dissertation) but that something like a year of full-time work needs to be spent in courses geared to the needs of the doctoral candidate and not necessarily appropriate for the M.B.A. student who is preparing himself for a career in business.

Financing the Doctoral Program

A good doctoral program is an expensive operation. The faculty costs are particularly high for several reasons. First, the student-faculty ratio must be lower than in M.B.A. or undergraduate instruction. Special seminars and advanced courses must be offered for relatively few students; the supervision of dissertations and individual projects represents a heavy drain on faculty resources; and so does the time that must be spent in consulting with students. Second, the faculty administering a doctoral program must be research minded. Only those who are themselves engaged in scholarly investigation can keep abreast of rapidly changing fields and teach in the more advanced courses, and only a research faculty can develop in prospective scholar-teachers the necessary skills and attitudes of scholarship. Finally, because of this emphasis on research, the faculty in a doctoral program should be more distinguished (and therefore presumably better paid) than a faculty which awards only the master's degree.

Perhaps no more than half of the schools which have awarded at least one doctorate in the last few years are financially able to offer quality work at the doctoral level. And few of the schools now hoping to launch doctoral programs for the first time have the financial resources or quality of faculty needed. The latter group would be well advised to delay indefinitely inauguration of work for the doctorate and to concentrate on improving the quality of their undergraduate and master's programs. It would also be no more than frank concession to reality if those schools now offering the doctorate to few students, with inadequate faculty and course offerings, were to suspend their programs for the time being.

Even in the better graduate programs (with very few exceptions) resources are not sufficient to provide all the financial aid to doctoral candidates that is needed to permit them to secure the degree within the time limits we have suggested. More aid is needed to permit graduate students to study on a full-time basis, at least until they pass their qualifying examinations. As a minimum they should have the opportunity for one or two years of full-time study. More advanced students should not work more than half time. In universities with large undergraduate enrollments, a large number of teaching appointments are likely to be available to graduate students, but the use of this form of financial aid should be attended by certain safeguards. The completion of one year of full-time graduate work should be required; a half-load of course work should be carried concurrently; continuous progress toward the degree should be a requirement for continuation of the arrangement; after two years of half-time teaching the student should be given an opportunity for full-time study for at least a half year and preferably a whole year; and no more than half-time teaching should be permitted during the first year of the dissertation.[31]

The financial burden of prolonged, part-time doctoral work is certainly a strong argument for extending fellowship and loan funds to the utmost so that every student will be able to do as much full-time work as possible. Outside fellowship help has already been expanded, in part as a result of the 1955 Arden House Conference and the several programs of the Ford Foundation, but much remains to be done. One section of

[31] We are fully aware of the problem, in today's market, of dissuading students who have reached the dissertation stage from leaving to take full-time positions elsewhere. But an effort should be made to have the dissertation at least started in residence.

the National Defense Education Act of 1958 provides for a large number of graduate fellowships, for which, presumably, students in business administration will be eligible. An increase in faculty research activity can also contribute to the support of graduate students, particularly if research funds can be used to finance doctoral candidates while they are writing their dissertations.

We suspect that more financial support can also be made available from business firms, particularly through the organization of a group of "Associates" or "Friends" of the school. Funds from this source can be used for student loans and fellowships as well as for research, case collection, and other purposes. Earnings from a school's management development program have also been used to support graduate students.

A Final Comment

At the doctoral no less than at the lower academic levels, there is room for marked improvement in the quality of the training that the business schools are providing. But, in addition to the improvement in quality, there is need for a large increase in quantity. The scale of the better doctoral programs needs to be considerably enlarged. But an increase in the number of doctoral candidates should go hand in hand with improved training for tomorrow's teachers and research workers in the field of business. There are already too many in the faculties of the business schools who are poorly trained. Doctoral programs should become more rigorous at the same time that they seek to train a rapidly growing number of graduate students.

The goals of quantity and quality can be reconciled only by limiting doctoral training to those schools which have an adequate base of (actual or potential) financial resources and a faculty that is actively engaged in pushing outward the frontiers of our knowledge about business and administrative behavior. The major research contributions in the years ahead are likely to come from a fairly small number of schools, and the number qualified to offer doctoral training of high quality is not a great deal larger. It is smaller than the number now offering doctoral programs. To the extent that support is mobilized to increase the supply of doctorates in business, efforts should be concentrated on the best of the existing programs and schools. There is little excuse for wasting resources in expanding some of the marginal programs now in existence—and even less excuse for supporting some of the present plans for new programs by schools not now offering the doctor's degree, particularly when those schools are not even members of the AACSB.

PART V

The Need for Action

chapter 18

SOME FINAL SUGGESTIONS

A PARTIAL summary of our findings has already been provided in Chapter 7. In that chapter we considered the educational implications of the analysis of business competence attempted in Part II, and we described the direction in which, in our opinion, collegiate business education should seek to move in the years ahead. The recommendations offered in Chapter 7 were then elaborated in considerable detail in Part III, dealing with curriculum, and in Part IV, which was concerned with students, faculty, teaching, and research.

The general tenor of our recommendations was that the business schools (and departments of business) need to move in the direction of a broader and more rigorous educational program, with higher standards of admission and student performance, with better informed and more scholarly faculties that are capable of carrying on more significant research, and with a greater appreciation of the contributions to be made to the development of business competence by both the underlying non-business disciplines and the judicious use of clinical materials and methods.

In this final chapter, we propose to consider some of the implications of our recommendations and to suggest some things that might be done to implement them. The years immediately ahead offer an unusual opportunity for significant reform throughout business education. The business schools will not be alone if they insist on higher standards; there is an increased awareness nationally of the need for more rigor both at and before the collegiate level; and, perhaps most important of all, enrollments are rising rapidly. All this means that substantial reform will entail fewer problems of adjustment than might otherwise be expected.

The Need for Further Study and Appraisal

We still know too little about the kinds of qualities that make for success in business and other administrative careers and in what ways formal education can most effectively contribute to the development of managerial competence. We have made use of such information as was available and have attempted to contribute some additional evidence of our own in Part II. But only a start has been made. There is need for further research, in which business and the universities should cooperate, on the basic elements in different kinds of management jobs, on the qualities and training needed for various types of management positions, and on the specific roles to be played by different types of experience and formal education in the development of the kinds of competence that are required.

There is particular need for a large-scale study of the relation between education and business career. This should include a survey of business school alumni drawn from a broad cross-section of schools and departments of business, in which an attempt would be made to evaluate the kinds of business training received. With this should go a companion study of a large sample of businessmen of varied educational backgrounds that would investigate in some detail the relationship between career pattern and type of education. The present report would have rested on a more solid foundation had it been possible for us to make these studies or to have had them already available.

There are many more areas that cry for further investigation—for example, the identification (by tests and other means) of the kinds of talents that business requires, ways of judging the relative effectiveness of various teaching methods, and the value from different points of view of the various courses that enter into the standard business curriculum. We have tried to supply a rationale for our particular curriculum recommendations on the basis of both *a priori* reasoning and some empirical evidence, but we should be the first to admit that our analysis is incomplete and in some respects inconclusive.

THE NEED FOR SELF-APPRAISAL

Enough has been said to suggest that there is a paucity of verified knowledge on which to base effective educational planning. Nonetheless, such planning must be done, utilizing the best information that is available. Essential to such planning is a thorough stocktaking, in which, it seems to us, every business school and department of business should periodically engage. Most schools and departments could benefit at the present time from such a self-appraisal.

Such a self-study might well begin with a critical review of the school's objectives, include an inventory of its resources and special problems, and go on to a thorough evaluation of its present programs and ways of improving them. The program evaluation should include such matters as the relative emphasis to be placed on undergraduate and graduate teaching, ways of revising the curriculum so as more effectively to achieve the school's objectives, elimination or overhaul of obsolete courses, the desirability of raising standards of admission and performance, consideration of new teaching methods, ways of making more effective use of faculty time, means of raising the scholarly quality of the faculty, and so on through the range of problems considered in this report.

A considerable number of business schools have made self-studies of varying degrees of thoroughness in recent years. This is a reflection of the uncertainty and soul-searching that we described in Chapter 1. We hope that this report will stimulate many more schools to engage in such self-examination, in which they will make use not only of the material presented in this and the Carnegie Corporation reports but also of the experience of other, particularly the more progressive, schools. These evaluations will, we hope, stimulate schools to look more to the future than most of them are now doing. Every school should ask the question: In what respects will the problems facing business a generation hence be different from those which business faces today, and what effect should these prospective changes have on present teaching and research?

Stocktaking should extend beyond curricula, course content, standards, and teaching methods in the school's regular degree programs. It should encompass also the scholarly activities of the faculty and the school's relations with the business community. We have already pointed out the need for reappraisal of what the schools are doing in the field of adult business education, for taking a new look at bureaus of business research, for reviewing the amount and kind of consulting done by the faculty, and, most important, for finding ways of raising the general competence of the faculty and stimulating their desire to engage in significant research.

One implication of these suggestions is that a self-appraisal, to be effective, should be comprehensive. Piecemeal consideration and revision of a school's total program should, so far as possible, be avoided. Since every school's resources are limited, and since its activities are interdependent, a revision of any particular part of the school's activities must be considered in the light of its possible effects on all other, and particularly the most important, parts of the overall program.

This leads us to repeat another warning, which has already been made several times in connection with the discussion of curricula in Chapters 8-11. The business schools should keep their programs under continuous review. The world in which business operates does not stand still. Knowledge in the underlying disciplines and in the various business fields will continue to accumulate. Ideas will change as to what to teach and how to teach. The need for reform today will not remove the need for further improvement tomorrow, and the day after.

Not only the full-fledged business schools but also the departments of business administration not separately organized as schools need to re-appraise their programs. As we saw in Chapter 10, most departments of business are seeking to do something which, by the nature of the case, they cannot do well and which, in a liberal arts setting, they should not even attempt. Here, as in the case of many business schools, the central administration of the college or university should probably take a hand to insure that the necessary studies are made and that needed changes are put into effect.

We hope that, in planning revisions of their programs, the more imaginative schools will not be afraid to experiment, and in earlier chapters we have suggested some of the kinds of experimentation that would be desirable. There is considerable room for variation in curricula, methods of teaching and kinds of teaching materials, and the like. Indeed, considerable variation is essential if each school is to make the most effective possible use of its particular strengths and minimize the handicaps imposed by its particular weaknesses. Within the broad framework outlined in the preceding chapters, there is room for wide variation in detail and for an unlimited amount of imaginative experimentation. To this only one obvious qualification has to be made. Within the broad standards suggested in this report, there should be as little compromise with quality as possible.

It is to be hoped that the more progressive business schools will continue to pioneer in curriculum planning, in the development of new teaching methods and materials, and in research. It is also important that such pioneering schools accept some responsibility for disseminating the results of their experiments so that other schools can learn from their experience. As we shall point out later in this chapter, there is a serious lack of communication among business schools, and we shall at that point venture a few suggestions as to how some of the leading schools can help to disseminate knowledge regarding the best educational practices.

Stimulating Curriculum Reform and Improvements in Teaching

USE OF REGIONAL MEETINGS

We hope that one immediate result of this report (and that prepared under the sponsorship of the Carnegie Corporation) will be a series of regional and national meetings which will concern themselves with the recommendations in these two reports, particularly those that deal with curriculum reform and raising standards at both the graduate and undergraduate level. These meetings should be accompanied by the kind of individual self-studies suggested in the preceding section.

A number of regional groups of business schools now exist on a more or less informal basis. Although the AACSB has a committee on regional meetings, relations between the regional groups and the Association are rather loose and informal. We think it would be wise to expand and formalize these regional groups, to draw them closer to the Association, and to bring more faculty members into their meetings. Specific issues regarding changes in curriculum, raising of standards, improvement of teaching materials, and the like can be debated at these regional meetings, and schools taking the lead in instituting improvements can report on their experience. Active regional groups not only serve a useful informational purpose; they can also help to build up pressure for some of the kinds of action which the AACSB should take at a national level.

ELIMINATING SPECIALIZED COURSES

We need say little about reducing teaching loads (particularly where they exceed twelve hours per week), providing faculty members with more clerical assistance, and raising salaries. While we can urge the need, we can add little to what was said earlier regarding ways to bring about these ends. We would stress again the substantial savings that would result from a drastic pruning of overspecialized and vocational courses, particularly at the undergraduate level. Here, probably, central university administrations will have to intervene more firmly than in the past, both to insist on reduction of needless course proliferation and to educate the university's trustees, alumni, students, and parents to accept less vocational emphasis and higher academic standards.

In this connection, we should like to repeat a suggestion made in Chapter 12. Many of the more specialized courses which do not belong in the daytime degree curriculum can be moved to the evening or extension program to satisfy the demand for specialized training by those already in business. Those instructors in these courses who cannot readily adapt themselves to a broader type of teaching can move with their courses to the evening program. In this way, the school can proceed with the necessary reform of its daytime curriculum and at the same time protect the tenure of those faculty members who cannot adjust to the new situation.

OTHER STEPS TO IMPROVE TEACHING

As suggested earlier, information should be widely disseminated regarding innovations in curriculum planning, course content, and teaching methods at the more pioneering institutions. The latter should be encouraged to take more initiative in publicizing educational innovations. In addition, all schools should be prepared, with their own funds or with outside help, to give individual faculty members sufficient free time to revise their courses and develop new teaching materials.

We believe that a strong effort should be made to develop at least one really strong business school in each part of the country. The advantages of having a strong regional center to provide leadership for the smaller schools are fairly clear. Outside support for such a center should be contingent upon the latter's accepting responsibility for exercising some leadership, for example, through holding conferences and seminars to which faculty members from other colleges would be invited and providing fellowships for teachers at nearby schools.

Some things can be done to improve teaching materials and teaching methods. Regional or national conferences on teaching in particular business fields—especially those which have been undergoing rapid change—might be desirable. Such meetings can also be held (as they occasionally have been in the past) at the annual conferences of such professional societies as those in accounting, finance, insurance, management, and marketing. Certainly more effort should be made to stimulate the publication of high level textbooks that rest on a solid foundation in the underlying disciplines and incorporate the latest scientific and business developments. Handbooks and review articles might also help to bring to the more isolated teachers knowledge of significant developments that can be incorporated in their teaching.[1] Textbooks and handbooks, since they are usually commercially profitable, should ordinarily require no subsidy. Enterprising publishers might, with the help of a committee of experts, seek to commission improved texts and handbooks in various fields. Gradually, we hope, the market for the low-level descriptive texts that make up so much of the business school market will tend to dry up.

A good many schools need to be encouraged to make greater use of business cases in their teaching. We hope that the summer seminar at the Harvard Business School on the preparation and use of cases will be continued and perhaps duplicated at one or two other institutions and that the intercollegiate collection of cases will be widely used.[2] It is to be hoped, however, that the larger schools will restrain their institutional pride and avoid carrying their own case preparation to excess if adequate cases are available elsewhere. This is not to deny the value of a modest program of case collection to the faculty concerned.

More experiments in teaching methods would be desirable—for ex-

---

[1] The Ford Foundation has already taken some initial steps along these lines.

[2] See the description on p. 370–71, above, of the Intercollegiate Case Clearing House, administered for the AACSB by the Harvard Business School.

ample, on the effectiveness of case teaching in different kinds of courses, on the effectiveness of large and small classes, on what can be done to develop more skill in human relations and communication, and on the possible use of organizational experience outside the classroom. We hope, also, that more schools will experiment with imaginative honors programs. The results of such experiments should be widely disseminated.

RAISING STANDARDS

We are not sure what can be done to force the poorer business schools to raise their admission and performance standards. Here again much depends on the attitude of the AACSB, which could take a number of steps to raise standards at both the graduate and undergraduate level. At the graduate level, such steps might include suggesting the requirement of a minimum score on a test such as the ATGSB or some minimum undergraduate scholastic record, and the development of performance tests which the business schools could use as guides. For undergraduates, measures might be taken to insist on essential kinds of secondary school preparation, minimum grade records in college, essential college-level nonbusiness prerequisites (as in mathematics, the social and physical sciences, and English), etc. We also suggested at the end of Chapter 13 that the Association should initiate studies on the form which higher academic standards should take and how such standards can best be implemented. We also think it would be desirable to explore the possibility of an aptitude test to be given to undergraduates, perhaps at the beginning of their junior year.[3]

While we did not take a firm stand on this point in the body of our report, a strong case can be made against including all four undergraduate years in the business school. If the school waits to take students until the beginning of the sophomore or junior year, it is much easier to impose admission standards that are high relative to the rest of the university. Otherwise, unless admission requirements are raised for the whole campus, the business school can keep its standards high only by forcing an extremely high attrition rate during the freshman year. While there are important exceptions, it is generally true that the two-year or three-year schools have higher standards and can do a more effective educational job than the four-year schools. The situation is worst where a four-year school is part of a university that accepts virtually any high school graduate.

---

[3] It has also been suggested that a national test might be given to graduating seniors and the results publicized. This would, it is argued, force the poorer business schools to raise their standards.

COOPERATION WITH OTHER DEPARTMENTS

Some business schools now work closely with related departments in other parts of the university, but much more can be done to extend and deepen such cooperation. On the side of teaching, cooperative efforts should be directed along three lines in particular.

1) The business schools, in conjunction with other professional schools and departments, should intensify their efforts to secure the kinds of general education courses they need for their students—in English, mathematics, the natural and behavioral sciences, and so on.[4]

2) Cooperation from the engineering schools is required in two different ways. Business students need to have available to them a few broad survey-type courses in engineering, designed for nonengineering students. And the engineering schools should be prevailed upon to design a broad type of undergraduate engineering program that would be suitable for those not planning to be engineers but desiring a background in engineering and the physical sciences for a career in business. This type of undergraduate education, if it paid sufficient attention also to the humanities and social sciences, would provide an excellent foundation for the kind of M.B.A. program recommended in Chapter 11.

3) Cooperation is a two-way street, and we should like to repeat here the recommendation made in Chapters 7 and 10 that the business schools undertake to make available to nonbusiness students a carefully designed set of service courses in the more important areas of business and administration. In Chapter 10 we described the kinds of courses needed.

Aiding the Faculties of the Business Schools

Substantial improvement in collegiate business education depends first and most of all upon the faculties of the business schools. While administrative leadership is important, it is ultimately upon the faculties of the schools that we must depend for curriculum reform, higher standards of student performance, better teaching materials and teaching methods, and more significant research. The faculty must provide the initiative for a general improvement in the intellectual atmosphere, and the faculty can also have an important influence on admission standards.

Improvement must clearly start with the *present* faculties of the business schools. It is they who are training not only a future generation of businessmen but also many of tomorrow's teachers who in turn will train yet another generation of businessmen. And today's faculty, by their in-

---

[4] Chapter 8 described some of the kinds of nonbusiness courses that are needed but which are frequently not available.

fluence on recruiting policy, will have much to say about the quality and kind of new teachers who join their ranks.

KEEPING ABREAST OF NEW DEVELOPMENTS

A number of steps can be taken—and some have already been started —to help faculty members keep pace with important scientific developments that are beginning to affect the practice of business and should be influencing teaching and research in the business schools more than is now the case in most institutions.

A highly important step in this direction are the Seminars in New Developments in Business Administration, sponsored by the Ford Foundation, which are now being conducted during the summer by the Carnegie Tech Graduate School of Industrial Administration and the School of Business of the University of Chicago.[5] This program needs not only to be continued but expanded further. As additional programs of this sort are established, they should be made available to selected teachers from schools which are not members of the AACSB. Until now, the program has been available only to faculty members from Association schools.

The Ford Foundation has taken another important step in establishing an Institute of Basic Mathematics for Application to Business. According to the public announcement, this program, which is to run for only one year, is to be available to business school faculty members concerned chiefly with graduate teaching and who are active in research, although undergraduate teachers are also eligible. Additional training programs of this sort are needed. The initiative could come from some of the leading business schools or from the AACSB. Training programs could be set up in the applications to business of mathematics, statistics, or some of the behavioral science fields. Outside support would undoubtedly be necessary. The institutions that should take the lead are those that have been pioneering in these newer applications and have close working relations with the other departments in their universities which might need to cooperate.

The enterprising business school should also be able to help itself in this kind of retraining for interested faculty members. The support of, say, the local mathematics department might be solicited in establishing a special seminar on the campus for the business school's faculty members.[6] Squeezing out the time needed for study by already overburdened faculty members would be a serious problem, but the school might be

---

[5] The first seminar was begun by Carnegie Tech in 1957. The School of Business at Chicago began a similar seminar in 1959.

[6] Something of this sort has been tried in a few business schools, not always successfully. If the business school has some mathematicians on its own staff (and a number of them now do), the help of the mathematics department may not be necessary.

able to offer a modest reduction in course load or administrative assignments for those who agreed to participate in such a seminar.

Other ways of encouraging faculty members to bring themselves abreast of new developments are feasible, even at schools with limited budgets and heavy teaching loads. Every school should have in its budget one or more rotating nonteaching positions, which a faculty member can hold for, say, a semester at a time. During this semester he would be relieved of teaching in order to strengthen his background in particular areas, to learn the use of new analytical tools, to develop new teaching materials, or to engage in research that looks forward to publication. While this may be beyond the means of some of the poorest schools with only a few faculty members, most schools could readily create one or more positions of the sort suggested by eliminating unnecessary courses. The leading schools now permit arrangements of this sort, either through research leaves or sabbaticals. The need is greatest in the poorer schools (poor in terms of both quality and resources), where faculty members have not had either the time or inclination to engage in the study necessary to remain fully abreast of new developments, particularly in the underlying disciplines, that bear on the particular business fields in which they teach.

In this connection, we suggest that many business schools would find it useful to establish regular faculty seminars at which faculty members would take turns evaluating and reporting on new developments in their own and related fields. Occasional part-time relief from teaching might be made conditional on presentation of a substantial report to such a seminar (whether or not the paper was intended for eventual publication). Such seminars would serve to improve the general intellectual atmosphere in the school as well as provide a more specific stimulus to the particular faculty members who were asked to report.

There have recently been made available a small number of fellowships for business school faculty members wishing to pursue studies in the behavioral sciences, mathematics, or statistics. Further foundation support of this kind is desirable in these and other fields, but the amount that is likely to be available from this source can meet only a very small part of the need. The schools themselves should take the initiative and develop their own programs for encouraging and supporting faculty retraining where retraining is necessary.

The business schools should try to find the funds to finance a limited number of summer research or study stipends for their faculty. Such summer grants would permit a few faculty members to use the summer for study and research instead of, as is typically the case, devoting their summers to earning additional income by teaching or consulting.

THE FACULTIES OF THE FUTURE

Considerable attention is already being paid to increasing the supply of future faculty members, and none of our recommendations on this score is new. Doctoral programs are now being expanded in perhaps a half dozen of the leading business schools, in some cases with substantial outside support. A concerted effort should be made to improve the quality and expand the size of the doctoral programs in perhaps another dozen schools. Improvement in quality, along the lines suggested in Chapter 17, is as much of a need as is the increase in number of doctoral candidates. Schools with doctoral programs that have not recently been reviewed need to restudy their programs in the light of recent developments, strengthen their faculties as needed, and build up financial support, particularly in the form of doctoral fellowships. As suggested in Chapter 17, the weakest of existing doctoral programs should be eliminated, even at the expense of some injury to institutional pride.

It is common practice for doctoral candidates to move to full-time teaching jobs before they have completed all the requirements for the degree. The employing schools should have a liberal program of paid leaves (or special summer grants) for these young faculty members so that they can complete their dissertations.

Faculty members, particularly the younger ones, face an irresistible temptation to seek extra income through additional teaching or part-time assignments with business firms. To protect itself and the future quality of its faculty, the business school should keep a tight control over these arrangements. The school itself should coordinate the consulting activities of the faculty and enlist the cooperation of the business community in making available consulting arrangements that offer fruitful professional experience for the younger as well as older faculty members.[7] Too often now, as we have already noted, "consulting" work consists of routine jobs that absorb the time and drain the energies of business school teachers without adding much if anything to their professional competence.

[7] By "coordinate" in this context we mean having the school itself receive requests from business for faculty consulting help and distributing the consulting opportunities in a way that makes the most effective use of the faculty talents available and contributes most to developing the professional competence of the faculty. Such coordination should also include more careful screening of consulting arrangements which faculty members make on their own initiative.

As noted in Chapter 14, there is growing interest in recruiting faculty members for the business schools from those whose training has been in one of the underlying disciplines, such as the behavioral sciences, mathematics, and statistics. The more conventional business schools need to utilize this source more than they now do, perhaps through the device of joint appointments with the relevant departments in other parts of the campus. Foundation support has recently become available to encourage senior men and graduate students in these other fields to apply their disciplines to business problems. This support needs to be continued, and it may lead to a modest increase in the number of doctoral candidates from these fields who will be attracted to faculty appointments in the business schools.

IMPROVING CHANNELS OF COMMUNICATION

Many business school faculties fail to keep informed of important new developments that should be influencing their thinking, teaching, and educational planning—not to speak of their research (if they are doing any). This is particularly true of the more isolated schools but seems to be the case also with many of the faculty members in the larger state universities and urban schools. The problem is partly one of poor channels of communication through which information about innovations in educational practice can be conveyed to the rank and file of business teachers. In part, it is a lack of desire to be informed; in part, it is a lack of knowledge of where to look.

We think a number of things can be done to disseminate more widely information regarding improvements in educational philosophy and practice and concerning important advances in knowledge that bear on our understanding of business behavior. We shall mention only a few of the possibilities.

The business schools, with or without outside financial support, should invite distinguished scholars (and scholarly inclined businessmen) to come to their campuses for varying periods of time. The arrangement can vary from a year's or semester's visiting professorship to a visit of a few days or a few weeks during which the visitor would give lectures or conduct seminars (chiefly for the faculty) on important new developments in his particular field of competence. The visitor need not be a specialist in one of the conventional business fields. With the increasing applications of mathematics, statistics, and the behavioral sciences to business problems, a visitor from one of these fields can provide a highly constructive stimulus to a faculty that is not yet aware of the importance of these developments or how they can be incorporated into their teaching. Foundation support has made it possible for first Harvard and then a number of other business schools to benefit from this kind of visiting arrangement. Here again, however, while foundation support is certainly to be encouraged, the main effort must be made by the business schools themselves with local support.

The AACSB or some other agency might take the initiative in establishing a panel of leading scholars in business and nonbusiness fields who would be willing to pay more or less extended visits to particular schools on the latter's invitation. Some foundation support for such an arrangement would almost certainly be necessary.

Communication can also be improved through the medium of the regional centers suggested earlier in this chapter. The leading business school in a region might extend visiting appointments to faculty members from surrounding schools and also send members of its own faculty to other schools for varying periods of time. As suggested earlier, it could also arrange for regional conferences and take a number of other steps to improve communication among the schools in its region.

Beyond this, we suggest that for a decade or more there should be some centralized system under which particularly the more isolated schools can be visited by persons who are conversant with the best of current thinking and practice in business education. Despite the numerous professional journals that exist in particular business fields, the majority of schools are not well informed regarding developments elsewhere with respect to such matters as curriculum planning, experiments in course content and teaching methods, or new teaching materials. In this connection, it would be helpful if one or two promising faculty members could be detached from their universities for a year at a time in order to be vehicles of communication among the business schools. In their visits to particular business schools they could both transmit information regarding important developments at other institutions and receive information regarding worthwhile activities at the host institution. Such visits might be at the initiative of this "peddler in ideas" or on the invitation of the school.[8] At present, this kind of information service is provided to a limited extent by foundation personnel, by the travelling representatives of textbook publishing firms, and by *Collegiate News and Views*, a magazine distributed by one of the publishing houses.

---

[8] It should be possible also for these traveling experts to be used as consultants by schools considering revision of their educational programs, perhaps along the lines suggested in this report.

This suggests that possibly the business schools need their own journal, similar to those which now exist in some of the other professional fields. While there are numerous professional business journals for the dissemination of research findings and for reports on new developments in business practice, there is no medium (other than the one mentioned in the preceding paragraph) through which business school deans and faculties can keep currently informed regarding new developments in business education at the university level.[9]

Views are mixed as to the desirability of establishing such a journal. While a need clearly exists for some formal channel of communication beyond what is now available, it may well be that a regular monthly or quarterly journal is not the best way of meeting the need. It is unfortunately true that a journal devoted primarily to pedagogical issues is not likely to be of high quality, although it is not inevitable that this be so. In any event, the proposal deserves further study. The logical agency for such a study is the AACSB.

The AACSB serves as an important communication channel among deans, but for a number of reasons it fails to meet the special informational needs of deans who have just been appointed to their posts. Hence it would be desirable to have a special summer seminar for newly appointed deans (and perhaps associate deans).[10] These would be working sessions of two or three weeks' duration, during which the participants could learn not only about the standard administrative problems associated with their jobs but, more important, about such matters as the educational programs at the more progressive schools, new experiments going on at various institutions, and how other schools had raised standards, stimulated research, and created mutually more beneficial relations with the business community. In addition, it should be possible for a newly appointed dean to travel widely in the early months of his tenure so that he can quickly develop the background he needs for progressive leadership. Such travel, chiefly to other business schools, would, we think, supplement rather than remove the need for the kind of summer seminar suggested.

[9] Some material on business education may occasionally appear in general business journals like the *Harvard Business Review*, *Journal of Business*, *Business Horizons*, or the *California Management Review*, or in the monthly reviews issued by particular business schools. In addition, information of interest to teachers in particular fields appears in such specialized journals as the *Journal of Marketing*, *Journal of Finance*, or *Accounting Review*. There are also journals dealing specifically with business education, but chiefly (although not entirely) at the subcollegiate level, which the typical business school teacher never sees and of whose existence he may be unaware.

[10] Such a seminar was held for the first time in the summer of 1959.

Improving the Quality of Research

As we stated in Chapter 16, research in the business schools needs to become more analytical, to develop a more solid theoretical underpinning, and to utilize a more sophisticated methodology. Steps to improve the quality of business school faculties along the lines suggested in this chapter will obviously also raise the quality of research now being carried on. A better trained and more scholarly faculty, with a sound grasp of analytical tools and well informed regarding recent developments in the relevant scientific literature and in business practice, will produce more significant research.

We must, however, face the cold facts of life and differentiate here among both schools and faculty members. While the measures suggested in this and earlier chapters should produce better informed and more scholarly inclined teachers in virtually all business schools, we must rely on a relatively small number of schools and a minority of faculty members for significant research results.

As we said in Chapter 16, one of the most pressing needs is to provide sufficient free time for those capable of significant research. Greater use needs to be made of the summer grant that will permit able scholars in the business schools to devote their summers to research rather than to extra teaching or other income-producing work. Every school with research minded faculty members should have funds in its budget so that full or part-time relief from teaching can be provided from time to time for its most productive faculty members. Fellowships or grants should also be available to permit young faculty members to complete their work for the doctorate or to secure advanced training that will help them in their teaching and research. We have already referred to the need to make it possible for more members of business school faculties to secure additional training in mathematics, statistics, and the various social sciences. The Ford Foundation has instituted a number of programs to stimulate progress in these directions, but the schools need to show more initiative along these lines than they thus far have. Some funds for these purposes can be raised locally, and other activities which are much less important (for example, proliferation of courses, some of the present activities of bureaus of business research, or, in a few instances, excessive emphasis on case collection) can be trimmed to help the more scholarly faculty members find the time and acquire the analytical tools they need for useful research careers.

We also strongly recommend that the business schools take more initiative in establishing closer working relations with other departments and schools on the campus—psychology, sociology, economics (if not a part of the school), mathematics, statistics, engineering, etc. Business school deans and faculty members frequently complain that their colleagues in other departments stand aloof and show no interest in the possible applications of their fields to business problems. As often as not, there is fault on both sides. The foundations should encourage the universities, even more than they thus far have, to develop cooperative research projects, seminars, workshops, and the like in which faculty members from the business school and other parts of the campus would cooperate.

We have already referred in Chapter 16 to the need to reorganize the activities of most bureaus of business research. Some should become no more than simple service agencies for the local business community. Others can serve a useful research function in ways that we suggested earlier.

Various means have been suggested to facilitate the work of the more able scholars who can find the time and have the ability and inclination to pursue active research careers. More ample research funds would help, although this is not a critical issue in the few leading schools. Closer working relationships with scholars in the underlying disciplines on which business administration depends would help. There is need to interest able men in these other disciplines to work on problems of interest to business and the business schools. Another need is for more conferences, perhaps in the summer, of scholars from different institutions working in the same general field. Business firms and the universities could cooperate in bringing closer together the more able staff specialists in industry and their counterparts in academic life.

We saw in Chapter 17 that doctoral programs in business administration need to provide more rigorous research training than most of them now do. If resources are to be used most effectively, the best of the doctoral programs should expand substantially and the weakest should contract or disappear. An expanded supply of better trained PH.D.s implies more financial support in the way of loans and fellowships to graduate students, a closer tying together of faculty research and graduate training (in part, through the wider use of faculty-student workshops), and closer cooperation with scholars in the underlying disciplines.

It might be worth mentioning again another suggestion made in Chapter 16—namely, that the time has probably come to try to distill some significant research generalizations out of the steadily accumulating mass of case materials that the business schools have in their files. While case preparation itself is not what we mean by research, the systematic study of a large number of business cases, particularly if supplemented by other types of materials, can probably provide the basis for significant generalizations about business behavior. Such studies must, of course, have an analytic framework; other materials must also be used; and the research worker will have to develop considerable skill in drawing inferences from a miscellany of cases prepared for a variety of teaching purposes and under widely varying conditions.

Ways in Which Business Can Help

There are many ways in which business firms can contribute to improving the quality of business education and of the research going on in the business schools. Money is, of course, a prime consideration, but it is by no means the only one.

We have already indicated some of the ways in which financial support can help the business schools. Among the more important needs, in addition to the always urgent need to raise faculty salaries, are fellowships for doctoral candidates, time off for study and research by faculty members, and support for preparation of cases and other teaching materials. One method of mobilizing financial support from the business community is through an organization of Friends or Associates of the business school.

A strong obligation rests upon the business community to provide liberal support on a continuing basis to collegiate business education. Indeed, from a purely selfish point of view, business has more to gain from its financial contributions to the business schools than to most other forms of education. American business stands to lose a great deal if the quality of collegiate business education is not raised significantly in the years ahead.

THE NEED FOR MORE THAN FINANCIAL SUPPORT

Equally important are the other forms of help that business can provide. Business firms ought to create more opportunities for faculty members to observe and participate in their operations. This can be done in several ways. Business firms might establish faculty internships, whereby faculty members might be given the opportunity to work at various assignments in a company and to observe different aspects of the firm's operations. Such internships could be for varying periods up to a year.[11] Faculty members would benefit in obvious ways. They would accumulate useful teaching material, including problems and cases; they would have an opportunity to observe business decision-making at first-hand; new types of questions for research would be suggested; and, with the company's cooperation, useful research materials might be made available. Continuing relationships between faculty members and business firms would be encouraged; and, in some cases, continuing consulting relationships might develop that would be profitable to both the faculty members and the companies concerned.

While we have spoken of such internship arrangements in terms of their probable benefit to the faculty members involved, substantial advantages could accrue to business also—directly and in the short run as well as indirectly and in the long run.

Reciprocally, some companies might lend some of their executives and high level staff specialists to the business schools for varying lengths of time. These visitors from the business world would not be given assignments teaching full time in the school's regular courses. Rather they should have roving assignments (as we suggest for the faculty interns in industry) which are tailored to their qualifications. These assignments could include, for example, occasional lectures, participation in graduate seminars, and joint research projects with faculty members.[12]

Business firms should to be more generous than they are now in making information regarding their operations available to faculty members for both teaching and research. They can quite reasonably insist, however, that individual requests be screened through some agreed channel. In this connection, individual schools might seek to establish a panel of firms to whom their faculty can go for information. There could be an agreed point of contact in each firm; and, on the school's side, it might be understood that requests for information or other forms of cooperation would be endorsed by an official or committee of the school.

[11] Scott Paper Company has had such an arrangement during the last several years with the University of North Carolina. A number of companies have summer programs for college teachers (not necessarily in business administration), but most of these programs fail to provide the kind of experience that most business school faculty members need. Some of these summer programs are little more than a form of public relations activity for the companies concerned.

[12] An arrangement of somewhat this sort now exists in the Program in Executive Management at the Stanford Business School, under which twelve young executives work with six PH.D. candidates in a special program lasting eight months. This is intended as a special kind of management development program, but it serves some of the purposes we have in mind and, in this case, also makes a special contribution to the training of the participating PH.D. candidates.

If such a panel of business firms existed, it might be able to cooperate with the school in other ways, for example, in setting up internship arrangements of the sort just described or in utilizing faculty members on responsible consulting jobs. If contacts were already established through such a panel under joint school-business auspices, faculty members would be more inclined to seek the kinds of rewarding materials and experiences that business can contribute. The official sponsorship and the opportunity to control these arrangements on both sides would serve to prevent exploitation of the relationship either by some faculty members or by particular business firms.

Once a panel of companies was organized, representatives of the school and of the business firms involved might set up a coordinating committee which, among other things, would plan activities of mutual interest and increase the flow of information in both directions between the business community and the business school. A number of business schools now have advisory councils of leading businessmen. But in the typical case these councils meet infrequently, active cooperation by the members' firms is not necessarily involved, and the councils are used more for their public relations value and as a means of soliciting financial support than as active working committees of the sort that we are suggesting.

Some schools might find it useful to have two kinds of liaison committees of businessmen. One would be an advisory committee of leading businessmen who would serve as individuals and provide advice on questions of policy, help the school secure financial support, etc. The other would be a working committee, the members of which would represent the companies included in the panel of cooperating firms.

Business needs to be educated to make more fruitful consulting arrangements available to competent business school faculty members. Many business firms make no use of the technical help available in the business schools. On the other hand, many faculty members (as we noted in Chapter 16) neglect their academic responsibilities as they take on any outside job available, even if it is of a low-level, routine sort, in their search for extra income. A larger number of more responsible consulting arrangements should be developed that will provide fruitful experience, as well as some extra income, for faculty members. While the responsibility must rest on business to create more such opportunities, the business schools have the obligation to see that only competent men are recommended for such arrangements and that the consulting work does not interfere with the faculty member's academic duties.

A NATIONAL INSTITUTE OF BUSINESS RESEARCH

We should like also to propose that a national study group be formed to investigate the possibilities of what we shall call a national institute of business research. There may exist in such an institute the possibility of a new and fruitful kind of cooperation between business and the academic world in an area in which such cooperation needs to be developed. What we have in mind is a nonprofit organization operating in large part with endowed funds contributed by business. The institute would be controlled by a governing board which would include leading businessmen, educators, scientists, engineers, and others prominent in their respective fields.

The institute would have a small core of full-time staff engaged in fundamental research in the area normally implied by the term "business administration," but the research would also involve delving into the underlying disciplines to whatever extent was considered necessary. This core of full-time staff would consist of outstanding scholars. In addition, the institute would have a number of rotating positions, which faculty members from the business schools (and from related fields) might hold for periods of a year or two at a time while they worked on research projects either of their own choosing or which were parts of the institute's planned research program. There might be also a number of fellowships for younger men either to assist the senior research men, to carry on their own research projects under supervision, or to engage in advanced study. Fellowships might also be made available to research minded staff specialists from business firms.

Such an institute would invite business firms to present research problems to it, but it would be free to reject any on which it did not care to work. Any "contract research" undertaken would be subject to the normal academic safeguards: the problems must be of general interest; the institute would have complete freedom in the way it chose to carry on the work; and the results could be published. Information regarding the institute's activities would be disseminated widely.

Once such an institute was well established, it could take on additional responsibilities for which there was clearly a need. It could call conferences of specialists in particular fields; it could conduct training programs in new fields of knowledge having applications to business; it could sponsor summer seminars and workshops to which both business firms and the business schools might send representatives.

An institute of this sort appeals to us particularly because it could help to meet a number of needs simultaneously. It would, for example, provide leadership in stimulating both pure and high-level applied research on business problems, create a research relationship between business and the academic world resembling that which now exists between practitioners and professional schools in other fields, and provide a center for advanced research training, particularly in new fields. While there may be reasons why an institute of this sort would not succeed, the idea impresses us as at least deserving careful study.

The AACSB

As we suggested in Chapter 2, the key to widespread improvement in business education lies with the comprehensive multipurpose business schools in the urban and state universities. These are, for the most part, the great middle class of collegiate business education, and they play a dominant role in the American Association of Collegiate Schools of Business.

THE PRESENT ROLE OF THE ASSOCIATION

Membership in the Association provides no guarantee of excellence. It is merely a certificate of a minimal and conventional kind of respectability. While the Association has served a useful purpose in helping to establish these minimum conditions of academic respectability, thereby narrowing the gap between the average and the poorest schools, it has not shown much leadership beyond this; and it has done little to narrow the gap between the average and the best. It has shown no leadership whatsoever in helping the best to become still better.

Widespread and significant reform will be difficult to achieve through the Association, which thus far has not been noteworthy for bold and vigorous action or imaginative and progressive leadership. While it has succeeded in raising the standards of minimum acceptability and in bringing about some uniformity in such matters as what should be included in the undergraduate core curriculum, its standards have not been high; nor have they been very well implemented. Because of the interests of the bulk of its membership, it has concentrated on problems of the undergraduate school. Only very recently (in 1958) did it suggest some standards for graduate programs—standards which, as we saw in Chapter 11, hardly touch even the fringes of the problem. Yet the failure of a school to live up to even these inadequate standards would not jeopardize its membership in the Association.

The Association is, according to its constitution, "composed of institutions offering approved programs of instruction in business subjects." Nothing is said in the constitution as to who should represent the member schools and serve as officers and on committees. In fact, the Association is an organization of deans, and there is essentially no faculty participation in the affairs of the Association.

Once a school is a member, its representative is eligible for any position in the Association, regardless of the quality of the school or whether it continues to conform to the standards of the Association. As a result, important assignments have sometimes been held by deans of schools that were in current violation of the modest requirements of the Association.

The Association gives the appearance of both strength and weakness. Its influence is strong among the weaker schools, which eagerly seek membership if they are not yet members. As a result, the Association has been influential in, for example, reducing teaching loads and increasing the minimum amount of general education required in the poorer schools. But its voice carries no weight at all in the best schools, whose standards are far above anything that the Association dares require. Further, the Association does not have the funds for any large scale program. The modest dues it collects from member schools do little more than pay for a part-time executive secretary and the expenses incidental to its annual meeting. Some member schools seek to keep it weak in this sense. Greater activity by the Association might impose new standards on them, force them to adhere more closely to existing standards, or otherwise disturb the tenor of their ways.

While it is not likely that there will be any dramatic change in the policies and activities of the Association, we think the following suggestions are worth making.

ORGANIZATION

Without any question, there should be greater faculty participation in the affairs of the Association. The present lack of active participation by faculty members has two related results. The Association does little to meet the critical need for greater communication among faculty members in different schools, no matter how conscientiously the deans may try to report to their faculties on the Association's activities. Second, because deans talk almost entirely to deans at the meetings of the Association, these sessions are primarily concerned with administrative matters. Even when substantive issues are discussed, the contributions that faculty members might make to the discussions are missing. And many important matters are never discussed at all.

We recommend that faculty members as well as deans represent member schools at all meetings and in all activities of the Association.[13]

[13] The precedent for this exists in some other associations of professional schools, for example, the Association of American Law Schools.

Faculty members should serve on standing committees and be eligible to serve as officers. They should have a major voice in planning the annual meetings, at which they should be liberally represented. They should serve on examining or inspecting teams (for both new and old schools).[14]

The Association also needs to be supported by a broader base of regional groups and meetings. Regular meetings now occur in some areas of the country, and the Association has a standing Committee on Regional Conferences. But still there is insufficient faculty participation; and the meetings do not provide an effective channel of communication between the faculties of the various business schools, although it is our impression that recently there has been some improvement in this respect. Membership in the AACSB should automatically carry with it membership in a regional group, which should meet frequently with liberal faculty representation. In addition to regular (say, annual) meetings, the regional groups can, among other activities, plan conferences on special topics, arrange for a full exchange of information among schools, take some responsibility for improving and coordinating relations between member schools and the larger business firms in the region, sponsor summer seminars at particular schools, stimulate research programs of regional interest, and coordinate relations between the degree granting schools and the junior colleges in the area.[15]

The Association ought also to have a larger income for its activities. At present, it operates on an annual budget in the neighborhood of $10,000. The Association probably needs a budget several times the present size for adequate operations. If it could offer more of value to business school faculties—for example, printed proceedings of annual meetings that dealt with important and challenging questions—it might be able to collect a modest amount from individual faculty members, perhaps in the form of subscriptions to the proceedings of the annual meetings.

All of this suggests that the time has come for the Association to consider a substantial reorganization both of its structure and its activities. As a start, it might be desirable to establish a national committee to consider the problem and recommend the form which such reorganization should take. The chairman and a significant number of the members of

----

[14] The Association might be wise to appoint a continuing panel of examiners whose names would be made public, much as the engineers now do. The present practice is to appoint *ad hoc* inspecting teams as schools apply for membership. These teams are usually composed of deans without too much regard for their competence or educational philosophy as reflected, for example, in the quality of the educational programs in the schools with which they are associated.

[15] See what was said earlier in this chapter regarding the role which the leading school or schools in a region might play in connection with some of these activities.

this committee should be distinguished persons who are not deans of member schools.

RAISING STANDARDS

The Association needs to impose higher standards on its members and to enforce more effectively those that it already has. In earlier chapters we indicated the more important respects in which requirements should be raised. These include, at the undergraduate level, increasing the minimum of general education to 50 per cent and specifying minimum requirements in essential nonbusiness areas, revision of the core program, a strong stand against overspecialization and course proliferation, the introduction of more analytical content into courses, and higher admission and performance standards for students. At the graduate level, reasonably rigorous standards along the lines suggested in Chapter 11 ought to be imposed. As already noted, the present graduate standards of the Association are largely nominal.

Before it raises its standards, the Association should try more vigorously to enforce those it now has. Continuous reinspection of member schools is necessary, and suspension or expulsion ought to be a real rather than a nominal threat. Evaluation of schools should emphasize, more than it now does, such criteria as the scholarly quality of the faculty, facilities for research, admission and performance standards in the undergraduate and graduate programs, and the degree of vocational emphasis and course proliferation. Inspection committees should include distinguished faculty members as well as deans and should be chosen from the superior schools.[16]

The present statement of the Association's standards ought to be rewritten in more explicit and forthright language. This is necessary if the spirit as well as the letter of existing standards is to be enforced.[17]

Perhaps most important of all, the Association should become more of an active force for improvement than it now is. Not only should it have minimum standards which all member schools are expected to meet fully but it should engage in an active educational program that has as its purpose stimulating schools to raise the quality of their programs much beyond the minimum levels which all schools are now expected to achieve.

[16] See the suggestion in footnote 14 on p. 447.

[17] For example, the Association is on record that "a proliferation of courses which might serve to diminish the effectiveness of the staff in meeting its obligations toward fundamental areas of training is not to be encouraged." (Standards for Membership, 1958). This is hardly an enforceable standard and, as noted in Chapter 9, it has done nothing to reduce the extreme specialization and course proliferation that exist in some member schools.

FUTURE ACTIVITIES OF THE ASSOCIATION

The AACSB could become a powerful force for improving the quality of business education being offered by American colleges and universities. The recommendations in this and earlier chapters suggest the general direction in which it should move if it is to become such a force. At present it seems to be content to act primarily as the guardian of a respectable kind of academic mediocrity. It is probably too much to expect that the Association can immediately begin to exercise the bold and far-ranging kind of leadership that we think is necessary. Even under the most favorable circumstances, the Association will probably have to confine itself to a limited program and to a cautious leadership that reflects to some extent the fears and inhibitions of many of its member schools.

But even cautious progress with a limited program can do a great deal of good. Such a limited program could include a restatement of its standards aimed at bringing about needed curriculum revisions in both undergraduate and graduate programs, stricter enforcement of the spirit as well as the letter of present and future standards, improving the flow of information among business school faculties so that important new developments become more promptly and widely known, and taking more initiative in improving the quality of both teaching materials and the competence of the weaker members of business school faculties. Even this much is a large program, particularly when it is added to the present activities of the Association. If progress is to be made along these lines, a reorganization of the Association is likely to be necessary, particularly in order to bring greater participation by faculty members and to give the Association the financial support needed for a wider range of activities.

While revitalization of the AACSB is badly needed, individual schools can act without waiting for leadership from the Association, as the better ones have already been doing. Some of the measures we have suggested call for concerted action on a national or regional scale. But most of the steps needed—whether they involve curriculum reform, higher academic standards, or improving the scholarly quality of the faculty—are within the reach of the individual school, particularly if it can enlist the aid of the central university administration, the local business community, and other sources of support. Other measures will require concerted action, but cooperative effort can readily take place outside the Association if the latter cannot exercise the leadership to which its position entitles it. There is no question, however, that vigorous leadership by the Association will greatly accelerate the improvement in collegiate business education that is so badly needed.

APPENDIXES

appendix A

THE LITERATURE ON PERSONAL

QUALITIES CONTRIBUTING

TO BUSINESS SUCCESS

In the first part of Chapter 5 we attempted to summarize the relevant literature bearing on the personal qualities which are presumably important for success in business. This appendix describes in more detail than was possible in Chapter 5 the studies which we consulted.

The list of qualities presented on page 78 was derived from a study of the books and articles listed below. Those which were found most useful are indicated by an asterisk. The attempt to collate the findings of a number of disparate studies—each using different premises, each surveying a different group, and each using different procedures—raises the problem of constructing a common set of categories into which the qualities listed by each author can be placed. We attempted to fit the findings of each author into the framework we used in interviewing business firms on the qualities they felt were important for success in business management. This necessitated combining overlapping categories in several of the studies. The list presented on page 78 represents the qualities which were most often emphasized by the authors cited below.

*Bach, G. L. "Where Do Executives Come From?" *Personnel*, XXIX (July, 1952), 51.

Bowen, Howard R. "Future of Business Education," in *The Challenge of Business Education*. Chicago, University of Chicago Press, 1949. Pages 36–44.

*Calkins, Robert D. "Objectives of Business Education," *Harvard Business Review*, XXV (Autumn, 1946), 46–57.

Cleeton, Glen U., and Charles W. Mason. *Executive Ability*. Yellow Springs, Ohio, The Antioch Press, 1946. Page 26.

*Endicott, Frank S. "Employment Trends in 1955," *Journal of College Placement*, XV (March, 1955), 41–51.

Gardner, Burleigh B. "What Makes Successful and Unsuccessful Executives?" *Advanced Management*, XIII (September, 1948), 116–25. See also William E. Henry. *Executive Personality and Job Success.* Personnel Series, No. 120, American Management Association, 1948, pp. 3–13.

Goode, Cecil E. "Significant Research on Leadership," *Personnel*, XXVII (March, 1951), 342–50.

Kirkpatrick, Forrest H. In *Collegiate Business Education in the Next Quarter Century*, West Virginia University Business and Economic Studies, V (February, 1958), 14–15.

*Mandell, Milton M. "The Selection of Executives," in M. J. Dooher and Elizabeth Marting (eds.). *The Selection of Management Personnel.* I. New York, American Management Association, 1957. Pages 225–56.

*National Industrial Conference Board. *Employment of the College Graduate.* Studies in Personnel Policy, No. 152, 1956, p. 24.

*Randle, C. Wilson. "How to Identify Promotable Executives," *Harvard Business Review*, XXXIV (May–June, 1956), 122–34.

*Trickett, Joseph M. *A Survey of Management Development.* New York, American Management Association, 1954. Pages 42–45.

Wald, Robert M., and Roy A. Doty. "The Top Executive—A First-hand Profile," *Harvard Business Review*, XXXII (July–August, 1954), 45–54.

What Makes an Executive? Round Table on Executive Potential and Performance. Eli Ginzberg, chairman. New York, Columbia University Press, 1955.

In addition to the works cited above, studies on leadership and executive performance by psychologists and personnel and other experts were examined. Although the work in this area by psychologists and other experts is often superior in research design to the writings found in the business literature, their findings are largely inconclusive and their methodology leaves much to be desired, as we noted in Chapter 5. The list of studies cited below is by no means exhaustive, but it may serve to give a representative picture of the work in this area. We are indebted to Mr. Irving Krauss and Professor Lyman Porter, both of the University of California, for help in surveying this literature.

Bibliographies and surveys of the literature

Fox, Harland, *et al. Selected Annotated Bibliography on Leadership and Executive Development.* Maxwell Air Force Base, Air Force Personnel and Training Research Center, 1955.

Jenkins, William O. "A Review of Leadership Studies with Particular

Reference to Military Problems," *Psychological Bulletin*, XLIV (January, 1947), 54–79.

Stogdill, Ralph M. "Personal Factors Associated with Leadership: A Survey of the Literature," *Journal of Psychology*, XXV (January, 1948), 35–71.

Other studies

Bell, Daniel. "Screening Leaders in a Democracy," *Commentary*, V (April, 1948), 368–75.

Gibb, Cecil A. "The Principles and Traits of Leadership," *Journal of Abnormal and Social Psychology*, XLII (July, 1947), 267–84.

Gouldner, Alvin W. (ed.). *Studies in Leadership and Democratic Action*. New York, Harper & Bros., 1950.

Guilford, Joan S. "Temperament Traits of Executives and Supervisors Measured by the Guilford Personality Inventories," *Journal of Applied Psychology*, XXXVI (August, 1952), 228–33.

Henry, William E. "The Business Executive: The Psychodynamics of a Social Role," *American Journal of Sociology*, LIV (January, 1949), 286–91.

Meyer, Henry D., and Glenn L. Pressel. "Personality Test Scores in the Management Hierarchy," *Journal of Applied Psychology*, XXXVIII (April, 1954), 73–80.

Miner, John B., and John E. Culver. "Some Aspects of the Executive Personality," *Journal of Applied Psychology*, XXXIX (October, 1955), 348–53.

Porter, Lyman W., and Edwin E. Ghiselli. "The Self Perceptions of Top and Middle Management Personnel," *Personnel Psychology*, X (Winter, 1957), 397–406.

Selznick, Philip. *Leadership in Administration*. Evanston, Ill., Row, Peterson & Co., 1957.

Shartle, Carroll L. *Executive Performance and Leadership*. Englewood Cliffs, N. J., Prentice-Hall, Inc., 1956.

Stogdill, Ralph M., and Alvin E. Coons (eds.). *Leader Behavior: Its Description and Measurement*. The Ohio State University, Bureau of Business Research, Research Monograph No. 88. Columbus, Ohio, Ohio State University, 1957.

Stogdill, Ralph M., and Carroll L. Shartle. "Methods for Determining Patterns of Leadership Behavior in Relation to Organization Structure and Objectives," *Journal of Applied Psychology*, XXXII (June, 1948), 286–91.

Stryker, Perrin. Series of articles on executive qualities in *Fortune*, LVII and LVIII (June–December, 1958).

appendix B

SURVEY OF BUSINESS FIRMS

In Chapters 4, 5, and 6 we cited evidence compiled from intensive interviews held with officials of a sample of business firms. The companies included in this survey were not selected randomly, nor is the sample representative of the population of all business concerns. Since the survey was primarily designed to secure information regarding company practices, experiences, and policies in reference to the employment of college and university graduates, we felt that the smaller companies, which individually employ few graduates, would not have enough experience in this area to provide meaningful responses. The responses obtained from the small firms which were included in the survey substantiated this opinion. In addition, we did not have the resources to undertake a sample survey which would include both a substantial and representative panel of small firms as well as an adequate sample of medium and large firms. Ordinarily it is considerably more difficult to develop an adequate sample of small companies and to secure cooperation for intensive interviews than it is in the case of large firms. To secure information by personal interview from a representative sample of small firms would have entailed considerable expense in compiling a "universe" of such firms from which to derive a stratified sample; we should have had to cope with a high rejection ratio in making the first approach; and we should have needed for interviewing more staff, time, and funds than were at our disposal.

Thus, small companies (those with fewer than 1,000 employees) are significantly under-represented in our sample. As company size increases, the ratio of firms included in our survey to all firms in the United States in that size class increases. This design with its emphasis on the larger companies seems defensible for our purposes. In general, there is a positive association between the size of firm and the degree of attention given by a company to problems of selecting and training management personnel. Within the universe of large firms in the United States we were careful to secure a representative panel of firms in terms of industry classification and geographical location.

Given these considerations, we selected a panel of 111 firms as the basis for a survey based on intensive personal interviews. For various reasons it was not possible to arrange interviews with nine firms. For approximately ten other firms, the interviews were generally too incomplete to be of much use. Thus, the findings of the survey reported in Chapters 4, 5, and 6 refer to about ninety firms. All firms visited are listed at the end of this appendix.

The questionnaire around which the interviews were structured was framed in preliminary form after extensive discussions with business educators, business consultants, and businessmen. It was then pretested in six company interviews and modified as seemed necessary. This modified form of the questionnaire was the final form utilized in the remaining interviews.

While it does not appear necessary to reproduce the complete questionnaire here, it may be useful to indicate the general areas covered. The following is a list of the sections in the questionnaire:

1) The company's definition of "management," the types of management positions in the company, and the numbers and education of the persons filling these positions.
2) Recruitment and use of college graduates.
3) Promotion procedures, policies, and experiences.
4) Respondent's views as to the important management qualities and their relation to education.
5) The company's use of management training programs.
6) Relation of business firms, businessmen, and business practices to current teaching and research in the business schools.

This questionnaire was the basis for the personal interviews in each of the companies. These interviews were conducted over a period of a year (ending early in 1958) by the authors, by Mr. Donald S. Bridgman, formerly Director of College Relations, American Telephone and Telegraph Company, and by Professor Thomas L. Whisler of the School of Business of the University of Chicago.

In each firm, the interview was solicited through a letter to the chief executive. Respondents almost always included those officials of the firm particularly concerned with personnel and educational policies. In addition, brief interviews were frequently held with the chief executive and sometimes with operating executives. The interviews usually took the better part of one day to complete. Many of the questions in the questionnaire required qualitative rather than quantitative answers. This meant that extreme care and considerable judgment had to be exercised in presenting the questions and interpreting the responses. (These difficulties are illustrated by the fact that sometimes two respondents from the same firm would give conflicting answers to a question.)

It was not always possible to secure from a company answers to all questions on the questionnaire. Some questions simply were not applicable to the firm in question, while for others the respondents did not have an answer. In particular, the estimates of the size of the management group presented in Chapter 4 are based on a very limited number of responding firms. Not only was this information not available for some of the firms, but also the replies of some firms were so ambiguous that they could not be used.

The firms at which interviews were conducted during the course of the study are the following. The location of the interview is given in parentheses except for those which were conducted in New York.

Abraham and Strauss (Brooklyn, N. Y.)
Aldens, Inc. (Chicago)
Aluminum Co. of America (Pittsburgh)
American Brake Shoe Co.
American Molasses Co.
American Sugar Refining Co.
American Telephone & Telegraph Co.
American Tobacco Co.
Armour & Co. (Chicago)
Armstrong Cork Co. (Lancaster, Pa.)
Arthur H. Andersen and Co. (Chicago)
Atchison, Topeka & Santa Fe Rwy. (Chicago)
Austin, Nichols & Co., Inc. (Brooklyn, N. Y.)
Bank of America National Trust & Savings Assn. (San Francisco)
Blue Bell, Inc.
Broadway-Hale Stores, Inc. (Los Angeles)
Burlington Industries, Inc. (Greensboro, N. C.)
Cannon Electric Co. (Los Angeles)
Carrier Corp. (Syracuse, N. Y.)
Chase Manhattan Bank
Chrysler Corp. (Detroit)
Cluett, Peabody & Co., Inc.
Columbia Broadcasting System, Inc.
Commonwealth Edison Co. (Chicago)
Connecticut General Life Insurance Co. (Hartford, Conn.)
Connecticut Light & Power Co. (Hartford, Conn.)
Continental Can Co., Inc.
Continental Casualty Co. (Chicago)
Continental Copper & Steel Industries, Inc.
Continental Illinois National Bank & Trust Company of Chicago
    (Chicago)
Crown Zellerbach Corp. (San Francisco)

Detroit Edison Co. (Detroit)
Doubleday and Company, Inc. (Garden City, N. Y.)
E. I. du Pont de Nemours and Co. (Wilmington, Del.)
Eastman Kodak Co. (Rochester, N. Y.)
The Emporium Capwell Co. (San Francisco)
Fidelity-Philadelphia Trust Co. (Philadelphia)
Ford Motor Co. (Dearborn, Mich.)
General Electric Co.
General Foods Corp. (White Plains, N. Y.)
General Petroleum Corp. (Los Angeles)
George A. Fuller Co.
Hart Schaffner & Marx (Chicago)
Hexcel Products, Inc. (Berkeley, Calif.)
Inland Steel Co. (Chicago)
International Harvester Co. (Chicago)
International Shoe Co. (St. Louis)
Jackson-Cross Co. (Philadelphia)
Johns-Manville Corp.
Johnson and Johnson (New Brunswick, N. J.)
Kroger Co. (Cincinnati)
Lane Publishing Co. (San Francisco)
Lee & Cady (Detroit)
Lockheed Aircraft Corp. (Burbank, Calif.)
Longines-Wittnauer Watch Co.
Lytton's, Henry C. Lytton & Co. (Chicago)
Macmillan Co.
R. H. Macy and Co., Inc.
Magna Power Tool Corp. (Menlo Park, Calif.)
Marshall Field & Co. (Chicago)
Mason-McDuffie Co. (Berkeley, Calif.)
McGraw-Hill Publishing Co., Inc.
McKinsey & Company
Minnesota Mining & Mfg. Co. (St. Paul)
Missouri Pacific RR. (St. Louis)
New York Life Insurance Co.
Olin Mathieson Chemical Corp.
Pacific Telephone & Telegraph Co. (San Francisco)
Panellit, Inc. (Skokie, Ill.)
Pendleton Tool Industries, Inc. (Los Angeles)
J. C. Penney Co.
Pennsylvania RR. (Philadelphia)

Pettibone Mulliken Corp. (Chicago)
Previews, Inc.
Riegel Textile Corp.
St. Paul Fire & Marine Ins. Co. (St. Paul)
Scott Paper Co. (Chester, Pa.)
Sears, Roebuck & Co. (Chicago)
Seidman and Seidman
Shand and Jurs Co. (Berkeley, Calif.)
Simmons Co.
Southern Ry. (Washington, D. C.)
Standard Brands, Inc.
Standard Oil Co. of California (San Francisco)
Standard Oil Co. (New Jersey)
J. P. Stevens & Co., Inc.
Sylvania Electric Products, Inc.
Texas Gulf Sulphur Co.
J. Walter Thompson Co.
Thompson Products, Inc. (Cleveland)
Turner Construction Co.
Union Oil Co. of California (Los Angeles)
United Air Lines, Inc. (Chicago)
United Parcel Co.
U. S. Plywood Corp.
U. S. Rubber Co.
United States Steel Corp.
Wachovia Bank & Trust Co. (Winston-Salem)
Western Electric Co., Inc.
Western Pacific RR. Co. (San Francisco)
Wisconsin Motor Corp. (Milwaukee)
Wisconsin Power & Light Co. (Madison)
Young and Rubicam, Inc.

In addition to the companies that were included in our sample, a number of other organizations and individuals helped us in planning and carrying out our study of the policies and experience of business firms in recruiting and developing managerial talent. This help was offered through informal interviews and in other ways. We should particularly like to acknowledge the help of the following organizations and individuals.

American Management Association
Donald S. Bridgman, formerly with American Telephone & Telegraph Co.
James F. Brownlee, J. H. Whitney & Company

Bureau of Applied Social Research, Columbia University
Robert D. Calkins, The Brookings Institution
Dun & Bradstreet, Inc.
Frank S. Endicott, Director of Placement, Northwestern University
Fortune Magazine
Harold Guetzkow, Northwestern University
Harvard University Graduate School of Business Administration
Edwin R. Henry, New York City
Fred Lazarus, Jr., Federated Department Stores, Inc.
Arthur D. Little & Company
National Industrial Conference Board
William H. Newman, Columbia University
Bruce Payne, Bruce Payne & Associates, Inc.
Ewing Reilly, McKinsey & Company
Richardson, Bellows, Henry & Company
Beardsley Ruml, New York City
O. N. Serbein, Columbia University
Harold F. Smiddy, General Electric Co.
R. Webb Sparks, Manpower Development Corporation
Time Magazine, Research Department
U. S. Department of Labor
U. S. Office of Education, Department of Health, Education, and
    Welfare
Lewis B. Ward, Educational Testing Service

appendix C

TECHNICAL NOTE ON
THE SURVEY OF COLLEGE
PLACEMENT OFFICES

THREE questionnaires were prepared for submission to college and university placement directors. The basic form of the questionnaire was that designed for the directors of centralized university placement offices, that is, placement offices which handle students from all the component schools of the university. This form was then modified (primarily by omitting inapplicable questions) for the directors of placement offices under the jurisdiction of schools of business, and again for the directors of placement offices in liberal arts colleges. This procedure enabled us to compare answers between two or among all three of the variously affiliated placement offices.

We selected as respondents the directors of twenty-four centralized university placement offices, fourteen business school placement offices, and ten placement offices in liberal arts colleges. This selection was not random, though an attempt was made to secure an adequate geographical distribution of institutions for each of the three types of placement offices. Institutions were selected primarily by the possibility of identifying the placement director to whom we could direct the questionnaire. Such identification was secured by consulting college and university catalogues and bulletins, regional placement officer associations' publications, etc. A list of the institutions cooperating in the survey is given at the end of this appendix.

The questionnaire designed for the directors of the centralized university placement offices was tested by submission to four institutions. After incorporation of the minor revisions suggested by this test, the questionnaires were mailed on September 1, 1957, to the forty-four remaining placement offices. A second mailing to nonrespondents was undertaken in the middle of October. Tabulations were begun on the completed questionnaires in December, at which time all but one of the questionnaires had been returned. (This last questionnaire was finally returned, but it was too late to be included in the tabulations.) Thus, the tabulations refer to replies from the directors of twenty-three centralized university placement offices, fourteen business school offices, and ten placement offices in liberal arts colleges.

Tabulations based on the completed questionnaires yielded a set of fifteen tables, which were used in the discussion of company recruiting practices in Chapters 5 and 6. Only one table, however, is actually reproduced in the text. The authors hope to make available at a later date additional material derived from this survey.

The following institutions cooperated in this survey:

I. Universities with centralized placement offices

Boston University	Michigan State University
Bowling Green State University	University of Oregon
Brigham Young University	Pennsylvania State University
University of Buffalo	Rutgers University
University of Cincinnati	St. Louis University
University of Connecticut	San Francisco State College
University of Detroit	University of San Francisco
Duquesne University	San Jose State College
University of Georgia	University of Santa Clara
Hofstra College	Seattle University
University of Louisville	University of Tennessee
University of Maryland	Texas Technological College

II. Universities with placement offices located in business schools or departments

University of Akron	Miami University
University of Alabama	University of Michigan
College of the Pacific	University of Minnesota
University of Florida	University of Missouri
Louisiana State University	Ohio State University
Loyola University (New Orleans)	Oklahoma State University
Marquette University	University of Richmond

III. Liberal arts colleges

Baker University	Duke University
Bowdoin College	Knox College
Carleton College	Lewis and Clark College
Colgate University	Macalester College
Davidson College	Yale University

appendix D

TECHNICAL NOTES TO
TABLES IN CHAPTER 2

THE DATA on business degrees in Table 1 are from a work sheet prepared for this study by the Research and Statistical Services Branch of the U. S. Office of Education. We are indebted to Mrs. Mabel C. Rice, Supervisor of the Statistical Services Section, for her cooperation in making these data available to us. These data refer to the aggregate United States (continental United States plus outlying parts) for all years except 1939–1940, 1941–1942, and 1943–1944, when they refer to the Continental United States. Data on degrees were not collected by field in 1945–1946.

The figures for "all fields" in Table 1 are from *Biennial Survey of Education* and *Earned Degrees Conferred by Higher Educational Institutions* (annual), both published by the United States Office of Education. These data refer to the Continental United States only. The limitations of the basic series have made it impossible to eliminate discrepancies between the series on degrees in business and in all fields which arise from differences in the geographical area covered. We believe, however, that these discrepancies are of minor importance.

Prior to 1931–1932 the estimates of business degrees do not include any degrees conferred by teacher training institutions. From 1931–1932 through 1954–1955 degrees in business conferred by teacher training institutions are included in the estimates. The business degrees conferred by teacher training institutions from 1931–1932 through 1954–1955 must include (in addition to "legitimate" degrees in business administration and commerce) some degrees in the field of business education. Only in 1955–1956 and 1956–1957 does the reporting form specifically identify degrees in business education (as opposed to business administration) and indicate that they are to be counted as degrees in education, not business. For the period 1931–1932 through 1954–1955 the decision on how to classify business degrees in teacher training institutions was left to the responding institutions; therefore some business education degrees must be included in the totals. This fact may account for some part of the decline in the percentage of business to all degrees from 1954–1955 to 1955–1956 shown in Table 1.

The fact that the Office of Education reports its degrees as "Bachelor's and First Professional," "Second Level Degrees (Master's except First Professional)," and "Doctorates" means that some master's degrees in business which were considered "the first degree granted upon completion of a course of study in a given field" (e.g., the Harvard M.B.A.) were included at the "Bachelor's and First Professional" level. For our purposes it was considered desirable to classify business degrees as "Bachelor's," "Master's," and "Doctorate." Hence, we adjusted the Office of Education data by reclassifying those master's degrees which were reported as "Bachelor's and First Professional" degrees. This was a problem only in the case of institutions which had exclusively graduate business programs, since those institutions which had both graduate and undergraduate programs would report their bachelor's degrees in business as "First Professional" degrees and their master's as "Second Level" degrees.

The Office of Education data have been adjusted, where necessary, over the period covered by Table 1, by transferring the master's degrees conferred in business by the exclusively graduate schools from the "Bachelor's and First Professional" level to the "Second Level" or master's level. These adjustments were made through a comparison of the Office of Education data with information supplied us by the six schools (Harvard, Dartmouth, Stanford, Cornell, Columbia, and Chicago) on the number of master's degrees they conferred.

We should add that the data for 1957–1958 in Table 1 are based on unpublished tabulations which were supplied to us through the courtesy of the United States Office of Education. We wish to thank Mrs. Mabel C. Rice of the Office of Education for her help in this as well as other ways.

Tables 2 through 4 are derived from data on earned degrees conferred by higher educational institutions between July 1, 1955 and June 30, 1956. The source is the U. S. Office of Education, *Earned Degrees Conferred by Higher Educational Institutions, 1955–1956* (Circular No. 499, 1957), which reports degrees by field of study and by conferring institution. In the field of Business and Commerce, degrees are reported in six subcategories: 1) Accounting, 2) Hotel and Restaurant Administration, 3) Secretarial Studies, 4) Business and Commerce, Other Specific Fields, 5) Business and Commerce, General, and 6) Business and Commerce, Not Further Classified. We defined the universe of business institutions in which we were interested as any institution in the Continental United States appearing in categories 4 or 5 or 6, or appearing in *more than one* of categories 1, 2, and 3. Thus, those few institutions conferring business degrees only in accounting, only in hotel and restaurant administration, or only in secretarial studies were not included.

For each of the 592 institutions in this selected universe we totaled the number of business degrees conferred in the six subcategories for each degree level, in order to derive the total number of business degrees conferred at each of the three degree levels by that institution. We also tallied the total number of degrees in all fields, business and nonbusiness, at each level for each institution.

As in Table 1, it was necessary to reclassify master's degrees in business reported by the Office of Education as "Bachelor's and First Professional" degrees. This reclassification was necessary only in the case of six graduate schools of business. The following adjustments (based on information from The Carnegie Survey of Business Education, correspondence with the schools involved, and other material in our files) were made in the Office of Education data to redefine their degree levels as "Bachelor's" and "Master's":

	Bachelor's and First Professional	Second Level
Columbia	−95	+95
Cornell	−52	+52
Dartmouth	−68	+68
Harvard	−577	+577
Stanford	−175	+175
Chicago	−193	+193
	−1,160	+1,160

These adjustments were also made in the degree totals for all fields.

When our tallies by institution were totaled over all institutions they compared with the Office of Education totals as follows:

The Office of Education (*Earned Degrees, 1955–1956*, p. 6) reported the following totals for business degrees:

Bachelor's and First Professional	42,195
Second Level (Master's Except First Professional)	3,106
Doctorate	121

Our totals were:

Bachelor's	40,370
Master's	4,241
Doctorate	121

The Office of Education total for bachelor's degrees is 1,825 larger than our total. Subtract from this 1,160 First Professional business degrees which we have reclassified as master's degrees in the preceding section. The difference between the adjusted U.S.O.E. total and ours is now 665. Subtract from this figure 356 noncontinental (Puerto Rico, Hawaii, Alaska) degrees, leaving an adjusted difference of 309. Subtracting from this figure 40 degrees (conferred by the Carnegie Institute of Technology) that have been reclassified as Industrial Engineering degrees yields a difference of 269. Finally, subtracting 392 degrees conferred by schools not included on our list—schools conferring business degrees in only one of the fields of accounting, secretarial studies, or hotel and restaurant management—gave us a difference of −123. Thus, our estimate of bachelor's degrees is approximately 125 degrees larger than the adjusted Office of Education estimate.

The Office of Education total for master's degrees is 1,135 smaller than our master's total. Subtracting from this figure the 1,160 First Professional degrees reclassified as master's degrees leaves an adjusted U.S.O.E. estimate 25 degrees larger than our estimate.

The above adjustments also account for the difference between Tables 2 and 3 in Total Business Degrees. Table 2 presents this figure as given by the Office of Education, while in Table 3 it has been adjusted.

The institutions in our universe were classified by type of institutional program. The Office of Education (*Education Directory, 1955–1956, Higher Education*, p. 8) recognizes eleven types of programs, which we have combined into three categories, "Colleges," "Technical Institutes," and "Universities." The Office of Education lists the following subgroups for our three categories: *Colleges*, b) liberal arts and general, c) liberal arts and general and terminal-occupational, d) primarily teacher-preparatory, f) liberal arts and general, terminal-occupational, and teacher-preparatory, and j) liberal arts and general with one or two professional schools; *Technical Institutes*, g) professional or technical only (not including teacher-preparatory), h) professional or technical and teacher-preparatory, and i) professional or technical and terminal-occupational; *Universities*, k) liberal arts and general with three or more professional schools. (The Office of Education classification "a) terminal-occupational [below bachelor's degree]" was excluded.)

The organization of the degree-granting unit as a School (or College) of Business or as a Department (or Division) of Business was taken from the institutional exhibits in American Council on Education, *American Universities and Colleges* (Mary Irwin, editor; 7th ed., 1956), and from the catalogues of those few institutions not listed in *American Universities and Colleges*.

The U. S. Office of Education's *Education Directory, 1955–1956, Higher Education*, identified women's colleges ("those institutions where the undergraduate student body is composed of women") in our list of business institutions. The same source was used to identify public and private institutions. AACSB members in 1955–1956 were reported in the U.S. Office of Education, *Accredited Higher Institutions, 1956* (Bulletin No. 1, 1957).

We recognized seven regions as follows:

New England: Connecticut, Rhode Island, Maine, Massachusetts, New Hampshire, Vermont.

Middle Atlantic: Delaware, Maryland (including District of Columbia), New Jersey, New York, Pennsylvania, West Virginia.

Central: Illinois, Indiana, Iowa, Michigan, Minnesota, Missouri, Ohio, Wisconsin.

Southeast: Alabama, Arkansas, Florida, Georgia, Kentucky, Louisiana, Mississippi, North Carolina, South Carolina, Tennessee, Virginia.

Southwest: Arizona, New Mexico, Oklahoma, Texas.

Northwest: Colorado, Idaho, Kansas, Montana, Nebraska, Nevada, North Dakota, South Dakota, Utah, Wyoming.

Pacific Coast: California, Oregon, Washington.

It is not possible to reconcile our list of 157 institutions having schools or colleges of business with the 187 institutions reported in the Carnegie Corporation's *Summary of Preliminary Findings* (revised August 1, 1958) as having schools or colleges of business, since the latter apparently includes an unknown number of departments and/or divisions of business. In May, 1958, Professor Pierson, director of the Carnegie Corporation Survey of Business Education, supplied us with a list of 162 institutions having schools or colleges of business which may be compared with our list of 157 institutions (which is raised to 158 if we count the University of California twice, as is done in the Carnegie list). Four of the schools on the Carnegie list are not included in our universe; the University of Hawaii (excluded as noncontinental), Georgia State College of Business Administration, Massachusetts Institute of Technology, and Purdue (all excluded because they were not reported as conferring business degrees in the Office of Education's *Earned Degrees, 1955–1956*). Of the remaining 158 institutions on the Carnegie list, we classified ten institutions as conferring degrees through departments or divisions since they were so reported in *American Universities and Colleges*. Thus the Carnegie list includes 148 institutions that are comparable to our definition of institutions conferring business degrees through schools or colleges of business. We included, in addition, ten institutions not on the Carnegie list since they appeared in *Earned Degrees, 1955–1956* and were identified as having schools or colleges of business.

Nonaccredited institutions were not excluded from our universe of schools if they appeared in *Earned Degrees, 1955–1956.* The U. S. Office of Education considers an institution accredited if 1) it is accredited by a nationally recognized regional accrediting institution, or 2) if it is accredited and/or approved by state departments of education, state accrediting commissions, and state universities. Sixteen institutions which are included in the universe of business degree granting institutions were not accredited in the Spring of 1956. The total number of nonaccredited institutions (16) and the number of degrees in business they conferred (397) are not large enough to suggest adjusting our summary totals. However, 263 of these degrees were concentrated in the category "departments of business in technical institutes" and accounted for about 27 percent of the 966 business degrees in this category. Only one of the nonaccredited institutions was in the school or college category. For details of accrediting, see U. S. Office of Education, *Accredited Higher Institutions, 1956.*

The figures on doctoral degrees in Table 22 (Chapter 17) for the years 1955–1956 and 1956–1957 came from the annual volumes of the U. S. Office of Education on *Earned Degrees Conferred by Higher Educational Institutions,* in the same way as did the figures for Tables 2 through 4. The figures on doctoral degrees for 1957–1958 were supplied directly by the Office of Education through the courtesy of Mrs. Mabel C. Rice.

appendix E

TECHNICAL NOTE ON
SAMPLES OF SCHOOLS

THE descriptions of curricula presented in Chapters 8, 9, 10, and 11 are based upon detailed analysis of the business curricula of approximately 125 institutions conferring earned degrees in business. In each case use was made of the 1955–1956 or 1956–1957 catalogues and bulletins of the included institutions. In many instances, additional information (from the authors' visits to the institutions, the Carnegie Corporation Survey of Business Education work sheets, and reports supplied directly by the institutions concerned) was used to supplement descriptions in the catalogues.

The 592 institutions conferring earned degrees in business in 1955–1956 through schools and departments can be classified as follows:

School of Business—member of AACSB	80 (7 graduate schools)
School of Business—not member of AACSB	79
Department of Business	435

(The total number of schools differs from the 157 presented in Table 3 in that here the business schools on the Berkeley and Los Angeles campuses of the University of California and the undergraduate and graduate schools at New York University are each counted separately.) Representative samples were selected from each of these three classes of institutions.

One or the other (or both) of the authors visited thirty-seven undergraduate schools which were members of the AACSB in 1955–1956.[1] These thirty-seven institutions constituted the first sample. These institutions were selected as follows. All AACSB member institutions were carefully stratified by size, location, type of control (public, private, and Roman Catholic), and type of business program. We then selected thirty-seven undergraduate business schools which we felt best represented all characteristics and strata, with the qualification that several substitutions

---

[1] We visited more than thirty-seven member schools. The others were graduate schools, in engineering schools, or were admitted to the AACSB later.

were made in the original list when it became apparent that a school originally selected could not be conveniently visited (because of transportation difficulties or because it was not possible for the dean to receive us at a mutually convenient time). The undergraduate programs of these schools are described in Chapters 8 and 9. The thirty-seven institutions in this sample are: University of Alabama, Boston University, University of California (Berkeley), University of California (Los Angeles), University of Cincinnati, University of Colorado, University of Denver, Drake University, Emory University, University of Florida, University of Georgia, University of Illinois, Indiana University, University of Kansas, University of Kentucky, Lehigh University, Louisiana State University, Loyola University (New Orleans), University of Michigan, University of Minnesota, New York University (undergraduate), Northwestern University, Ohio State University, University of Oregon, University of Pennsylvania, University of Pittsburgh, St. Louis University, University of Southern California, Syracuse University, Temple University, University of Tennessee, University of Texas, Tulane University, University of Utah, Washington University, University of Washington, University of Wisconsin.

For our second sample we randomly selected thirty-seven of the seventy-nine schools which were not at the time members of the AACSB. One or the other of the authors visited eleven of these thirty-seven institutions. Their undergraduate curricula are described in Chapters 8 and 9. The institutions included in this sample are: University of Akron, American University, Arizona State College (Tempe), Babson Institute of Business Administration, Bob Jones University, Bradley University, University of Bridgeport, Butler University, Clark University, University of Connecticut, Duquesne University, East Tennessee State College, Fenn College, Golden Gate College, University of Idaho, University of Kansas City, Kent State University, Lamar State College of Technology, Long Island University, Manhattan College, Mississippi State College, University of Nevada, University of New Mexico, North Texas State College, University of Omaha, Oregon State College, Pennsylvania State College, Rhode Island University, University of Richmond, St. Peter's College, University of South Carolina, Southern Illinois University, Southwestern Louisiana Institute, Texas Christian University, Utah State Agricultural College, Wayne State University, and Western Reserve University.

The final sample consisted of thirty-seven institutions conferring degrees in business through departments. Eighty institutions were selected at random, and for these catalogues were collected, as available, until a total of thirty-seven had been accumulated for analysis and description. This method of deriving the sample has probably introduced some bias in the form of selecting the larger, better-known institutions whose catalogues are more readily available. However, we do not consider this bias disturbing. The business curricula of these institutions are described in Chapter 10. The institutions included in this sample are: Albright College, Arkansas Agricultural and Mechanical College, Atlantic Christian College, Austin College, Bethany College, Bethany Nazarene College, Canisius College, Carroll College, University of Chattanooga, Colby College, College of the Pacific, College of St. Thomas, Doane College, Fisk University, Hillyer College, Idaho State College, Lake Forest College, Lewis and Clark College, Louisiana College, Maryville College, Midland College, Mississippi College, Muhlenberg College, North Central College, Norwich University, Ohio Wesleyan University, Rockhurst College, St. Lawrence University, St. Mary's University of San Antonio, Sam Houston State Teachers College, University of Scranton, Texas Western College, Valparaiso University, Wheaton College (Illinois), Whittier College, Winthrop College, and Yankton College.

In addition to the schools visited which were included in the above samples, we also visited the following institutions: Case Institute of Technology, DePaul University, Duke University, Fresno State College, Hofstra College, University of Houston, and University of Miami, as well as several additional liberal arts colleges. In all, including the graduate schools mentioned later, we paid personal visits to something over sixty-five colleges and universities. We also had access to the reports on visits made by Professor Frank Pierson's staff to a number of additional schools and departments of business.

Samples Used in Chapter 11 (Master's Programs)

The graduate programs studied in detail in Chapter 11 come from the following samples: the thirty-three member schools in the list of thirty-seven described previously which had master's programs; the twenty-one having master's programs in the sample of thirty-seven nonmember schools; the exclusively graduate schools at Chicago, Columbia, Cornell, Dartmouth, Harvard, New York University, Stanford, and Virginia; and a sample of five master's programs in industrial administration or management at the Carnegie, Georgia, Illinois, Massachusetts, and Stevens Institutes of Technology. Data are, in general, for the academic years 1955–1956 or 1956–1957, but we have tried to take cognizance of important changes since then where they have come to our notice. Where more recent information is used, this is indicated in the text or footnotes.

We personally visited all of the eight graduate schools mentioned in the preceding paragraph, as well as the Graduate School of Industrial Administration at Carnegie Tech and the School of Industrial Management at M.I.T.

INDEX

INDEX

TITLES IN THIS SERIES